CHRISTOPRAXIS

CHRISTOPRAXIS

A PRACTICAL THEOLOGY OF THE CROSS

ANDREW ROOT

Fortress Press
Minneapolis

CHRISTOPRAXIS

A Practical Theology of the Cross

Cover design: Laurie Ingram

Cover Image: Peeter Viisimaa/Vetta/Getty Images

Library of Congress Cataloging-in-Publication Data

Print ISBN: 978-1-4514-7815-0
eBook ISBN: 978-1-4514-8428-1

The paper used in this publication meets the minimum requirements of American National Standard for Information Sciences — Permanence of Paper for Printed Library Materials, ANSI Z329.48-1984.

Manufactured in the U.S.A.

This book was produced using PressBooks.com, and PDF rendering was done by PrinceXML.

to my mom, who prayed for me

WbB 3.21
Book 3.15
Run

CONTENTS

PREFACE

Years ago James Loder said that "practical Theology is the generative problematic of divine and human action."[1] This statement has been my own personal rudder as I've sought to sail the seas of practical theology. Yet, I have embarked on this project because it appears that the major approaches in the field of practical theology have not always embraced Loder's definition and mission for the field. Practical theology has been able to create rich projects on human action in relation to church life, society, and pastoral practice. But these fruitful articulations have not always sailed practical theology into the deep waters of exploring divine action, therefore missing, in my mind, the generative and problematic nature of practical theology.

In this project I hope to make a case for the central place of divine action in practical theology. Like Loder, I believe deeply generative possibility rests in contemplating divine action next to human experience and agency. And yet to do so is problematic, for divine action, if we are to contend that it is real—that is, a reality—is a transcendent mystery.

There, then, is possibility and peril in practical theology making such a voyage into the waters of divine action, for we must contemplate how potentially incongruent forms of action that exist in different layers of reality (God is in heaven and we on earth, for example) can and do nevertheless relate. It confesses the possibility of the event of God encountering us in our concrete and embodied lives. Overall, I'll argue (to melt down my project to a single line) that it is in *ministry*, as distinct and related forms of action, that these apparently incongruent forms of reality are fused. The event of ministry associates the divine to the human, taking the human into the divine (time into eternity). I

---

1. Paraphrased from James Loder, "Normativity and Context in Practical Theology: 'The Interdisciplinary Issue,'" in *Practical Theology: International Perspectives*, ed. Friedrich Schweitzer and Johannes A. van der Ven (Berlin: Peter Lang, 1999).

will then make a case in this project that practical theology *is* ministry (both in its operations and its attention).

Most books are written in parts. This book is particularly organized around its parts as I seek to present a practical theological approach I call a Christopraxis practical theology of the cross.

Part 1 seeks to reveal that there is something missing in the rich discourses on practical theology. While practical theology has become a force in the last half of the twentieth century and first decades of the twenty-first, it has nevertheless struggled to articulate its theological, or even normative, character. I argue that practical theology has been magnificent at articulating rich approaches to human action but has been deficient, as I hope to show, in articulating divine action in the same depth.

I believe this inability to discuss divine action has happened because practical theology has erroneously seen divine action as *impractical*. Practical theology's commitment to the lived and embodied realities of concrete persons and communities seems to draw practical theology like a magnet toward conversations with philosophy, the social sciences, and forms of empirical research. Within discourse in these fields and disciplines practical theology has found the dialogue to move into rich approaches to human action. But, most of these perspectives (with exceptions like that of T. M. Luhrmann, whom I'll discuss more below) overlook or are disinterested in divine action. This disinterest in the possibility of a divine or transcendent reality has made it harder for practical theology to attend to the theological.

Yet, the idea that divine action or transcendence is impractical seems to me to be a misstep. I will seek to show that divine action itself is not impractical, but rather is a deeply practical and lived reality, that people do have distinct experiences with God that they believe are concrete, lived, and *real*. These very experiences direct their lives in formative ways, moving them to do one thing or another in their embodied practical life. These experiences are bound in a reality that they claim is beyond them, a reality that transcends them, but which is nevertheless *real* to them and real in the most practical way, directing them to quit high-powered jobs or forgive themselves for not seeing a husband's illness, for example.

There are many people that assert they have had concrete and lived experiences of divine action. It is my contention that practical theology has missed this, and in so doing not only has failed to be truly "practical" (not attending to the depth of people's practical experience), which has therefore led to a "theological" deficiency within practical theology itself. Practical theology has rightly started with people's experience, but because it has been blind to the possibility that people have *real* experiences with God, it has neglected to wade deeply into conceptions of divine action that would move practical theology further toward unique theological contributions.

In the four chapters of part 1 I seek to show how practical theology has missed what I call the "evangelical experience." By "evangelical experience" I *do not* mean to make a case for American Evangelical Christianity. This is not a practical theology for Evangelicalism (though Evangelicalism is part of my own story, as I'll discuss in the first chapter). I ask the reader to be diligent in recognizing where I say "evangelical" and where I say "Evangelical" (noting the capitalization).

By "Evangelical" I mean something more like the sociological category of American Evangelicalism that is a loose set of denominations and churches forming a cultural coalition. There are places throughout this book where I have critical things to say about this cultural coalition. Yet, while so doing I want to honor these people and many others (who live out their faith beyond this coalition) that nevertheless assert that they have had real experiences of God coming to them, that they have experienced God speaking to them, directing them, or caring for them.

I call these real experiences of God's coming to people in concrete and lived ways the "evangelical experience." So by "evangelical" I mean something broader and connected back to the Protestant Reformation—experiences like that of Luther, who contends that he had a distinct occurrence of divine action, that Jesus came to him. By "evangelical experience," I mean the centrality of the commitment to a God who comes to us, calling each of us to confess our sin and follow the Jesus who lives. The practical theological approach that I'll present in this book can be read as a deeply committed Protestant perspective of practical theology, an approach that honors the concrete "evangelical experience" of God's coming to us as *pro me* and *pro nobis*.

Therefore, I make this case by articulating the "evangelical experience." The evangelical experience, then, is a realist sense that people have experiences of God's coming to them, that they have experiences of Jesus. T. M. Luhrmann adds texture to what I mean by evangelical experience when she says, "People seem to call themselves evangelical to signal something about their own sense of spirituality. . . . They are asserting that they want Jesus to be as real in their lives as the Gospels say that he was real in the lives of the disciples. . . . For many of them . . . this involves an intense desire to experience personally a God who is as present now as when Christ walked among his followers in Galilee."[2]

Luhrmann, a Stanford professor, has provided a unique argument from within psychological anthropology for what I call the evangelical experience.

In her book *When God Talks Back*, Luhrmann shows the possibility that those who claim such experiences of God actually may have encounters with a divine reality. Luhrmann shows that these claims of experiencing divine action are not mad, but may truly open people up to real experience with the ministering activity of the living Jesus.

I wish to show how practical theology has not always been open to these experiences as real encounters with divine action. I believe that doing so *could* move practical theology onto more significant theological ground, to attend as deeply and concretely with the reality of divine action as practical theology has with human action.

The first part of the book then makes the case that people have concrete experience of divine action and that practical theology has missed this. I use the first two chapters to locate myself and define practical theology. Chapter 3 presents the voices of those whom I interviewed, exploring the shape of their real experience with divine action. Part 1 concludes by examining the most formative approaches to practical theology in North America, showing how these perspectives have, perhaps unwittingly, overlooked divine action.

Following the possibility that people do have concrete and lived experience with the living Jesus, as Luhrmann says, in part 2 I present my own approach to practical theology called Christopraxis practical theology of the cross. This part moves into three distinctly theological chapters that are centered around the concrete and lived experience of divine action itself. I mobilize theological discourse to help make sense of people's concrete experience of God's coming to them as seen in part 1. This coming to them I call *Christopraxis*, which is the continued ministering presence of Christ. The very shape of God's coming to people takes the form of ministry; encounters with divine action come as ministry.

Therefore, I argue that practical theology *is* ministry and that as ministry it is both practical and theological. Ministry is the shape of divine action itself. God is minister. People in my interviews who spoke of the evangelical experience, of encountering divine action, spoke of this action coming to them as ministry, either through the feeling of God's care and healing or through the ministerial activity of another (or themselves to another) that mediated the depth of divine encounter. Therefore my approach to practical theology, called Christopraxis practical theology of the cross, places ministry at the very center, claiming that ministry is practical theology because ministry directs human

2. T. M. Luhrmann, *When God Talks Back: Understanding the American Evangelical Relationship with God* (New York, Vintage, 2012), 13.

action as a response to the nature of divine action. Ministry is the shape of God's very act and being, coming to us as a concrete and lived reality.

But, just as "evangelical" can be confused in my argument, so too can "ministry." By ministry I do not mean clerical or institutional functions, but a relational, personal, and embodied (even emotive) encounter of love and care, a willingness to share in the other, to join in the concrete experiences of homelessness, imprisonment, and hunger, to enter the experiences of suffering for the sake of participating in the transformation toward new life. In these acts of ministry that join concrete humanity, Jesus is present through the ministerial action of the Spirit (Matthew 25). Chapter 5, the first chapter of part 2, explores Christopraxis as ministry, extending and deepening the thought of Ray S. Anderson. Chapter 6 explores ministry as the shape of justification, entering a dialogue with Eberhard Jüngel and seeking to connect practical theology to the heart of the Reformation (justification by faith alone). And by making this connection, this chapter also makes a pitch for practical theology to move away from the Aristotelian framework of actuality to possibility that it has been so embedded within, claiming that such a framework pushes practical theology away from divine action as ministry.

The *consursus Dei* is the focus of the final chapter of part 2, which explores how divine and human action further come together as participation in the divine being through the act of ministry with concrete and lived people. The reader will notice, especially in chapters 6 and 7, both the Lutheran and Reformed elements in my thought. My own history stands equally between these two theological perspectives, as they are linked in the early Reformation. I seek not a Lutheran or a Reformed practical theology, but a practical theology that attends to people's real experience of divine action. I have used Lutheran and Reformed concepts (justification and God's otherness that comes to us in freedom) as hermeneutics of God's action next to concrete human experience; I assert that these perspectives provide lenses with which to understand people's concrete and lived experience of God's coming to them.

The first two parts of this project take distinct steps away from the established conceptions of practical theology, using concrete experiences as a way of critiquing and then reconstructing a practical theological approach. The third part leads me to defend how I can even claim divine action as a reality. After all, since its renaissance in the 1970s, most practical theology has been constructed on antirealist frames (that is, the hermeneutics of suspicion, postmodern deconstruction, and the like). I have said boldly that people have real experiences of God and that God's ministerial being and act may very well be a true reality. But how can I claim this?

I make references throughout the first two parts that my Christopraxis approach rests on critical realism. Critical realism becomes the direct focus of the third part of the book. Here I show how divine action is a possibility through the framework of critical realism. I therefore place my Christopraxis practical theology of the cross on what Christian Smith has called a "critical realist personalism."

In this final part I make a strong case for a realist practical theology, but this realism must be a critical postfoundationalism that sees divine action as a real possibility but always recognizes the need for judgment and evaluation. In other words, it is possible that our experiences of God are truly that, but it is also possible that we are confused or misguided. I claim, with critical realism, that parts of reality exist outside the human mind, that there is a real world that human minds cannot possess. But because this is so, we are always in need of judgment and discernment of our experiences. Because reality is more than us, there is the possibility that we do have real encounters with God. But in the same way, because reality is more than our minds, it is also possible that we are misguided and the evangelical experience is just a stomachache. Therefore, critical realism allows us to honor the evangelical experience, claiming that these experiences of Jesus may be real, but also recognize that they may be erroneous and that we must enter into judgment and discernment as an act of ministry itself. Placing my Christopraxis perspective on a critical realist personalism allows me, in the final chapters of this project, to explore normative conceptions of human action and an interdisciplinary method that places ministry itself as the mechanism that orders the conversation between theology and the sciences.

While this project is uniquely my own, it nevertheless stands within a stream of practical theological projects that have gone before it. These projects have not rested at the center of established practical theology in North America or beyond. The focus on the evangelical experience and its movement into the theological swims in the currents of a certain kind of Princeton practical theology. Princeton practical theology has been both correctly and erroneously perceived as a practical theology concerned with theology. It is quite true that the Princeton school has sought from its beginning to do practical theology always in deep conversation with theology. But what has often been missed is that this embrace of theology has most often been for the purpose of deeply articulating the lived experience of divine action itself—this cannot be ignored, for example, in the introduction of James Loder's *The Transforming Moment*. I'm following then the likes of Charles Erdman,[3] Elmer Homrighausen,[4] and James Loder,[5] who turned strongly to the theological in practical theology to help make sense of the experiential, to help them testify to the very shape of God's coming to them.

Richard Osmer more than anyone else has tended, curated, deepened, and, in the last few decades, shaped the Princeton form of practical theology. I am personally and greatly indebted to Rick Osmer. I came to Princeton Seminary as a PhD student, fresh from the mentoring of Ray Anderson at Fuller. Rick not only encouraged my own unique voice but broadened my theological purviews, motivating me to embrace passionately the theological in the practical theology that Ray had taught me and to move further into conversation with the wider world of practical theology. I'm thankful for Rick's continued encouragement and wisdom around this project.

---

3. Gordon Mikoski and Richard Osmer describe Charles Erdman's theological commitments for practical theology, which were embedded in his own evangelical experience. They state, "Charles Erdman represents the beginning of a trajectory of practical theology that would continue to develop at PTS over the course of the twentieth century. It placed emphasis on theology as central to the identity of so-called 'practical fields.' . . . Moreover, it attempted to develop a theology that was a clear alternative to Reformed orthodoxy, on the one hand, and theological liberalism, on the other." *With Piety and Learning: The History of Practical Theology at Princeton Theological Seminary* (Berlin: LIT, 2012), 85. They continue by describing how Erdman embraced the evangelical experience: "Charles Erdman is best described as a Reformed evangelical. While subscribing to orthodox, Reformed doctrine, he was evangelical in his emphasis on ecumenism in the church's mission and on the spiritual life, which take precedence over confessional distinctives." Ibid., 96.

4. Mikoski and Osmer state, "At the heart of Homrighausen's project is the recovery of the theological grounds of Christian ministry—the ministry of clergy, laity, and the congregation as a whole. This is central to Homrighausen's sense of vocation. When asked why he entered the field of Christian education in the department of practical theology, he responded: 'It is primarily because I regard the practical field as in desperate need of being undergirded by sound theological structure.' Later, reflecting on his time at PTS, he put it this way: 'I felt that all Practical Theology needed to become centered more fully in a theology of the Word. Practical Theology needed to become theological.' Homrighausen's emphasis on theology continues a central feature of the trajectory of practical theology established by Charles Erdman. This will continue to be the case in future decades at PTS." Ibid., 120.

5. Loder's whole project was to makes sense of experience like my own, shared in chapter 1, and those I interviewed, shared in chapter 3. Most famously Loder's own experience of God's coming to him in the Spirit is described, dramatically, in the introduction to *The Transforming Moment* (Colorado Springs: Helmers and Howard, 1989). But before this experience Loder describes another that, because it is less dramatic, connects more directly to the experiences I share in this book. Mikoski and Osmer report, "In an interview with one of his former students, Dana Wright, Loder shared a significant experience that took place during his first year of seminary. His father was diagnosed as having brain cancer and died fairly quickly. At home and in deep grief, Loder grew seriously ill and was confined to bed. He called out to God, 'Do something!' To his surprise, his body was enveloped by a 'warming presence,' leading him to get up out of bed and begin singing, 'Blessed Assurance, Jesus is Mine.'" *With Piety and Learning*, 148.

Jessicah Duckworth and Theresa Latini read many of the chapters as part of a review group the three of us created at Luther Seminary. This group met once a month to discuss each other's writing, providing feedback and encouragement. I'm thankful for their friendship and insight. Blair Bertrand also was kind enough to read the manuscript, providing, as usual, insights and direction. Blair has been one of my most treasured dialogue partners. My Norwegian friend Bård Norhiem was also kind enough to read more than half the manuscript, providing very insightful feedback. Bård and his family have become dear friends to my family over the last five years. It is one of the great blessings of academic life when fellow conference attendees become friends, and when these friendships stretch as deep as children and spouses. Will Bergkamp at Fortress Press has been wonderful to work with. He enthusiastically supported this project from the start. I'm thankful to him and his team, especially Lisa Gruenisen, for all their hard work.

Yet, the greatest thanks go to Erik Leafblad. Erik tediously read through each chapter with me, seeking to make it as clear and consistent as possible. Erik is one of the most talented budding practical theologians that I know, and I'm greatly honored by the attention he gave to each word of this manuscript. Of course, all shortcomings of the book are my own, but without Erik's insight and hard work they would be more glaring.

Finally, Kara Root, my wife, also took great pains to proof and interact with this project; she clarified and deepened my writing, as she has done with all of my work. She is my greatest blessing and it is for her and my children, Owen and Maisy, that I continue to write, hoping to provide something of value to the church that they make their lives within. I have dedicated this book to my mom, Judy, who prayed for me; it was in the context of these prayers that Jesus came to me, to minister to me and give me life.

PART I

1

Introduction

A Theobiographical Starting Point

There was an apple tree that sat just beyond the yard of the first house in which I grew up.[1]

At least in my memory, this apple tree sat right between my house and the house of Benjamin—my first friend. Its low-hanging branches served as the canvas in which my first friendship was painted. As far as I can remember, Benjamin was a good friend, the perfect companion with whom to spend my fourth and fifth years.

Our friendship took the shape of all good childhood friendships: playing. We climbed and pretended, eating apples right from the tree, throwing the rotten ones from the ground at the older neighbor girls. That tree became our universe, a place to be together. Like monkeys in our habitat, we felt as powerful as children can when we climbed the tree's branches. I can remember nothing we talked about, even now I can't remember the sound of Benjamin's voice, but his person, because he was my friend, is somewhere lodged in me. I've taken him with me.

But the idealistic heaven of the apple tree couldn't protect us from forces that indiscriminately crush bodies of children and the hearts of their parents. Benjamin was my first friend, and he was my first friend to die. Cancer got him.

One day he was fine, running and playing, laughing and singing, and the next day a lump appeared in his armpit. Then cancer over took his body, and within months the happy, healthy child was thin as a rail, weak and bald. Once able to outclimb me to the top of that apple tree, he now couldn't even stand.

---

1. I'm stealing the phrase "theobiographical starting point" from Pete Ward in *Participation and Mediation: A Practical Theology for the Liquid Church* (London: SCM, 2008).

Marlen, his mother, fought hard for him. Marlen was a European caught in the Midwest; she had relocated after marrying Benjamin's dad. She still spoke with a deep Dutch accent; she was an anomaly in this whitewashed suburb, a true manifestation of the Old World. Marlen was liberal, brash, and an outspoken and deeply committed (if that is possible) atheist. Culturally, Marlen was three or four decades before her time.

When Benjamin became sick, Marlen wasn't sure she could bear her fate, but bear it she did, with the force and will of a lion. Benjamin's sickness only dug in Marlen's atheism, forcing her to refuse even more forcefully a God who would create a world where she loved her boy so deeply, but lost him so horribly.

But Marlen's brokenness couldn't keep her spirit from yearning for something transcendent and bigger than herself to come, to arrive. She now hated a God she didn't believe in, cursed a Jesus she thought didn't care.

It may be true that there are no atheists in foxholes, but it seems just as true, or maybe more so, that there are no atheists in children's hospitals either. While the solider in a foxhole pleads with God to save him, the parent in the children's hospital does just as much pleading. But after pleading relentlessly hits against the cold wall of impossibility, the pleading turns to cursing. In the wake of parents' misery God surely exists, but sometimes as a brutal thief.

After Benjamin's death Marlen wore her theistic rage like a cloak around her atheism. She claimed her atheism all the more; she lived like a prophet from the Old Testament blaming God for forsaking God's people, giving diatribes about the stupidity of an invisible Man in the clouds and the ignorance of people who see religion or faith as anything other than a language game given to you by your family and its culture.

As fate would have it, Benjamin's little sister would become my little sister's first friend. Elizabeth and my sister now ran and played as Benjamin and I had.

One warm summer night Elizabeth had an experience. Only a very small child herself, and only a few months after Benjamin's death, she awoke to tell her mommy that she had seen Benjamin in her room in the middle of the night and that he was standing with Jesus. She explained that Benjamin kissed her and told her to tell Mommy that he was OK, that Jesus had him.

Marlen, the rigid European atheist, burst through our front door early that morning with tears in her eyes, repeating as she tried to catch her breath, "Benjamin is OK! Elizabeth saw him. He is OK; he is with Jesus."

The very thought that her boy was bound in something she didn't believe was enough. It was a real experience to her, an experience ministered to her by her small daughter, an experience of God, of divine action, that was so real it gave her broken heart comfort. The woman who did not believe in God grasped onto this experience with both hands, trusting it as real, *believing* that Jesus had really come to her daughter to minister to her. Like Saul and the blinding light (Acts 9), or Peter and the vision of the sheet filled with animals (Acts 10), or Mary Magdalene witnessing that the once-dead Jesus now lives (Luke 24), the experience of God's presence, the divine act, shattered what was believed. It came to her in the most concrete and lived experience of her own suffering of nothingness. It was real, she just kept saying; she "believed up against her unbelief" (Mark 9).

Like some forbidden fruit that correlates so shockingly close to the story of Genesis, being with Benjamin, loving Benjamin, gave me, even as a child, the awful knowledge that I and all those I loved "will surely die." I saw clearly that I was no creator, but a creature that must face nothingness. Because of Benjamin, I knew, even as a child, that I possessed the knowledge that Adam and Eve were never meant to know, the knowledge of good and evil, the knowledge of life and death. Watching Benjamin die, I could hear God speak a word of judgment, with an apple in my hand as the token of our friendship, holding it for my emaciated friend, I heard God say (or maybe it was the voice of death itself), "Now *you* shall surely die."

With my paradise lost and Benjamin dead, my childhood experience was haunted. I needed a minister, someone to share this experience with me, but in the aftermath of his death and my seeming resilience I was left alone to bear my experience of nothingness. The denial-based Midwestern culture in which I was raised lacked the capacity to confront such realities with children. No one said anything, imagining I was fine as I ran around the neighborhood with my hand in a baseball glove.

I'm not sure how many months it was after Benjamin's death that they started, but they started with force. Nothingness had snatched my friend from our apple tree and now I feared, I knew, it was coming for me. Some months after Benjamin's death I started having terrible dreams, frightening dreams that seemed to blur the line between awake and asleep. I had deep, dark experiences. I was being haunted and often "awoke" screaming that something was in my room, that something was after me. It felt so real that, once awake, I couldn't sleep again, shaking in fear, terrified of what might meet me when my eyes shut.

The only way to get me back to sleep was for my mom to pray for me, to minister to my person through prayer. And pray she did, often sitting on my bed for hours, praying all the while I worked myself back to a place of sleep. She prayed for me, but, with the help of the old Lutheran ladies at church, she also taught me to pray. Frozen in fear, I'd call my mom, demanding that she pray with me. I'd say, "*please, please, Mommy, pray with me*," grabbing her hands. I wouldn't wait—I'd just start speaking, praying and praying. It seemed to be the only thing to help me stand up against the reality of nothingness. The only thing to witness toward an experience of new possibility, the only thing that I believed brought Jesus close to me. But still the fear was palpable.

When we moved to a new house, leaving the apple tree behind and all the heartbreak it now represented, I suppose Benjamin's death was seen to be behind us. He had lived two doors away from us in our old house—just one house sat between his and ours. Now, in our new house, on our new street, two houses away rested a hole, a cavernous dug-out foundation for a new house. Our first summer in our new house, I had few friends. I was the new kid in a new neighborhood, still carrying the afflictions of haunting nightmares.

I found myself those lonely summer days wandering around that hole, walking its perimeter, throwing rocks into what my childhood self saw as its gaping belly. I think I was fascinated with this hole not only because I was bored, but also because it sat at the same distance, in the same direction as Benjamin's house had. It just simply seemed so fitting that now in this new house a hole, a dark pit sat in its place, as if Benjamin and his family had been sucked from the earth.

I'd roam around that hole, peering into its center, like staring down the nothingness that existed in the world. And, oddly, its greatest appeal, its beckoning for me to come and explore it, almost always came at dusk. Just as the dark was coming, I would hear it whisper to me to come and see, to come and dip my foot into its yawning mouth.

On a summer night in the upper Midwest, the sun does not begin its descent until 9:30 p.m., a time when bedtime is near and the prospect of bad dreams hovers. So I'd walk out to that hole as an odd way of facing the darkness that haunted me, moving me to visit the hole, a hole left where Benjamin once lived.

My dusk walks into my existentialism didn't comfort my mom. She made no connection between Benjamin and that hole; rather, like any good mom, her fear was the danger of a fall and a concussion, so she'd warn me, "Andy, stay away from that hole; it's dangerous." Yet, it called to me. So one night as dusk was descending toward black, I walked over and stood next to the hole, throwing three rocks at its center, staring into its belly, and bending my knees to spit into this hole I despised without knowing why.

But, as I extended from my crouch to propel my loogie into the eye of the hole, my feet lifted from the ground, returning inevitably to a different place, closer to the edge of the hole. And when my toes touched the loose ground, the hole swallowed me into its nothingness. Like a scene from a movie, I slid down, knowing I had just done the one thing my mom had directly warned me against, the thing I knew she was most anxious about. Dropping down its wall into the hole's nothingness, fear gripped me.

Now, in my enemy's grasp, the fear overtook me as dusk faded completely into darkness. In retrospect, I was in little danger. A few more minutes or a few loud yells and adults would have come looking for me. But in the moment, even in my memory, the fear enveloped me. I had come eye-to-eye with nothingness, with the danger that had threatened me, that I imagined had taken Benjamin.

Finding myself now in the pit of nothingness, I did the one thing anyone else would: I ran! With every effort to hold back my tears I ran for the wall of the hole, trying to free myself, but every effort to reach the top led only to my sliding back down into the belly of nothingness, kicking as the nothingness seemed to grab and pull me back.

The tears could no longer be contained as fear pushed big, round drops from my intensely frightened eyes. I looked again at the walls of the hole, scanning its sides for another way out. Stuck with the nothingness that took Benjamin, feeling its eyes penetrating me as it followed ever more, I returned to the action my mom taught me brought the nearness of the ministering Jesus. I had learned from my night torment that I needed Jesus to minister to me, to bring divine action into my nothingness and secure my being. Prayer was the action that drew me into the ministering action of Jesus.

So I prayed for Jesus to come and minister to me. Praying, I felt moved to turn, walk, and sit at the very middle of that hole, the middle eye that I loathed, the middle that represented all the nothingness in the world, that had so concretely taken my friend.

I sat there and I prayed, at the foot of the cross. I pleaded with God to free me from this hole, to rescue me from this nothingness. Like some modern-day Joseph and his fancy coat, I pled with God to minister to me, to rescue me from this hole—from all the nothingness that threatened me.

I then heard two things, as real and concrete as could be, spoken to my spirit. I heard God say I was loved, that Jesus would always be near me to minister to me, that God smiled at the thought of me, that God's delight could not be shaken and Jesus would *always* be for me, coming to me. And then I heard God say, "Run, run, run, run!" Yet, it was not the call to run from something but to it—to the very presence of Jesus that was present to minister to me. So in my Kangaroo tennis shoes I took off like lightning, lightened enough by the embrace of God in the ministering action of Jesus to race up the side to the top of that hole, never stopping as I ran from the belly of the hole's nothingness to my own front door.

Bursting through it, I could do no other than proclaim, to witness to the act of God, to herald the ministering action of Jesus as real. I shouted that Jesus had come to me, meeting me in my experience of hell. So like a mini tornado I swung the screen door open and shouted, "I fell in the hole and prayed and Jesus rescued me! Jesus got me out!"

I announced it with the excitement and shock of Mary Magdalene seeing the angel at the tomb of Jesus. I proclaimed with the same assurance and joy that she did to Peter and the others. I was *not* speaking of a mishap, of the fall into a hole—a situation truly not needing a miracle—but I was testifying to much more: I was confessing that I had been in hell, that I knew it, but in that hellhole I had found Jesus, right there, right where Benjamin's house once sat. It was in that very hell that Jesus found me, ministered to me, and acted to save me. Jesus was real to me in that hole. I screamed over and over, "Jesus rescued me! Jesus rescued me!" My nightmares never returned.

Toward Practical Theology

If practical theology is committed to the concrete and lived, then these experiences of divine encounter, *real* experiences of the presence of God like Marlen's and mine, must make their way into the center of practical theological reflection. If practical theology is to be *practical* (attending to concrete experience) but yet *theological*, then it must make central the encounter of divine and human action. It is my hope in this project to reimagine practical theology through the experience of divine action. The centrality of divine action has not in my opinion been central to practical theology—leading some, as we'll see, to wonder about what makes practical theology theological. My goal in this project is to push practical theology headlong into the theological, but to do this without losing the centrality of the concrete and lived, of the experiential. It is then these experiences, like Marlen's and mine, like Saul's and Peter's, that become central to, and yet often have been neglected by, practical theology.

Because practical theology is about the concrete and lived, I must be upfront and start this project by articulating what it is about my own experience that moves me into this project, seeing both the vitality and missteps of the field.

I have three competing narratives that make practical theology of interest to me and help me make sense of my experiences like the one in the hole. They are narratives that rest in my own biography but nevertheless point, in my mind, to both the potential and peril of the field of practical theology itself. These narratives overlap, making it possible for someone like me to be drawn from one to another. But they also compete.

These three narratives center around (1) practical theology itself and its attention to the concrete and lived, coupled with my upbringing in (2) evangelicalism and (3) my theological heritage in an equally significant neo-Barthianism, laced with strong Lutheran propensities.[2] As I will articulate below, many evangelicals, Lutherans, and Barthians (for their own distinctive reasons) have *not* embraced the reimagining of practical theology that began in the last decades of the twentieth century. And many of them have looked at this reimagining with a raised eyebrow, for while practical theology seeks the concrete and lived, it has not always been able to see experiences like mine as real.

My Narrative

Raised in a conservative Lutheran *evangelical* community,[3] a community who's discourse surrounded (almost equally) Luther and Dobson, the small catechism and the Willow Creek association, a certain pietism that connects the heart, head, and hands was clear in my upbringing.[4] Faith was to be lived; it was to

2. "Nevertheless, while there is a good deal of diversity, there remains a good deal of continuity. Irrespective of the theological and methodological diversity, the common theme that holds Practical Theology together as a discipline is its perspective on, and beginning-point in, human experience and its desire to reflect theologically on that experience." John Swinton and Harriet Mowat, *Practical Theology and Qualitative Research* (London: SCM, 2006), v. Fowler says something similar: "Practical theological approaches are contextual, local, and stay close to experience.""The Emerging New Shape of Practical Theology," in *Practical Theology: International Perspectives*, ed. Friedrich Schweitzer and Johannes van der Ven (Frankfurt: Peter Lang, 1999), 85. Bonnie Miller-McLemore continues, "Methodologically practical theology begins with the concrete and local." "Introduction: The Contributions of Practical Theology," in *The Wiley-Blackwell Companion to Practical Theology*, ed. Bonnie J. Miller-McLemore (Oxford: Wiley-Blackwell, 2012), 7.

3. Practical theology attends to the embodied and concrete, and therefore I present my narrative that leads me into this project. I do this as a way of showing the very personal elements that shape this project. I seek to present this as a way of revealing my experience and not claiming it as conclusive (for instance, my whiteness). My experience and positions in this text are no doubt impacted by this reality. But, even because they are, it is possible that my experience is real, and while it needs to be put in conversation with those with different background, I'm seeking a way to uphold *real* experience while attending to the particularities of gender, race, and the like that so impact our interpretation of these experiences.

4. I'm seeking to draw a distinction between "evangelical" and "Evangelical" throughout this project. My own story has its roots in "Evangelicalism" defined as a sociological category. I will not shy away from how this background has affected me for good or for ill. I have tried to be as critical as affirming of this part of my background. Yet, I'm most interested in making a case not for the cultural Evangelical

be put into action. And it was to be put in action because God was active. We were sinners, but God acted for us. God in Jesus Christ lived with and for me, calling me to *live* as a disciple.

EVANGELICALISM

Finding myself in a classic evangelical college in the mid-1990s directed me deeper into the commitment that faith must be lived. This commitment came with enough weirdness, spiritual elitism, and misguided theology to fill a book. But it also came with a commitment, bound in a form of discourse, that God was active, that we talk about God as moving and living, as a reality who impacts our being, and therefore God deserved to be the subject of active verbs connected to our lives.[5] I had personal experience with this living reality in the most emotive of ways; I had concretely experienced the presence of Jesus with me.

This attention to the concrete and lived made practical theology an ever-intriguing discipline to me. It *appeared* to connect the experience of faith with deep reflection, fusing the academy and the congregation, the church and the world. Its practicality touched my own narrative of faith, but its theological and intellectual depth pushed me into deeper reflective contemplations than my upbringing had invited. Practical theology became a vehicle for thinking deeply about faith and God on the ground and in experience, experience like what happened in the hole.

I was first introduced to the field in an evangelical institution, Fuller Theological Seminary, where I discovered for the first time that such a thing called practical theology existed. This was exhilarating, not only because I had found a new personal and intellectual love, but also because at Fuller practical theology itself was a rebel, a discipline given attention by only a few (perhaps one or two) faculty members and their half-dozen doctoral students. It was no mainstream field in this evangelical institution. And for a lowly MDiv (and then ThM) student to be invited into such closed conversations was thrilling. Like love at first sight, one glimpse of practical theology's possibilities and its evangelical avant garde nature and I was overcome, infatuated. It connected the concrete, lived experience of my upbringing with an intellectual, reflective disposition that I yearned for.

Yet, while I'd marry myself to practical theology, eventually completing a PhD in the subject at Princeton Theological Seminary and then teaching it

experience but for the broader theological evangelical experience, as a theological sense that God through Jesus Christ comes to us in our lives even today as a true reality.

5. As my colleague Roland Martinson often says.

at Luther Seminary (both mainline institutions), my love affair with practical theology was not always smooth. As I ventured deeper into the field, I began to understand why practical theology could never find firm footing in an evangelical institution like Fuller (or even a Lutheran one like Luther Seminary, for that matter). Not only was the discipline's reemergence in the last decades of the twentieth century propelled by thinkers from more liberal universities and divinity schools, but their very theological starting point invited evangelicals with one hand (with a concern for the concrete and lived) while also repelling them with an inability or unwillingness to talk about the agency of God, to see experiences like Marlen's and my own as real encounters with divine action.[6]

PRACTICAL THEOLOGY AND DIVINE ACTION

As I'll argue in the chapters below, practical theology has developed an incredible and admirable ability to discuss the complication and wonder of human action. But the field has been less imaginative (or attentive) to divine action (to the concrete and lived experience of God) in a way that doesn't equate it to or conflate it with human action. This struggle has left even stalwarts in the discipline like Bonnie Miller-McLemore to wonder about the normative theological nature of the field. She has even wondered what is theological about practical theology.[7] Miller-McLemore has called discussions around theological normativity a necessary growing edge for the field.[8]

6. Stephen Pattison also worries about practical theology losing its theological heart and becoming too enamored with human action through the social sciences. "In particular, I worry that this kind of emphasis may collude with a loss of theological focus and interest in the sort of conceptual and imaginative work that practical theology might engage with." *The Challenge of Practical Theology* (London: Jessica Kingsley, 2007), 245. Ted Smith asks something similar, "If theories of practice have been especially useful for the descriptive moments in practical theology, it is not clear just how they should be related to constructive or systematic theological claims." "Theories of Practice" in Miller-McLemore, *The Wiley-Blackwell Companion to Practical Theology*, 252.

7. "Of course, we must have something interesting to say: 'The primary justification for inclusion is the ability to produce an interestingly different angle on life.' This is where practical theologians face a challenge. No one says practical theology is not normative, constructive, or Christian. But do we have something theologically interesting to say? For decades, practical theologians have argued that attention to practice has a yield for theology but specifying this or even getting around to it has been difficult. If practical theology has been partly about transforming academic theology, then it has to show what it has contributed to theology as theology." Bonnie Miller-McLemore, "Misunderstanding about Practical Theology: Presidential Address to the International Academy of Practical Theology," presented at the 2011 conference of the International Academy of Practical Theology, Amsterdam, 2011, 58.

8. "Reformulating the final misunderstanding—that practical theology is largely, if not wholly, descriptive, interpretative, empirical—sounds a little like stating the obvious: practical theology is in fact theology. However, there are benefits of a more explicit correction as follows: As theology, practical

This project then seeks to push practical theology more fully in the direction of divine action (normativity), asserting that doing so does not undercut practical theology's commitment to the concrete and lived but takes it deeper into the experiences like those with which this chapter starts. The heart of the field (and, one might argue, the heart of ministry) is to attend to the encounter of the divine and the human, recognizing them as two *distinct* forms of action that nevertheless associate; this means being open, at least in part, to the idea that the field of practical theology may need to take a deeper ministerial turn as much as an empirical one.[9] This, needless to say, moves us headlong into normative theological conversations, into claiming boldly the *theology* in practical theology.[10] This is something dangerous to do in light of the establishment, but worth the risk, in my opinion, because of the field's severe theological deficiency.[11]

theology is normative. It makes demands on those who practice it to live by the sacred and transcendent convictions it professes. Greater clarity about our theological and not just our practical contribution is one of our challenges but success in this realm will advance the discipline and its value for religious communities and the common good." Ibid., 59.

9. I'm with Karin Heller on this concern and need for practical theology, she states "The constant temptation of practical theology is to come up with a mere translation of God's Word into a language style proper to each community, nation, and culture. The danger faced is to substitute human speech for God's speech. The challenge of practical theology, then, is to reply to this persistent temptation in two ways. First, practical theology has to approach the biblical text in a way that does not nullify God's Word. Second, it has to consent to a constant verification of man's speech about God, Christ, God's people, and ministers by an ongoing return to Scripture and to practical life." "Missio Dei: Envisioning an Apostolic Practical Theology," *Missiolog: An International Review* 37, no. 1 (January 2009): 53.

10. "It is important to return to Paul, the cross, and the great inversion implied in the incarnation because in academic theology we are constantly in danger of forgetting that the foundations of our subject matter and its raison d'être are a-rational, deviant and evangelical. Although we use the tools of critical reason and scholarship to understand religious faith and practice and its significance, we are explorers within a faith tradition; some of our most distinguished and creative predecessors have been labeled as mad!" Pattison, *Challenge of Practical Theology*, 283. Hawkes continues down the road on which Pattison has started us, "But truth is not simply logical; theological truth is certainly not. Nor is the understanding of truth reached purely by logical processes. This is understood now even by the philosophers of natural science. Scientific theories are not reached by 'simple' induction (still less by deduction). Frequently the process of theory-building involves the exercise of creative imagination which intuits a hypothesis, which must then be tested and can never be finally and absolutely proven. The hypothesis, or theory, always remains open to revision; and is always an approximation to rather than a complete description of reality." Gerald Hawkes, "The Role of Theology in Practical Theology," *Journal of Theology for Southern Africa* 49 (December 1984): 47.

11. Gordon Mikoski points to the theological challenges confronting practical theology. "As a cognate problem, practical theology has wrestled with the ways in which it is an authentically theological discipline. The Protestant emphasis on the authority of scripture has helped the field avoid devolution

Perhaps this is unfair. To say that practical theology is theologically deficient is to overlook a number of projects that have spilled ink on chapters addressing their theological frames. But what is interesting is that so often these theological conversations use theology as a frame to attend to human action (conflating the divine with the human). For instance, one of the most popular theological (call it *doctrinal*) perspectives in practical theology is creation. Since Don Browning's work, it has been nearly paradigmatic to use creation as the link between the human and the divine, or really between the human and the theological tradition. While other thinkers have turned to other (doctrinal) perspectives, it appears that the purpose of doing so is *not* to actually use the doctrine to speak of God's independent action, but to add texture to the presentation of human action. In other words, practical theology has become a discipline fluent in talking about concrete human action (practice), but hesitant in speaking of God's action and nature from the locale of the concrete.

MOVING WITHIN AND BEYOND A NEO-BARTHIANISM

My own narrative chafes against this unwillingness to talk of God's action; in the same years that I was falling in love with practical theology, I was being introduced to the work of Karl Barth. Coming from a hyperspiritualized evangelical college, where spiritual growth was a competitive sport, reading the great Swiss theologian was liberation. It was freedom to read of God's action stated so boldly and creatively. It was freedom to see the beauty of God's action done for me and to recognize that my action, while important, paled in comparison to the action of the triune God. While I had perspired pushing myself to spiritual growth, Barth opened my eyes to see all the work was God's own. Barth claimed that God's action comes upon us as an event of reconciliation. I had experienced this in the hole; I believed in the most lived way that Jesus had come to me and rescued me, not so much from the hole but from the nothingness in the world.

While Barth has been an enemy of many practical theologians, who feel perhaps that his perspective on the wholly Otherness of God is too firm to allow for human practice, he nevertheless gives us rich themes to speak of the possibility, of a realism, of God's action in the world, that ministers to mothers in despair and finds little boys who are lost in nothingness. I'll argue below that

into merely empirical social research into human experience of all things religious. Often, however, practical theology defines itself against the abstract and disconnected pontifications of systematic dogmatic theology. In seeking to correct or supplement such theology by attending to lived contexts, practical theology has often underdeveloped the theological dimension of its work." "Mainline Protestantism," in Miller-McLemore, *The Wiley-Blackwell Companion to Practical Theology*, 562.

this is fundamental to the concrete and lived nature of practical theology but is so often missing from the field's presentations.

Yet, outside of a discussion on Barth's articulation of the *concursus Dei* and its grounding for thinking of the partnership of divine and human action, this project will be appreciative, but critical of so-called Barthian practical theologians, asserting that too many have used Barth's perspectives as a cul-de-sac for their own thought; rather than the catalyst to construct more generative accounts of practical theology and its core in purview of divine action.

Therefore, one of my core dialogue partners in this work will be Eberhard Jüngel, who, while indebted to Barth's thought, is no simple commentator. Rather, Jüngel, while drawing on *some* of the material Barth gives him, builds his own constructive theological structure from those pieces. In part 2, I'll follow Jüngel, using him like he does Barth to construct my own perspective on practical theology. Following the path where Jüngel moves through Barth, I'll accompany the former in seeking to place practical theology on a lived articulation of justification.

Toward Justification

To move toward justification is not to make practical theology live as a slave of doctrine. Practical theology has defined itself over and against an applied theology that seeks to simply draw out the practical from the doctrinal, for instance. So my goal here is *not* to make justification applicable by accommodating Jüngel to practical theology. Rather, standing inside a practical theological perspective called *Christopraxis*, I'll use Jüngel as a mutual dialogue partner to see justification not simply as a static doctrine of thought but as an epistemological perspective that articulates a concrete, lived reality of God's ministering action in the world.[12] Justification, I'll argue, is the shape divine

---

12. James Fowler discusses this move away from applied or trickle-down theology. "That older arrangement of the division of labor in theological education rested upon an unfortunate understanding of the relation between theory and practice. The description of practical theology as applied theology indicates the problem: We were working with a 'trickle-down' understanding of applied theology. The assumption was that the creative work in theology went on in the fields of Biblical Studies, Historical Studies, and most especially, Systematic Theology. Ethics, because it touched on the practical and political, had a somewhat ambiguous position. Unconsciously, theological faculties absorbed the positivist bias toward what could be called pure reason, scholarship that proceeded in accordance with the canons of pure research in the sciences. In theological education the results of scholarly inquiry and constructive interpretation in the so-called classical disciplines of theology would be appropriated and applied in the work of church leadership and pastoral practices. That is what I mean when I say that practical leadership and pastoral practices. That is what I mean when I say that practical viewed its work as derivative and second-hand. In this perspective pastors and educators were encouraged to think of themselves as

action takes in the concrete and lived world, coming through nothingness to give new possibility.

In other words, I see justification as the epistemological articulation of an ontological reality of divine action and human impossibility (this points to critical realism that will support my perspective and will be discussed in depth in relation to practical theology in part 3). Justification, in this work, is not a container of thought (as it so often is in *some* Lutheran contexts) but an existential, ontological *reality*. It is an epistemological "best account" of an ontological state (both for God and human beings). This project then is a *realist practical theology* (as we'll explore in part 3, allowing experiences of Jesus like those articulated at the beginning of this chapter to be central in practical theological construction), and justification is the epistemological account of this reality. So, then, I'm not *applying* justification as a static idea but using it as lens to explore a dynamic reality, like that of an atheist celebrating the presence of Jesus. Justification as a lens allows me, in a critical realist way, to favor ontology over epistemology, asserting that what is most real (even real outside of our epistemological account) is human impossibility, the hole, and God's free action for us, to minister to us from nothingness to new possibility (we will explore this in depth in part 2).[13]

Justification has rarely if ever (at least in the English-speaking world) been the framework for thinking about practical theology, and it is easy to see why. Justification, especially in its Luther-inspired form (in the perspective of the *theologia crucis*) sees the human agent as utterly stuck, and stuck so severely that all human forms of thought and action are bent toward impossibility (this is the human being's ontological state). All human action is caught in a fever dream of circularity, leading in only one direction—toward death—with no possibility inside the human agent or its natural history for the fever to break.

In a field overemphasizing the human forms of action (practices constructed or reappropriated by human agents in socially constructed milieus), it is no wonder that justification has been ignored, for justification through the *theologia crucis* claims that human action (practice) is covered in impossibility.

---

consumers . . . of theology, but not as producers. And the laity were viewed as passive receivers of this second-hand theology transmitted by pastors and educators." "Emerging New Shape of Practical Theology," 76.

13. "Christian faith is the language of a community of which the depth grammar is described in its doctrines." R. Ruard Ganzevoort, "Narrative Approaches," in Miller-McLemore, *The Wiley-Blackwell Companion to Practical Theology*, 217. This is similar to my understanding of justification, though I would push the definition a little further to articulate doctrine as an epistemological best account of an ontological reality.

The cross is the end of human action; it claims only God and God's action can save (or even sustain the good). A practical theology from the cross then radically shifts the ground practical theology stands on. From this perspective, human action through justification is to receive the divine act, to receive the ministering presence of the living Jesus. And distinct forms of human action themselves must come after (as responses) to the divine act to save the human out of impossibility and death (or better, through death). It is after experiencing the nearness of Jesus in my hole of nothingness that I'm called into action, to run and to testify that Jesus is found in places of death, making them stages of resurrection, of new possibility.

The conservative Lutheran community in which I grew up gave me an ability to pray to a living and active God, and (in contrast to my college pietism) the old Lutheran ladies taught me that this piety was not bound in what I did. Rather, it was a pietism built on justification, and therefore it came with a deep existential core—not only in the sense of faith meaning something to my personal being, but also in the seeking for God, finding God in human impossibility (something Jüngel himself explores, as we'll see). While it was a pietism that meant faith was lived, it was nevertheless bound within a radical conception of justification as a commitment that human action has no inner redeemable natural core, that all human action, all practice, needs to face its impossibility. No human practice could justify, no human action can run itself out of the hole; only the act of the personal ministering God found in the cross of Christ could justify.

It claimed a deep level of realism: it stated that no matter what thought forms we construct or what new practices we take on (even in their goodness), there is a deeper reality, concretely bound in our death, that we cannot escape. Justification as a frame for practical theology, as I'll argue below, gives us a realism both of the human condition and God's free act in it that recalibrates practical theology away from empirical social constructionism and toward a critical realism where generative visions of divine action, truth, ontology, and reality may be articulated. This logic of *theologia crucis*, of the theology of the cross, stands as a reality (as the real) and thus rests in opposition to many of the core practical theological conceptions that have recently defined the field.

So I will try something very difficult and yet central to the theological commitments of those of us with evangelical, Lutheran, or neo-Barthian propensities in our background, as well as those of us who have concrete and lived experiences (a realism) of Jesus' presence coming to us; I will try to construct an understanding of practical theology that sees at its core an attention to divine and human action, a perspective that affirms such transcendent experiences as concrete and lived and therefore essential for practical theology to affirm and interpret theologically. Therefore, the construction of this project could be called a *Christopraxis practical theology of the cross*.

But before we can get to the constructive heart of the project (parts 2 and 3), it will first be important for me to set the terrain of the field itself, exploring in the next three chapters what practical theology is by first examining both its strengths and weaknesses (chapter 2). Chapter 3 will examine some concrete cases of encounter with divine action, listening to other people's voices of divine encounter like my own presented at the beginning of this chapter. Chapter 4 will, then, explore some of the most dominant models in the field, models I will mine for their attention and construction for normative visions of divine action.

2

Setting the Terrain
What Is Practical Theology, Anyway?

The forecast of religion in America remains tempered, with some spotting trends of decline and others reporting relative stability.[1] But almost no one is predicting clear skies and perfectly happy days for American religion as it moves into the next decades of the twenty-first century. While sociologists and cultural theorists (whether academic or popular) continue to discuss a (new or revived nontraditional) spiritual propensity of the populace, the institutions of religion in America are, it appears, unequivocally taking a hit.

And no institutions are impacted more directly than theological seminaries and divinity schools. Some predict that nearly a third of mainline seminaries will need to close their doors in the next decade or two. Many are already merging, even across denominational and theological traditions, to remain afloat. A radical reorganization, if not already here, has gathered on the horizon with force and is moving in our direction.

As leaders of denominations and educational centers rush to batten down the hatches to either prepare for or mitigate the damage of the high winds of change, they are often turning to practical theology. It is more than obvious that theological education as usual, a theological education that fails to prepare graduates for concrete and lived faith communities, will not do. In the storm of change only a more *practical* perspective, a *practical* perspective that connects

---

1. For an account of decline, see Robert Wuthnow's *After the Baby Boomers: How Twenty -and Thirty-Somethings Are Shaping the Future of American Religion* (Princeton, NJ: Princeton University Press, 2007). For reports of stability, see Mark Chaves, *American Religion: Contemporary Trends* (Princeton, NJ: Princeton University Press, 2011). Though Chaves sees a relative stability in American religion, he nevertheless mentions that religion has experienced slight declines since the 1970s, and particularly since the mid-1990s.

theory with practice, will provide any way to fortify the structures of local congregations and denominations.[2]

THE BASTARD CHILD

Practical theology has experienced a revival of relevance. It was born as the bastard child of another radical transition of theological education, born in the ferocious winds of the arrival of post-Enlightenment modernity, which saw a momentous shift in the location of theological education as it moved from monasteries, abbeys, and humanist classrooms to modern research universities. This shift uprooted theological education from places of formation and repotted it in the soil of empirical science. Because of such an environment, practical theology was pushed into the world.[3]

But its arrival was never celebrated. In the ethos of the modern scientific research university it had no claim to royalty; practical theology's bloodlines were too mixed with experience and practice (with the practical as opposed to the theoretical) to claim the right of the throne of science. Belittled and ignored, it rested at the bottom of the theological encyclopedia, and it was imagined to be a bottom feeder, hoping to gather up the intellectual crumbs that fell from the table of Bible, systematics, and history.[4] Practical theology was to use these scraps to *apply* the noble scientific theories of the university's high table to the peasants out in the practice of ministry. It was believed that if budding pastors had the scientific theory (the true meal) of the classic theological disciplines (systematics, history, and Bible), then with a few concluding courses (a little sweet and fluffy dessert) on management and liturgical organization, they were properly nourished and ready to lead.[5]

---

2. If one trend has been to turn to practical theology, another trend, arguably congruent with the practical theology, is the turn toward the missional. A number of thinkers in practical theology and missiology have begun to cross-fertilize with each other. For instance, Kenda Creasy Dean and Thomas Hastings have drawn on missional perspectives for practical theology, and Ben Conner has pulled from practical theology for his missiological work. See Kena Creasy Dean, *Practicing Passion: Youth and the Quest for a Passionate Church* (Grand Rapids, MI: Eerdmans, 2004); and Thomas Hastings, *Practical Theology and the One Body of Christ: Toward a Missional-Ecumenical Model* (Grand Rapids, MI: Eerdmans, 2007).

3. Richard Osmer, following Edward Farley and others, has made the point that before the modern research university all theology had a practical edge. Osmer calls such heroes of the faith like Luther, Calvin, Augustine, and Paul proto-practical theologians, explaining that for these fathers (and a number of mothers could be added) all theology was embedded in concrete communities and was never imagined outside of the "livedness" of a people.

4. See Gisbertus Voetius's seventeenth-century encyclopedia for an example.

Such a perspective held for centuries. With theological education housed in the brick buildings of universities and the church itself protected by the castles of nobles in Europe and the monocultural socialization of North America, the "university" system of theological education was firmly protected by any strong winds that might blow.

Winds of Change and a Bastard No More

But after a few centuries, and leading into the last decades of the twentieth century, the erosion of the brick walls created by the friction of positivist empiricism and cultural pluralism became evident. The winds of transition began to penetrate the halls of the theology department, coming with a bitter chill that made other empirical fields, such as the hard and social sciences, wonder why a university needed a theology faculty at all. As the church lost cultural relevance and faced the challenge of living in a context in which pluralism and doubt met it at every turn, new students stumbled into the cold lecture halls and seminar rooms already raw from the winds of transition, shaking their heads as the learned "men" spoke with little acknowledgment or concern for the state of change and how these winds had frozen brittle, applied, theory to practice perspectives into irrelevance.

In the 1970s and 1980s a handful of the very scholars teaching in universities made a push for a renewed understanding of practical theology. Recognizing the winds of transition and the erosion of the theological encyclopedia, and bolstered by the recovery of practical philosophies (from Aristotle to Marx to American pragmatism to postmodern deconstruction), people like Don Browning, James Fowler, Edward Farley, Lewis Mudge, and Thomas Groome sought to turn the bastard discipline into a prince (or at least mutual sibling).

---

5. Duncan Forrester explains, "In both Protestantism and Roman Catholicism this tradition has continued almost up to the present with little or no critical theological reflection or suggestion that the subject is or may be a systematic and rigorous discipline in volume after volume of good advice to ministers, and in hints and tips on how to perform traditional functions of ministry. F. D. Schleiermacher's suggestion that practical theology was the completion and 'crown of theological study' indicated the possibility of a better integration between practical theology and the other theological disciplines. But Schleiermacher saw practical theology as no more than the craft of church management, the channel through which the theories of biblical and systematic theology flow to nourish the life of the church. The present structures of church and ministry were accepted uncritically, as was the assumption that the subject addressed itself exclusively to the practice of clergy." "Can Theology Be Practical?," in *Practical Theology: International Perspectives*, ed. Friedrich Schweitzer and Johannes van der Ven (Berlin: Peter Lang, 1999), 8.

Arguing that all theology needed to make a turn to the practical, these scholars sought to move practical theology out of the basement of theological education and into a more constructive and essential place within the endeavor. These scholars made a convincing case that concrete communities of practice (whether congregations or other social forms of lived practice) are the very text of practical theological reflection because these communities are places of embodied theology, places of practical wisdom.

This effort has given practical theology a new relevance. Those standing against the stiff winds of transition are quick to point to practical theology as a way forward, as a way of connecting theory and practice, theological education and ministry, Christian practice and public engagement. After all, if the institutions of American religion are waning but there is nevertheless a potent (though maybe chaotic) spiritual propensity, then maybe theological education would do much better to turn toward these concrete organic communities of experienced practice.

More Complicated than It Seems

Practical theology has been ushered out of its basement room of shame, redefined no longer as bastard, and *maybe* even made leader in a way forward for theological construction. Practical theology has made a move to the concrete, to lived contexts and lived theology, leaving the stuffy library behind for fieldwork and questionnaires. This undertaking has not been done simplistically. But because it has *not* been done simplistically, it has *not* been free from slippage and confusion regarding what exactly practical theology is and how it goes about its work.

I will do my best to avoid this slippage as I seek in the following chapters to recalibrate the field within a lived conception of justification through a Christopraxis practical theology of the cross. Doing all I can to avoid this slippage is not only needed for my argument, but it also communicates my deep appreciation for other practical theological projects and work already offered within the field. I no doubt will be critical of some of this work (even in the paragraphs below) but nevertheless recognize that it also hoists me onto its shoulders, making it possible for someone like me to climb from the theological dungeon of bastard derision into theological partnership.

While many standing in the squall of transition have pointed to practical theology as a helpful way forward, these very advocates in seminary administrations or denominational offices have often found it hard to actually say what practical theology is and who does it—this is the very slippage to which I'm referring. Is it something done by pastors, professors, or laypeople? And what makes a practical theologian different than, say, a biblical scholar who is concerned with the practice of preaching or Bible study in her classroom? Is she a practical theologian as well as Bible scholar? And what exactly is a practical theologian? Practical theology's turn to the concrete and lived is essential (and something I deeply affirm), but how is this done? And where? And by whom?

What Is Practical Theology and How Does It Work?

Two leading scholars in the field of practical theology, Bonnie Miller-McLemore and Richard Osmer, on whom I'll draw first, have spotted this slippage and sought to answer the questions above. Osmer has provided what he calls his "reflective equilibrium model of practical theology."[6] He explains that this is not a method per se, though some have used it that way. Rather, it is a model that seeks to explore the shared operations of those calling themselves practical theologians. Osmer's model seeks to provide some traction on what practical theologians do, on the operations of practical theology.

Osmer has defined practical theology, then, as consisting of four core tasks: the descriptive, interpretative, normative, and pragmatic. These four core tasks, broadly done, articulate what practical theology is and does.[7]

These tasks surround four central questions. The descriptive asks, *what is happening?* and uses tools of thick description to answer it. These tools could include case studies, questionnaires, appreciative inquiry, participant observation, and so forth. The interpretative asks, *why is it happening?* and places the descriptive findings in conversation with frameworks that seek to explain the phenomenon experienced and examined. These usually are cultural, psychological, or anthropological frameworks.

---

6. See Tom Hasting's *Practical Theology and the One Body of Christ* for a critical exploration of Osmer's perspective.

7. In *Practical Theology: An Introduction* (Grand Rapids, MI: Eerdmans, 2008), 9, Osmer provides a summary of these tasks. •"*The descriptive-empirical task.* Gathering information that helps us discern patterns and dynamics in particular episodes, situations, or contexts. •*The interpretive task.* Drawing on theories of the arts and sciences to better understand and explain why these patterns and dynamics are occurring. •*The normative task.* Using theological concepts to interpret particular episodes, situations, or contexts, constructing ethical norms to guide our responses, and learning from 'good practice.' •*The pragmatic task.* Determining strategies of action that will influence situations in ways that are desirable and entering into a reflective conversation with the 'talk back' emerging when they are enacted."

These two core tasks of practical theology bind it unequivocally in concrete and lived contexts. Practical theology, whether it starts with a crisis, established practice, or lived belief, is placed first and foremost on the ground. This is a unanimous commitment across the field. Yet this also makes the field confusing in depiction to outsiders (and in function to some insiders). The need for rigorous attention to the descriptive and interpretive DNA of practical theology can makes it appear, to some, as "social science lite." It can be seen as a kind of sociology in the theological faculty, leading some to wonder about the difference between sociology of religion and practical theology.

For practical theology to continue to be concrete and lived, it must not expunge these tasks from it operation, yet it nevertheless must also think of how such moves (in themselves) point to the theological nature of practical theology. After all, it appears *en vogue* and ruled as good scholarship to nearly take off the theological hat when doing descriptive and interpretive work, before (maybe) putting it on again later. We will explore this assertion in more depth in the discussion of critical realism in part 3. But for now it is enough to ask whether practical theology, by taking off its theological hat and succumbing to the logic of the university (its birth mother that never wanted it), takes on a kind of social constructionism that sees reality as little more than socially constructed phenomena, making the objective of practical theology to articulate empirically human constructs rather than to articulate something about a complicated emergent and stratified reality.

When this happens, the descriptive and interpretive tasks become locked in epistemology (what humans *know* as constructed and observable) and escapes ontological articulations that touch on concrete and lived ways people lean into the mystery of reality itself, a reality bigger and more than socially constructed constructs. Taking on the social constructionism of a hyperempirical social scientific pursuit makes rich conversation about divine and human encounter (those that uphold God's own freedom) ever difficult; for the divine cannot be captured in strict social constructionism without severe reduction. While seeking to avoid reduction but still wed to a hard social constructionism, practical theology runs the risk of avoiding the *theological* and succumbing to the human agent's social construction of God. Or more often, it simply stops talking of God and instead turns to religious phenomena—staying only at the level of the congregation, for instance, and its interaction with political ideologies.

Two Other Core Tasks

Osmer explains that there are two other core tasks to practical theology, two tasks he calls the normative and pragmatic. The questions that mobilize these two tasks ask respectively, *what ought to be happening?* (the normative) and, *what then should we do?* (the pragmatic). Osmer explains clearly that though the normative is the heart of the specifically theological move in practical theology, theology has also been present prior to the operation of this task. As a matter of fact, Osmer in the appendix to his *Teaching Ministry of Congregations* explains that the outworking of these four core tasks, which are shared by all practical theologians, are nevertheless mobilized in different ways depending on an upper lens, which includes things like one's view of praxis, one's theological anthropology, and one's cosmology.[8] I would include one's epistemology in this frame.

Though there is contention about how these normative and pragmatic tasks are used, practical theology clearly needs them to secure its identity as a theological discipline with some value within the faculty and church. While I would argue that in a scholarly frame practical theology has given its most direct attention to description and interpretation, it has not forgotten its pragmatic and performative mandate. Practical theology has not been shy about distinguishing itself from pure sociology or anthropology by asserting that it is interested not only in describing and interpreting the world, but in changing it.[9] For this change to happen, renewed, reimaged, or newly created forms of action are needed. So practical theology hones classic practices of the Christian tradition like liturgy or counseling, helping those performing such practices reflect on them and do them better. Practical theology as pragmatic action may also seek more public, even political, engagement. This search to change the world as much as describe it leads some to assert that practical theology is simply a normative sociology or normative anthropology.

Said either in disparagement or affirmation, such a comment reveals, nevertheless, that this attention to pragmatic action places practical theology within normative commitments. To seek to change things is to make some normative assertion about the deficiency of the present and the new direction

---

8. Richard Osmer, *The Teaching Ministry of Congregations* (Louisville, KY: Westminster John Knox, 2005).

9. "In [practical theology's] focus on concrete instances of religious life, its objective is both to understand and to influence religious wisdom or faith in action in congregations and public life more generally." Miller-McLemore, "Introduction: The Contributions of Practical Theology," in *The Wiley-Blackwell Companion to Practical Theology*, ed. Bonnie J. Miller-McLemore (Oxford: Wiley-Blackwell, 2012), 14.

the future needs to take. Osmer's question, *what ought to be happening?* has most often been taken in this kind of ethical framework, leading practical theology to be seen by some (particularly Don Browning) as a kind of pragmatically engaged ethics.

While honoring the concrete and lived commitments of practical theology, such a perspective nevertheless tends to flatten out divine action, choosing to see normativity as dialogue with the Christian tradition that sets ethical (normative) directions for engagement. Divine action, then, as an independent and free reality, runs the risk of being lost.

Therefore, from my perspective, it may be better to see Osmer's normative question, *what ought to be happening?* not solely in an ethical frame, but also in a revelatory one, that is, asking, *what ought to be happening (what ways should we perceive of reality, ourselves, the church, our practice, and conceptions of God) now that God has encountered us? What ought to happen now that we have experienced the event of God's encounter?* I might change this question to, *now what?* After we've had an experience with the living Christ, now that the divine presence has come to us in hole or dream, in our very concrete and lived experience, ministering to us. Now that we've called these experiences *real*, now what?[10]

The heart of the normative question in the perspective I'll be articulating is the "ought," defined not as moralistic or epistemological (Kantian) but as an event of encounter, as an ontological reality, as the unveiling of God's being next to our own. What ought to happen now that the Spirit has come upon us (Acts 2)? Therefore, my Christopraxis practical theology of the cross frames the normative question of *what ought to happen* not within a philosophical ethic, but as the experience of Pentecost.[11] *Now that the Spirit of the living Christ has fallen on us as a very ontological reality, as something we experience as real, now what?* From the experience of this encounter Peter and the disciples are pushed to performative action (Acts 2)—to preach in such a way that is not only a "best practice" (three thousand are added to their number, as all hear them in their own languages) but is the very participation in the continued action of God (the Spirit moves to build Christ's church by overcoming the curse of Babel in the communion of Word heard and responded to).[12] I could add little to

---

10. This shifting of Osmer's question is actually the heart of this project—Christopraxis.

11. Ray Anderson, whom I am following in my Christopraxis perspective, discusses this Pentecostal starting point. See part 4 of *The Soul of Ministry* (Louisville, KY: Westminster John Knox, 1997).

12. "While we have suggested that the starting point for Practical Theology is human experience, in fact this is not strictly the case. God and the revelation God has given to human beings in Christ is the true starting point far all Practical Theology." John Swinton and Harriet Mowat, *Practical Theology and Qualitative Research* (London: SCM, 2006), 11.

John Swinton's excellent definition of practical theology: "Practical Theology . . . is dedicated to enabling the faithful performance of the gospel and to exploring and taking seriously the complex dynamics of the human encounter with God."[13]

Gripping the Slippage

Osmer's consensus model of the four core tasks has provided helpful traction as we grapple with the slippery nature of practical theology. Osmer has helped us see the core operations of this diverse intellectual makeup of practical theologians. I used the model earlier in a dual manner, both as a way of defining the *shared* movements of practical theology *and* as a way of seeing the problematic way these shared movements have been operationalized in practical theology.

But Osmer's perspective too is not completely free of slippage. In his book *Practical Theology* Osmer explains that these four core tasks explicate what academic practical theologians do. But he also hopes that these four core tasks connect to those directly in the practice of ministry. And I, personally, from work in the classroom, think they can be helpful to practitioners.

But this doesn't alleviate tension around who does practical theology. While the four core tasks may be insightful for those in ministry, is practical theology something done by scholars or something done by pastors? And even in the academy, is the Bible scholar whom I discussed above, who teaches the Pauline epistles with an eye toward preaching and gives assignments to write Sunday morning Bible studies, not also doing practical theology? Confronted with these questions it appears that we want to say yes, but no, confused as to why both the affirmative and negative is in us.

What Is the Definition of Practical Theology? Who Does It?

Bonnie Miller-McLemore has explained that invariably, whenever a conversation on practical theology occurs, someone will say, "Well, what really is practical theology after all?" In other words, who does practical theology and where is it done? If Osmer helps us deal with the slippage in the function of practical theology, then Miller-McLemore helps us deal with the slippage in who does practical theology and where it occurs.

Miller-McLemore explains that practical theology is done in four related but distinctive locales, which therefore possess unique audiences and objectives.

13. Ibid., 4.

She explains that practical theology is (a) a *discipline* done by scholars, yet it is also (b) an *activity of faith* done by believers. But she doesn't stop here, explaining that practical theology can also be defined as (c) a *method* used for studying theology in practice and finally, (d) as a *curricular area* of subdisciplines (like pastoral care, homiletics, liturgy, and youth ministry) located in seminaries and universities.[14]

A) Scholarly Discipline	B) Activity of Faith
C) Method of Study	D) Curricular Area

Figure 1. Four Locales of Practical Theology (from Bonnie Miller-McLemore)

So the biblical scholar described earlier is not a practical theologian in the sense of (a) a discipline done by scholars, and her work is not located in a practical theology department in the sense of (d) a curriculum area, but she is using practical theology inside her Bible course in the sense of (c) a method for studying theology in practice, with the hopes of impacting her students to do practical theology in the sense of (b) an activity of faith done by believers. So in some sense she is involved in practical theology, turning theology to the practical. But she has not exhausted or eliminated the field in her classroom operations.

In my own school there has been a significant turn throughout the institution toward concrete congregations of practice. All faculty are called to attend to these concrete locales in all courses. We are a school that has sensed the winds of transition. But this turn has actually worked to tacitly subjugate the division of practical theology (called "leadership") to a group of misfits that do not fit squarely into Bible, theology, or history. When an argument is made for more clearly affirming the pursuits of practical theology within the division itself, colleagues outside the division will return with, "Well, I also do practical theology in my systematics classes." But what is missed is that yes, they may do practical theology in the sense of (c) a method for studying theology in practice and (b) an activity of faith done by believers, but not as (a) a discipline done by scholars and (d) a curriculum area. We continue to talk past each other because of the slippage in locales, which Miller-McLemore helps us see.

---

14. See Miller-McLemore, "Introduction: The Contributions of Practical Theology," 4.

Therefore, in conversation about practical theology we must be clear about which of the four dimensions of practical theology we are discussing. Miller-McLemore has helpfully shown that we cannot flatten the essential texture of the field itself.

So when I talk of practical theology in this project I mean to keep in mind all four dimensions but will focus directly on practical theology as (a) a discipline done by scholars and (b) an activity of faith done by believers, exploring how it is that a Christopraxis practical theology of the cross might impact and address the scholarly field of practical theology, giving it normative footing within a revelational realism that nevertheless still attends to the concrete and lived. *By focusing on (a) and (b) I am seeking to assert that those in (b) have real experiences of divine action, and it is the job of those in (a) to attend to these concrete experiences, giving theological shape to them.*

Therefore, while the primary audience for this thought experiment is the field itself, I hope to also provide ways that it might impact the vista of those in ministry, most directly because of the centrality that ministry plays within my perspective (I'll argue below that I think practical theology is ministry). I hope to show how practical theology as a discipline done by scholars is connected to practical theology as an activity of faith done by believers, who, as I'll show in the next chapter, have concrete experiences of God's action, of Jesus' presence, coming to them through ministry.

CONNECTING THE A WITH THE B

Practical theology has tended to stick to the phenomenal (to borrow Kant's language), believing that attending to the phenomenal and ignoring the noumenal is, in the end, more *practical* (that is, concrete and lived).[15] Practical theology then attends to phenomenal religious experience.

It has been a great pursuit of practical theology as a discipline to make "practical" or obvious this link between the field as (a) a discipline done by scholars and as (b) an *activity of faith* done by believers. By this I mean that it has worked to make the link close at hand for the human agent. Practical theology has had a certain aversion toward metaphysical assertions about noumenal realities. This knee-jerk disdain for any metaphysical starting point, ruled out as impractical, has tended to make practical theology, at least in North America, uneasy with *even* the revelatory realism that I will be forwarding. I too will stand against a firm metaphysic that is claimed to be beyond experience and

---

15. This, in my opinion, also shows how ingrained practical theology is in eighteenth- and nineteenth-century liberalism.

intangible. But, my assertion is that experiences of transcendence, experiences of Jesus coming to us, may actually be concrete and lived—may be *practical*; they get us out of holes and heal our broken hearts. And because they do, we can claim them as real. Below, I'll ground my perspective not in a disconnected metaphysical but in a commitment to the mysterious nature of reality that comes to us as event. Transcendence, experiences like Marlen's and mine, may be contested but may nevertheless possess the possibility of being real experiences of higher strata of reality, of divine action, not as a pure metaphysic but as an event of ministerial encounter.

There have been three connected ways, like Russian nesting dolls, to make the connection between (a) and (b), between scholarly reflection and the action of practitioners, and each of these ways has tried to avoid some of the pitfalls of nineteenth-century liberalism while not always being opposed to it. These three ways have been an attention to *phronesis*, an exploration of human flourishing, and, most richly, an analysis of practice itself.

Phronesis is a concept taken from the thought of Aristotle. It is practical wisdom as opposed to formal knowledge of the theoretical (*theoria*). It signals a practical form of knowing that stands in contrast to *theoria*. *Phronesis* is a form of knowledge that is acquired by doing through practice; it is more than simply *techne*, but in the end it is attentive to the lived rather than turning to articulations or explorations of universal truths. Its attention rests in the generative depth of human actions, whether those actions are rationally conceived or tacitly formative. It stands in contrast to the theoretical, but it nevertheless is a form of rational knowledge blooming from the concrete, lived experience of reflective doing (from praxis).

Phronesis connects (a) and (b) because it is a form of knowledge that those operating in (a) can attend to that is bound within the practical phenomenal experience of those in (b). Therefore, those in (a) can study those in (b) to see how *phronesis* is operating and formed. Concrete communities, through their practice, take on practical forms of wisdom that deeply impact their communities. Therefore, the practical theologian in (a) can study these actions to see how the practical wisdom is either benefiting or hurting the concrete community. Those engaged in these communities of *phronesis*, those in (b), also are practical theologians because their stewarding of practical wisdom is deeply formative. But this focus on practical wisdom takes little account of the concrete and lived experiences people have of God. *Phronesis* makes the experience of the transcendent of little concern.

What, then, is the objective of *phronesis*? While *theoria* has an objective goal—to be right, to rule, to possess the truth—*phronesis* seeks the virtues necessary for living well together. So we could say that the objective of *phronesis*, and then the next way that practical theology has sought to connect (a) with (b), is to cultivate human flourishing.

The origins of the centrality "of human flourishing" rest in the biblical text: Jesus comes to bring life and bring it abundantly (John 10:10).[16] But this abundant life, in the discourse of the field, also comes from within the phenomenal where it lacks the cruciform conception of abundance that I believe Jesus is pointing to. Human flourishing happens through liberative (or at least engaged and reflective) action that has its core foundations in *phronesis* itself. Because the human agent and her actions in the phenomenal are the source of *phronesis*, attending to her pursuit for flourishing reveals an experienced "good." This anthropological "good" reveals the direction and value of human agency.

The experience of the "good" is equated with the experience of God. To examine actions toward the "good" of human flourishing is to study people's experience of God. So those in (a) explore how those in (b) are acting for the sake of human flourishing, equating, maybe downstream, such action with the work of God. If *phronesis* is rational knowledge, an epistemological way of knowing within practical operations, then teasing out "human flourishing" from within *phronesis* gives practical theology over to the human realm. Human beings determine what it means to flourish because human communities create *phronesis*. It is true that these rationally formed conceptions of human flourishing are born in *phronesis*, which takes its shape through interactive dialogue with tradition (that is, Scripture, creeds, and so forth). But this very dialogue of determining human flourishing happens not with a living God, within transcendent experiences, but with a tradition. While a tradition may be made to live through the hermeneutical operations of a community of *phronesis*, this perspective remains locked within human action. It may be a dynamic interpretative human action, but it nevertheless runs the risk of being human action locked in its own echo chamber.[17]

16. This is the central theme or objective of practical theology as defined in one of the field's most important texts: Dorothy Bass and Craig Dykstra, *Life Abundant: Practical Theology, Theological Education, and Christian Ministry* (Grand Rapids, MI: Eerdmans, 2008).

17. Claire E. Wolfteich articulates what a practice is and shows the tradition-based, human action echo chamber I critique. "Practices are theory-laden; they embody and enact belief. Practices also are deeply formative; they shape belief, religious identity and community. . . . Practices also invite us into spiritual wisdom and transformation. Practice is built into ancient Christian traditions of passing on spiritual

Later we'll need to face how the very act of God, and the very life of the Spirit in a community, changes the frame of human flourishing from a natural and historical logic to an eschatological one bound in the starting point of the cross. In other words, no community of *phronesis* outside the movements of divine action (the Spirit) would imagine that to live is to die (Phil. 1:21) and to be first is to be last (Matt. 20:16). But this is the wisdom of the Spirit; it is the reality (the realism) of God's action, a reality that chafes against *theoria* (the Greeks) and *phronesis* (the Jews) (1 Cor. 1:23). From the perspective of the *theologia crucis*, human flourishing is bound in a deep foolishness. Paul is not trying to construct his communities as practical theologians around *phronesis* that leads to human flourishing but in and through the foolishness of the cross that opens up an all-new ontological realism to them—that makes them not wise but new creations.

This then moves us into the third and final—and the most formative—of our Russian nesting dolls. If *phronesis* is a practical wisdom bound in the phenomenal experience of acting for human flourishing, then these actions of practical wisdom are bound most powerfully in practice.[18] Practices done well together mediate human flourishing and produce *phronesis*.

Practice has become such a paradigmatic concept in practical theology that it has almost become inseparable from the definition of practical theology in North America. Such a definition asserts, at least in the dimension of (a), that while systematics attends to the history of doctrine, practical theology attends to practice. Practice itself has become a text to study, linking (a) and (b). In some practical theologies practice becomes the locale where the divine and human associate or, for some, even merge. Practice is the human-constructed vehicle that brings God's presence. These practices may not have their origin in human constructs; they may be practices given by God. But when they are studied or examined, the methods of the social sciences lead practical theologians to attend to them first and foremost as phenomenal human constructions.

—[?] *Phronesis → Practice*

wisdom." "Re-Claiming Sabbath as Transforming Practical: Critical Reflections in Light of Jewish–Christian Dialogue," in *Religion, Diversity, and Conflict*, ed. Edward Foley (Berlin: LIT, 2011), 254.

18. Swinton and Mowat see practices differently than for human flourishing only and see them in a way I would affirm. "The key thing in this understanding is not that the practice brings particular benefits to individuals or communities (although it may do). The important thing is that the practice bears faithful witness to the God from whom the practice emerges, and whom it reflects, and that it enables individuals and communities to participate faithfully in Christ's redemptive mission. Thus the efficacy of practice (the good to which it is aimed), is not defined pragmatically by its ability to fulfill particular human needs (although it will include that), but by whether or not it participates faithfully in the divine redemptive mission." *Practical Theology and Qualitative Research*, 22.

Ted Smith brilliantly articulates the limits of practice, limits I see bound strongly in the realist perspective on justification that I'll be articulating. Smith shows here how practices that attend only to the cultural can miss the larger purviews of reality itself.

> Theories of practice have opened up significant ground for constructive work in practical theology. But attention to practice, as Certeau saw, eventually runs into limits. The limits of practice are closely linked to the limits of the cultural turn more broadly. They appear at the boundaries of the category of "culture," and especially at the edges of three allegedly foundationalist "others" against which the turn to culture defined itself: nature, material relations, and doctrine. . . . Can we turn to culture as a source and object of study and still make claims about a God who is not identical to culture?[19]

From the level of the theology of the cross, from its very foolishness, we can see that all practice, all forms of action, that do not go through death possess no transformative (soteriological) power.[20] Practice itself must take on this paradigm (hence the reason baptism and communion remain central for Paul and Luther, as they are practices that exist in death-to-life paradigm).[21] They are also bound in the emotive over the linguistic—more on this in part 3.

Practice has become so central to practical theology that it may be fair to organize the multiple projects in the field around their conception of practice. Building on or pushing off from a hermeneutical framework, many recently have constructed their projects around a pseudo neo-Aristotelian conception of

19. Ted Smith, "Theories of Practice," in Miller-McLemore, *The Wiley-Blackwell Companion to Practical Theology*, 251–52.

20. Swinton and Mowat point in the direction I will be headed: "Practical Theology is critical, theological reflection on the practices of the Church as they interact with the practices of the world, with a view to ensuring and enabling faithful participation in God's . . . redemptive practices in, to and for the world." *Practical Theology and Qualitative Research*, 6.

21. It is interesting that in Dykstra and Bass's work on practice, baptism and communion are not as richly articulated as the other practices. Benjamin Conner has critiqued them for this in *Practicing Witness* (Grand Rapids, MI: Eerdmans, 2011). I believe that attending to these two practices (sacraments) pushes the practices into the death-to-life paradigm I see in the theology of the cross and its Christopraxis method I develop. I see practices in a way much more like the way that Swinton and Mowat explain them. "Christian practices are a reflection of the Church's attempts to participate faithfully in the continuing practices of the triune God's redemptive mission to the world." *Practical Theology and Qualitative Research*, 24.

practice, a postmodern Bourdieuian view, or even a critical, liberative take on practice. These philosophical frameworks have become bridges linking (a) and (b), and thus they have also become frames of the ways the human associates with the divine.

Because this has been so central and poignant, in chapter 4 I'll use these differing grounds of practice to explore multiple and significant projects in practical theology. I'll do this not with the intention of disparaging these perspectives but with great appreciation as a way of exploring how my own Christopraxis practical theology of the cross may differ in the way it conceives of divine action, human encounter of the divine, the human condition, and the ontological realism it rests on.

In chapter 4 I will also explore four perspectives of practical theology.[22] I will examine a hermeneutical (Gadamerian) perspective represented by Don Browning; a postmodern Bourdieuian perspective represented by Bonnie Miller-McLemore and Mary McClintock Fulkerson; a pseudo neo-Aristotelian perspective represented by Dorothy Bass, Craig Dykstra, and Kathleen Cahalan; and a strict Barthian perspective represented by Andrew Purves.[23]

But, before I can move to this, it is important to honor the concrete and lived nature of practical theology, broadening my own experience by listening to the voices of others, by placing my own experience of the ministering Jesus in conversation with others. To do this, the next chapter will present interviews with a number of laypeople who tell stories of their encounter with God, of Jesus coming to them to minister to them and to send them out into ministry.

---

22. I am following Richard Osmer, with some notable additions and subtractions, in my mapping and exploring of the dominant models of practical theology in the next chapter. Osmer states, "We can identify at least five paradigms of practical theology in contemporary American practical theology, which cross ecumenical lines: (1) a postmodern transforming practice approach (Mary McClintock Fulkerson, Bonnie Miller-McLemore); (2) a hermeneutical approach (Charles Gerkin, Thomas Groome, James Fowler, Don Browning); (3) a Christo-praxis approach (Ray Anderson, Andrew Root, Richard Osmer); (4) a neo-Aristotelian practices approach (Dorothy Bass, Craig Dykstra); and (5) a neo-Barthian approach (James Loder, Deborah Hunsinger)." "The United States," in Miller-McLemore, *The Wiley-Blackwell Companion to Practical Theology*, 503.

23. I call the third perspective "pseudo" because both Bass and Dykstra affirm their indebtedness to Alasdair MacIntyre, the leading philosophical neo-Aristotelian thinker on practice, but also distance themselves from him. Their distancing has much to do with a desire to infuse a rich theological perspective to the conversation. Therefore, the "pseudo" signals their distancing, but the label nevertheless highlights their indebtedness to the perspective.

3

Concrete Lived Cases of Ministerial Encounter with Divine Action

I began chapter 1 by articulating one of my own concrete experiences with divine action. This experience and others that have followed it, I claimed, are real; God's presence has come to me, and come to me in the most practical and lived ways. But all experience is contested. Its contested nature *does not* prevent it from being real, but it does mean that all such experiences must be placed in dialogue. I must remain open to the possibility that my interpretation of my real experience, through dialogue, may be reworked.

It is possible that I did not experience God in the hole and that there are other explanations. The reader may have already thought of a few. But these other explanations, too, must be put back into dialogue, continuing the conversation, for no interpretation stands on a foundation that can conclusively rule on others.[1] We can no doubt provisionally evaluate one interpretation over another, having very good reasons for this interpretation and not the next (I'm foreshadowing the discussion in part 3 around critical realism's postfoundational judgmental rationality).

I then claim, for good reasons, that my experience in the hole was real, that Jesus came to me, ministered to me, and set me free. I claim that I've had a concrete and lived experience of divine action, one not equal, but nevertheless similar, to Paul's, Peter's, and Mary Magdalene's. It is possible that these biblical foremothers and forefathers point to the concrete and lived encounter with divine action (with the living Jesus) that is central to all Christian faith. Christian faith, at least in its broad evangelical commitments, claims the necessity of experiencing Jesus, of God showing up as an event of encounter.

---

1. For a direct social-scientific perspective that uses interview data, see T. M. Luhrmann, *When God Talks Back: Understanding the American Evangelical Relationship with God* (New York: Vintage, 2012).

As a theological enterprise that attends to experience, practical theology should use (a) the constructions of scholars to help (b) believers make sense of such experiences (see figure 1). It may be that practical theology is to give critical and constructive assistance as individuals and communities make sense of their encounters with the living Jesus, with the moments and episodes of the Spirit descending upon them. Embracing such experiences as real, I believe, helps practical theology claim its theological (normative) center, which it so often has been missing since its renaissance in the twentieth century. Practical theology is lived and theological through its exploration of such concrete experiences, as it attends to divine action as a lived reality. Luhrmann shows in her own extensive study how such experiences of God's action are deeply concrete and lived for those who claim them as real. She says, "[People] map [their] abstract God from their own particular lives. They use their own experience of how conversation happens and how they relate to trusted friends to pick out thoughts and images in their minds that are like those ordinary moments, but different in certain ways."[2]

The Anselmian call for "faith seeking understanding" may start and gather its energy not in rational study of past theological points but in the pursuit to make sense of our concrete and lived experiences of Jesus who finds us in a hole, knocks us from our horse, or comes to our daughter in her sleep.

Dialogue

As I said earlier, these experiences of the divine are contested and must be placed in dialogue. So within this chapter I will take one step to place my own experience in *one* kind of dialogue with others. After all, this project is not an apologetic for my own experience; rather, it has started with my own experience only to honor the experiential and lived heart of practical theology. But because it is not an apologetic for my own experience, my experience must be placed in dialogue with the experiences of others. It is now time to examine other experiences of divine action.

Clearly, I could have chosen to place my experience in dialogue with those who claim no such experience (Margaret Archer explains beautifully that the experience of the absence of transcendence is no more authoritative than the experience of transcendence).[3] I could have chosen to place my experience in dialogue with those who believe my experience of Jesus is an illusion, a psychological yearning, or the imaginative hiccup of a stressed, fearful small

2. Ibid., 47.

3. See part 3 for a long dialogue on this point.

boy. And much like Paul, I do have to entertain the possibility that it may not have been the voice of Jesus that came to me, but just the thunder (Act 9). But, considering this possibility seems not quite to square with my experience, and my own experience seems to find congruence with the testimony of others who have also claimed to encounter divine action.[4] So if it is possible that it was only a psychological illusion, it is also possible that it was real—real enough to reorder my psychological state. For just as Paul was blind and then made to see, was a killer made follower, I was haunted by my dreams and then released to sleep well, night after night in peace, after Jesus came to me.

THE LOCATION

I have chosen to conduct interviews as a way of placing my own concrete experience in conversation with others. The people I interviewed were members of two congregations, both located in the Pacific Northwest. I chose the Pacific Norwest because its larger cultural locale is not soaked in church talk, as some parts of the Bible Belt are, for instance. Rather, the Pacific Northwest is often considered to be one of the more secular regions of the United States. Only the Northeast rivals it for secularity. But speaking in broad terms, unlike the Northeast, the Pacific Northwest, both because of its recreation culture and the historical ethos of western immigration in the United States, tends to be a place where people are open to the possibility of transcendent, even spiritual, experiences (of course, these are often connected to nature and distinctly disconnected from the church).

I talked with people only in churches (due to the pursuits of the study) but picked these churches because of the ethos of their locale. My desire in interviewing these people was to see if they too had experiences of divine action and if they would describe these experiences of Jesus and God coming to them. I wanted to explore what shape these experiences had for them and whether it was similar to or distinct from my own experience.[5] Therefore, at points I did

4. The ten interviews that I did found congruence with my own experience. And importantly, my own experience and these ten interviews found correction with another (much more expansive) research study conducted by Luhrmann, as described in *When God Talks Back.*

5. My own experience is not eliminated in this form of research, as Rubin and Rubin explain, "In qualitative interviewing, the researcher is not neutral, distant, or emotionally uninvolved. He or she forms a relationship with the interviewee, and that relationship is likely to be involving. The researcher's empathy, sensitivity, humor, and sincerity are important tools for the research. The researcher is asking for a lot of openness from the interviewees; he or she is unlikely to get that openness by being closed and impersonal." Herbert J. Rubin and Irene S. Rubin, *Qualitative Interviewing: The Art of Hearing Data* (Thousand Oaks, CA: Sage, 1995), 12.

not shy away from describing my own experience, asking if it matched their own—I was open to encountering difference and seeing my own experience in a new light.

All those invited to be interviewed were laypeople, chosen by their pastor because in their pastor's mind they were able to talk in an articulate manner about their faith. This was the only criterion. My approach was not to do a congregational study but rather to do semistructured life-history interviews.

Because this was not a congregational study, my concern in picking the congregation was only in its ability to provide me with interesting people to interview. And because I was listening for their experience of divine action, I chose to ask pastors of a moderate Evangelical (PCUSA) congregation located a half hour outside Seattle and a moderate Mainline (ELCA) congregation just outside Portland.[6] I thought it would be more interesting to interview people from congregations not often known for talking easily about experiences of God but nevertheless not allergic to them. I chose to stay away from more conservative Pentecostal congregations, not because I am suspect of their experience of divine action, but because such language is more socialized in such churches.[7] I also stayed away from more classically liberal congregations, not because I believe people are absent such experiences at these churches, but because their socialized patterns often discourage such talk. Therefore, I chose two congregations that did not necessarily reward talk of real experiences with Jesus but also did not discourage it.

The Approach: The Ministry of Interviewing

As mentioned, my research method was semistructured life histories as developed by Rubin and Rubin in their book *Qualitative Interviewing*. The

---

6. On the West Coast and especially in larger parts of Washington, PCUSA congregations tend to identify more as Evangelicals. This particular congregation most definitely did.

7. So while Luhrmann's study looked at Vineyard Church, I sought to see if people in more moderate denominations without a history of talking in such a breezy way about divine action would nevertheless do so. They did, and in very similar ways to the people in Luhrmann's study. They were perhaps more hesitant, but all spoke of at least one concrete experience of God, and they told of this experience as hearing God speak to them. It was a deeply emotive experience and never simply intellectual. Like in Luhrmann's study, the ten people I interviewed spoke of direct experiences with God but spoke of them as rare. They would say, "God did speak to me once." These were not weekly occurrences, but rather events that happen only one to four times in people's lives. Yet, when they happened, they were transformational. Luhrmann explains, "These special moments are not common in the life of the believer, but they are extremely important. They demonstrate that God matters, not just as an abstract principle of the universe, like gravity, but that God is present for you in particular, and that he cares." *When God Talks Back*, 127.

"semistructured" refers to the loose structuring of the thirty-minute interview. I prepared a list of six questions but entered the interview anticipating, even hoping, that we would get to no more than two or three. This hope rested in the "semi" element of the structured interview.[8] As Rubin and Rubin say, this kind of interviewing method is like planning a vacation; you plan enough to get going, welcoming new directions and opportunities as they come.

My desire was to hear these people's experiences. My interview questions only existed to invite conversation, allowing the answers to take our conversation in new and unique directions. Rubin and Rubin explain, "The purpose of main questions is to encourage people to describe their lives, providing narratives, stories, and examples that the researcher can analyze and follow up on."[9]

The structuring of these questions revolved around life history. Rubin and Rubin explain life-history research, "In life histories, what is being studied is the major life events of those being interviewed. . . . Questions are asked that tap the interviewee's experiences."[10] I invited the people I interviewed to discuss the experience of divine action, exploring such experiences throughout their life of faith (whether that be long or short).[11] The advantage of life-history research is that it mines experiences of reality in and through biography.[12] This is why I began this project not only with my own experience but also with the biographical elements that led to its deeper narration. In a much more truncated

8. Rubin and Rubin explain the difference between quantitate and qualitative research. Their explanation nicely states why I chose to do this research with these two congregations. I was not looking for generalizable data but rather seeking to hear and share in peoples' stories. "One of the key differences between qualitative interviewing and survey interviewing is that the surveyors are trying to generalize relatively simple information, such as who are you going to vote for, whereas the qualitative interviewers are trying to learn about complex phenomena. Qualitative interviewers don't try to simplify, but instead try to capture some of the richness and complexity of their subject matter and explain it in a comprehensible way." *Qualitative Interviewing*, 76.

9. Ibid., 178.

10. Ibid., 6, 10. Rubin and Rubin give guidelines for how to avoid hearing only what affirms the interviewer's position. I sought to keep this in mind. "By being aware of your own specialized vocabulary and cultural assumptions, you are less likely to impose your own opinions on the interviewees. It is the interviewee's ideas you want to hear, and you don't want to block that communication by putting your own assumptions in the way." Ibid., 19.

11. Rubin and Rubin say more, "Life histories focus more on the experiences of an individual and what he or she felt as he or she passed through the different stages of life. . . . Life histories involve a combination of narratives and stories that both interpret the past and make it acceptable, understandable, and important." Ibid., 27

12. Rubin and Rubin state, "In teaching, as in interviewing, biography affects what is shared." Ibid., 14.

manner I was seeking the biographical elements that surround the experiences of divine action of those I interviewed.

The great surprise of doing this research is how it was quickly transformed from being merely research; the interviewing itself became an experience of Christopraxis (as I'll unpack in part 2). The stories shared became fertile ground for new experiences of divine action as mutually we testified to God's moving in our lives. At a few points, people actually said through tears, "I've never told this story before; it is such a blessing to do so."

It became clear to me that this approach was not just an adequate way to gather information but an experience of ministry itself. As this project unfolds and I present my own Christopraxis practical theology of the cross, I will critique the empirical turn that has occurred in practical theology. But my critique of this empirical turn is not that it has sought to move deeply into the concrete and lived but that it has been done more so as science than as *ministry*.

I'm not suggesting that because this form of empirical research takes the shape of ministry that it doesn't work hard to hear correctly. As a matter of fact, seeing qualitative research as a possible event of ministry may push us harder to hear correctly, to not impose our own position but to do what Rubin and Rubin say a good researcher does: "To understand what people are saying, interviewers learn to hear the taken-for-granted assumptions of the interviewees and try hard to understand the experiences that have shaped these assumptions."[13] Qualitative research can, perhaps, participate in the ministry of divine action as it bears witness to the concrete reality of people's experience with divine encounter.

For this reason, I will argue, particularly in part 2, that practical theology is ministry. And my semistructured life-history interviews witnessed to the possibility of even the qualitative research of those in (a, the discipline done by scholars) being an action of ministry with and for those in (b, an activity of faith done by believers) and that hearing the stories of those believers may minister back to those in the scholarly discipline of practical theology. It may be ministry (as sharing the personhood of the other as testimony or witness, or as participating in the real experiences of God's presence) that allows (a) and (b) to find their link. Even the methods and approaches of the academic study of those in (a) should wear the marks of ministry itself—this was the surprising realization I had in doing these interviews.

13. Ibid., 9.

REPORTING

I interviewed a total of ten people (five per congregation). Interestingly, all ten people told stories of unique experiences of God; many talked specifically of Jesus encountering them and coming to them in transcendent and eventful ways. For the sake of the reader I will not report all ten of these interviews in depth but will instead organize the interviews based on the two churches in which they were done, providing an overview of each of the interviews and offering significant snippets from our conversation.

As we move into part 2 and the construction of a Christopraxis practical theology of the cross, we will return to the experiences and stories of these people to give flesh to my perspective. So this reporting serves two larger purposes. It stands alone as the articulation of people's concrete and lived experience of divine action, providing experiences other than just my own for practical theology to consider, to recognize that attention to divine action (as a theological pursuit) may be close to the heart of practical theology. I desire for practical theology to see that if it truly wishes to attend to the concrete and lived, then it must not neglect the concrete and lived experiences some (*many*) people have of divine action. Attention to people's experience of divine action, I believe, moves practical theology like an undertow into deeper theological waters. But, these interviews do more stylistically as I seek to construct a complicated approach called a Christopraxis practical theology of the cross. These interviews provide the reader with the fleshy, lived experience that will make my more complex argument breathe.

THE LUTHERAN CHURCH

The ELCA congregation in which I did my first interview session is located outside Portland. It is an area that many professionals come to retire, a place to get away outside the urban and suburban centers of greater Portland. It is still close enough to allow easy back and forth to the city, yet far enough to allow for the change of pace that many seek who move here. It is a beautifully scenic community that this church rests in, and all the people I talked with took pride in its natural beauty.

Because of the congregation's locale as a retirement destination, there is a strong presence of older folks in the church, but this is coupled with a growing number of younger families as well. My five interviews were representative of this demographic.

My first interview was with Shirley.[14] Shirley is a woman in her early seventies who has been a member of the church for three years, coming after her husband's retirement. She is a lovely soft-spoken woman who spends most of her free hours running the quilting ministry of the church. She is unassuming in every way, so it was quite a shock when she told me that at the age of thirteen (in the 1950s) she had been a spy for the FBI, with her parents infiltrating the budding Communist groups of Washington by posing as Communists themselves. She had even, when she was eighteen, spent time in Prague, behind Communist lines, spying on assemblies of gathered party supporters. She explained that at the end of each day she had to write entries of the day's happenings for the FBI, careful of what she said aloud in her hotel room, aware that it was bugged.

Shirley now sits before me a grandmother and quilter, similar to the thousands that fill our churches, and yet the intrigue of her story is beyond imagination. I'm aware of the privilege of hearing it as she tells me that only in the last four years and only to a handful of people has she ever told these details of her life.

Yet, even before her clandestine operations, Shirley had a significant, eventful experience with Jesus. As a nine-year-old she had become ill and bedridden. The illness was so severe that it kept her from school for years, most days restricting her to her bed. Her parents, as she explained to me, were not churchgoing people and, while she had been baptized, she had not been back to church and knew nothing of Jesus.

To pass the hours bound to her bed she would listen to the radio. When her programs of choice ended, she would listen to the radio preachers and their words about Jesus. One day in the middle of a difficult moment, when the pain was nearly more than her nine-year-old being could take, she called out to Jesus and asked Jesus to be with her. She says, "I had this feeling of Jesus' presence. And I laid there and it was so dark, I was in a lot of pain. But God—I asked God, 'What God, please God,' and then I went to sleep. I was aware that I had been not exactly rescued but cared for."

Much like my own experience in the hole, in my own childhood, Shirley experienced a God that comes not to fix but as the ministering Spirit of Jesus who comes, as she says, to "care for." She says directly, "I had this sense of God's presence taking care of me."

Lynn, a woman in her late fifties, would also tell me of an eventful experience of God's coming to her. I asked her, as I had Shirley, "When did faith become important to you?" With nearly all of the ten interviews it

14. All names and identities of those interviewed have been changed.

was in response to this open life-history question that they would share their experience of divine action, relaying it in deep eventfulness. This points in the direction of my earlier statement that Christian faith may be intertwined with such experiences of divine action.

For Lynn, this experience happened on an airplane. She had become deeply involved in a woman's prayer group in her thirties; this group supported and cared for her. She felt like these women had ministered to her by sharing deeply in her life and by praying for her, as the Lutheran old ladies had done for me. One of the women from the group suggested that Lynn read Augustine's *Confessions*. She finally got to it on a plane, and as she did, God's presence came upon her. She says, "I had been reading St. Augustine and I just felt like I was floating off the airplane. I said 'OK, God, I know who you are and that you really exist now,' and it was a physical feeling as well as an emotional feeling. . . . It was just a wonderful feeling. It was physical, all the way from my head to my toes. It must be what total love feels like."

It is interesting that Lynn says, "I know who you are"; through the experience of divine action, of God coming to her as event, she received the knowledge of who God is. Within the experience, not outside of it, she is transformed. Much like Paul, it is not until the event of personal, experiential encounter with divine action that knowledge falls into place. It is also interesting that Lynn speaks of this experience as a deeply physical reality. Through cause that impacts the emotive, according to Archer, we are moved to call something real. This experience feels so real—Lynn cannot be persuaded it wasn't real—because she *felt* a *cause* impact her very person.

Both Shirley's and Lynn's experiences of divine action came to them as a felt cause of love and acceptance. They experienced Jesus come to them to minister to their person. Yet, interestingly, Greg, Sarah, and Mark had experiences with divine action in the act of ministry itself.

Greg is a no-nonsense man who has just entered retirement. He is not the *feeler* that Shirley and Lynn could be interpreted to be. In the first half of our interview he is very rational and reasoned. Speaking in the ethos of, "God helps those that help themselves," he is skeptical of those who speak too often of divine action. But as our conversation continues, he says, "I *feel* there's one time that God did speak directly to me." Greg explains that his good friend's father had just died. This friend shared a Lakota heritage with Greg, and watching him grieve the loss of his father was deeply painful. Greg says, "I didn't have the words to bring comfort, so I asked God for help." Greg asks for divine action to lead him into ministry. As he was gardening, Greg explains, he heard God speak to him, giving him, he is sure, the words to say to his friend, words that could minister to his friend's broken person.

Through the action of ministering to another person Greg had an experience of divine action—God eventfully "showed up." Greg frames it as a time God spoke directly to him. Both Shirley and Lynn felt the ministering presence of God come to them; Greg experienced God's presence though the participatory act of ministry itself.

Sarah too had an experience of divine action through the act of ministry to another. Sarah is in her mid-twenties and returned to the congregation after college. Since then she has become the leader of the youth group. I asked her, "Have you ever had an experience of God's presence?" Sarah, responded, "Yes, many." Asked to pick one she described an experience of ministering to another.

Sarah said that she was at wedding and saw a former youth group kid named Erin that had grown up and now had a family of her own. She felt this overwhelming feeling that she should reach out to her. It had been a number of years, and truth be told, Sarah explained, she didn't know her that well even back when she was in the youth group. Yet she couldn't shake this feeling she needed to talk with her. To Sarah's shock, a day later her sister informed her that she had run into Erin, not knowing that Erin "had been laying heavy on [Sarah's] heart." Feeling that God was up to something, Sarah says, she sent Erin a Facebook message. Sarah received a nearly immediate response, with Erin saying that she had been thinking about how she wanted to talk with Sarah.

Sarah met Erin for coffee, and within minutes Erin was sharing the deep pain of her parents' recent divorce. Sarah explained to me that she heard clearly God's voice directing her, communing with her in the action of ministry itself. Sarah says,

> Every time I opened my mouth to say something to Erin, there was a big loud voice in the back of my head saying, "Sarah, do not say one word. Not one word. Don't say it. You are not here to talk. You are here to listen." And it was such an odd place to be because it was so clear the two voices that I was hearing. Erin telling me X, Y, and Z and the one that for me was absolutely God saying, "Don't talk. This is not about you. You need to listen." And then sitting there going, "OK, but what do you want me to do?" And it wasn't about me doing anything.

In a manner similar to Greg's encounter, Sarah encountered divine action as real in and through the action of ministry itself. Divine action came to her as Christ's own praxis, as Christopraxis, binding her own human action with the divine. She heard God directing her, telling her not to do anything but be present with Erin's broken person, sharing in her person as an act of ministry.

Matt, the final person I interviewed at the Lutheran church, highlights this point. Matt is in his early fifties. He was raised Catholic but since childhood has found it hard to connect to either a church or God. He explains that he always believed God existed but had no real experiences of God. After moving to this community Matt and his wife visited the church, feeling they had a fresh start. Matt said, "I'd never really dipped my foot in the pool with regard to doing any type of ministry. And so, I decided, you know, blank slate, I could do that now. So I asked [the pastor] if he knew of anything that I might be able to do."

Matt soon found himself engaged in the congregation's homeless ministry, traveling into Portland weekly to share a meal and clothing with people on the streets. Matt was surprised how much he saw himself in the homeless faces he met. He explained to me that in the late 1980s after a few failed business endeavors he'd almost found himself on the street.

Matt figured, as he started in homeless ministry, that he was there simply to do the grunt work of carrying boxes and unloading trucks. But this personal experience affected him deeply, and soon he felt drawn closer particularly to the men he met in the streets, and he felt God leading him deeper.

Something changed for Matt: he was no longer simply volunteering but was doing ministry. And this doing of ministry drew him near the persons of these homeless men, leading him into an experience of divine action, of feeling Jesus coming to him. He says, "I never really had my own church or an experience of God. And so, when I did the homeless ministry here, it clicked, and then I knew, OK, this is what Jesus is all about. You know, this is what my connection is. This is how I feel closest to Him, this made me realize there's a God, there's Jesus, and he's working through me." It was in the action of ministry that Matt felt himself taken near divine action. Matt experienced the presence of Jesus as he joined Jesus' own action of ministry to these homeless men.

This divine action that comes to Matt through ministry is bound in one person sharing in another, in Matt sharing in these homeless men's lives (this is the hypostatic shape of ministry that we will explore in part 2). Matt goes so far as to say that he experiences the presence of Jesus not simply in the doing of activities but in the personal encounter with the concrete and lived humanity of these men. Matt says he feels Jesus near them, ministering to them, so when

Matt joins their person, he is taken into the movements of Jesus' own praxis. Matt says it in his own way: "I feel close to God in doing this ministry. But I feel that He's [Jesus is] also with them—I know He is, and He's giving Himself to me through them. I have done some volunteering, but it was never on this level. I just feel very touched, you know, by God, in doing this."

Matt witnesses through his words that the act of ministry draws him into the experience of divine action. He feels his past volunteering is important, but his experience in ministry is different, and it is different in his mind because the presence of God encounters him through the ministering praxis of Jesus. Matt states as much when he says, "I always had some faith, even when I was young, but this really made me feel like, OK, now God's really in my life. And, it has changed me." Matt has a real experience of God's coming through the action of ministry itself.

Evangelical Presbyterian Church

The Presbyterian church is located in a large suburb of Seattle. The church itself is large, with dozens of programs for all ages packed around three weekly worship services. Yet, while the church is large, the leaders have worked hard to make sure people don't fall through the cracks, encouraging them to get involved, and not as volunteers serving programs but as ministers seeking the presence of God.

Margo is in her mid-fifties; she is a thoughtful woman who works hard to answer my questions precisely, pausing between each sentence. She explains that she has particularly experienced the presence of God in the dark pit; as in my own story, Margo too has faced the nothingness of a hole. She says, "My son has a lot of mental health issues and I've been desperate for strength and wisdom, and I'm thankful that I've turned to God and found Him there."

She explains with beauty, dignity, and deep pain the struggles she has faced with her son. These are unequivocally concrete and lived experiences; in the dense experience of this struggle of love for her son Margo articulates the nearness of God. There is nothing more concrete and lived for Margo than the experience of her son's struggle. And right in the middle of these struggles with nothingness she has a profound experience of God's coming to her, caring for her, and seeing her through, as God provides strength and wisdom from God's own hand. Her son's situation has pushed Margo to the point of breaking, but it has also given her the distinct and sure feeling of God's presence, coming to her, helping her make it through the day. Margo is even brave enough to say, "I think when things are going well you don't feel that same presence, but when there's difficulties, I feel God near me." Margo explains there is a sense of God's particular nearness in experiences of suffering.

This could no doubt be interpreted as the weakness of the human consciousness, saying that when we are up against the uncontrollable, we turn to an invisible reality to do what we cannot do for ourselves. This is possible! But it doesn't square with Margo's experience. And, therefore, it is just as possible that we experience God near to us in our suffering *because* this God who encounters us through the Spirit in the person of Jesus Christ comes to us as a minister (this is to foreshadow the heart of my Christopraxis approach), joining the reality of nothingness with the new, the possibility born from God's own ministering presence. Margo's experience of God in the nothingness correlates with my own story.

Through prayer that seeks strength and wisdom, Margo has experienced God's presence, kneeling at a particular place in her living room to pray for her struggling son. Her prayers are desperate cries for direction on what to do for her boy; they are prayers that plead for the strength to be a minister—to care for and uphold the humanity of her beloved son. In these moments of prayer up against nothingness, she explains, she has experienced the coming of Jesus, ministering to her with mercy and endurance, leading her to care for (to minister to) her child.

Margo's experience has similarities to Stanik's. Stanik is in his late twenties and is the son of Indian immigrants. Through his twenties he climbed quickly up the culinary ladder, making himself into a successful chef at a renowned restaurant. Yet with every new success Stanik felt more and more depressed. When I asked him if he's ever experienced the presence of God, he responds quickly, "Yes, it was two years ago at 2:35 a.m." Stanik can recall it so clearly—it is so significant to him—that he remembers the exact time. Of course, he remembers this experience so clearly, because, like the Apostle Paul, it redirected his life. He explains further,

> I was driving home from work, exhausted. I'd been there for twelve hours, I was just done. Wiped. And I remember just sitting in my car, just going, "I'm ready for something new." And, if I could describe it as every cell in my body saying that, that's how it felt to me. I just felt, really overwhelmed to say that—*I'm ready for something new*. Like, I didn't say anything else the rest of the way home. But, I knew in saying it, I was heard by God. That God was with me.

Stanik explains that this "I'm ready for something new" was his deepest prayer and one that every cell his body witnessed to as a holy reality, an event of God's presence. He says that he felt heard, like God had come to him not only to embrace him but to do more, to redirect his life in a new direction—into ministry.

The next day the feelings of God coming to him, of God redirecting his life, were confirmed. While Stanik was spending his day off with a friend, she received a phone call from the camp she was a board member of, informing her that the cook had quit, just days before the summer camp season was to begin.

The same feeling as the night before came over Stanik, and before he knew it, he heard himself saying, "I'll do it; I really think I'm supposed to do it." Within forty-eight hours he was quitting a lucrative, competitive job cooking entrees for seventy dollars a plate to live in a cabin and make grilled cheese sandwiches.

The foolishness of the gospel (1 Corinthians) came to him as a concrete experience of a God who heard his cry, leading him into a foolish ministry that transformed his life. From the cry within the nothingness of his stuck situation the ministering Christ came to him with a new possibility, a possibility that looked foolish to the world, for he gave up his self-fulfillment to minister to others. But having done so, Stanik explains, he was given new life.

Ken is in his mid-forties; he is the father of three and is very involved in the men's ministry at the church. Like Stanik, Ken too had an experience of God coming to him in foolishness. He explains that years back, he and his wife were going through some intensely painful marital struggles. Needing a counselor, they found themselves by chance in the home office of an eighty-year-old, six-foot-one-inch-tall Mormon woman in a bright red wig. Ken explains that if they had not been so desperate and hurting they would have run in the other direction. Yet, in the foolishness of gospel Ken says, "Over the next three years, this person was ministering to us in incredible ways; she was just loving us, and encouraging us, and transformed our lives, not only as a couple, but as individuals. She could see the vision of what we could be and who we were, even though we couldn't. And so she would paint that picture, but knew we needed time; she gave us that time, gave us a lot of grace."

Through the sharing in his broken person, Ken, a more directly conservative Evangelical than most of the other people I interviewed, was willing to call the action of this Mormon woman the very ministry of Christ. In the experience of this other person sharing in his suffering, he not only felt ministered to but also, because he felt ministered to, sees it as a real experience of the presence of God. Divine action came to him through the ministry of another, right at the center of his most central lived experience (the tensions in his marriage).

Ken explains that experiencing the presence of God through the person-to-person ministry in and through suffering led him to join in ministry himself, sharing in this woman's own experience of nothingness. Ken says, "What is interesting about that story is, not only was she ministering to us, but her husband during that time was dying. We ended up ministering to her during that time of grieving." Through another person ministering to him, Ken was led to participate in ministry himself. And this experience of ministry was so powerful that it led him into, and then shaped, his ministry in the men's group at the church.

Ron, too, is very involved in the ministry of the church. He entered our interview and began talking about his involvement on the church session, explaining how different it is from his experience in the corporate world. Ron is in his early seventies and retired a decade ago after running a few very successful businesses. He continued to talk about how the financial work of the church session has felt like a real ministry to him. He explained, "Never have I felt anything like it; I've never done a budget in prayer. But there was this Jesus factor, this sense that Jesus was leading us. I've never had that experience in finance and it was impactful."

I asked Ron if he ever had an experience he would call the presence of God, and he reminded me of the experience of Jesus on the church session. But then Ron thought back through his life, and this former vice president and CEO of successful corporations, responded, "I did hear God speak to me very specifically." Just like my own experience of God speaking to me in a hole and Elizabeth seeing Jesus in her room, so Ron too, the leader in the business world, had a lived experience of hearing God's voice. He explained that fifteen years ago his wife passed away, and something happened. "I would say it was within a couple of weeks of Martha's passing and I was down—there's nothing worse than returning to an empty house after you lose somebody. I was lying in bed on Sunday morning in misery, and I heard this clear voice that said, 'Martha is safe at home.' No doubt about it. People might question that, but it's clear in my mind. I didn't have to think, oh, what was that all about?" Ron had a concrete and lived experience of divine action that came to him through the nothingness of the loss of his wife. He heard God speak to him, and he is sure that it was an act of God ministering to him, speaking to the new possibility that God has given his beloved wife. From this experience Ron's life was reordered; he found the strength to get out of bed and continue to have his person ministered to by his friend Hank, who also had lost his wife. Ron says, "I think [this experience] affirmed some of the discussions that Hank, the mentor from the men's group, and I had, and affirmed what I know is true, that God speaks to us either through nudges or occasionally verbally. I can't explain that phenomenon any other way!"

Though Rachel is only in her late thirties, she too, like Ron, has lost her spouse. Rachel has two elementary school-aged children. When they were just three and one, eight years ago, Rachel's husband died while on a business trip in Chicago. She explains the deep, deep loss that this thrust her into. She describes the deep blessing of people taking her children at church so she could sit in the worship service and cry. I asked her if she felt like this was an experience of being ministered to, and she said, "Yes, of course." I then asked her if she had any other experiences of being ministered to that she would call an experience of God's presence. Rachel says,

> A pet peeve of mine is the whole "It's a God thing" phrase. But there were a lot of moments where I felt like I was at the absolute end of my rope and someone would throw me a line. Like, my husband died in Chicago and I had to go and identify his body. I didn't know anybody in the city, and so my cab driver dropped me off and he walked in with me, and brought me a bottle of water, and stood by me, and put his hand over my shoulder when they showed my husband's body. This cab driver I didn't know whatsoever, but he saw where he was taking me, and he came in, and so I wasn't alone in that moment. At that point I was so thankful and knew God was involved.

Rachel has such a deep experience of suffering and nothingness that she will not settle for trite platitudes about the presence of God—she hates the "it's a God thing" phrase. But, here in the hellish nothingness, the foolishness and absurdity of ministry breaks forth again as an event she can only call divine action. In her own hole, in the pit of loss, a cabbie joins his person with her own, participating in a real experience of divine presence, sharing in her nothingness by giving his own person to hers. She can only thank God for being present, giving forth God's ministering presence through the beautifully foolish act of a taxi driver, a bottle of water, and a hand on her shoulder.

But Rachel had another experience of divine action that, coupled with the cabbie in the morgue, caused her to reorder her life. She explains, "My husband died of heart disease and there was one day where I was feeling like it was my fault; I can't believe I didn't see it, why didn't I catch it, I should have sent him to the doctor. If I had he'd still be here and my kids would have their father." She was swirling down deep into nothingness. She continues,

> So I was on this walk crying out to God and feeling like it was my fault. I got home, and I opened the paper, and the first thing I saw was a rookie baseball player who had died at training camp with the exact same condition my husband had, the baseball player had a huge physical [exam] and they missed it. And it was this relief of OK, if that can happen to him with all of that scrutiny, it wasn't my fault—I felt peace. These were moments where I felt like I was crying out and I just got a response.

Rachel articulates two significant experiences of divine action. These experiences came to her as ministry, the joining of her person (the first story) that causes her to reorder (the second story) her very conception of things, bringing her peace. Like my own story, Rachel was in a hole, cried out to God and heard God speak to her, telling her it wasn't her fault, giving her the strength to run from the hole, providing peace as a result of what she believes is a real experience of divine action.

CONCLUSION

In this chapter I've sought to show that if practical theology truly wishes to honor the concrete and lived experience of people, then we have to make room for divine action itself. Practical theology does not need to turn toward conceptions of divine action so it can prove it is a true theology; rather, practical theology, more fundamentally, must turn to divine action so that it can honor the lived experience of concrete people.

Not all people would claim to have such experiences, but I contend that many do, and the visions and approaches of practical theology have tended not to honor these experiences as real—as real encounters with the Spirit of Jesus Christ. All those that I interviewed had such experiences, and their own experiences were similar to my own. I believe that by embracing these experiences of divine action, practical theology can recover, and even contribute, deeply theological projects that may be meaningful to the academy and even more so to the church.

It will now be my pursuit in chapter four to turn to four of the leading approaches to practical theology in North America. While all four of these approaches are rich, they tend to neglect or obscure the very concrete and lived experience of divine action we have seen in this chapter. In the next chapter

I'll show why and how they have overlooked the experience of divine action, further presenting the need for the Christopraxis approach I will set forth in the second part of the book.

4

Dominant Models of Practical Theology

The objective of this chapter is to map the field of practical theology. But maps are always of a particular place, and when you have your feet on the ground of a locale it is always helpful for the maps to be specific. When trying to get around the streets of Chicago, it is of little help to have a globe. Therefore, the purpose of this chapter is to map the field of practical theology in *North America*. While practical theology is undoubtedly an international project (and if my map included that breadth, I'd certainly need to include Johannes Van der Ven, Friedrich Schweitzer, and Stephen Pattison), for space I'll give my attention to North America. However, the thinkers I will analyze, though located in the States, have all had a global impact on the field. I believe it is fair to argue that all of them are, in their own ways, involved in field-defining work.

I should say something more in the way of warning and intention. Maps, while incredibly helpful, particularly when you're lost, are in themselves always prone to reduction. And there is no way to avoid this. We want our maps reduced to give only the information we need to get us to where we need to go. It isn't helpful for Google Maps to tell us of every billboard or native plant that grows next to the road's shoulder. To be helpful it cares little about the aesthetic of the drive and sticks to the important details.

So, too, my map of the dominant North American models of practical theology will (can only) attend to the important details. Each author has written much more than I can address. In every case I'll attend to only the most significant methodological work of the author as it relates to practical theology. And because I am mapping them, I have placed these authors in categories that they no doubt spill out of (for instance, hermeneutical, pseudo neo-Aristotelian, and the like). I admit that as thinking, reflective persons they are much more than I can capture in these few paragraphs—the personalism embedded in the Christopraxis practical theology of the cross, which I'll be constructing following this chapter, demands this affirmation.

Therefore, it is essential for me to restate once again my objective in doing this mapping in the first place. My goal is simply to explore how these field-defining authors have conceived of divine action and how this divine action is appropriated and experienced by human agency (even within cultural/societal structures). To that end, and because of what I'll be constructing, I'm interested in what frameworks move an author's imagination for this divine and human association (that is, how and which doctrines possess hermeneutical weight or priority in interpreting divine action). To summarize all this in two overarching questions, I desire to know each author's epistemology of divine action and view of soteriology.[1]

A HERMENEUTICAL PRACTICAL THEOLOGY

If there is a father of practical theology, it is Friedrich Schleiermacher (1768–1834), the great nineteenth-century theologian. He not only reimagined theology in a modern world but placed practical theology as the crown of the theological tree in his 1830 work *A Brief Outline to the Study of Theology*. But as the father of the field, Schleiermacher has received as much derision as praise from his progeny, most especially those late children born in the second half of the twentieth century. Practical theologians have been prone to tear Schleiermacher down as they stand in the field he cleared. There has been a certain Greek mythological drama in practical theology, a kind of need to kill the father to move forward.

So if Schleiermacher is the confirmed and yet despised father of practical theology, then Don Browning is practical theology's big brother. In the scope of the family line that runs from Schleiermacher to today, Browning is a late-born progeny (born in 1934 and dying in 2010), but Browning came on the scene at just the right intellectual and cultural time for his impact to be massive. Browning's impact—made evident through the publication of *A Fundamental Practical Theology* and through his kindness and willingness to mentor so many—cannot be overstated. Like the best of big brothers, Browning was not only talented in his own right but caring and supportive of his fellow siblings.

---

1. A soteriological view is significant because it operationalizes a thinker's view of divine action. It reveals views of divine action because soteriology cannot ignore the need for some kind of imagined agency for God.

Before the publication of *A Fundamental Practical Theology* Browning had already asserted himself as a significant thinker in pastoral theology, writing particularly about pastoral care and blending with incredible precision psychology and pastoral practice. Browning had asserted that religion was actually embedded within many of the formative psychological theories, showing that religion was a more central actuality than the social sciences would have liked to admit. Browning sought to prove a religious propensity in the practical social sciences. He would turn this on its head in *A Fundamental Practical Theology* in which he showed religion/theology itself to actually be practical.

Browning continued this rich interdisciplinary focus of his earlier work, but now moved his focus wider in *A Fundamental Practical Theology*, arguing that it was time for the whole of the theological enterprise to be reimagined in a *practical* way. Much like father Schleiermacher, Browning took on the whole of the study of theology, turning it practical, and by so doing gave a new identity to "practical," or what Browning called strategic or fully practical, theology.

However, Browning was in no way *simply* reviving the project of Schleiermacher; Browning actually had a critique of Schleiermacher. Though, like father and son, both intended to make the whole of theology practical and sought to do this by attending to "religion," Browning critiqued Schleiermacher for not having the foresight to escape the trap of a theory-to-practice perspective.[2] Browning held with iron force to the idea that for theology to be practical, and for practical theology to be generative, it must move into a practice-to-theory-to-practice perspective. From practice itself one

---

2. Speaking of his position in contrast to Schleiermacher, Browning says, "It differs somewhat from Schleiermacher's organization of theology into philosophical theology, historical theology, and practical theology. Although Schleiermacher saw practical theology as the teleological goal and "crown" of theology, his view of theology still had a theory-to-practice structure. He understood theology as a movement from philosophical and historical theology to application in practical theology. It is true that this structure is altered by the fact that Schleiermacher understood the whole of theology as a positive science in contrast to a pure or theoretical science. By positive science, Schleiermacher meant 'an assemblage of scientific elements which belong together, not because they form a constituent part of the organization of the sciences, as though by some necessity arising out of the notion of science itself, but only insofar as they are requisite for carrying out a practical task.' Such a view of theology clearly emphasizes its practical, conditioned, and historically located nature and makes all theology a basically practical task. It has, therefore, some affinities with the close association of historical reason and practical reason that we noticed in Gadamer's hermeneutic philosophy. Nonetheless, Schleiermacher saw theology in general as moving from historical knowledge to practical application; he had little idea how the practices of the church form the questions we bring to the historical sources." Don S. Browning, *A Fundamental Practical Theology* (Minneapolis: Fortress Press, 1991), 43.

moves into reflection, and that reflection, Browning asserted, leads to refined action.

The problem with theology proper and practical theology itself was that both were stuck in a theory-to-practice perspective and therefore could not become practical because their first step, or first attention, was given to the unlived and abstract. Browning did not come up with this practice-to-theory-to-practice perspective out of the blue; rather, drawing on the work of hermeneutical philosopher Hans-Georg Gadamer, Browning showed that this perspective was endemic to interpretation itself. Practical life is fundamentally a process of interpretation; it is hermeneutical. This is how communities, like the congregations Browning studied, formed practical wisdom.[3] Having an experience in practice, such as being confronted with the decision to sanctuary illegal immigrants, communities reflected on a tradition (the classics of religion) to decide what to do (what new practice to take). By moving from practice to reflection to practice, Browning saw a fusion of horizons that led to the creating and deepening of practical wisdom.[4]

Throughout *A Fundamental Practical Theology* it is hard to miss practical wisdom as the objective for Browning; the formation of practical wisdom becomes the focus of practical theology. And (Gadamerian) hermeneutics, because of its focus on practice, tradition, and fusion of horizons, creates this practical wisdom (this *phronesis* as we discussed in chapter 2). In this summary of Browning's method there is no articulation of divine action as an independent and free reality:

> Rather than envisioning practical theology as primarily theological reflection on the tasks of the ordained minister or the leadership of the church, as was the view of Schleiermacher, these newer trends

3. Gerkin, too, uses Gadamer and a hermeneutical perspective of practical theology to articulate his pastoral care perspective. So in a number of ways he is similar to Browning (and Browning dialogues with his work in *A Fundamental Practical Theology*), yet Gerkin has a much richer conception of divine action in his eschatological vision in chapter 3. Drawing deeply from an eschatological and incarnational perspective, Gerkin is loosed to talk more of God's distinct freedom to act than Browning can. See Charles Gerkin, *The Living Human Document: Re-Visioning Pastoral Counseling in a Hermeneutical Mode* (Nashville: Abingdon, 1984).

4. Here the catalyst for transformation is not the act of God, but the hermeneutical process itself. "The main task of descriptive theology, however, is to form questions that are brought back to the classics for the creation of new horizons of meaning. These horizons of meaning are the most basic, most threatening, and finally most truly powerful sources of transformation. These new horizons transform our fundamental visions and narratives that provide the envelope for practical reason." Browning, *Fundamental Practical Theology*, 285.

define practical theology as critical reflection on the church's ministry to the world. I find it useful to think of fundamental practical theology as critical reflection on the church's dialogue with Christian sources and other communities of experience and interpretation with the aim of guiding its action toward social and individual transformation.[5]

From a Christopraxis practical theology of the cross, Browning's hermeneutical perspective is commendable. As we'll see in the next chapter, my Christopraxis perspective is highly hermeneutical as it also seeks a fusion of horizons. But for Browning, this fusion happens only at the critical correlational level (at the level of placing distinct traditions or fields of thought in discourse); this keeps the horizons bound almost fully in the realm of human agency. In other words, the horizons that Browning wants to fuse, through a correlational method, are religious traditions and human ethical actions, which takes little account of the concrete experiences of divine action such as those presented in the previous chapter. Ethics for Browning is the heart of practical wisdom because ethics teaches people how to act and does so not only reflectively but also practically. This is the best of a liberal conception that equates divine action with religious tradition, and human participation in the divine (if such a thing can be said) through ethical/religious practice.[6]

However, from my Christopraxis approach this isn't sufficient, for it flattens out too quickly the possibility of divine action. Divine action is actually lost in the hermeneutical operations of constructing practical wisdom within communities of ethical action. Browning has little conception (and where there is little, there is disdain) for conceiving of a qualitative distinction between time and eternity (Kierkegaard). Browning, through philosophical pragmatism, has defined reality not as an emergent, multidimensional reality but solely as a human-constructed interpretive process. Reality *is* hermeneutical, and hermeneutics is done by human agents that seek to interpret human actions through the best of human thought and action (tradition) for the sake of better human practice. Browning gives very little attention to the conception that reality may be more than the action of human agents. Human agents must act (ethically for Browning) in a particular time. But this perception of time is bound within the human knower who acts. I believe it is possible that reality

5. Ibid., 36.

6. This quote is informative because Browning doesn't seek to give weight to divine action as independent (revelatory), but as bound in classic tradition, in religion. "Christian practical theology, by virtue of being Christian, will give special weight to classic Christian texts." Ibid., 139.

is more than these human constructs and that practice and action themselves may exist outside of human constructs (this is what I mean by the qualitative distinction between time and eternity). With the remainder of this book, I'll show how this might be possible.

This can be most clearly seen in how Browning opens his book with a (polemical) critique of Karl Barth. Browning contends that Barth is a paradigmatic example of bad theology (unpractical theology) because Barth works from a theory-to-practice perspective, seeking to articulate a theory of theology and then mobilizing that theory into forms of practice, like preaching (if Barth ever even gets that far, Browning contends).[7]

Yet, what Browning misses (and my neo-Barthianism takes exception to) is that while Barth may have taken on the personal disposition of a classic theoretical theologian (writing lectures and volumes of dogmatics), his theological career started in practice itself, as a pastor. And as a pastor in practice, Barth discovered the central theme of his theological project, building his project not on a theory-to-practice perspective, but rather on an articulation of divine practice, of divine action in God's self-revelation. It starts with a conception that God acts outside of or distinct from human constructs but comes into human constructs through the humanity of Jesus Christ.

Unlike Browning, Barth (and I, too, for that matter) attend to an ontological realism that allows for reality to be constituted not solely in human epistemological structures (like Browning's Kantianism). Therefore, divine action, which for Browning is nearly infeasible (or, if a possibility, is now

---

7. Browning explains his opposition to Barth: "Although contemporary theology is less rationalistic, it may not seem less apodictic, impractical, and unrelated to the average person. A theologian as recent as Karl Barth saw theology as the systematic interpretation of God's self-disclosure to the Christian church. There was no role for human understanding, action, or practice in the construal of God's self-disclosure. In this view, theology is practical only by applying God's revelation as directly and purely as possible to the concrete situations of life. The theologian moves from revelation to the human, from theory to practice, and from revealed knowledge to application. A good deal of Barthianism is still present in modern theology. Barth's model of practical theology is partially right; many contemporary commentators, however, believe that it is partially, if not significantly, wrong." Ibid., 5. Browning continues, "The difference between this view of theology as practical and the Barthian view is apparent. The view I propose goes from practice to theory and back to practice. Or more accurately, it goes from present theory-laden practice to a retrieval of normative theory-laden practice to the creation of more critically held theory-laden practices. Barth, in contrast, was an epistemological realist. He believed that the interpreting community should empty itself of its usual attempts to verify things morally, experientially, or cognitively. The believing community should conform itself totally to the Word of God revealed in Scripture. This, I believe, is a classic expression of the theory-to-practice model of theology. Such a model dominated most theological education in both Europe and North America in the middle decades of the twentieth century. It also affected the thought and life of the churches." Ibid., 7.

locked in a classic tradition that we mobilize for human ethical discernment), is a reality from a Christopraxis perspective. Therefore, hermeneutics itself becomes transformed from only the human-to-human epistemological level to human epistemological "best accounts" of an ontological reality of divine action, of how the eternal breaks into time and does so in concrete, lived experience like these explored in the prior chapter.

To say it more directly, a Christopraxis perspective sees hermeneutics first and foremost at the level of divine and human action. It seeks to interpret the revelatory realism of God's action in concrete, lived experience. Browning's hermeneutical perspective sticks to human constructions of communities of practical wisdom rather than communities that wrestle with their individual and corporate experience of God's coming to them. Browning's perspective, while brilliant at the level of human action, is razor thin at the level of divine action and can say little about the experiences of Jesus like those of Shirley and Lynn.

How would Browning's project answer my two overarching questions? What is Browning's epistemology of divine action? As I said earlier, divine action is rendered nearly impotent in Browning's project, and if not impotent then captured in tradition that is mobilized only by human hermeneutical processes. The reality of divine action is either impotent at worst, or irrelevant at best. Yet, Browning is not antidivine, and even in the churches he studies he honors their language of divine action. But this then becomes the key for Browning's epistemology of divine action. Because divine action is locked in a lived religion, it is through descriptive theology (a hermeneutical sociology of religion) that we come to know the divine.[8] Through a process of deeply reflecting on practical wisdom we can understand human communities' conceptions of the divine. So it is through descriptive theology done in a critical correlational way that we conceive of the divine—but this divine conception is inextricably linked to human forms of practical wisdom and interpretation. Does descriptive theology ultimately collapse divine action into the human and lose the experience of God's coming to us?

8. "The description of theory-laden religious and cultural practices is the first movement of both theology and theological education. For want of a better term, I will call it descriptive theology. Its task is more important than its name. It is to describe the contemporary theory-laden practice that gives rise to the practical questions that generate all theological reflection. To some extent, this first movement is horizon analysis; it attempts to analyze the horizon of cultural and religious meanings that surround our religious and secular practices. . . . It would be a great mistake to believe that descriptive theology is simply a sociological task, especially if sociology is modeled after the narrowly empirical natural sciences." Ibid., 47. "Descriptive theology, however, would be close to sociology if sociology were conceived hermeneutically. A hermeneutic sociology sees the sociological task or conversation between the researcher and the subjects being research." Ibid.

What about soteriology? How does Browning conceive of salvation? One could articulate Browning's perspective as postcruciform.[9] It is not that Browning denies the cross; rather, through his dialogue with Reinhold Niebuhr he (apprehensively) affirms it. But Browning does see, by using the doctrine of creation and *imago Dei*, the cross as an unfortunate need for sacrifice that is not fundamental to human life and action.[10] Browning is so apprehensive about sacrifice, because he has so locked it within human forms of action, that he nearly refused to even imagine how the cross may reveal or articulate anything about the nature (being) and economy (act) of God. Rather, for Browning's mobilized soteriological frame, what he calls equal-mutual regard is that which is desired (and fully soteriological). The point of human life, and human life lived in step with divine desires, is to live in an ethical manner that treats the other as mutual and equal. One moves into this "soteriological" reality not primarily through divine action in itself but through the five levels of practical wisdom that Browning sets forth in the second and third parts of his book. It is hard to see either in Browning's epistemology or his soteriology how the foolishness of the cross, as Paul's central theological theme, is tended to at all.

POSTMODERN BOURDIEUIAN PRACTICAL THEOLOGY

If Don Browning has his own direct progeny, it is Bonnie Miller-McLemore. Miller-McLemore not only did her doctoral studies with Browning at the University of Chicago but afterward worked on a number of projects with him.[11] Throughout her writing Browning pops up often, not only because she follows his disciplinary pursuits in practical theology and interdisciplinary

9. Referencing Niebuhr's place for the cross, Browning is affirming but wary of giving it too much of a place. "Although Niebuhr was wrong to say that self-sacrificial love is the end and goal of the Christian life, he was right to find a definite role for it." Ibid., 199. Here Browning explains further, "This is true not because self-sacrifice is the goal of life; the fellowship of mutuality and equal regard is the goal of life. Sacrifice is the necessary step required to bring equal regard back into focus. It is precisely the forgiveness and grace of God's own outpouring agape that make our sacrificial agape possible. . . . The goal is fellowship and enjoyment between God and humans, and mutuality, sisterhood, and brotherhood between humans themselves. Because sin will never disappear—and for that reason mutuality can never be perfect—self-sacrifice will always and everywhere be a part of the Christian life even though it is neither its proximate nor its ultimate goal." Ibid., 160.

10. "The doctrine of creation reinforces what practical reason through its radical empirical experience also gradually learns—that the limits of nature and human institutions place constraints on practical reason that it must recognize and accept." Ibid., 196.

11. Specifically, *From Culture Wars to Common Ground* by Don S. Browning, Bonnie Miller-McLemore, Pamela Couture, Brynolf Lyon, and Robert Franklin (Louisville, KY: Westminster John Knox, 1997).

discussions around religion and psychology but also because in formative ways Browning's work is paradigmatic for her own.

It must be stated clearly that Miller-McLemore is *no* derivative thinker or simple commentator on Browning (if she were, there would be no reason to place her in a different category from Browning in my map). Rather, where Browning leaves off, Miller-McLemore goes further, taking the step from Gadamerian hermeneutics into postmodern theory, driving deeper into the social and cultural (constructed) locatedness of knowledge, most directly religious knowledge.

Miller-McLemore may be best known for her field-impacting rearticulation and broadening of Anton Boisen's assertion that practical theologians (CPE students) attend not to books as their primary text but to human beings. The "human living document" is the central text of practical theologians. While agreeing with Boisen, Miller-McLemore nevertheless deepens his perspective, arguing that it would be more helpful to think of the text not as a "human living document" as much as the "living human web." Her conception has since been taken in a number of directions, all of which honor the central kernel of her perspective.[12] But what Miller-McLemore was most centrally seeking in her reimagining was a deeper appreciation for the cultural location of the individual, recognizing that we all live in cultural webs like gender, race, and economic realms.[13] While remaining, à la Browning, a correlationalist, Miller-McLemore draws most generatively from postmodern theory to articulate more deeply the cultural experience of people, the cultural experience she correlates with religious propensities (like mothering).[14]

While early in her career Miller-McLemore was *helpfully* driving practical theology into deep conversations with feminism and liberation theology, all generative to her deep cultural turn, later in her career she would take this cultural focus in the direction of practice theory, which allowed her to further articulate the living human web connecting religious experience with concrete bodies.[15] This practice theory (gleaned from Pierre Bourdieu) allowed the

---

12. See Osmer's appropriation in *Practical Theology: An Introduction* (Grand Rapids, MI: Eerdmans, 2008).

13. Miller-McLemore explains, "Genuine care now requires understanding the human document as necessarily embedded within an interlocking public web of constructed meaning. Clinical problems, such as a woman recovering from a hysterectomy or a man addicted to drugs, are always situated within the structures and ideologies of a wider public context and never purely interpersonal or intrapsychic." *Christian Theology in Practice: Discovering a Discipline* (Grand Rapids, MI: Eerdmans, 2012), 81.

14. "Mothers also have accessibility to certain invaluable ways of knowing, particularly bodily knowing." Ibid., 126.

cultural (particularly the experience of gender) to connect with the religious. Now practice itself mediated religious experience. While for Browning the community came up against the religious within the dialogical correlation (within the hermeneutical), in Miller-McLemore it was within practices done by culturally constituted persons. The great advantage of this perspective was that it allowed Miller-McLemore to speak more robustly about the "on the ground," even technical, actions of (embodied) practitioners than Browning's more philosophical perspective would allow.[16]

The themes with which Miller-McLemore was working would be picked up and mobilized in a rich and exciting way by Mary McClintock Fulkerson, a systematic theologian turned practical theologian.[17] Her book *Place of Redemption* would resound not only in the field of practical theology but in theology more generally. Doing her own ethnographic research (sight observation) at a small interracial, interabilitied community in Durham, North Carolina, Fulkerson explored what allowed this unique and beautiful community to be a *place* of welcome, a place where black, refugee, and disabled people all found a home.[18]

15. She explains, "In the movement between knowing and acting, I use a mode of circular bodily reasoning that interweaves physical sensation, momentary cognition, behavioral reaction, and a physical sensing and intellectual reading of the results—a trial-and-error, hit-and-miss strategy that in its bodily ethos surpasses that described under the rubric of Catholic moral casuistry. When it works, I relax; when it fails, I repeat it ceaselessly because I must; when it fails one too many times, I must master a physical desire to retaliate in stormy, mindless abuse." Ibid., 130.

16. She states directly, "As I will ultimately conclude, the field of practical theology needs to learn a lot more about practical theological know-how: how to teach it, how to learn it, and how to demonstrate it." Ibid., 165.

17. Mary McClintock Fulkerson explains her turn to practical theology and what it allows for: "Attention to the worldly, situational character of Christian faith directs me to the task of practical theology." *Places of Redemption: Theology for a Worldly Church* (London: Oxford University Press, 2007), 7. She continues, "In contrast with the definition of normative memory or systematic and philosophical judgment, the practical theological task has to do with the way Christian faith occurs as a contemporary situation." Ibid.

18. "Since the majority of Christians in the United States are 'traditioned' or habituated into the faith in racially homogeneous communities and are isolated from those with physical and mental disabilities, the argument for a complex framing of Good Samaritan is, in effect, a recognition of a woundedness much larger than this faith community. This suggests that we may think of Good Samaritan as a complex text about difference and a variety of positionings in relation to difference—about 'whiteness' as well as 'color,' and 'normal' and 'not-normal,' at the very least." Ibid., 17. "In this introductory chapter, I have argued that practical theology, the task of theological reflection upon this contemporary situation, is at least two things. It is, first of all, full attention to the structure of situation, its shape and demand, in such a way that the complex of radicalized, normalized, and otherwise enculturated bodies and desire are as much a part of the analysis as the presence of biblical and doctrinal elements." Ibid., 21.

With incredible sophistication Fulkerson moved beyond cognitive beliefs and cognitive theological catechesis as the factors that allowed this community to become a place of welcome.[19] Rather, turning headlong to the cultural, Fulkerson argued, through Bourdieu and postmodern place theory, habituation was the engine that drove this little church. In other words, through and by practices, a habitus of seeing and being with was created.

The community was actualized not through intellect (as so often is assumed by theology) but through bodies, through the bodies of those in the community. Fulkerson shows, through Bourdieu, that our bodies possess culture, and in our bodies a habitus of culture is created. We feel culture's strangeness when we do not know what to do with our bodies or contort our bodies in shame, revealing our unwelcome. But we are welcomed when our bodies are seen and embraced for their actuality. The community that Fulkerson studied was experiencing divine action because it created a habitus that avoids the obliviousness (the deep unwelcome) of so many racist and homophobic church communities.

For Fulkerson and Miller-McLemore, then, practical theology attends to embodied realities of culture. Miller-McLemore turns practical theology toward issues of gender, and Fulkerson to race and disability, both attending strongly to the cultural realm of embodiment.

Divine action for Fulkerson and Miller-McLemore comes through bodies embedded in culture. Much like Browning, they see little need for a distinction between time and eternity—or for a sense that reality is stratified and therefore can account for the eventfulness of divine action. Fulkerson even states that the world takes shape through our bodies.[20] And while clearly part of the world does, not all the world, not all of reality can be deduced to the cultural habitus of embodiment. While our bodies may clearly be receivers of experiences of the divine, the divine itself cannot be captured by or equated to the embodied cultural realm. Fulkerson does not go this far, necessarily, but leans heavily in this direction.

---

19. Fulkerson explains, "To avoid the inadequate (modernist) model of Christian community as a coherent system of beliefs, the next move in the argument is a proposal to frame Good Samaritan with the categories of postmodern place theory, a framing that will further specify these items, powers, and events, their gathering and evoking of response in such a way that brings to focus the social problem of obliviousness as well as the means of its redress. A much improved alternative to the charting of beliefs, or activities or attempts to cobble them together, postmodern place theory allows for a needed expansion of the results of my ethnographic research, which, despite its thickness, does not represent the continuum of human experience that is needed." Ibid., 22.

20. "The world takes shape through our bodies." Ibid., 25.

So, to return to my first question, what is the epistemology of divine action in a postmodern Bourdieuian practical theology? It appears that divine action itself comes through embodied practices of people. When habituated forms of action (practices) in cultural realities oppose sexism and racism, divine action (or the religious) is seen. Because Fulkerson has her hesitation about doctrine and Miller-McLemore feels uncomfortable with it, divine action is articulated within the cultural itself.

But this is not to say that either thinker has some kind of transcendent propensity in her work. Fulkerson speaks often of people's articulations of divine agency and even moves in this direction herself before always returning squarely to the cultural. Yet, both thinkers do move into the transcendent in their articulation of human suffering (Miller-McLemore) and human finitude/wound (Fulkerson) as realities that *can* open the cultural to the religious.[21] In my Christopraxis practical theology of the cross, I too will see experiences of suffering (brokenness and need, what I call below the ex nihilo) as central frames for articulating the association of the divine and human.

Yet, what is fascinating is that while both thinkers turn to suffering or wound as an opening to the religious or theological, neither articulates anything near a robust sense of the presence of Christ.[22] Miller-McLemore, by her own confession, is uncreedal and therefore, other than a few sentences about eschatology, says little about divine action outside of equating it to religion (which too is cultural).[23] And she says almost nothing about Jesus.[24] It is not that she is allergic to theology. For instance, she quotes James Nieman's helpful

21. Miller-McLemore explains: "To develop the idea that one studies religion in pastoral theology at the point where human suffering evokes or calls for a religious response and sometimes at the point where a religious response is given and/or experienced." Miller-McLemore, *Christian Theology in Practice*, 146. Fulkerson notes: "The earlier image says it well, namely, creative thinking originates at the scene of a wound. And such creative thinking is formed by a combination of convictions—theological and faith-driven at the same time as cultural, political, and autobiographical." Fulkerson, *Places of Redemption*, 234. This is a beautiful comment, but I think it needs a christological core. "The latter recognizes that equally constitutive of Christian community is openness to new focus of relationships, to new definitions of the neighbor." Ibid., 216.

22. This kind of statement is powerful, but not really developed by Fulkerson. "While 'normative' is traditionally designated through some form of divine authorization, its material form has to do specifically with ensuring faithfulness to the ends of Christian community, what we can call 'faithfulness to Jesus.'" Ibid., 36.

23. "I have gone back time and again to Clark Williamson's more appealing portrait of Disciples as professing a belief in behavior and enactment rather than creeds, clergy, ritual, and theological doctrine. 'In a behavioral practical system,' I write, 'how things are done, what one does, is a primary form of confession and a witness of faith. More oriented to the world than to the church, to ethics than to piety, Disciples seek to verify faith propositions by literally seeking to make them true.' Granted, there are

definition of theology, "Theology is, in Nieman's words, less 'a fixed set of direct, positive claims about divine being' and more 'indirect gestures . . . to a sense of divine activity.'"[25] I would agree with Neiman wholeheartedly; it appears, however, that Miller-McLemore, by turning so strongly to the cultural, is not able (or willing) to gesture to divine action with any conception of Jesus' encounter that was representative of the people's experiences recounted in chapter 3.

While Fulkerson repeats often how persons in the community she studies talk about Jesus, her theological articulations at the end of the book are absent of any developed sense of the living Christ.[26] Fulkerson's talk of Jesus is all about remembering him (from a Christopraxis approach more than remembering is needed; one also needs to attend to the living/active Christ present in and through the Spirit).[27]

Fulkerson's approach runs the risk, which I believe both thinkers fall into, of conflating everything to the cultural.[28] A well-developed Christology may allow for practical theology to attend deeply to the human through the incarnational humanity of Jesus but nevertheless seek for the otherness, the divine, that stands outside of the cultural, in Jesus' divinity. Therefore, it may allow practical theology to give attention to the cultural but, in the end—through the hypostatic union, for instance—to be more ultimately concerned with the mystical (how the divine and human relate and indwell) than simply the cultural.

---

problems with this outlook, including an overachieving Protestant work ethic and a righteousness about earning our salvation through works." Miller-McLemore, *Christian Theology in Practice*, 17.

24. "Although no doubt there are some who would see my low sacrificial Christology, high incarnation, non-creedal, non-patriarchal view of God as unorthodox, I remain a Christian who believes God can be found anywhere God chooses. And I think God sometimes favors trees and children." Ibid., 20.

25. Ibid., 199.

26. Fulkerson has a very rich theological anthropology but doesn't connect this to Christology.

27. Here is an example that also articulates Fulkerson's cultural bent: "The familiar 'inscribed' form of tradition is illustrated by culture as it shapes the social world through memorized values and mores, or in the way Christian communities maintain a faithful identity by 'remembering Jesus'." *Places of Redemption*, 43.

28. Fulkerson has a place for doctrinal/creedal language, but much as in Browning, it is frozen in the tradition and not connected to the living God. "The vision or telos of the community, the creation of a place for all to appear, will be rooted in an inscribed tradition—the authoritative written and stored memories of Christian communities that are found in Scripture, catholic creeds, and denominational commitments. But Connerton's point is that tradition—social memory—is not just comprised of these practices of inscription, but of distinctive bodily practices as well." Ibid., 50.

Both thinkers avoid discussion of the cross of Christ, but, as I'll try to argue below, it may only be through the cross of Christ that human wounds can be healed enough to allow for the kind of person-to-person encounter Fulkerson hopes for. The place of redemption for Fulkerson is the human-to-human encounter. I couldn't agree more, but without a Christology this moving perspective can be too quickly equated with the cultural and miss divine action. And it may be only by the cross that the human suffering which Miller-McLemore sees as the engine for religious attention is drawn into new life and is made the place where the divine breaks the hold of the cultural and places us fully in participation in the life of God, where there is no Jew or Greek, male or female, for all by the Spirit are one in the life of God. (Gal. 3:28)[29]

This leads us to ask our final question: what is the soteriological perspective of this position of practical theology? It is most clearly stated by Fulkerson who articulates it as a place where difference is affirmed and the faithfulness of being with different others is clear in our bodies. Soteriology is experienced in a more inclusive conception (or even an obliteration) of "normal," allowing all bodies to be seen as included. This soteriological reality comes though an embodied habitus of welcome.[30] Again, one wonders about the work of the Spirit in this habitus, how divine action is a catalyst for this embodied place of welcome, and if there is any room for experiences like those in chapter 3. It appears that, because it is a habitus, it is formed by human action, making soteriology embedded in a world/cultural realm, locked in time. Thus, this place of welcome in our bodies rests only on the plan of the human, potentially missing the eventful dynamic that may be possible within divine encounter, that may be opened up in a revelatory realism.

---

29. I personally think Fulkerson's theology doesn't match the robust way that these people talk about the activity of God in their lives. "A different kind of appeal to God characteristic of some Good Samaritans occurs as a piety that understands God to intervene in personal life, from the smallest events to the providential guiding of nations and history. An example is Letty's belief that God led her to a particular biblical passage that spoke to her fear about her husband's work life. Citing instances of God's direct work in his life, Miguel spoke of God using him when he preached a sermon at Good Samaritan. His assertion that 'God never lets the church fall on its face' was God's intended message for the community." Ibid., 205.

30. Here divine action becomes the habitus. "The faithfulness of a habitus will not be evaluated in terms of its success at a mental search for the correct Christian teaching or doctrine to 'apply' to or direct a situation. Nor does the model that Christian practices must be 'grounded' on 'adequate beliefs' prove sufficient to the dynamic and experiential nature of faithfulness and the necessarily changing character of the discourse that qualifies as 'belief' or inscribed tradition. Bourdieu's habitus entails a level of wisdom that cannot be reduced to such second-order reflection and precludes prescribed, fixed forms of normative discourse." Ibid., 48.

Pseudo Neo-Aristotelian Practical Theology

While all practical theologians give attention to lived and concrete communities, believing, at least in part, that their work should impact the action of practitioners, few have been able to bridge this gap to actually give back *useful* perspectives to practitioners themselves. In other words, academic practical theologians have studied communities and practitioners, but these studies have rarely been meaningful to the practitioners themselves, remaining instead in academic papers and monographs.

Yet, if there is an exception to this, it can be found in the work of Craig Dykstra and Dorothy Bass. Over the last two and a half decades, Dykstra and Bass have not only had tremendous impact in the field of practical theology—as a discipline done by scholars, those in part (a) of Miller-McLemore's definition—but have also impacted pastors on the ground—those seeing practical theology as an activity of faith done by believers, those in part (b).[31] Their shared work has reverberated loudly within both the academy and the church.

This is due in part to the resources standing behind Dykstra as former senior vice president for religion at the Lilly Endowment. While these resources have allowed for conferences, research, and conversations within and between the academy and the church, it is not *only* such resources that have led to the impact Dysktra and Bass have had. Rather, Dykstra and Bass have curated a deep practical theological conversation by shaping it with their own intellectual project.

As a practical theologian at Princeton Seminary in the 1980s, Dykstra sought a perspective that would move Christian education beyond the stale paradigms of knowledge appropriation and/or development and into seeing Christian education as a way of life. Dykstra worked to turn the field from its infatuation with psychological development theory back toward a theological language, but a theological language that could connect to concrete life.

In order to do this, Dykstra not only returned to theological language but to the very actions, the very practices, he believed that theological language possessed or pointed to. So instead of attending to developmental theory, Dykstra's perspective of Christian education revisited what he called "the disciplines," the classic actions of prayer, worship, hospitality, and so forth.

---

31. Not to mention how they have impacted (c) though conversations and books like Miroslav Volf and Dorothy Bass's *Practicing Theology* (Grand Rapids, MI: Eerdmans, 2002), a work within which systematic theologians discuss practice, and (d) through the teaching and learning initiatives like those centered at Wabash College and in books like Gregory L. Jones and Stephanie Paulsell's *The Scope of Our Art: The Vocation of the Theological Teacher* (Grand Rapids, MI: Eerdmans, 2001).

He saw these disciplines as providing "a way of life" that attended to the individual but was not individualistic, that sought a way of life in the present but was bound to a past, to a tradition embedded in generations of practicing communities.[32]

Eventually, Dkystra (and Bass) would find a dialogue partner for this perspective in the groundbreaking philosophical work of Alasdair MacIntyre and his neo-Aristotelian "practice" perspective. MacIntyre contends that practices are coherent cooperative human activities that encompass within themselves, and therefore lead to, a good. As cooperative human activities, they are done in communities and given to communities by a tradition of doing the practice itself. This attention to practice as a way of life in a community with a tradition was essentially Dykstra's point in turning to the disciplines, what he now called "practices," in the first place.

But while inspired and pushed along by MacIntyre, Dykstra had begun moving in this direction before finding him. While turning his attention to practices, Dykstra, with Bass, was doing more than merely appropriating MacIntyre's thought (which is why I call this perspective pseudo neo-Aristotelianism).[33] Rather, while Dykstra and Bass sought to attend to how practices were, following MacIntyre, cooperative human activities done in a community through a tradition for the sake of a good, they would not follow MacIntyre in seeing practices as solely and finally socially established.[34] They were socially established enough that concrete lived communities *did* them, and did them for the sake of a good (life abundant), but their origin (and indwelt potency) rested outside the social and instead with God. "Indeed, we believe," say Dykstra and Bass, "that it is precisely by participating in Christian practices that we truly come to know God and the world, including ourselves."[35] This

---

32. Dorothy Bass says it this way: "Those who participate in practices are formed in particular ways of thinking about and living in the world." "Ways of Life Abundant," in *For Life Abundant: Practical Theology, Theological Education, and Christian Ministry*, ed. Dorothy Bass and Craig Dykstra (Grand Rapids, MI: Eerdmans. 2008), 29.

33. In Dykstra and Bass's own works, "Our own understanding of practices reflects the influence of MacIntyre . . . while also differing in crucial ways from MacIntyre." Bass and Dykstra, "Theological Understandings of Christian Practice, in Volf and Bass *Practicing Theology,* 21.n8.

34. They state, "Our present understanding of practices differs from MacIntyre's account in *After Virtue* in that ours is now theological and thus normed not only internally but also through the responsive relationship of Christian practices to God." Ibid., 21n8.

35. Ibid., 24. Bass states further, "Dykstra's and my work on practices began with Alasdair MacIntyre's account of social practices, but the theological turn we have taken marks a significant break with the concepts developed there. The 'goods' that concern us are not 'internal' to a practice but are oriented to God and God's intentions for all creation. In addition, our concept of Christian practices is differentiated

can be seen in their succinct and helpful definition of Christian practices: "Christian practices are things Christian people do together over time in response to and *in light of God's active presence* for the life of world."[36]

In other words, these practices were socially done but given to the church by God, cementing these practices in normative theological language. For Dykstra and Bass, practices (worship, prayer, and hospitality, to name three of their twelve) become the very link between divine and human action.[37] There is much to be commended in this perspective, and much that connects (at least in intention) to my own Christopraxis practical theology of the cross. I believe their project is a rich offering to practical theology. It is one of the few (or at least leading) projects that attends so *directly* to divine and human encounter and speaks so boldly, as I will try to do below, of the continued and active presence of God.

Dykstra and Bass, in my opinion, do a much better job than Browning and Miller-McLemore in (bravely and clearly) articulating the locus of divine and human encounter. They name a place where the "happening" occurs, and this "happening" is free from *solely* the religious.[38]

from that of MacIntyre, on the one hand, and from social scientific concepts of practice, on the other, in that our notion is shaped by a theological anthropology that posits the existence of certain fundamental needs and conditions as belonging to human existence as such. 'Christian practices,' as we use the term, are clusters of meaningful action (including thinking and representation) that are sizable and significant enough to address these needs (e.g., for relationship with one another, creation, and God; for physical care in illness or injury; for certain material goods) and conditions, (e.g., finitude, mortality, and physical and psychological vulnerability). Dykstra and I developed this understanding most fully in 'A Theological Understanding of Christian Practices.'" "Ways of Life Abundant," 30n11.

36. Bass, Dykstra, and Wuthnow, "Practicing Christian Faith" presented in a paper at Louisville Presbyterian Seminary, September 25-26, 1997 and quotes in Conner's *Practicing Witness.* Dykstra and Bass continue, "Rather than speak of a Christian way of life as a whole, therefore, we shall speak of the 'Christian practices' that together constitute a way of life abundant. By 'Christian practices' we mean things Christian people do together over time to address fundamental human needs in response to and in the light of God's active presence for the life of the world. Thinking of a way of life as made up of a constitutive set of practices breaks a way of life down into parts that are small enough to be amenable to analysis, both in relation to contemporary concerns and as historic, culture-spanning forms of Christian faith and life. At the same time, practices are not too small: each Christian practice is large enough to permit us to draw together the shards and pieces of particular understandings, beliefs, events, behaviors, actions, relationships, inquiries, and skills into sets that are capacious and cohesive enough to show how they might guide one into a way of life." *Life Abundant,* 18.

37. See Bass, *Practice as a Way of Life* (Grand Rapids, MI: Eerdmans, 2008).

38. "Dykstra, an astute Reformed theologian, is careful to add that practices do not allow us to manipulate revelation. Revelation, knowledge of God, and the things of God are always a gift. Nonetheless, certain practices have proven 'efficacious' in the long history of the church." Benjamin Conner, *Practicing Witness* (Grand Rapids, MI: Eerdmans, 2011), 78.

Therefore, we could say, that for Dykstra and Bass, unlike for Browning and Miller-McLemore, there is attention to *the distinction between time and eternity*. While Browning and Miller-McLemore seem to lock everything within the constructs of human action, Dykstra and Bass speak of an eternal/divine reality that cannot be flattened into human action only. These practices of the church are done by human agents in time, but they are given as gifts to human communities by the eternal God.[39] So it is by participating in these divinely gifted practices that we (the community of practice) participate in the divine life (connecting the divine and human). Practice itself becomes a means of grace because practices are the gifts given to humanity that draw the human agent into divine action.[40]

But the outworking of participation in the divine life through practice has its results, for Dykstra and Bass, *almost* completely on the plane of the human, and this is where my Christopraxis approach begins to differ. For Dykstra and Bass, participating in the divine through practice has the effect of bringing forth the good of life abundant to concrete communities. This life abundant looks much like (or is) the result of doing a practice; the very good of doing the practice is seen as a manifestation of God's act in the practice.[41] They

---

39. Conner explains, "In this sense the practices are understood to be 'arenas' that 'put us where life in Christ may be made known, recognized, experienced, and participated in.' They are the means of grace by which the presence of God is palpably experienced and our doubts, fears, and suspicion that there are no realities behind the language and liturgies of the Christian faith are quelled: 'In the midst of engagement in these practices, a community comes to such an immediate experience of the grace and mercy and power of God that the "nasty suspicion" . . . simply loses its power.' So through these large-scale ways of being in the world, communities and individuals are transformed and reoriented, in response to God's active presence in the world." Ibid., 59.

40. Kathleen Cahalan gives a rich overview of practice that connects to Dykstra and Bass's normative/theological interests. "First, a practice is understood as an intentional action, which, secondly, takes place within a community and tradition of shared meaning and purpose. Third, practice is an embodied action, an expression of identity, knowledge, and conviction through bodily action. Fourth, practices are corruptible, meaning they are intertwined in personal sin and failings as well as oppressive forms of systematic power and evil. And fifth, practice is a spiritual exercise that requires attention to the immanent and transcendent presence of God." *Introducing the Practice of Ministry* (Collegeville, MN: Liturgical Press, 2010), 99.

41. "A practice is a practice in our meaning of the term only if it is a sustained, cooperative pattern of human activity that is big enough, rich enough, and complex enough to address some fundamental feature of human existence. Christian practices also have a normative dimension that is thoroughly theological in character. That is, our descriptions of Christian practices contain within them normative understandings of what God wills for us and for the whole creation and of what God expects of us in response to God's call to be faithful. Christian practices are thus congruent with the necessities of human existence as such, as seen from a Christian perspective on the character of human flourishing." Bass and

state, "Normatively and theologically understood, therefore, Christian practices are the human activities in and through which people cooperate with God in addressing the needs of one another and creation."[42] This allows wonderfully for concrete actions to have theological depth, but nevertheless, in its concrete focus, it misses the potential eventfulness of divine encounter that may very well exist outside the practice itself.[43]

So here too, while understood with much more theological depth, divine action nevertheless ends only on the plane of human action—even though it starts independently of the human. Dykstra and Bass speak little of a more eventful encounter of divine action that allows for the human to be taken and bound in the life of God through the Spirit: "I no longer live, but Christ lives in me" (Gal. 2:20). In other words, there is little articulation of the ontological binding of the human with the divine (as the verse from Galatians points to). Rather, all divine and human encounter becomes equated with functional action done on the plane of human good (abundant life). There is little discussion, in an ontological frame, of how human *being* itself is bound and now lives in the very life of God as a practical but also spiritual reality.[44]

Paul's own experience of the eternal (I am thinking here of Acts 9), for instance, happens not through practice but through revelatory encounter, where he is informed that the young church, which he is persecuting, is in Christ and Christ is in the church. This encounter of the living Christ, once dead, now resurrected and ascended, means the eternal is not only in time (through incarnation and crucifixion) but time is in the eternal (through ascension and the outpouring of the Spirit at Pentecost). This ontological mystical union, as biblical scholar Mora Hooker calls it, seems to escape a practice-orientated pseudo neo-Aristotelian practical theology.[45]

For a pseudo neo-Aristotelian perspective, practices allow the eternal to connect with time, but Dykstra and Bass are not as clear about whether and

Dykstra, "A Theological Understanding of Christian Practice," in Volf and Bass, *Practicing Theology,* 22.

42. Ibid.

43. I'm not saying that they reference this perspective or point in this direction. They say, "Christian practices share in the mysterious dynamic of fall and redemption, sin and grace." Ibid., 27. I'm saying only that it is not developed enough or central enough in their practice perspective.

44. Ben Conner wonders something similar, though in the end thinks they avoid a problem that I see with the perspective. "I do not believe that the Practicing our Faith discussion has fallen into this trap. Nonetheless, one must ask what compromises, if any, have been made theologically by investing so heavily in MacIntyre's definition of practices. As Sarah Coakley has convincingly laid bare, MacIntyre's oft quoted definition of a practice from *After Virtue* is about socially established human activity and human projects." *Practicing Witness,* 54.

45. Morna Hooker, *From Adam to Christ: Essays on Paul* (Eugene, OR: Wipf and Stock, 1990).

how time is taken into the eternal.[46] Dykstra and Bass explain richly how practice brings the eternal to earth, but because of the lack of ontological language (particularly about the humanity of Jesus and union with Jesus in Spirit), we are unsure from their explanation whether time itself, the human, is taken into the eternal life of God (for instance at the level of pneumatology, eschatology, or even soteriology).

This can all be seen further in Dykstra and Bass's attention to discipleship. Practices as means of grace give the human actor "a way of life," and a way of life, in theological language, can be understood no more directly than as discipleship. This attention to discipleship shows the positive elements of their perspective, as they articulate that the point of practical theology is to help people into following Jesus Christ. But it also has the possibility of binding discipleship too much in time, running the risk of making all discussions of discipleship only about *imitatio Christi* and saying little about the more dynamic (from my Christopraxis approach) *participatio Christi*.

This can be seen most clearly in the work of one of Dykstra and Bass's most consistent contributors and colleagues, Catholic practical theologian Kathleen Cahalan.[47] In her book *Introducing the Practice of Ministry*, Cahalan provides a rich articulation of ministry in a practice framework.[48] She, like Dykstra and Bass, also sees discipleship as the focus of practical theology (and the work of ministers). What constitutes discipleship is practice itself; following the practices done (in time) by Jesus gives shape to discipleship. In the vein of the *imitatio Christi*, discipleship is not so much following the *person* of Jesus Christ as the practices of Jesus, practices like *follower, worshipper, witness, forgiver, neighbor, prophet, and steward.* We too are disciples as we follow Jesus in *doing* these

46. Calahan points in the direction of the eternal in light of time in her discussion of kataphatic and apophatic later in *Introducing the Practice of Ministry*.

47. In congruence with Dykstra and Bass, Cahalan and Nieman state, "The basic task that orients practical theology is to promote faithful discipleship." Kathleen A. Cahalan and James R. Nieman, "Mapping the Field of Practical Theology," in Bass and Dykstra, *For Life Abundant*, 67. Cahalan herself says, "Ministry is leading disciples through the practices of teaching, preaching, worship, pastoral care, social ministry, and administration; for the sake of discipleship lived in relationship to God's mission." *Introducting the Practice of Ministry*, 55.

48. To provide one example of the *imitatio Christi*, Cahalan says, "Clearly the first step of discipleship is responding to the call to follow Jesus. A disciple is a follower first and foremost. But what does following mean? What must a follower learn along the way? Who do we become when we follow Jesus? To be a disciple means learning a way of life that embodies particular dispositions, attitudes, and practices that place the disciple in relationship to, and as a participant in, God's mission to serve and transform the world." Ibid., 4. She continues, "These seven features—follower, worshiper, witness, forgiver, neighbor, prophet, and steward—are the central aspects of the life of the disciple that I will elaborate here." Ibid., 5.

practices, meaning that practical theology connects (a) the work of scholars with (b) the activity of faith in the life of believers by giving direction and leadership in doing these practices.

Much of this is helpful, but it misses one of the core commitments of a Christopraxis practical theology of the cross, which is to think of practical theology from the locale of *participatio Christi*, of how, from the ontological level, the human being participates in the life of God through Jesus Christ (this foreshadows my definition of Christopraxis). It is not only that God is active and present in the world, as Dykstra and Bass affirm, but also that we participate ontologically in the divine life itself, that our life is hidden with Christ in God (Col. 3:3). Matt, Sarah, and Greg experienced ministry not as an *imitatio* of Christ but as an experience of *participatio*. Experientially, their ministry was more real than the practice itself.

This participation, I'll argue, happens only through a death-to-life, life-through-death paradigm of divine action (this is the *theologia crucis* element of my perspective and the fundamental core, I will argue, of ministry itself). We participate in Jesus, are called disciples, because we have died with Christ, and we are now given life through Christ's ministry of cross and resurrection (this is Christopraxis). Through the cross, through death (a reality bound fully in time but nevertheless shared in by the eternal God), we are ushered into the life of Godself, a life where death is overcome in the eternal love of Father to Son.[49]

A pseudo neo-Aristotelian practical theology, while wonderfully attending to discipleship, here too leaves it only on the plane of time (in the context of the human knower) by connecting it too fully to practices themselves. After all, the most significant work in discipleship in the last hundred years has been done by Dietrich Bonhoeffer; Bonhoeffer asserts boldly that discipleship is not primarily about practices but first and foremost about following Jesus (it may be secondarily about *imitatio Christi*, seen for instance in *Life Together*). And this following is about participation (*participatio Christi*), not through practice but through death (*theologia crucis*). As Bonhoeffer says, "When Jesus Christ calls a man [*sic*] he calls him to come and die."

Bonhoeffer's perspective of discipleship is one constructed fully on a *theologica crucis*, which grows from the soil of justification. We come and die

---

49. Cahalan moves in this direction in the final chapter of her book, "The Practice of the Trinity." But she makes this Trinitarian move without enough discussion of Christology, particularly, from my perspective, the hypostatic union, therefore breaking down how time enters the eternal community of Godself. This has been a major shortcoming of social trinitarianisms and most especially those in practical theology. For further critique of social trinitarianism see Kathryn Tanner's *Christ the Key* (London: Cambridge University Press, 2010).

because none of our own actions (practices) can save us. All our actions (all our desires for *imitatio*) are bound too fully to death and sin. Even our best intentions to follow, even our best practices, demonstrate the impossibility of full discipleship as instead we follow the sons of Zebedee (Matt. 20:20), seeking reward and power.[50] We follow to die as a confession that no practice can save us, and yet "follow to die" becomes "in dying with Christ we are saved" (Rom. 6). We live a life abundant in this time as a deeper witness to a time when the eternal turns from promise to actuality. A perspective on discipleship too bound to *imitatio Christi* locks practice too tightly into a form of sanctification that is disconnected from justification. The practices of faith can only be a means of grace if they too bear the death-to-life, life-out-of-death paradigm (a core sense of transformation through justification) as both baptism and communion do![51]

So discipleship may have the result of life abundant but only as it ontologically shares in Christ by passing through death, and it is abundant not because it is a good in time but because though in time, though we are passing away, we are being renewed (2 Cor. 4:16ff.), for we participate through our being that knows death in the being of God that overcomes all that is dead with the eternal (as a higher stratum of reality).

This leads us to conclude with my two questions, questions we have already explored, and therefore answering them more directly serves as summary. First, what is a pseudo neo-Aristotelian epistemology of divine action? Divine action is known in the functional act of a community doing a practice in time. This is more than religious socialization because these practices

50. All practical theologians working from this perspective affirm that practices can be corrupted, though this possibility doesn't eliminate practices' potential.

51. Both Dykstra and Bass are committed to the power of communion and baptism. Though they do point to the life-death paradigm, my critique is simply that it is not central enough (or formative enough) to their perspective of practical theology. They say, "And [baptism] incorporates that person into the very mystery of Christ. 'Do you not know that all of us who have been baptized into Christ Jesus were baptized into his death?' writes Paul to the Romans (6:3-4). 'Therefore we have been buried with him by baptism into death, so that, just as Christ was raised from the dead by the glory of the Father, so we too might walk in newness of life.'" "A Theological Understanding of Christian Practice, p. 30 in Volf and Bass *Practicing Theology*. And this is seen in how the preceding quote leads to the next, in which baptism is summation of practice rather than the existential reality bound in justification that I hope to point toward. "At its heart, baptism is not so much a distinct practice as it is the liturgical summation of all the Christian practices. In this rite, the grace to which the Christian life is a response is fully and finally presented, visibly, tangibly, and in words. Here all the practices are present in crystalline form—forgiveness and healing, singing and testimony, Sabbath-keeping and community shaping, and all the others. Unlike each particular practice, baptism does not address a specific need; instead, it ritually sketches the contours of a whole new life, within which all human needs can be perceived in a different way." Ibid., 31.

are gifts given by God; they are realities of God's active presence. This active presence is joined through *imitatio*, by practice itself. We experience divine action as we communally practice the faith.

And what is a pseudo neo-Aristotelian view of soteriology? Soteriology is life abundant; it is to join in God's own practice of bringing the good in time itself by doing practices of good ourselves for the world that God loves. Life abundant is *not* simply a program for betterment, but a form of working with God for the salvation of all. However, this soteriological reality happens within time; it is not necessarily (at least functionally) an eschatological or mystical reality, but one that is unfolding now and can be tangibly experienced when practices are done with the result of life abundant.

A BARTHIAN PRACTICAL THEOLOGY

Throughout this chapter we've mapped three dominant North American models of practical theology. Our first two models (a hermeneutical practical theology and a postmodern Bourdieuian practical theology) had very strong resemblances to each other, giving rich attention to human action. A pseudo neo-Aristotelian practical theology differed from these two perspectives in its confessional attention to divine action but, like the other two, did most of its heavy lifting on the plane of human agency.

I have critiqued all three of these perspectives, emphasizing the inability of each perspective to attend to the qualitative distinction between time and eternity, noting also that all three subsume practical theology within human operations and zones of practice, interpretation, or embodied cultural action and that all have a hard time articulating the concrete experience of divine action seen in the interviews in the prior chapter. As I've tried to show, I have appreciation for each of these perspectives and find each provisionally helpful in articulating *part* of the operations of practical theology. But I feel that all three fall short of presenting a dynamic articulation of divine action.[52]

Yet, this articulation of divine action is far from missing (or given short shrift) in our final model. Andrew Purves (particularly in his text *Reconstructing Pastoral Theology*) has presented a thick, unabashed, and unrelenting articulation of divine action. And while Purves does this in sophisticated dialogue with

---

52. My own perspective too will be provisional; as a critical and revelatory realist, I cannot presume that my own thought experiment can possess, in itself, reality. I'm hopeful that it says something true, but even in saying something true it will only be *a piece* of reality. Therefore, while I critique others, I wish to possess humility, knowing in the end my own position is simply a "best account" of a reality bigger than me (a "best account" I'm willing to argue for but still recognize as only "an" account).

Calvin, T. F. Torrance, and John McLeod Campbell, Karl Barth rests at the foundations of his work.

While Barth is not absent from practical theological constructions, he nevertheless has been seen as an odd and unwelcomed dialogue partner.[53] This unwelcome can be seen in Browning's critique of him and rests on the perception of Barth's hostility to human action.[54] Barth's perspective is perceived as hostile because of his uncompromising starting point in revelation and his foreclosure on any possibility for natural theology (this is why Browning interprets Barth as starting with theory). This seems to leave little for practical theology to do, methodologically, pastorally, or curricularly, other than articulate the actuality of divine action. While some may argue this is actually a lot, it nevertheless runs the risk of making practical theology almost completely the handmaid of systematic or dogmatic theology, because in the end there is no reason to study human communities or explore human practice, for all is shown to be but dry bones next to the heat of God's own act.

While neo-Barthian practical theologians (like Deborah van Duesen Hunsinger, James Loder, and Theresa Latini) have sought to balance this reading of Barth (hence, my calling them neo-Barthian), Purves seeks, in *Reconstructing Pastoral Theology*, to lean into it, articulating a pastoral theology from within just such a strong articulation of divine action and in the tone of a systematician (hence, my calling him Barthian).[55]

53. Others, like Deborah van Deusen Hunsinger (VDH), Theresa Latini, and James Loder, can all be considered neo-Barthian practical theologians. And in some way my own biographical neo-Barthianism finds intellectual partnership with their projects. Yet, here I'll be placing *theologia crucis* in connection to a certain Barthian perspective. In that sense the authors above are neo-Barthian because, jumping off from Barth, they seek to make more room for interdisciplinarity and conversation with other forms of knowledge, showing that critiques of Barth like Browning's are not conclusive. The "neo," then, is a pushing beyond. My own "neo"-Barthianism finds support for this but is more directly focused on mining Barth's own *theologia crucis* and placing his revelatory realism in conversation with an existential actuality toward which the cross points. Joyce Mercer, in her book *Welcoming Children: A Practical Theology of Childhood* (St. Louis: Chalice, 2005), admits that Barth can be unwelcome, sheepishly confessing she'll be using Barth in that text, nearly apologizing for doing so, explaining that a feminist practical theology wouldn't normally use Barth.

54. Latini explains, "With the exception of a few people, practical theologians by and large have veered away from Barth as a source for their constructive work. While the reasons for this are likely diverse and varied, one criticism stands out among the rest: that Barth's theology leaves little room for human agency." *The Church and the Crisis of Community: A Practical Theology of Small-Group Ministry* (Grand Rapids, MI: Eerdmans, 2011), 193.

55. Latini explains what she and other neo-Barthians are trying to do: "Rather, I have built on aspects of his overall methodology, at times extending his argument and at other times going beyond it. In this sense I have been working from what I call a 'neo-Barthian practical theology.'" Ibid, 194. By calling

One could argue that Purves is seeking to rewind the very history of pastoral theology in North America, fretting that the inspirational intellectual forefather is Seward Hiltner and his attention to shepherding as a theological and psychological reality is primary.[56] Purves grieves that Edward Thurneysen, the dear friend of Karl Barth who presented pastoral theology (pastoral care) as proclaiming the forgiveness of sins and the actuality of God's action of reconciliation, is the not leading figure. Thurneysen turns so forcefully in this kerygmatic (dogmatic) direction that nearly all human pathos is sucked from his argument, leaving not even an analogy or case example to ponder.

Purves not only presents an apologetic for Thurneysen but follows his methodological lead in seeking to present a pastoral theology that articulates this same actuality, seeing practical theology (pastoral care) as the proclamation

Purves "Barthian," I am not asserting that Purves is closest to the actual Barth. Rather, I could argue that the neo-Barthian perspective, or maybe even my Christopraxis perspective (especially as Anderson constructs it), may be what Barth himself would find affinity with. Calling Purves a Barthian affirms his connection to Barth's thought, but much as Barth said himself at the end of his life, "I am no Barthian." See *A Karl Barth Reader*, ed. Rolf Joachim Erlaer and Reiner Marquard (Edinburgh: T&T Clark, 1986).

56. Purves states his discomfort with Hiltner. "Hiltner, as noted, argues for two-way communication at all points within the body of divinity. This means a rejection of the kerygmatic approach, I found, for example, in the theology of Karl Barth. Hiltner's theology is constructed ostensibly upon both biblical bases and reflection upon acts and events of ministry, when theological questions are asked of them. It is, however, especially constructed upon reflection on acts and events, with a notable absence of biblical and classical theological references and content. The Word of God, Hiltner believes, is found in many areas of inquiry into human experience, and especially from inquiry into psychological and psychotherapeutic processes. He develops what we might call an immanentalist pastoral theological method that is heavily influenced by the empirical theology movement that came out of the University of Chicago, and a precursor of process theology, and Paul Tillich's method of correlation. Thus, according to Hiltner, the theological study of Anton Boisen's notation of "living human documents"—people, in other words—is the study not merely of psychology but also of theology when theological questions are put (what this means is not defined). The method of correlation, which Hiltner actually advanced beyond Tillich to anticipate by about twenty years David Tracy's own correction of Tillich, states that there is a correlation between our deepest existential questions and the answers of faith. It allows for culture to raise questions and for Christian faith to show its relevance by answering them. According to Hiltner, the correlation must also go the other way, from questions raised by faith to answers found in human experience. Thus Hiltner opened the way for a profound dialogical relationship between the personality sciences and pastoral care under the rubric of pastoral theology. This was a remarkable achievement, for he offered a systematic construal of pastoral theology that has guided the practice of care for two generations of ministers." Andrew Purves, *Reconstructing Pastoral Theology: A Christological Foundation* (Louisville, KY: Westminster John Knox, 2004), xxxii. "Shepherding has been developed as an imitative rather than as a participatory approach to ministry. This approach follows the example of Jesus in some regards—*imitatio Christi*—without having at its core a vital way in which the church's ministry shares in Christ's continuing personhood and ministry—*participatio Christi*." Ibid., xxx.

(something near preaching) of the action of God in reconciliation.[57] Purves follows Thurneysen not only in method but in style as well (Purves waits until page 162 of 231 to present his first analogy, story, and example from pastoral ministry itself).

This central kerygmatic focus leads Purves to see practical theology as the articulation and living out of doctrine.[58] If Miller-McLemore is admittedly uncreedal and undoctrinal, then Purves is überdoctrinal. While his focus may sound initially like the retreat of practical theology into applied theology, Purves shows that this need not be the case. Rather, through an articulation of revelatory realism (of a rich understanding of divine action) practical theology gives attention to the *continued* ministry of God.[59] Doctrine, Purves believes, is the trusted interpretation of divine action. *Doctrine, itself, is the epistemology of divine action.* So practical theology remains, not applied but dynamically about action. This action is just turned from human to divine, Purves believes.[60]

This is where Purves's Barthian practical theology and my Christopraxis practical theology of the cross differ. While sharing with Purves this attention to a revelatory realism of God's ministry as a central engine of practical theological

57. I mean this "apologetic" ironically, because of course Thurneysen, Barth, and Purves are critiqued for being overly *kerygmatic* and having no place in any form for apologetics—and *kerygma* and apologetics have historically been seen as the two poles of theology. "First, the indicative of grace means that pastoral work must give the highest priority to the kerygmatic affirmation 'You are forgiven.' The whole movement of the gospel pulls in this direction. This was Thurneysen's primary point in his *Theology of Pastoral Care*, where he developed an understanding of the pastoral conversation as moving a person from the ground of his or her own human experience to the ground of the Word of God. The conversation does not become pastoral until that shift is made. For Thurneysen, the actual content of this ground was the proclamation of grace, meaning forgiveness of sins through Jesus Christ. The goal of pastoral work, he contended, was a restored communion with God." Purves, *Reconstructing Pastoral Theology*, 35.

58. "In its preaching, teaching, and serving, the church depends on the acts of God in Christ. To borrow from and rephrase Karl Barth, it is not Jesus Christ who needs pastoral work, it is pastoral work that needs Jesus Christ. The relation between God's ministry in, through, and as Jesus Christ in the power of the Holy Spirit and the ministry of the church is the proper concern. Because pastoral care is at all points both a ministry of God and a ministry of the church, it is tied to the gospel given in Word and sacraments." Ibid., 10.

59. I agree in so many ways with Purves's position here; both of us work from Anderson's perspective. "Practical theology is theology that is concerned with action: first, with God's action, the mission Dei; and second, with the action or praxis of the church in its life and ministry in faithful communion with the God who acts, the mission of the church. But God's acts are always first, and our acts, the church's acts, are always second, and even then, I argue, our acts are but a participation in the Holy Spirit in our Lord's human response on our behalf to the prior act of God. Even in response we find ourselves within the sphere of God's prevenient grace and the functioning of the Holy Trinity." Ibid., xxv.

60. See Purves, *Reconstructing Pastoral Theology*, 4 and 9.

attention, I believe Purves too quickly turns God's ministerial action into doctrine, keeping it from any connection to the dynamic movement of the Spirit and capturing it in a tradition controlled by theologians.[61]

Like Purves, I contend that doctrine, as articulation of divine action, has been overlooked in practical theology. And in chapter 6 I do not shy away from engaging a doctrine itself as paradigmatic for practical theology. Yet, to make doctrine live (an essential for practical theology), it must not only articulate the action of God, but do so next to the very crisis of reality that human beings experience.[62] Doctrine, in my position, is the church's (not the theologian's) articulation of God's action next to its contextual experience of the crisis of reality itself (human action, or better impossibility of human action). This articulation becomes doctrine because, though it is worked on in a context, it becomes trusted and helpful across contexts (across places and times the church lives in). Purves speaks of doctrine only from the divine side (the side of the theologian), not showing how it is embedded in the experience of communities. This prevents doctrine from living because, ironically, it keeps it from the event of encounter (the eternal) that doctrine seeks to articulate in concrete communities in time.[63]

61. Both of us draw on Anderson in our attention to the revelatory realism of God's ministry as a central engine of practical theological attention; see Purves, *Reconstructing Pastoral Theology*, 3.

62. Here Purves explains how his objective is to make pastoral theology fully dogmatic. This is why I say he emphasizes the theologian over the pastor, though he wants concrete community to do theology and the pastor to see herself as a theologian. There is just little articulation of how theology is done differently in church than in the library. "In what follows I attempt to reconstruct the foundations of pastoral theology. In this I will move away from Hiltner's *Preface to Pastoral Theology* altogether by the development of what might be called 'pastoral dogmatics.' By this I intend that we think of pastoral work in a rigorous way, out of the dogmatic or doctrinal content of Christian faith: our minds must be conformed to this way of thinking, for at its center is God as revealed and self-declared, rather than we ourselves." *Reconstructing Pastoral Theology*, xxxiv. Continuing these thoughts, he states how doctrine, as opposed to experience, will set the terms for him. My argument is to uphold doctrine as the articulation of human experience next to the event of God's act. Purves too may want this, but it is left undefined: "It stands over and against more recent perspectives in pastoral theology that begin with the human experience on its own terms." Ibid., 1.

63. This is a way of thinking of doctrine that I agree with. Clearly, Purves wants to push this out into the practice of ministry and the life of the church. But in the end he doesn't tell us how this happens from the human side and how it affirms (or even judges) people's significant experiences. "Theology that truly refers to God as the revealing and acting God in, through, and as Jesus Christ, and that the church through due process confirms, is known as doctrine. Doctrine is practical theology because it is church theology. With doctrine the church bears witness to the ministering God in the language of our knowing, to the acting God who reaches out in saving and serving love in Jesus Christ, not only in revelation but also to bring us into the joy of reconciliation and relationship with God." Ibid., 9.

So for Purves divine action is leveled so formidably and in such a way that human action is swallowed; human action becomes only attention to doctrine, which grounds and gives shape (if there is any) to human action. Purves can give no examples or direction to how the human spirit experiences the divine Spirit and how this is concretely transformational.[64] So instead of speaking in any way (even a biblical way, let alone an interdisciplinary one) of the human being's experience of the divine, Purves turns to doctrine in a manner nearly devoid of the pathos of the human experience itself.[65]

While divine action is robustly articulated in Purves's perspective (as we will see more fully below), human action is flat. If the models of practical theology I've described overemphasize human action or, more positively, articulate the richness of human action by flattening divine action, then Purves does the opposite. Emphasizing divine action so fully, Purves, like the caricature of Barth, leaves little room for human action other than to live out the beliefs found in doctrine, given by systematic theologians. Then we could say that Purves attends wonderfully to the eternal, doing what the other authors fail to, keeping the qualitative distinction between time and eternity and affirming a stratified reality. But in drawing this boundary between time and eternity, Purves fails to give practical theology any ways of attending to time, making all his presentations of the associations between time and eternity too obscure and abstract to be helpful. Purves seemingly cuts loose talking about human action (time) altogether.[66]

---

64. It isn't that Purves has no conception of, or even a soft spot for, experience. He is willing to tip his hat to it but doesn't give us any handles to take it into his project in any deep way. "Because of the work of the Holy Spirit, God is active through the Scripture but also surely in situations of human experience. The basis for the interpretation of the latter is given by the former, and the meaning of the former is found as a lived reality in the latter. It is the present and continuing mediation of Jesus Christ through the Holy Spirit in and through Scripture and in and through the experiences of life that opens up Scripture as the hermeneutic of the church pastoral practice, and the church's pastoral practice as a necessary aspect of the interpretation of Scripture." Ibid., 12.

65. Purves here explains that he doesn't intend to eliminate human action but nevertheless seeks to push in a different direction, one that attends to God outside of human experience itself. "That my argument pulls strongly toward God, focusing on the God in whom we believe rather than on the experience or faith of the believer, must not be interpreted to mean that there is no value in or place for human experience or for the study of this experience. It is to make the claim rather that the former and not the latter is definitive and as such is the proper ground and subject matter of pastoral theology." Ibid., p. xxii.

66. For instance, Purves doesn't talk about praxis, a central theme discussed in practical theology, until the very end of the book, and only then in a quote by Ray Anderson. In this text Purves seems to have little interest in human action at all, which is a strange perspective for a book of pastoral theology.

Yet, even with that said, Purves's project takes shape in a number of ways congruent with my own project, especially as it seeks to articulate divine action. Following Athanasius and T. F. Torrance, Purves nicely articulates how the human being, through Jesus Christ, participates in the eternal, in the divine life. Purves refuses to limit practical theology in any way to *imitatio Christi*, seeing instead practical theology's need to articulate the actuality of our participation in the divine life.

My Christopraxis practical theology of the cross will also seek to turn practical theology from *imitatio Christi* to *participatio Christi*, believing that in so doing, divine action is freed from an inert tradition of interpretation or practice and can become a living personal reality. This *participatio Christi* allows us to articulate a mystical union through personhood—that is, through ministry—that binds the divine and human both in time and eternity. Ministry is the event in which time and eternity come together.

Purves also wants this (and in many ways articulates beautifully the eternal side of it), but because he cannot explicate human action more richly, his theological method ironically, like the perspectives described earlier, falls into seeing *theology* in practical theology as the mobilization of tradition (so in Browning this tradition is for hermeneutical reflection, in Dykstra and Bass for practices that mediate God, and in Purves for doctrines that proclaim).[67] In other words, because he cannot articulate how it is, from the human side, that we experience this divine participation, it becomes little more than a traditional doctrine.

My Christopraxis practical theology of the cross will seek to free divine action from "tradition" (whether for interpretation, giving practice, or providing doctrines) and see it instead as an existential encounter with the reality of God's coming to us—or, better, an encounter with the divine through the existential experience of impossibility, an experience where time and eternity are qualitatively distinct but mutually experienced. We share in Christ and Christ shares in us in and through the cross. Through the human pathos of impossibility, directed to God the Father in the abandoned plea of Jesus on the cross (as event), and the embrace by the Father through the restoration by death in the newness of resurrection, we are invited to share in God by now being in Christ.

Purves, through Christology, places ontological language back within practical theology, language lost in the orbit of practice theory and

---

67. This strong statement is what I want to critique: "Neither individual doctrines nor the system of doctrine, however, substitutes for God and the gospel, for doctrine does not have a reality and truth independent of that to which it refers." Purves, *Reconstructing Pastoral Theology*, 13.

philosophical pragmatism.[68] He explains that through Christ our very being is drawn into Christ's being, and with Christ our being is given complete union with God. *Soteriology, for Purves, is nothing more and nothing less than union with Christ.* And this too finds congruence with my project, making the objective of practical theology to speak of this union. But for Purves the way we speak of this union (in many ways, the only way we can) is by proclaiming it and participating in it through worship and sacraments (as constituted in our doctrines) and not by engaging in ministry of person to person (which is a deeply experiential reality of participation).[69]

Even here, Purves articulates how worship and sacraments connect to the eternal and are bound in divine action. But, again, Purves provides no direction, stories, or analogies of how worship and sacraments function and move in time itself. Practical theology (pastoral care) is equated with worship and sacrament, just as it starts with worship and sacraments. It is a never-ending circle constituted in divine action that runs the risk of making human action passive to the point of unimportance.[70]

While his Christological/ontological presentation is rich from the level of divine action, it is hard to decipher in Purves's project how the human being concretely experiences or is taken into this reality. Purves would just claim it as an actuality, as something that is: all humans are reconciled and found in Christ through their very *being* human as Jesus is human. But Purves never seems to articulate how it is that the human being *experiences* this reality. The reality may *be* (I'll go with Purves here), but it is hard to conceptualize how to articulate a form that connects to human experience itself.

And this is a major weakness of Purves's project (and one I hope to avoid in my Christopraxis approach). Purves seems to provide no place for human experience, for how the human being (from the ontological level) can articulate (or live into) the experience of divine action. It is simply an actuality with no emotional, and therefore personal, contact. While Purves attends uniquely (in comparison to other models) to divine action, to the eternal, he too misses

---

68. "The starting point in ecclesiology is the ontological connection between Christ and the church. The church exists as church only insofar as it is Christ's body, in union with him, meaning also our union in him, both of which are a matter of his free and gracious choice." Ibid., 97.

69. "Because this is the same Word preached in the sermon and celebrated in the sacraments, pastoral work comes from sermon and sacrament and returns to sermon and sacrament." Ibid., 161.

70. Purves says as much when he talks about preaching, explaining that because the preacher speaks the word of God and the Word does something, what is important is not *how* and *in what ways* the pastor preaches, but that in preaching the word moves. This is helpful theologically, but without some conception of human action it naively imagines no reflective action is needed from the preacher.

the death-to-life, life-out-of-death paradigm that a *theologia crucis* gives us, especially one mobilized in conversation with the critical realism my project rests upon.

Much like Thurneysen, Purves in my opinion misses the essential *theologia crucis* that rests in Barth himself (which connects my own neo-Barthianism with my relational justification perspective).[71] This *theologia crucis* allows us to speak of divine action as ontological union through the *participatio Christi*, but to see the opening for this participation in the experience of human impossibility (whether bodily, psychologically, materially, relationally, and so on). From the place of impossibility, the divine and human find association. Purves works wonderfully with revelation and reconciliation, but justification leads in the direction of seeing the association of divine love next to human impossibility as the very way that time and eternity are held distinct but associated in and through ministry (in the chapters that follow, I will argue that justification does this). From this perspective of justification, the practical theologian must attend deeply to human action, seeking to "call a thing what it is," as Luther would say. This calling a thing what it is means attending deeply to human action, but in the end seeing this human action as in need, even in its genius, of the action of God to pull us from impossibility to all new possibility in the life of Godself.

---

71. Purves does turn to the early Jürgen Moltmann at a few places in his project, but his dialogue with Moltmann never seems to move into a developed conversation with his *theologia crucis*.

PART II

5

A Christopraxis Practical Theology of the Cross

Through the appreciative critique of the four dominant models of practical theology in the last chapter, I began to articulate my own position, an approach I call a Christopraxis practical theology of the cross. The objective of this chapter will be more directly and more fully to lay out this position, leaving behind critique and moving headlong into construction.

This chapter signals a rhythmic change in the flow of the book. If the first four chapters were set to the anthem of definition and models of the field, then this chapter is a jam session laying out the tones and tunes of my perspective. It seeks to articulate directly what a Christopraxis practical theology of the cross is and how such a theology seeks to hold divine and human action together, honoring the lived experiences of divine action presented in chapter 3. Having laid these beats here, the following chapters will remix them with beats from justification, the *concursus Dei*, participation, and hypostatic personalism. The point of these following chapters is to show how their own beats accentuate or complement the beats of Christopraxis and its articulation of divine and human action in practical theology—that is, how the human agent encounters and participates ontologically in the divine life—providing an approach for practical theology that attends to the concrete and lived experiences of divine action.

While this chapter will signal the new rhythmic direction of the project, it nevertheless continues with some notes of the last. While it is different from the earlier chapters in its move from critique to construction, it is similar in its use of description. As I described the composition of each the models in the earlier chapters, so here I will describe the composition of a Christopraxis approach in more depth. But before I can do that, a confession is in order.

A Confession

To move into a description of my perspective after leveling my critique of other approaches seems unfair and makes it appear I've cooked the books, setting up the other models by critiquing them against my own, only to present mine in a secure vault with concrete walls six feet wide protecting it from any theft of its veracity. While my critique will come (in journal reviews and blogs), the organization of these chapters nevertheless forces a disclaimer that propels us forward.

A Christopraxis approach begins and in many ways ends with the *event* of revelation; it centers on what is God's being in God's becoming, as I will explain more below. This event of revelation I have sought to describe in the lived experience of people. And I will argue in the sections to come that God's being in becoming is seen and experienced in God's full identification with the perishing Jesus, who therefore identifies with us in our own perishing—this is the *theologia crucis* in my perspective. This view, then, seeks to construct a practical theological approach on the foolishness of God's act of perishing on the cross. This starting (and ending) point means that all attempts toward articulation of this foolish event must be done in humility (it is foolish after all) and with a wry rabbinic smile that admits that we seek to articulate what cannot be fully known and can never be possessed, but that we nevertheless will take joy in trying—pleased to look stupid to some and irreligious to others (1 Corinthians).

This means that my perspective, because it is constructed on the foolishness of the *theologia crucis*, is only, as critical realism would say, a provisional best account. And while I'll do it the service it deserves by passionately articulating it, it should be read as such a provisional account. My hope is that in some small way the Pauline truth of God's foolishness exceeding human wisdom will be recognized. But if it is, it will need to be recognized as the event of God's being in becoming.

For the Practice of Ministry

With this declaimer of humility pasted to the beginning of this chapter, why make the effort at all to construct a theory? Admitting that such a theory cannot possess reality, why not opt for a cold beer and an episode of *Pawn Stars*? After all, it is not only the admitting that reality cannot be captured in theory (even theory that starts in practice) that makes my pursuits seem odd, but even more so my desire to build a perspective on the spongy ground of foolishness.

In other words, why would an academic perspective, presented in the arena of ideas, seek foolishness? Even if foolishness is somehow a religious or transcendent or biblical reality, it nevertheless seems odd to make it the pursuit of (scientific) method—why not just stick with confession and move on?

The reason to do so rests squarely at the heart of practical theology itself. The foolishness of the cross, I contend, is the richest avenue for connecting practical theological method (done by scholars in Miller-McLemore's first quadrant) with ordained, professional, or lay ministers in the church and world (engaging as believers in an activity of faith in Miller-McLemore's second quadrant).[1] And this connecting through foolishness does something richer: by connecting the first quadrant with the second (and vice versa), it also connects the divine with the human. Foolishness becomes the economy of God while being the very state of our own being. It then is not the scientific that a Christopraxis practical theology of cross looks to attend to, but rather the ministerial. We saw this ministerial foolishness that became the event of God's coming in both Ken's and Rachel's stories above. The absurd acts of a cabbie in a morgue and an eighty-year-old woman in a bright red wig that embrace Rachel and Ken in their struggles, ministering to their persons, become the concrete experience of God's presence.

Therefore, my Christopraxis approach seeks to offer a vision and space for the practice of ministry itself, which is what matters in the end. Therefore, it desires not so much to be *scientific* as *ministerial*, making, I hope to show, *foolishness* a significant vision for practical theology. Christopraxis at its heart, as we will see, is about and for ministry, for it attends to divine encounter with the human through God's becoming, but this event of God's becoming is made concrete and lived (essentials for practical theology) in the foolishness of God's act to perish and humanity's experience of perishing itself.

With this said we turn now to the description of Christopraxis, showing, as we go, its DNA in the foolishness of the *theologia crucis*.

CHRISTOPRAXIS

Christopraxis, while not a household term in practical theology, is not absent from it either. Jürgen Moltmann uses the term in his book *The Way of Jesus*

---

1. As a reminder, these letters refer to practical theology's attention to the following: practical theology is (a) a discipline done by scholars, yet it is also (b) an *activity of faith* done by believers. But she doesn't stop here, explaining that practical theology can also be defined as (c) a *method* used for studying theology in practice and finally (d) as a *curricular area* of subdisciplines (like pastoral care, homiletics, liturgy, and youth ministry) located in seminaries and universities. See figure 1.

Christ. Richard Osmer, drawing from Moltmann, also uses Christopraxis in his important *The Teaching Ministry of Congregations*, pushing the conception into the purview of practical theology. But even before Osmer's use of Christopraxis, it had made its appearance in practical theology, though it appeared far from the university divinity schools and mainline seminaries that are the center of the practical theological establishment. Outside these Jerusalems, in the far country of the Galilee, evangelical Ray S. Anderson used the conception as a central theme in his 2001 book *The Shape of Practical Theology*.[2]

Anderson, like Moltmann, defined Christopraxis as the *continuing* ministry of Jesus Christ in the world. Yet, unlike Moltmann, Anderson mobilizes the term not for dogmatic purposes but for ministerial ones. While Moltmann uses Christopraxis as an essential component of Christology, Anderson is more interested in how this perspective effects pastoral action in the church and world. Christopraxis becomes for him a frame for a theological praxis that is embedded in Christology but is ultimately about concrete and lived experience.[3] Anderson states, "Christopraxis means the real presence of Christ as the one who has been raised from the dead and the one who is coming again, but also as the *eschatos* who is even now present in the world."[4]

This then makes Christopraxis (the praxis of Christ in the world) the criterion for practical theology itself.[5] Christopraxis is not simply a doctrinal

---

2. Anderson actually brings Christopraxis into his work before the appearance of this text, though it is the most directly laid out in this text. For his earlier articulation of Christopraxis see "Christopraxis: The Ministry and the Humanity of Christ for the World," in *Christ in Our Place: The Humanity of God in Christ for the Reconciliation of the World; Essays Presented to Professor James Torrance*, edited by Trevor Hart and Daniel Thimell (Exeter, UK: Paternoster Press, 1989) and reprinted in *Ministry on the Fireline* (Pasadena, CA: Fuller Seminary Press, 1993).

3. Here Anderson articulates the Trinitarian shape of Christopraxis. Later in this chapter I'll discuss why we should continue to call it Christopraxis and not Trinitarian-praxis. "The vicarious life and humanity of Christ continues to exist in this world as concealed in the history and life of the church, which is his body. . . . Both the doctrines of the church and its own praxis of ministry are thus bound to the reality of Christopraxis. Christopraxis is the act of God in Jesus Christ which occurred once and for all through his life as Incarnate Word, but which continues to occur through the mighty acts of revelation and reconciliation whereby the Holy Spirit glorifies Christ by coming into our sphere of historical and personal existence to manifest his resurrection power and presence (John 16:13, 14; Rom. 8:9-11). Thus, revelation as well as reconciliation, true knowledge of God as well as true life with God, true worship as well as authentic ministry, are derived from out of the same structure of reality which I call Christopraxis." "Christopraxis," 19.

4. Ibid., 28.

5. "Practical theology is thus grounded in Christporaxis as the inner core of its encounter with the Spirit's ministry in the world." Ray S. Anderson, *The Shape of Practical Theology* (Downers Grove, IL: InterVarsity, 2001), 52. Anderson continues, "Christopraxis, I have argued, is the normative and

Christological point, but an experiential one. For instance, both Shirley and Lynn felt Jesus come to them, ministering to them, providing comfort in their moments of need. Anderson is not *primarily* interested in how people think about Jesus (Christology) but rather how they experience the presence of Jesus.[6] There is a deep evangelical commitment in Anderson and his Christopraxis perspective that I am following. It rests on a commitment that lived and concrete communities have personal, though not individualistic (Anderson is opposed to this), experiences of the presence of the living Jesus, as we saw in chapter 3.[7] People experience a real sense of God's action, of the praxis of Christ, and this experience is not simply intellectual or religious, but also personal and spiritual.

Christology itself is transformed for Anderson into Christopraxis. Jesus's own ministry (Christopraxis) precedes theology (Christology). Christopraxis no doubt is dependent, for its depth of reflection, on thoughts about Christ (Christology), but these very conceptions themselves must bow to the very praxis of Jesus. All forms of theology for Anderson must contend (and even be reshaped) by the (practical) ministerial action of this living Jesus that comes to people like Shirley and Lynn.[8] The ministry of Jesus is not a past happening

authoritative grounding of all theological reflection in the divine act of God consummated in Jesus Christ and continued through the power and presence of the Holy Spirit in the body of Christ. Practical theology is an ongoing pursuit of competence through critical theological reflection. This competence does not arise merely through repetition and practice of methods but is gained through participation in the work of God in such a way that accountability for the judgments made in ministry situations are congruent with Christ's own purpose as he stands within the situation and acts through and with us." Ibid., 53.

6. Here he is like Fulkerson. Anderson says directly, "This is Christopraxis. Not a doctrine for which life is sacrificed, but the very being and life of God given for the sake of preserving and upholding human life. Not an ideology or strategy which fights inhumanity for the sake of becoming human, but the very humanity of God which seeks the transformation of all that is inhuman in humanity." "Christopraxis," 18. This quote also points to the core social paradigm that will be discussed at the end of the chapter.

7. Anderson's critique of oversubjectivism can be seen no more clearly than in the following quote: "Christopraxis as a form of the ministry of the church expects the eschatological presence of Christ to be released as a 'charismatic' experience. This has the danger of succumbing to the temptation of pietism, individualism, and corporate inwardness as a variety of Christian experience. To the extent that this happens, it is no longer 'dangerous' as a manifestation of the Kingdom of God in the form of Christ's real presence. The authentic charism which empowers is the charismatic power which redeems humanity from the social, political, and institutional powers which dehumanize." Ibid., 29.

8. "If there be an orthodox theology, let it be accountable to this Christopraxis as the primary dogma, seeking faithfully to interpret it on the basis of the humanity and ministry of Christ. If there be an authentic orthopraxy, let it dare to submit its concerns and its agenda for the healing and hope of humanity to the One who is the Advocate, The Leitourgos, and the Redeemer of all humanity. If there

for Anderson but is *the ongoing possibility of God's encounter*. Anderson explains, "Theological praxis means that truths of God are discovered through the encounter with Christ in the world by means of ministry. This is what I call Christopraxis."[9]

So for Anderson, Jesus lives, and lives as a dynamic event (as Christopraxis), not solely in memory or biblical text but as personal Spirit that can be experienced.[10] Attention to Jesus Christ is not (primarily) to find a tradition that gives us practices, ethical exemplars, or even doctrines, but rather primarily an experiential presence; it is an encounter like those described in chapter 3.[11] And this experientially encountered presence is personal, is a person, and therefore is experienced in *action*, in praxis.[12] "Jesus still does stuff," Anderson says in a folksy way to make his complicated point matter-of-fact.

Because this experiential center is bound in personal action (praxis), these experiences are not simply Christomystical for Anderson (this is where is he is critiquing his Evangelical tradition), but grounded in Christopraxis. The experience of the living Jesus in communities of persons is for ministry itself; the Christ who encounters us is Christ at work, ministering to our person by sharing in our lived experience. This experience is praxis, not only because it is action (not pure mysticism) but because it is action with a telos, for the sake of ministry (relationally sharing in the life of other). All the people whose experiences were recounted in chapter 3 discussed divine action within the context of ministry. They either experienced God in doing ministry themselves

be an authentic church, let it be found where Christ has his praxis—let it pay the price of its orthodoxy in its true ministry and so be empowered by Christ himself." Ibid., 31.

9. Ray S. Anderson, *The Soul of Ministry: Forming Leaders for God's People* (Louisville, KY: Westminster John Knox, 1997), 29.

10. With Christopraxis Anderson is connecting the work of Christ with the work of the Spirit. Christopraxis is embedded in the continued ministry of Jesus, but this continued ministry is made known to us (to be experienced) by the work of the Spirit. "Christopraxis is the continuing ministry of Christ through the power and presence of the Holy Spirit." Anderson, *Shape of Practical Theology*, 21.

11. Anderson explains how experience works in his perspective: "Experience itself is not the criterion for what is the truth of the Word of God. But the truth of the Word of God must be discerned in terms of its effect when applied to humans in their life situation. When the effect of a truth extracted from the Word of God contradicts the effect of the Word, then it becomes absurd, and to follow it consistently is folly. This was as true of the people in the Old Testament who turned the law of God into a law that dehumanized as of those in the New Testament who resisted the ministry of Jesus." *Soul of Ministry*, 15.

12. This is why, as we'll see, Anderson has a significant place for the Holy Spirit in his perspective but even so continues to use Christopraxis; because of the priority of "personhood" in this perspective, Spirit and personhood are linked in an important way. "Christopraxis grounds the criteria for competence in the very being of the truth as the personal being of God revealed through the historical and contemporary person and presence of Jesus Christ." *Shape of Practical Theology*, 58.

(listening to a friend, feeding the hungry) or felt God come to them as a source of ministerial action, hearing their cries and giving comfort, as in the case of Shirley, who said that as an ill nine-year-old she cried out to Jesus and "felt not so much rescued as cared for." Or like Ron, who heard God speak to him, telling him his deceased wife "is home," ministering to him, embracing his person and loving him through his wounds, so that like the man in Mark 2 Ron might take his mat and walk back into his life.

Our response to this Christopraxis is not to harvest spiritual experiences like a religious consumer, but rather to be led by the Spirit to participate in Jesus' own praxis, to act in ministry ourselves. For Anderson, then, practical theology may be (and even is) ethical, political, liberative, and even doctrinal, but *only* as an outgrowth of being first and foremost *ministerial*, of participating in the praxis of Jesus in and through human experiences of encounter, like those of Matt and Sarah, who experience God in and through the act of ministry itself. To participate in Christopraxis is to take on the form of and join Jesus' own action, which is to join the praxis of ministry itself.

Ministry before Theology: Why Theology Is Practical

For Anderson, this continuing action of Christ (Christ's praxis) becomes the criterion of theology. Because the criterion is the living, moving Jesus in ministry, theology and ministry are fused. This fusion, however, gives priority to ministry.

Anderson, *even more so* than Browning, contends that all theology is practical. I say "even more so" because, unlike Browning, Anderson justifies this statement in Godself; the reality of God's own being rather than the shape of human epistemology as a fundamental practical wisdom of interpretation makes theology practical. Theology is practical because God's being is given in God's act—God's act is the revealing of Godself for the sake of ministry.[13] So we can know God (epistemology) only through the priority of encountering God's being (ontology) as it is revealed in the act of God's coming ministry to humanity.[14] Anderson says, "What makes theology practical is not the fitting of orthopedic devices to theoretical concepts in order to make them walk.

---

13. Bonhoeffer explains this actualism that we're working on: "God remains always the Lord, always subject, so that whoever claims to have God as an object no longer has God; God is always the God who 'comes' and never the God who 'is there' (Barth)." *Act and Being* (Minneapolis: Fortress Press, 1961), 85.

14. This is why in a following chapter I'll make a turn to critical realism, following this perspective in asserting that the ontological has priority over epistemology. Douglas John Hall says something similar: "We affirm that, in the relation between reason and revelation in Christian epistemology, revelation has noetic priority." *Thinking the Faith* (Minneapolis: Fortress Press, 1991), 420.

Rather, theology occurs as a divine partner joins us on our walk, stimulating our reflection and inspiring us to recognize the living Word, as happened to the two walking on the road to Emmaus on the first Easter (Lk24)."[15]

And what has to be emphasized is that this ministerial action is not God's simple transcendent function (God's hobby), it is not naively asking what God is up to as if it were an obvious catchphrase or trivial knowledge—Christopraxis is much deeper than this. Rather, *ministry as the act of God is the event of God's being* coming to humanity; this being is always becoming because this being is always moving and active. It is, then, the *event* of God's moving that makes ministry an ontological encounter of the divine with the human; it is the infusing of time with eternity, the making of the event in history the place of the transcendent God's becoming.[16] *God's being as becoming is God's very ministry, God's giving Godself to humanity so humanity might be with God.* Jüngel's point echoes Christopraxis when he says, "God's being is moved being."[17] God moves toward humanity in the shape of ministry, as the invitation to take action to share in another's being.

God does stuff in Christopraxis; however, it is not really stuff (functions) but rather the unveiling of God's self (becoming)—it is the event of ontological encounter.[18] It is ontological, shattering trivial knowledge, because God gives

---

15. Anderson, *Shape of Practical Theology*, 12.

16. Jüngel explains this focus on event: "God's taking form is thus not an accidental characteristic of God 'but . . . an event' and, indeed, an event which presupposes a self-distinction in God, 'something new in God, a self-distinction of God from Himself, a being of God in a mode of being . . . in which He can also exist for us.'" *God's Being Is in Becoming: The Trinitarian Being of God in the Theology of Karl Barth* (Grand Rapids, MI: Eerdmans, 2001), 30.

17. Ibid., 14–15.

18. We are following Jüngel in our attention to ontological language. We are not discussing God as if God could be captured in a general ontology, but instead we are connecting all ontology to the very act of God that reveals God's being (and therefore, following Bonhoeffer's *Act and Being*, places us ontologically into the truth of reality). Jüngel justifies this ontological language in relation to Barth's project. "Barth directs strong protest to the 'threatened absorption of the doctrine of God into a doctrine of being,' from which he certainly does not exempt Protestant orthodoxy. Yet he does not shy away from making ontological statements. All statements about the knowledge of God and thus about God's being-as-object possess a thoroughly ontological character." *God's Being Is in Becoming*, 76. He says earlier in this text, "'Becoming' thus indicates the manner in which God's being exists, and in this respect can be understood as the ontological place of the being of God." Ibid., xxv. Jüngel continues, "To prevent any misunderstanding, let me say at once: the ontological place of God's being is the place which God chooses. However, when God is understood as the one who chooses, his being is already thought of as a being in becoming. This hermeneutical circle is grounded in an ontological circle which will be located by the designation 'God's being is in becoming.' The ontological location of God's being in becoming is an attempt to think theologically in what way God is the living one. Unless it has the

God's very self in ministry for humanity and gives it to us at the level of our own ontological personhood, becoming the ministering Christ who reveals God (revelation) to humanity and bends this humanity back into union with Godself (reconciliation).[19] God's ministry is the revelation of God's being in God's coming to humanity, making, as Jüngel says, "God's being essentially relational; God's being is 'pure relation.'"[20]

All knowledge of God (theology), then, is gleaned from encountering the event of God's ministry (this is why Christopraxis has priority over Christology).[21] Then, following Jüngel, we can say that God's being is in God's becoming. This pulls us deeper into practical theology by allowing us to add that God's becoming is for the sake of ministering Godself to humanity, that God's being as becoming is the event of ministry itself. Then God is ontologically a minister, God is ontologically (as Bonhoeffer says) *pro me*, giving Godself to humanity for humanity.[22] All the people's experience of God in chapter three came in and through the act of ministry. They were either being ministered to by God's presence or experienced God's presence in doing acts of ministry themselves.

Theology, then, can *only* be practical, because its very epistemological object is the pure subject of God's ontological state of ministering to creation.[23] Theology is practical because its subject is the practical action of Godself (Christopraxis). And this action is practical because it ministers to concrete persons.

Anderson sees this perspective deeply embedded in the biblical narrative, finding the footings of Christopraxis in the Hebrew Bible itself, where ministry precedes theology. For instance, Moses is given new knowledge of God (God's

courage to think God's livingness, theology will end up as a mausoleum of God's livingness." Ibid., xxvi.

19. In "A Theology for Ministry," in *Theological Foundations for Ministry* (Edinburgh: T&T Clark, 1979), Anderson articulates revelation and reconciliation as the singular, two-pronged ministry of God.

20. Jüngel, *God's Being Is in Becoming*, 116.

21. "One fundamental thesis will control this discussion—the thesis that ministry precedes and produces theology, not the reverse. It must immediately be added, however, that ministry is determined and set forth by God's own ministry of revelation and reconciliation in the world, beginning with Israel and culminating in Jesus Christ and the Church." Anderson, "Theology for Ministry," 7.

22. See Dietrich Bonhoeffer, *Christ the Center* (San Francisco: HarperCollins, 1978). Jüngel says something very similar to Bonhoeffer: "God wills certainly to be God and He does not will that we should be God. But He does not will to be God for Himself nor as God to be alone with Himself. He wills as God to be for us and with us, who are not God." *God's Being Is in Becoming*, 81.

23. "Thus: God is subject, predicate and object of the event of revelation. The question of what God is may, according to the biblical witness, be answered only when immediately and from the beginning we answer 'the two other questions: What is He doing? And: What does He effect?'" Ibid., 28.

name as Yahweh) because Moses encounters the action of God to minister to God's people in Egypt (Exodus 20). Moses himself is called into ministry, for this is the only response to encountering the divine being (the bush that burns but is not consumed). Encountering, experiencing the divine being as practical (as becoming), we join the divine being by taking on its form (by entering into ministerial practice ourselves). This is similar to Stanik's story. He felt with every cell of his body that God heard his prayer for a fresh start, experiencing the presence of this bush that burns but is not consumed at 2:35 a.m. He is next called to do the foolish act of ministry, to trade his high-powered chef's position for the apron of a camp cook.

We take the divine being's form not in the way of ontological essence (this is not possible) but through action, by ourselves becoming ministers, joining God's being (ontology) not through shared essence but through concrete shared action of ministering (Matthew 25 seems to point in this very direction, as does Stanik's experience).[24] Practical theology as Christopraxis is a form of human *ministerial* action that, by reflecting and acting in ministry, attends to the very being of God through God's own ministerial action. God calls out to Moses from the burning bush, revealing God's very being by becoming to Moses—God's very name given to Moses can be understood as "I am who I am becoming."

This very participation through action allows God ontologically to remain freely God (eternal), not taken into human systems in time. While allowing God to remain distinct (holding to the qualitative distinction between time and eternity), it nevertheless allows for humanity to be ontologically "in" God. This "in-ness" that holds to the qualitative distinction between time and eternity is made possible by action; God gives Godself to us by acting for us, which is the action of ministry. This means our very sharing "in" God happens not at the level of essence but of action. When we join in God's ministry (*going* to Egypt), we join God not just functionally, but ontologically.[25] This is so because in ministry we encounter God's being as the becoming action of ministry, and our being participates in God's through the action of ministry itself. This means for Anderson that the human minister always has vocational priority over the

---

24. This notion of taking the divine form by becoming ministers is a reinterpretation of Athanasius and *theosis*. I agree with Athanasius that we take on the divine form, but not in a sense of essence. Instead, remaining fully human, we take on the divine form through participation in ministry.

25. Paul Nimmo points to this conception in Barth's thought, "Barth contends that, where the Christian serves God, there is a 'fellowship of action . . . between Christ and Christians.'" *Being in Action: The Theological Shape of Barth's Ethical Vision* (Edinburgh: T&T Clark, 2007), 154.

theologian, for the human minister participates in the event of God's becoming, and the theologian tries to describe it.[26]

Ministry itself is conditioned by God's own action; ministry has its source in God's very self. This means, for Anderson, that because ministry is the unveiling of God's being in coming (going) to humanity, that ministry is fundamentally missional (ministry and mission as God's act are synonymous for Anderson).[27] So the human agent joins God's ministry and thus God's being by going with God (going to Egypt), much as Greg was sent to his friend with a word of comfort after his friend lost his father.

In a Christopraxis practical theology, ministry is *not solely* attention to church practices but also attention to these very "in-church" practices through a missional impulse that searches for God's ministry as it comes to humanity in the world.[28] Because God's being is becoming in ministry, God's very ontological state is missional. Thus the ministerial form that the human agent takes, the form that shares in the divine being, is not ministerial in a clerical,

---

26. In Anderson's own words, "The incarnational community is not merely the 'practical theology' department of the church, where truths learned in seminary are put into practice. Rather the praxis of ministry is itself the context in which both the authority and true order of theology is grounded. The theological task is that of interpreting the praxis of Christ, both in its revealed sense as the 'dogma' of the gospel of Christ and in its contemporary form as divine latreia, or reconciliation, as the ministry of the church. It is noteworthy that the primary theological documents of the New Testament were produced by the apostle Paul from the itinerant centers of his own praxis of ministry. Theologians who are first of all recognized as academic scholars and technicians may not be the theologians that the church needs in carrying out its own theological task of the latreia of Christ." *Shape of Practical Theology*, 128.

27. I hesitate to use the word *missional* because it has become so trendy of late, and using trendy words often puts someone in a camp. My conception is that most in the missional church conversations have not pushed their perspective into the act and being of God enough. This is what I mean in saying that the question "What is God doing?" is so trivial. There are major exceptions to this, like Darrell Guder, John Fleet, and Ben Connor; all three and others drive the missional church conversation deeply into discussion of the very being of God as active in mission. Anderson explains how ministry and mission as God's act are synonymous: "As a discipline practical theology has both a mission and ecclesial focus, set forth in that order. Mission precedes and creates the church. Mission is the praxis of God through the power and presence of the Spirit of Christ. As a result of this mission, the church comes into being as the sign of the kingdom of God in the world." Ibid., 31. Anderson continues, "This missological dimension is crucial for practical theology. It is the ongoing mission of God in the world and to the world that provides the aims and the goals, tests the methods, and adds the necessary energy and vision that guide the task of practical theology." Ibid., 31.

28. "The focus of practical theology is not simply the internal working of the church community (although it includes them) but the praxis of the church as it interacts with the praxis of the world. As such, there is a necessary critical and prophetic aspect to practical theology's reflective activity, the boundaries of which are defined by the boundaries of God's continuing mission." Ibid., 32.

bureaucratic, or even a religious sense, but rather in a *missional* sense. God's being is becoming in acts of ministry that are mission.

Thus, encountering God's being (God's name) in God's becoming (through the ministerial act of exodus), Moses is not called to write a systematic theology of God's name but to *go* to Egypt and join God's ministry (tell the Pharaoh, "Let my people go, for Yahweh is going to act, to minister to His people's groaning, becoming their God through my action"). Moses will only *logically* be a theologian *after* having been in ministry, having participated in the being of God by sharing in God's own action of ministry.

All knowledge we have of God, Anderson contends, is born from the practical encounter of God's (ministerial) action. "The 'practice' of ministry, then, is not only the appropriate context for doing theological thinking, it is itself intrinsically a theological activity."[29] Theology is only second-order (sideline) reflection on the event of God's action, and it is second order for soteriological rather than pragmatic reasons. Theology cannot save, but joining in God's being by sharing in God's action of ministry is salvation (is redemption from Egypt).[30] And it is a salvation, a soteriology, that is never devoid of praxis (of love for neighbor).

Covenant, creation, exodus—these are all ministerial events of God's action (of God's becoming) that are experienced by human persons, and when experienced they become the formative material of theology itself. So, for Anderson, ministry (practical theology) is not the handmaid of theology but rather, boldly, the other way around—theology is condition and therefore serves ministerial action, first as the event of God's becoming and then as human actions are swept up into it, fusing soteriology and vocation.[31]

Then, for Anderson, the praxis-to-theory-to-praxis loop is ironclad, but its very strength, paradoxically, is in the mystery of eternal moving into time itself. The praxis of participating in God's ministry, of Moses going to Egypt and proclaiming God's coming exodus, is the only road to theological construction (the Law and Torah) because the ontological act of God precedes all

---

29. Anderson, "Theology for Ministry," 7.

30. "The taking up of humanity into the event of God's being is, rather, humanity's salvation. And 'salvation is more than being. Salvation is fulfillment, the supreme, sufficient, definitive and indestructible fulfillment of being. Salvation is the perfect being which is not proper to created being as such but is still future. . . . To that extent salvation is its eschaton . . . being which has a part in the being of God . . . not a divinized being but a being which is hidden in God, and in that sense (distinct from God and secondary) eternal being.'" Jüngel, *God's Being Is in Becoming*, 75.

31. "Theology, thus, serves as the handmaid of ministry, proclaiming it as God's ministry and making known the eternal being of God." Anderson, "Theology for Ministry," 7.

epistemological assertions about God (this parallels the critical realism discussed in depth in part 3). Practical theology can never be the application of systematic theology. Rather, practical theology is the pioneer theology, ministry on the fireline, as Anderson would say, because practical theology attends most directly to contemporary ministry, to the becoming of God, to the action of Christopraxis. Practical theology therefore attends to experiences like Matt's experience with Jesus' presence in the eyes of the homeless men he ministers to. The action of ministry draws him into encounter with the reality of God (with divine action, connecting time and eternity).

Hermeneutical Christopraxis

To claim that practical theology is Christopraxis and that this theology is the lead theology because it attends contemporaneously to the event of God's being as God's becoming in the action of ministry means interpretation (hermeneutics) is central, but this interpretation is not primarily of human practice but of Jesus Christ.[32] Practical theology is the need to interpret the "where" of Jesus Christ in our experiences of the now.

Ministry, from the human side, is joining in God's contemporaneous becoming, in God's own ministry; it is doing God's work with God (going to Egypt), but doing so for the sake of being ontologically joined to God (being God's people). This makes the text of practical theological reflection the present ministry of God as it is discerned and participated in by human forms of ministry done in concrete and lived experiences like those described in chapter 3. So just as the New Testament scholar exegetes the Greek text, so the practical theologian's primary hermeneutical objective is to discern the movements of God's ministry (as mission), confessing God's ministry is God's being as becoming.[33]

---

32. Anderson sees practical theology as hermeneutical all the way through. He says, "Practical theology is essentially a hermeneutical theology. That is to say, theological reflection that begins in the context and crisis of ministry seeks to read the texts of Scripture in light of the texts of lives that manifest the work of Christ through the Holy Spirit as the truth and will of God." *Shape of Practical Theology*, 37.

33. This does not eliminate or minimize the place of the biblical text for practical theology and most directly for interpretation of Christopraxis. Rather, Anderson, as an evangelical, works hard to articulate how the biblical text functions in the hermeneutics of Christopraxis. For Anderson the Bible as written Word is made Word by the Christopraxis itself. The Bible as witness points to the living, ministering Christ. Therefore, the Bible is *used* to discern divine action, pulling the Bible into the contemporaneous. Anderson does some interesting things here, exploring how divine action always (it seems to him) has a biblical antecedent. Unfortunately, there is not the space to expand this interesting perspective here or add it to the text proper. Therefore, I leave the curious reader with Anderson's own words: "This leads into an answer for the second question. I have attempted to demonstrate from Scripture itself that the

This may mean empirical methods are needed to examine living human documents as locales of ministry, but even this is not the raison d'être of practical theology. *Practical theology is not concrete and lived because it is empirical, but because it seeks to discern (hermeneutically) the concrete and lived reality of God's becoming in ministry.*[34] Thus, description of concrete communities is not the lifeblood of practical theology (it may be one of its organs), but rather the description of *God's becoming* in these concrete communities is its very heart.

To discern God's ministry is to be led into it; it is to ontologically encounter its shape. For this hermeneutical process to be able to attend to God's becoming, it must be bound in ontology more than epistemology. We do not discern God's action through sheer knowledge but through an ontological experience of the Spirit (that conditions knowledge); God's being as becoming in the world encounters our own being-in-the-world, transforming it through the event of encounter itself (this is what makes practical theology *practical*). And this event of transformational encounter that is God's ministry is contemporaneously the work of the Spirit to align us with the ministry of Jesus, moving us into concrete forms of ministry ourselves as the circuits of ontological union with God *through Jesus Christ.*[35]

So the hermeneutical shape of practical theology is Jesus Christ, revealed to us in our concrete, lived experience by the Spirit (a number of the people in chapter 3 talked about "Jesus coming to them"). And this is so because Jesus is the ministry of God the Father, the one who *fully* participates in the ministry of God. Jesus participates in this so fully, with no division or separation, that Jesus becomes the ministry of God. Jesus so fully indwells God's being through God's becoming of ministry that Jesus becomes ontologically *the ministry*, becomes *the* revelation and *the* reconciliation. "To see him is to see the Father" (John 14:9)

Word of God is not a textbook of doctrinal truths that can be stated in so-called objective propositions. Rather, Scripture is a revelation of God's nature and purpose through its faithful proclamation and teaching. While the biblical text must be taken as an authoritative Word of God, discerning its meaning is related to its application in a contemporary context with the Holy Spirit as a guide." *Soul of Ministry*, 16. Anderson says further, pointing to the biblical antecedent, "At the same time, there was another movement in the first century that followed the leading of the Holy Spirit and looked back into historical revelation for antecedents rather than precedence. Such a movement as made by the apostle Paul." *Shape of Practical Theology*, 110.

34. This does not eliminate empirical studies in practical theology but conditions them theologically. For an example of this, see the splendid work of John Swinton.

35. Anderson says it this way: "Theology must be as contextual as it is metaphysical, and it must be as visual as it is cerebral. Another way of putting it is to say that theological reflection must be done in the context of the Spirit's ministry in the world. Theological reflection must also be a 'way of seeing' as well as a way of thinking." *Shape of Practical Theology*, 103.

for Jesus "does only what the Father tells him" (John 5:19); Jesus is revelation and reconciliation in action. Through the *doing* of ministry Jesus is shown to be the one sent by God, "Tell John, the dead rise!" (Luke 7:22).

Christopraxis then is Trinitarian, for it is constituted in God's own being as becoming in the action of ministry.[36] And this ministry finds it fullness and completion in Jesus Christ, allowing the ontological reality of God's becoming to rest in humanity itself, making the way for our humanity to find ontological union with God. But this union can only be substantiated in the form of God's being itself by being drawn into ministerial action. So Jesus ascends to heaven (Acts 1), giving another, the Spirit, to make our ontological union complete by sending us into practical theology as an activity of faith done by believers, leading us into ministry, which is participating in Christ's continued ministry through the hermeneutical criterion of the Spirit's "making known" in the now through an ontological experience.[37]

But why then call this Christopraxis and not Trinitarian-praxis, or something else? It is Christopraxis because Jesus is the *hermeneutic of God's ministry, and as the hermeneutic of God's ministry Jesus is the hermeneutic of God's very being.* Jesus alone is the hermeneutic of God, and through the cross and resurrection remains so for eternity. Possessing the divine and human natures (the hypostatic union), Jesus Christ's own person binds eternity and time; this is why Jesus is the unique, singular hermeneutic of God. And this hermeneutic *of* the Father, that *is* the Son, is given to us to experience concretely through the Spirit that descends at Jesus' baptism (Luke 3:22), empowering Jesus to be the ministry of God, and then ascends on us on Pentecost (Acts 2:1-4) so that we too might be in the continued *ministry* of Christ and, as such, be bound in the being of God.

It then is *not* the Spirit's job to take over Jesus' own ministry, falling into a modalistic trap. This is not possible, for Jesus is the resurrected and alive one;

---

36. Anderson explains how Christopraxis is itself Trinitarian, giving significant place for the Spirit. "The practical theologian is the theologian of the Holy Spirit, who points to and participates in the creative indivisibility of the God who holds all things together. The Holy Spirit is the revelation to us of the inner being of God as constituted by the relations between Father and Son. For this reason, practical theology is grounded in the intra Trinitarian ministry of the Father toward the world, the Son's ministry to the Father on behalf of the world and the Spirit's empowering of the disciples for ministry." Ibid., 40.

37. Here Anderson connects his pneumatological focus with Christopraxis itself. "The Spirit of God does not come to us 'unclothed,' as it were, but comes clothed with the very humanity of Christ. Every feeling and every sensation that Jesus experienced as a complete human person became an expression of the divine being, revealing the truth of God through the humanity of God. Every feeling, need, and aspiration of the human spirit has its correspondence in the humanity of Jesus, which bears all human experience directly into the divine heart." *Soul of Ministry*, 74.

Jesus' ministry is not over but continues eternally. Jesus' resurrection stands as certification of Jesus' ontological fusion with God's ministry as God's being. As God remains eternally the being that is becoming, so Jesus is eternally *the ministry of God as the one in ministry*.[38] The Spirit's work is not to take over Jesus' own but to distribute it, to reveal its location (ascending at Jesus' baptism), and through concrete experience to call people into joining it (descending on Pentecost).

Pentecost, itself, Anderson asserts, is the Spirit working to give ontological union between humanity and God, opening eyes to see the continued ministry of Jesus Christ. The Spirit, Paul says, gives us the ministry of Christ (2 Cor. 3:6). The Spirit clears the way to discern Jesus' ministry. Before the Spirit comes, Peter and the others are confused, hidden behind locked doors (Acts 2). But when the Spirit descends, binding the being of those gathered to God's own, hiding them in Christ (Col. 3:3) so that they no longer live but Christ lives in them (Gal. 2:20)—inescapable ontological language—they respond by leaving their fearful hiding place and entering into *ministry* by preaching (pointing/ witnessing) to God's becoming in Jesus Christ—that is, by joining Christopraxis (Acts 2:14).

The Spirit's work rests in the same paradigm of Christopraxis. The Spirit unveils God's ministry as God's being in Jesus Christ (revelation) to and through human experience (encounter), calling the human agent into ontological union with God, through Christ, connecting the human spirit with God's own Spirit (reconciliation). Yet, this connection comes not through a magical transcendental state but by a calling of the human agent into ministry (as mission)—to swing open the doors and preach (Acts 2), to feed the widows (Acts 6) and orphans, to go to a friend with a word of comfort, to feed the homeless, to listen and not talk, to leave the kitchens of the powerful and cook comfort food for campers. Union with God comes to us through the act of ministry itself that takes us into divine encounter.

Practical theology (as a discipline of scholars) has its own concrete operation in studying those in the practice of ministry—not solely with the rational or scientific formal logic (as we will discuss below) but with the desire to witness and articulate how concrete actions of ministry are movements of the Spirit into God's becoming through Jesus Christ.

---

38. "We must remember that the living Christ is Lord of Scripture as well as Lord of the church. The resurrected Jesus is not a criterion of new revelation that replaces Scripture; rather he is the hermeneutical criterion for interpreting Scripture in such a way that his present work of creating a new humanity fulfills the promise of Scripture." Anderson, *Shape of Practical Theology*, 101.

Just minutes ago the disciples are blind and timid, but with the Spirit's coming they are given eyes to see, they are given a new hermeneutic that connects their spirit to God's through participation in Jesus' own ministry.[39] Through the ontological experience of the Spirit's indwelling, they are given knowledge.[40] Now, bound *in Christ*, all the odd happenings of Jesus' life, death, and resurrection, while minutes earlier strange and confusing, now take on a logic in which they themselves, through this ontological union, are called to participate. All their own concrete experiences now must be examined through this lens of the logic of the Spirit to reveal the ministry of Christ.[41] Through this new hermeneutic, Christopraxis is interpreted in the present moment, and through the empowering of the Spirit, Christopraxis is joined as ministerial action.

And it is necessary that the Spirit is operator of this hermeneutical process, interpreting human experiences and directing human agency into the ministry of Jesus, because this process of discerning God's becoming stands in opposition to what Anderson, following T. F. Torrance, calls "formal logic."[42] The action of God in becoming is never obvious within the structures of time and outside the leading of the Spirit could never be considered as the work of God. This action of God's ministry is fundamentally a "foolishness" (1 Corinthians), a "foolishness" only made wise by the ontological encounter itself with the bush that burns but is not consumed.

Christopraxis is foolishness from the formal logic of human epistemological structures. "They are drunk!" (Acts 2:14–15) is the formal logic of Pentecost that calls it foolish; Moses is an old, stuttering man sent to overthrow a king with the world's greatest military-industrial complex (Exodus 3). Moses has only one weapon, a Word from the God who is "I am who is becoming," and this Word is pure foolishness in the shadow of a mile of chariots. It is foolish for Ron to assume that a tall eighty-year-old woman in a red wig can help him, but she

---

39. "Pentecost can serve as a compass that performs two functions: theologically it orients us to the inner logic of God's incarnational manifestation in the world through Jesus Christ, and experientially it orients us to the eschatological vision of redemption for the world through Christ's presence and coming." Anderson, *Ministry on the Fireline*, 24.

40. This perspective finds significant connection to critical realism by seeing the priority of the ontological over the epistemological.

41. I use this phrase with a different emphasis than in the brilliant work of James Loder.

42. Anderson defines these: "Formal logic [is] defined as a way of thinking in accordance with concepts that are timeless . . . with regard to personal being. Inner logic is discovered as one discerns the relation between the invisible and visible as an objective structure of reality in which one participates." *Soul of Ministry*, 16.

joins his person, ministering to it, rescuing his marriage from crashing violently against the rocks.

This is why we said that practical theology is asking, where is Jesus Christ? And answers to this "where" cannot be discerned in formal logic but only in the foolishness of Jesus' own ministry. And because it is foolish, only the Spirit can awaken us to see this continued ministry of Christ.

But this Spirit that leads us into ministry as participation in God's being is not a Spirit of chaos (Corinthians)—it has a form and shape. Therefore, God's ministry is foolishness on the backdrop of formal logic, but nevertheless, though appearing as such, has its own logic. This foolishness, while appearing to be so to the wise and strong (to those unwilling to be in ministry), is the splendor of what Anderson calls "an inner logic" to those who have experienced God's being in God's ministry of becoming. This inner logic can only be known through the event of encounter—through a bush that burns but is not consumed (Exodus 3). And this inner logic, given to us by the Spirit, is the very form of Jesus Christ, the very form of the divine being as ministry. This inner logic is the *theologia crucis*; it is the logic of moving from death (impossibility) to life. While formal logic rests itself squarely in the empirical fact of nature that all moves from life into death, the inner logic of the cross, the foolishness of the gospel, asserts the opposite: that from death comes life. And this coming out of death is God's own ministry as an ontological identification with the perishing Jesus (Jüngel), who dies but is made alive. This inner logic is the hermeneutical shape of Christopraxis. Jesus is "where" he is in ministry and where he is in ministry is places of death (cross as revelation) bringing forth life (resurrection as reconciliation). Jesus is where a cabbie leaves his car to join in ministry to a heartbroken woman who just lost her husband. Jesus is where a scared child hears God's words of love and runs from a hole to testify (to do the ministry of preaching) that God has acted for him, leaving his nightmares behind.

DEATH-TO-LIFE PARADIGM: THE *THEOLOGIA CRUCIS* IN CHRISTOPRAXIS

This death-to-life, life-out-of-death paradigm is simultaneously an epistemological structure embedded in an ontological reality. It is the logic of God's ministry; it is a lens, even a pattern, that allows events to be discerned as God's own action. But this pattern as epistemological structure rests in an ontological reality; to epistemologically discern God's ministry is to encounter God's ontological being. And no one, *no one*, can experience (see) God's being and still live (Exod. 33:20). There is no road that leads from time into eternity, no honed formal logic in time that can give shape to the movements of the eternal God. Time, and all in it, wilts in sight of the eternal. Therefore, to bring time into eternity God too must enter at the level of the union's rupture, at the level of death. All ten of the people I interviewed, when asked the life-history question of whether they had ever experienced God's presence, spoke of times of death—experiences of the loss of a spouse, illness, a meaningless job, and so on. It was out of these experiences that God came to them.

The divine and human are associated not through practices, culture, or even doctrine, but through death (this is the heart of the *theologia crucis* in my Christopraxis perspective), and it is God's ministry to enter death. In this manner, as I hope to show more fully in the next chapter, time and eternity are neither conflated nor left unattended to.

The difficulty of examining time and eternity has led some systematic theologians to focus solely on the history of doctrine and some practical theologians to focus only on empirical descriptions of religious communities, steering clear of the hard, nearly impossible work of articulating the event of the eternal breaking into time.[43]

Others take another route, turning the eternal into a pet, asking naively what God is doing without recognizing that to ask of God's action at the epistemological level is like Jacob (Genesis 32) wrestling with God at the ontological level; it is to enter into the locale of God's being coming to humanity, and this locale is death itself, most fully happening in the perishing Jesus. No one lives when the epistemological gives way to the ontological; no one leaves this encounter in the same shape he or she entered it. You leave dead, burying the man Jacob to leave as Israel, pulling your leg behind you in the sand as a witness that no one encounters the eternal God without being taken through death to be given new life. And this new life is the reality (if only a taste) of the eternal. This movement through death to life is the very shape of God's ministry.

To participate in God's ministry and therefore know God is to die; if to encounter God's being is to encounter God in the practical, then this

---

43. John Caputo beautifully articulates this place of impossibility as the very event of God's coming. "The name of God is a name of an event, the event of our faith in the transformability of things, in the most improbable and impossible things, so that life is never closed in, the future never closed off, the horizon never finite and confining. The name of God opens what is closed, breathes life where there is desolation, and gives hope where everything is hopeless. The name of God is powerful, not with the power of brute strength, but with the power of an event. It opens up like an abyss, like a word of abyssal power—which means a groundless ground, not a grounding and foundational one—by means of which it shatters every horizon of representation or imagination, of foreseeability or programmability." *The Weakness of God: A Theology of the Event* (Bloomington: Indiana University Press, 2006), 88.

practicality comes forcefully in death itself, for instance, in the fear of a son's mental illness (Margo's story). But this is no masochistic occurrence; this is the good news of the gospel itself, according to Paul. For we die under God's judgment so that we might live by being in God, doing ministry with God (Col. 3:3). Anderson says it this way, "Grace must first kill and then make alive. This is the reformation of human existence into the humanity of Christ. And it is the nature of the incarnational community to bring the world under the same judgment and therefore into the same hope; this is what the church, as the community bound to Christ, affirms."[44]

But this ministry that we do with God is born not in our strength, but in our weakness—this is the heart of its foolishness. Our weakness actually becomes our essential competence in ministry (the thorn in the flesh; 2 Corinthians 12); weakness (death) becomes the epistemological source that leads into an ontological encounter, for this God enters time in and through death.[45] Greg wants to help his friend but feels powerless. As he gardens, he confesses his weakness, and in so doing, through his impossibility, comes the word of God to go and say a word to his friend. Having no words, and through his own weakness, Greg is given the word of ministry to speak (to embody). Weakness as the core component both allows eternity to enter time and keeps those in time from thinking they can possess eternity, yet through weakness those in time can join eternity! Our weakness, our deaths, become the field of ministry, for these places of weakness are where God's being is released in becoming, where the eternal God gives the divine name to one in time. But this becoming by giving God's name only occurs in and through Moses' own weakness, through God identifying with the aged and stuttering Moses, through impossibility, by joining those in the death throes of slavery.[46]

Moses is a fugitive, a murderer, and a stuttering old man. Yet here, in the reality of his weakness, he is called to the bush that burns but is not consumed. His weakness, as an ontological reality, becomes the epistemological criteria for

---

44. Anderson, *Shape of Practical Theology*, 117.

45. John Douglas Hall explains this perspective through Kierkegaard: "Existence, for Kierkegaard, was participation in despair and contradiction; and the only route to God across the 'yawning qualitative abyss' that separates the divine from the human was the one that exists as God's possibility, namely, God's own willing entry into the impossibility and absurdity of our condition." *Lighten Our Darkness: Toward an Indigenous Theology of the Cross* (Lima, OH: Academic Renewal, 2001), 123.

46. "Why did the Lord wait until Moses was eighty years old, a failure and fugitive, with no possibilities? Because the element of human possibility must be removed. The people were powerless and helpless. They cried out to the Lord. Moses was chosen to be the redeemer because he was also without power on the human level. Moses understood that this 'powerlessness' is itself a necessary ingredient in the chemistry of divine grace." Anderson, *Soul of Ministry*, 45.

his election—he is invited into God's ministry (that is, God's being) through the weakness of his own being. Moses is as good as dead out in the desert when God moves, using his very death as criteria for election in ontological union with God by joining God's ministry. God choses the stutterer to herald God's name, for the epistemological knowledge of this God is hidden in the ontological union of God with all that is broken and near death.[47]

So to say that when we encounter God we are made dead is no doubt a word of judgment, but a word of judgment that is in itself grace. It is judgment because it calls us what we are, it calls a thing what it is (in the language of the *theologia crucis*): we are weak, broken, and have no way of saving ourselves. And yet this judgment that is our ontological state is made grace, and grace not simply as a concept, an epistemological trait, but as the reality of God's own being as becoming. Grace is God's being as becoming, for grace is the label given the experience of the human who encounters Godself given to her at the level of her experiences of deaths—at the ontological level. Grace is the cabbie's hand on Rachel's shoulder and the seemingly random article in the newspaper that becomes God's word that it is not her fault. *Grace is the human experience of God's being as becoming in the ministry of bringing life out of death.*

To encounter the divine being, then, is not to be murdered but to be loved and loved at the deepest level, in and through the experience of death.[48] It then is love that reveals weakness, making known the ontological places where we are broken and near death. For God's ministry, which is God's very being, seeks to move in and through those places, drawing us into the eternal not through our own action of strength but its impossibility, through loving us in our brokenness and sending us into the brokenness of the world to participate in God's ministry by participating in the broken being of our neighbor. Jüngel says beautifully, "It is only short-circuited criticism which wants to see here a final triumph of death. Rather, what happens here is that turning around of death into life, which is the very essence of love. . . . Death is not turned around

---

47. Anderson explains, "The grace of God requires bareness, not our own belief, as a precondition. True faith and true obedience come as a gift of God's grace, and the inner logic of that gift requires that where we have inserted a human possibility the grace of God must remove it. This was true for Moses as he experienced his own failure and futility, only to witness God's power and grace through that weakness." Ibid., 47.

48. "Therefore, God's being does not first become love because love is necessary to counter nothingness. Rather, because God is love as he is himself, he counters nothingness and its power. Because God is love, this is then God's being: to be related to nothingness." Eberhard Jüngel, *God as the Mystery of the World* (Grand Rapids, MI; Eerdmans, 1983), 222.

apart from love, because love alone is able to involve itself in the complete harshness of death."[49]

Practical theology as Christopraxis happens in the world. It attends to the church, but the church *only as* a community of ministry; in contrast, it stands against the church as inner-directed stale institution. The church is the body of Christ and as such it must be in motion, in ministry, in the world, in the embrace of our context, by seeking for the ministering Christ (Christopraxis) that is out ahead of it, entering death for the sake of life.[50]

This Christopraxis perspective that rests on the *theologia crucis* begins to point in the direction of the next chapter, hinting toward the justification perspective we will explore through the thought of Jüngel. For now this Christopraxis perspective introduces the ex nihilo, the final component in Anderson's Christopraxis.[51]

An Ex Nihilo

Anderson asserts that there always seems to be an "ex nihilo" at the center of God's ministry, that to discern Christopraxis as a hermeneutical reality is to give attention to the ontological experience of the ex nihilo, to go to the cross.[52] In other words, God's being as becoming in ministry as an ontological reality finds its epistemological ground zero in the action of ministry itself, in embracing our experiences of ex nihilo (for example, human limitation, finitude, and need). We discern God's presence next to human weakness, not human strength.

Anderson shows that in the biblical events of God's being as becoming in ministry, the paradigm is there. "Why is it," he asks, "that Sarah must be ninety years old and barren before God moves?" Because human possibility must be removed. The event of God's becoming always comes out of death,

---

49. Ibid., 364.

50. Jüngel explains, "Understood this way, this discourse directs us toward the task of thinking God himself as the union of death and life for the sake of life, Since the 'union of death and life for the sake of life' is a way of defining the essence of love, we shall have to think God as love together with the christologically understood humanity of God." Ibid., 299. He writes elsewhere, "The fundamental aspect of the victory over death is not the 'standing outside of nothingness' (*extra nihilum sistere*) which flees from nothingness, but rather the creative 'standing into nothingness' (*in nihilum sistere*)." Ibid., 224.

51. As we'll see in the next chapter, Jüngel too makes the *ex nihilo* central to his perspective, showing, I believe, the generative link between these things I'm trying to accentuate for practical theology.

52. Caputo, whom I have quoted elsewhere in the notes for this chapter, stands against the *ex nihilo*, but my two main dialogue partners find it formative. We've seen how Anderson does, and here Jüngel says, "Thus God's being is understood as creative, as the being which creates 'out of nothing' (*ex nihilo*)." Ibid., 218.

for it seeks life, and death as the ontological break of union between God and humanity can only be healed by suffering its separation, by becoming weak in it so it might be healed. Broken union is healed only by inner logic; no force or coherence can renew. Only parties willing to confess, repent, and forgive—becoming weak one to another—can find it; only ministry itself can heal the rupture of relationship.

After the fall, instead of abandoning creation, God enters creation as a foolish minister, seeking to minister it back into union with God's very self. Because God's ministry is God's being as becoming, it is ontological, and this ontological ministry is to give back to humanity the union in time with the eternal that has been broken, taking the union so deep that those in time are bound in eternity itself. But this union will be achieved through God's own foolishness, through God identifying completely with the perishing Jesus, making the cross both the place of God's being, ontologically, and the shape of God's ministry, epistemologically.

This from-death-to-life paradigm is so deeply the epistemological criterion of God's ministry, for Anderson, that not only is Ishmael, the son of a fertile concubine, ruled out as the promise and ruled out because Ishmael wears no mark of impossibility (Genesis 16), but Isaac is chosen, Isaac whose life story begins with the impossible, with the assertion, "I am Isaac, the son of an old barren woman." Ishmael is loved but is not the epistemological criterion of God's ministry, for Ishmael is the product of human possibility. He is formal logic. It is Isaac that stands as the inner logic of God's ministry, for his mother's womb is dead with no possibility of resuscitation. Here his life springs forth as sign of the eternal breaking forth in time, through the portal of death, turning its very ontological reality into new life and new possibility.

And if Abraham (or the reader of the text) should miss the depth of this paradigm, this epistemological criterion that is bound in the ontological reality of impossibility in the birth of Isaac, Abraham, who has believed God's word of promise (Genesis 21) that he will be father of a great nation (Gen. 17:5), is told to take the impossibly born boy to the mountain and put the knife to his throat (Genesis 22).

The old man who saw the impossible, who saw with his own old eyes the boy push himself into the world between the knees of his old barren wife, is told to give him back to death. Abraham goes to the mountain in faith, trusting that if God has done it once, God will do it again, God will take what is dead and bring it to life, so even if the boy's blood soaks the dirt, God will, God can, impossibly, bring him back.

And surely God does, stopping Abraham from bringing the knife's plunge but forever writing the epistemological criterion into his being, that this God who called you out of Ur (Gen. 12:1-20) is the God who brings life out of death, who makes the dead alive. Isaac is the boy of promise, the one who stands on the ground of God's ministry, for this boy has twice moved from death into life.[53] Isaac knows (epistemologically), for it rests in his being (ontology), that when all is lost, when the impossible has dawned, his God's being is revealed as the one becoming who enters death to turn it new. Caputo says something similar to Anderson, "In the kingdom, things happen by the impossible. To be very precise, everything is possible just in virtue of being impossible."[54]

The God of ministry that gives us union with Godself by joining in ministry is a God whose ministry starts in death and breaks it through with life—most fully in the Christopraxis of cross to resurrection, of ascension to Pentecost. Anderson says it this way, "Out of impossibility, God's Word becomes God's ministry. . . . God's ministry takes what is impossible and creates possibility. But it does this in such a way that the creature himself is incorporated into the new possibility."[55]

Practical theology as Christopraxis attends to concrete human experience by seeing it through this very lens of God's ministry, by performatively helping human ministry take this shape of death to life. So many of the stories in chapter 3 bear witness to this pattern. In experiences of death and impossibility they witnessed to the experience of God's coming to them, giving life they do not doubt comes from the hand of God. For they were sick, grieving and stuck, and God ministered new life to them.

THE CROSS

This very epistemological paradigm becomes central for Luther's *theologia crucis*. Jesus Christ bears the paradigm of the ex nihilo; Jesus Christ is validated as son of God because ex nihilo runs through Jesus' life. Born impossibly of a virgin, Jesus impossibly dies on the cross as God's chosen one. The *theologia crucis* is the claim that the cross itself is the epistemological criterion of God's very self,

53. "Abraham's faith was not believing in an absurdity but believing in the power of God to do what is impossible for humans. 'Is anything too wonderful for the Lord?' Abraham and Sarah are told (Gen. 18:14). The faith of Abraham and Sarah in the Word of God was demonstrated as they embraced the barrenness that lay between them. Without that act there would have been no Isaac!" Ibid.

54. Caputo, *Weakness of God*, 102. Caputo, however, would not agree with my interpretation of the Isaac story. Caputo, as matter of fact, has a hard time with Kierkegaard's interpretation of the text (which is similar to my own). See *How to Read Kierkegaard* (New York: W. W. Norton, 2007).

55. Anderson, "Theology for Ministry," 14.

God is no more God for us than when God is on the cross.[56] God can only be recognized in the hiddenness of death on the cross; this is the epistemological criterion of Christopraxis.

And this hiddenness has soteriological ramifications, but these soteriological ramifications are embedded in revelation itself. God is revealed in dead places, and in dead places God not only identifies with us but saves us, by filling these very dead places with God's own being through God's becoming in fully identifying with the perishing Jesus.[57] The cross becomes the place of God's very being because God's being is in becoming, in the action of giving to humanity in ministry.

Then because God's being is given in God's act, God is crucified, Luther asserts, because the perishing Jesus is *the hermeneutic of God*, because this same Jesus who is perishing is *the ministry of God*.[58] God then is not outside of the perishing Jesus but perishes with Jesus, for God is no more God than in being through becoming in the death of Jesus.[59] And this is how death is ripped open, made the very portal of God's being in becoming in ministry; this is how the

56. Hall and Jüngel both articulate this perspective of Luther's. Hall says, "The true God, we are told, is not the omnipotent monarch whose glory the religious attempt to reflect. To the contrary, the true God is the One who is willingly divested of power and who hides under the opposite of what the world recognizes as omnipotence. Luther does not even hesitate to employ the term (shocking to every theology of glory) *Deus crucifixus* (the crucified God), for his doctrine of God, like every other aspect of his theology, is determined by the decision to know only 'Christ crucified.' God therefore is not distinguishable from the One who is revealed on the cross. 'He who has seen me has seen the Father.'"*Lighten Our Darkness*, 112. Jüngel writes, "According to his nature God cannot die, but since God and man are united in one person, it is correct to talk about God's death when that man dies who is one thing or one person with God. So far Luther. From this it is evident that it is wrongly put to say or to write that the cited locutions, 'God suffered,' 'God died,' are merely empty words which 'do not correspond to reality.' The Formula of Concord makes these statements in the context of its discussion of the doctrine of the communication idiomatum (the 'communion' or 'exchange' of the properties), which defines the relationship of the divine and human characteristics of Jesus Christ. The first implication of this doctrine of the 'exchange of the properties' is that "any property, though it belongs only to one of the natures, is ascribed not only to the respective nature as something separate but to the entire person who is simultaneously God and man." *God as the Mystery of the World*, 96.

57. "If it is then true that God has defined his deity in that event which we have understood as God's identification with the dead Jesus, then we must say that God is not only the one who is identical with himself for his sake alone. As the one who suffers endlessly, God is rather the one who exists for others. Being for others he is identical with himself. The localizing of nothingness within divine being is, as an act of God, an act of divine being, an act of divine self-determination. Whoever really is for others and seeks to be himself in that, always subjects himself immediately to nothingness." Jüngel, *God as the Mystery of the World*, 219.

58. Here I am not only following Luther, but also more directly, Jungel's articulation in *God as the Mystery of the World*.

eternal enters time. Through God so identifying with the perishing Jesus, God's being as becoming in this identification takes death into Godself, locating death through the cross in God's own being. So now "we die, in Christ" (Romans 6:8). Given Christ's death we live, for in the death of the perishing Jesus God is inseparably there.[60] As Jüngel explains, death is given a place inside the life of God's very self, taken into God's ministry.

When God perishes with Jesus, death and nothingness itself is filled with God's being, surrounding it in love, turning it to serve God. God's ministry of being as becoming is given its fullness in its complete identification with the perishing Jesus. And the perishing Jesus is the hermeneutical key to discern God's action. It is not Jesus in divine glory that is the epistemological criterion, but the perishing Jesus in the world, the *theologia crucis* asserts.

So while God is no more God than when God is identified with the perishing Jesus, giving God's very being to death, death cannot hold God. God enters time through realities of ex nihilo, through barren wombs (Genesis 20) and the cries of slavery (Exod. 3:9), but when the eternal enters through death (the impossible), death is taken into the eternal and life bursts forth. The *theologia crucis* claims the cross as the epistemological location of the being of God. And while the being of God experiences the fullness of death in the perishing Jesus, this God is eternal, raising the dead Jesus into the eternal. Through death, life springs.[61]

Jesus then is the hermeneutic, is the ministry of God, for in Jesus' body lives the movements of death to life, life out of death. So while the *theologia crucis* gives epistemological attention to death, it looks through it toward life. It is a hopeful hermeneutic that, while bravely placing itself in dead places to

59. This is where Athanasius cannot go, but many theologians of the cross since him, including my main dialogue partner Eberhard Jüngel, have.

60. Anderson pushes this perspective into his view of the atonement, also highlighting his attention to resurrection. Anderson is known for this as a response to a substitutionary perspective, yet the careful reader will see how this attention to resurrection is conditioned by a *theologia crucis* of existential *ex nihilo*. Anderson says, "It is the resurrection of Jesus, not just his death on the cross, that completed the atonement, I went on to suggest. The reason for this is that it is not just sin that needs to be forgiven, but death that needs to be overcome. The consequence of sin is death, as I have argued in a previous chapter. And the great human dilemma is death, not merely sin." *Soul of Ministry*, 98.

61. "Thus the Father, too, participates with the Son in the passion, and the divine unity of God's modes of being proves itself in the suffering of Jesus Christ. God's being is a being in the act of suffering. But even in suffering God's being remains a being in act, a being in becoming. God persists in the historicity of his being. And this persistence of God in the historicity of his being allows this being to remain even in death a being in becoming. In giving himself away God does not give himself up. But he gives himself away because he will not give up humanity." Jüngel, *God's Being Is in Becoming*, 102.

find God's ministry, knows that in these dead places the glory of the eternal dawns, but dawns in the foolishness of sharing death. God's ministry is to enter death, but by entering to give it life through union with God's own being made now in the act of ministry itself. The resurrection, new life, is brought forth by "sharing in" death so that when death is shared in God's being as becoming in the perishing Jesus, it is broken and life seeps into its cracks with the speed of light. Matt, Sarah, Greg, and Rachel can witness to this.

The *theologia crucis* asserts that God's being comes to us to share in our deaths so that death might be broken by resurrection. While the epistemological criterion of God's ministry starts in the cross, it does not end there; death that leads to only more separation and "aloneness" is demonic, but death shared *is* God's ministry, becoming the shape of our own. Our ministry is to foolishly enter death, sharing in death, knowing that when we share it, it is broken as determinative power, giving life.

We join God's ministry by going to Egypt, by walking with a heartbroken woman into the morgue, by entering the impossibility of death, but in so doing we are drawn into God's act of giving God's eternal being through Jesus so those ministered to might live and experience God's presence as coming to them.[62]

Practical theology as Christopraxis seeks to reflect on and move into this practice, into this Christopraxis, helping concrete communities and persons articulate their experience of death, discerning in them, giving language to

---

62. Hall points in the direction of ministry that I'm imagining here from the theology of the cross: "If that is so, then the task of Christian theology in our time and place must be to help people enter into that darkness—that is, into conscious participation in our corporate failure. The task is not to offer a refuge from the darkness, although this has been the principal function of religion among us. . . . But the light to which the Christian gospel bears witness in every age presupposes conscious exposure to the darkness of that age. After all, it is light for the darkness. Whoever refuses to enter the darkness can have no glimpse of this light." *Lighten Our Darkness*, xxiii.

them of God's presence in working life through them.[63] It is my contention that they already have these experiences.

These narratives become formative when people say, "When I went through the death of my husband I was lost; I still hurt so bad, but the willingness of so many at church to stand with me, to be my strength, to care for my children, has meant everything." Practical theology as the ministry of Christopraxis interprets these stories as the ministry of God, for they move from death to life. And practical theology as Christopraxis helps those in or preparing for ministry interpret concrete experiences in and through this paradigm itself, to hear people's articulation of their experience with the reality of God's ministry. This makes the very identity of practical theology inseparable from ministry itself, not because ministry is a practical wisdom but because it is participation in the very being of God. Practical theology is made a *theology* only because it is first an attention to ministry (the ministry of the human being as conditioned by the ministry of God).

This then also points to the core social paradigm in Christopraxis.[64] It is a form of ministry that seeks to share in humanity (hypostasis, as we will see) that is broken, trusting that in this shared brokenness of human suffering, the very being of God as becoming in the identification with the perishing Jesus, is made active, as it was for many in the stories of chapter 3.[65] A practical theology

63. Hall articulates how this theological perspective opens up a focus on context, driving deeply into practical theology. "Precisely here lies the point of inescapable convergence between the *theologia crucis* tradition and theological contextuality. Theology done in the spirit of this tradition is bound to be a contextual theology. For it would be the height of contradiction to insist that what is revealed in the suffering, death, and resurrection of Jesus Christ is God's abiding commitment to this world, and then to enucleate a theology which in effect ignored the specific realities of the here and now. If it is taken seriously that the whole movement of the God of the Bible, culminating for Christians in the incarnation and humiliation of the Word, is a painful but determined journey towards creation ("he set his face steadfastly to go to Jerusalem," Luke 9:51, KJV), then the faith which emanates from such a gospel must be a matter of praxis, i.e., of an ever more intensive concretization of the divine solidarity with creaturely being. It is possible that there are other types of theological emphases which provide a basis and rationale for Christian involvement in this world; but the *theologia crucis* not only offers the believing community such a basis and rationale, it positively drives the church out into the world." *Thinking the Faith*, 30.

64. Anderson says, "Humans exist essentially in concrete social relationships or what I have called a social paradigm." *Shape of Practical Theology*, 162. He then shows how this core social paradigm is embedded in his theological perspective. "The neighbor is not first of all an ethical construct based on some general ethical principle of duty or even of love. The neighbor is both God and the other. To deny the other as neighbor is to deny God. To recognize the other a neighbor is to recognize the good and the right as the demand of God on me through the neighbor." Ibid., 138.

65. This core social paradigm gives Anderson's Christopraxis perspective a heavy incarnational bent. "The incarnation of God does not take place in a privileged sphere nor in something less than real

of Christopraxis seeks to examine human relationships of shared humanity as places where the ministry of God as event is occurring, using the very epistemological criterion of sharing in death for the sake of life as its hermeneutic that allows for both discernment and reenvisioned practice, which we will explore further in chapter 6.

CONCLUSION

With this chapter I have tried to lay out the contours of a Christopraxis practical theology of the cross. I have done this mainly by looking at the work of Ray S. Anderson, connecting his thought with the actualist ontology of Godself as articulated by Eberhard Jüngel. The chapter concluded by articulating Anderson's contention that at the center of God's ministry is the reality of *ex nihilo*. We then saw how this was in itself a *theologia crucis*. To continue in this direction and elicit more fully some of the more provocative assertions surrounding God's being-in-becoming in the perishing Jesus, the next chapter will turn to justification, exploring it not as a doctrinal perspective but as a hermeneutic of God's ministry of becoming in and through human impossibility. Therefore, Anderson, while remaining in our discussion, will recede to the background, and Jüngel, who played an important but nevertheless supporting role in this chapter, will take the lead in the next.

humanity. In the humanity of Jesus Christ the actual humanity of every person has been taken up, judged, put to death and justified. Jesus Christ is not only the Son of the Father, he is at the same time the brother of every brother and sister. Through the incarnation it is determined that humanity, in its concrete and particular form as cohumanity, is a more fundamental and authentic humanity than that which exists merely as 'nature,' including all racial and cultural forms." Ibid., 139.

6

Practical Theology into Nothingness
Exploring Jüngel, Justification, and Creation Ex Nihilo

In the last chapter I sought to describe a Christopraxis practical theology of the cross. In the next two chapters I will deepen this perspective by drilling into a number of the central themes described earlier. For instance, in this chapter I will explore how Christopraxis and its theme "from death to life" and its hermeneutical paradigm of God's being in the ministerial becoming through ex nihilo is embedded in a certain perspective on justification, a perspective that Eberhard Jüngel has beautifully laid out. Jüngel has done this with his feet resting squarely in philosophical theology; it will be my pursuit to turn his ideas loose, letting them run in the field of practical theology, using them to interpret experiences of divine action like those in chapter 3, furthering my Christopraxis practical theology of the cross.

The turn to justification in this chapter is particularly interesting because almost no perspective gleaned from justification has been formative to practical theology (at least in English-speaking North America).[1] At one level this is odd, seeing that justification has been a (if not the) central theme in the ecclesial communities that trace their history back to the European Reformation and therefore a central focus of an evangelical commitment (whether evangelical is defined broadly or narrowly). This is why, I believe, as I said in chapter 1, that practical theology has been seen with suspicion or ambivalence by American Evangelicals, neo-Barthians, and American Lutheran communities.

---

1. No doubt certain dogmatic perspectives that center on justification see preaching as central. These perspectives enter the area of practical theology, but often do so without the desire to *do* practical theology. Rather, their objective remains only dogmatic, never touching on concrete communities or giving any sense of performative action. A good example of this perspective is Rudolph Bultmann, or in a more contemporary view Steven Paulson.

These particular perspectives and communities (of which my own history is part) have tended to focus both intellectually and pragmatically on issues of soteriology, making justification the essential frame of divine action, exploring how God justifies and therefore saves the human being. Even in American Evangelical communities with heavy attention to piety and human actions of sanctification, a focus on soteriology through justification has allowed participants to speak passionately of the agency of God. These soteriological views framed by the Reformation's conception of justification see the human being's action as holding little to no merit in the soteriological economy of God; human action, even at its best, holds no ability to connect itself with the eternal.[2]

This may be the very reason that the English-speaking world has steered clear of justification as a lens for practical theology. It may still have a place in confession but lacks much, it is perceived, in helping shape a practical theological approach. If justification claims that the ontological state of the human being is one of impossibility, then practical theology is seen as having little left to work with. And this perception is so because practical theology has made the potency of human action its text of study, and so often human action is studied for its potential to bring forth essential actualities, whether those are named as ethical actions of mutual regard (Browning), habituated welcome (Fulkerson), or life abundant (Dykstra and Bass). Practical theology has tended to study the potential and potency of human action as a way of studying the concrete and lived.

But justification claims neither potential nor potency for human action. It states the very opposite, claiming that sin and death have turned human action in on itself, impossibly separating it from the eternal. Whether at the level of soteriology or even history, justification claims that human action alone lacks the potency to achieve even justice for the oppressed. Sin and death are so bound with human action, muddying time so fully, that humanity's feet are too stuck to move into the eternal, into divine action. At the very least, practical

---

2. Eberhard Jüngel explains how I am defining evangelical and what is at stake in it. Following him, I'm contending that practical theology has not taken the living presence of Christ as central enough. His justification perspective allows for this possibility. "The possibility of thinking God is, for evangelical theology, not an arbitrary possibility, but rather a possibility already determined by the existence of the biblical texts and claimed already by faith in God. Theology must think God in the concrete context of a history which, beyond the momentary aspect of the 'I think,' implies experiences of God which have happened and are promised." *God as the Mystery of the World* (Grand Rapids, MI; Eerdmans, 1983), 154. Leo O'Donovan adds, "It is evangelical . . . because it centers on God, stressing God's address to humanity rather than humanity's search for God or our purported discovery of God." "The Mystery of God as a History of Love: Eberhard Jüngel's Doctrine of God," *Theological Studies* 42, no. 2 (1981):252.

theology's attention to the potential and potency of human action has led to a raised eyebrow of suspicion or confusion for those who see both divine action and theological anthropology through justification (that is to say, through the core commitment of the early Protestant Reformation).

It will be the objective of this chapter to show how a Christopraxis practical theology of the cross stands distinct from the other North American projects of practical theology by showing how Christopraxis attends to just such a perspective on justification. This chapter then will lean into human impossibility, making it the very arena of the possibility of divine action. I will draw a heavy distinction between actualities and possibilities as this chapter unfolds, exploring how the impossibilities facing people like Stanik become the stage for them to experience the ministerial act of God's becoming to them. Stanik confesses his impossibility as prayer ("I need a change"), and from this confessed impossibility comes the act of God, meeting him not only experientially ("I feel it in every cell") but reordering his life, moving him from chef to minister.

Through Jüngel, this will be my very definition of justification: divine action that comes in and through human impossibility, bringing forth the all-new possibility of life through death. And because this new possibility born from the impossible is new life through death (and sin), it is an ontological union with God, a union given to us not through our human effort but in and through God's becoming, God's coming to us in the ministry of identifying with the perishing Jesus (Christopraxis). Justification is not used here as a blunt instrument against established approaches of practical theology. Instead, I push justification beyond legal or forensic ghettos of atonement and into the practice of ministry itself, moving beyond intellectual doctrine to lived and concrete existence. Not only is practical theology transformed by justification, but justification too is transformed by a practical theology of Christopraxis.

To do this mutual transformation, we will also need to unhinge practical theology from a foundational dialogue partner—Aristotle. North American practical theology has been particularly impacted by Aristotelian perspectives. After all, Aristotle is the originator of the concept of praxis, which in so many ways is the central theme of practical theology. So, while in one way Aristotle is inextricably linked to practical theology, in another way Aristotelian thought has penetrated deeper. Browning, Miller-McLemore, and Dykstra and Bass, all following Aristotle, have been inclined to affirm that human actions can create actualities, particularly as it relates to character and community. They assert that right action leads to right living, which leads, in their perspective, to God. Aristotelianism has served practical theology by claiming a paved, hard road for human action, obscuring the Reformation commitment to human "stuckness" and the muddied impossibility of this action to reach anywhere near the eternal (Kierkegaard).

As we will see, Jüngel's project is to echo and then intensify Luther's opposition to Aristotelianism. Following Jüngel, this chapter desires to link practical theology and justification, distinguishing my Christopraxis practical theology of the cross significantly from the other dominant models, as it does not seek a basis in Aristotelianism's overattention to human action and its potential for actualities but turns instead to divine action and its ontological becoming next to human death and impossibility. Such a perspective shifts its vision from human actuality to divine possibility as the frame for ministerial action. I will seek to show how this perspective, which moves away from Aristotelian praxis toward justification, may actually be a more helpful framework for the conceptualization of the practice of ministry itself, connecting it to the life histories presented in chapter 3.

A Doctrine?

Earlier I said that all the dominant models of practical theology lean heavily on Aristotle, whether in the practice perspective of Dykstra and Bass or in the central attention paid to *phronesis* by Browning and Miller-McLemore. Yet, this assertion is not completely true. Andrew Purves has not bent a knee to Aristotle and has avoided him by attending so fully to doctrine.[3] Purves, as we saw in chapter 4, makes doctrine the form and pursuit of practical theology itself.[4]

It may appear at first glace that I too am running to historical doctrine, throwing my arms around it as a way of doing practical theology; such a turn to justification may be seen as a desire to prop up practical theology against the

---

3. Purves avoids Aristotle so fully that he barely even discusses or attends to praxis.

4. The following statement by Dietrich Bonhoeffer, in my mind, stands in direct opposition to Purves's desires with doctrine: "When God is bound within a doctrine of the divine nature, then God is to be found in that doctrine, understandable and subject to classification within the human 'system.' But this makes for no encounter with the existence of human beings. Even a doctrine of a gracious God, one which declares that wherever God and human beings come together there must stand the cross, is, certainly to our modern way of thinking, no offense at all but, rather, an entirely welcome addition to our 'system.' The offense arises for the first time when our existence is actually encountered, when we, wherever we hear about cross and judgment, must ourselves submit to them so that grace may abound. To declare that doctrine can be appropriated only through a divinely created faith is to make clear that there is something to revelation as a doctrine which somehow goes beyond human ontological possibilities. From this it follows that wherever revelation is understood only as doctrine one comes short of the Christian idea of revelation, because God is tied down by an ontological conception of that kind." *Act and Being* (Minneapolis: Fortress Press, 1961), 104.

sturdy (even rigid) wall of the dogmatic (moving into a foundationalism). But this is not my intention. Justification itself, as Jüngel asserts, is not so much a doctrine—or better, is only a doctrine—because it is a hermeneutic of God's very being as becoming.

My problem with Purves is not the attention to doctrine per se but rather the use of doctrine as an iron mold that freezes human experience within a hard historical past, making the practice of ministry the retrieval of doctrinal history rather than an experience with the being of God as becoming.

I use justification here *not* as the retrieval of doctrinal history but as a hermeneutic, a lens, that gives vision to the action of God in and through the concrete experience of human beings as they encounter the event of God's action of ministry.[5] I use justification as a way of understanding concrete experiences like that of Ron, who experiences Jesus come to him in the despair of his lost wife, or experiences like my own, where Jesus comes in the impossible stuckness of a hole and the fear of nightmares. In other words, I'm using justification not as historical artifact but as a lens of Christopraxis itself.

From this perspective, doctrine is freed to be of essential importance for practical theology. Practical theology has tended to have a kind of doctrinal deficit disorder, choosing dialogue with social sciences or anthropology as a way to propel it into the concrete and lived (Purves has rightly diagnosed this; he just threatens the health of the patient by overmedicating the problem). I believe that seeing doctrine as an interpretative lens for Christopraxis, as a frame to discern God's ministry of becoming, makes such doctrinal reflection generative within the zone of the concrete and lived to which practical theology attends.

Seen in this way, justification, Jüngel argues, is the protodoctrine (at least for Protestants) because justification encompasses the shape of divine action next to concrete human existence. It is attention to the association of divine and human action at the deepest level of both, binding conceptions of revelation with anthropology—making it quite germane for practical theology. Jüngel states, "The doctrine of justification deals equally with God and human beings: with the God who justifies and sinners who are justified."[6]

---

5. There I define doctrine much as Ellen Charry does in *By the Renewing of Your Mind: The Pastoral Function of Christian Doctrine* (New York: Oxford University Press, 1997).

6. Eberhard Jüngel, *Justification: The Heart of the Christian Faith* (Edinburgh: T&T Clark, 2001), 147.

From the Legal to the Existential

For justification to be nimble enough to do this, we must follow Jüngel further by seeing it within an existential/experiential framework rather than a legal one. By existential/experiential I mean to see justification as the articulation of the depth and contradiction of human existence. It is a wrestling with human existence next to the being of God in becoming in ministerial love. Justification is bound in the experience of human agents and their many experiences of sin and death.

I am claiming that justification is the central hermeneutic because, more so than almost all other doctrinal perspectives, it is bound to human experience (making it generative for practical theology), yet this experience has no possibility in itself of leading to the eternal. Rather, it is the concrete experience of impossibility. Justification is deeply experiential, but only in the articulation of human finitude and impossibility (this is its existential depth). Doctrines like the Trinity, eschatology, and soteriology are formative (essential) conceptions (dogma), but none is bound directly within the existential/experiential *being* of humanity itself. What I mean is that they cannot be accessed through the concrete experience of the human being. But all the people I interviewed had distinct experiences of being stuck and facing impossibility.

Justification as experience of the impossible within human being and acting is existentially concrete. Justification as a hermeneutical frame, Jüngel contends, opens up deep veins to the actual encounter with God's being as becoming, with God's ministry, known as Trinity, for instance. Having been given life out of death, having encountered the new possibility in and through the perishing Jesus who now lives, we claim Christ as Lord, as sure God. We are moved to claim this God as the relationship of three in one by the concrete experience of God's being as becoming in the act of justification in and through Jesus (through the act of God's ministry itself). This existential/experiential frame for justification frees it from stale doctrinal history and makes justification the very hermeneutic of Christopraxis, the very shape of God's ministry of love as God's being as becoming in taking on all experiences of death for the sake of life.

Often when justification becomes about the retrieval of doctrinal history, it is captured in a legal framework. Attention turns to a just God and the human offense against this God's legal honor as bestowed Lord of creation. Sin is immoral duty breaking, and God the offended king. Yet, such a metaphysical drama of offense rarely can connect to the very wrestling of the human being itself, seeking for God and life in the ontological experience of existence and death, of yearning in deep pain for why, for instance, one's husband died of heart disease in Chicago.

And so too in the legal framework does God become inert in some heavenly realm, offended and appeased to justify without any dynamic articulation of God's very being in becoming through the perishing Jesus. *In the legal frame of justification, God is not a minister but an offended monarch.* There is no Christopraxis, no continued and active ministry of Christ in the world moved by love, for Jesus stands only as a passive sacrificial lamb.

Jüngel pushes justification from a legal framework into an existential one, allowing for justification to become a hermeneutical doctrine, thrusting us into the now, into the lived. It then is a lived and concrete perspective that seeks for the becoming of God in and through the existential experience of impossibility. So unlike Purves, who is such a heated apologist for doctrine that all human experience is dried brittle from his perspective, I turn to justification as a way to embrace and explore human experience as the location for the encounter with God's own ministry of being in becoming. This human experience, it must be said again, is not one of strength and power but of death and impossibility (foolishness); it is the beautiful yearning for new life next to concrete and lived experiences of impossibility, the impossibility of sick children, grieving friends, absent spouses, and soul-smothering jobs.

As a hermeneutic, justification no doubt frames a certain way of interpreting human experience, with its darkness at center stage.[7] But this interpretation, I hope to show, creates many vistas for the articulation of the event of divine encounter in and through such human experience. This, at least, was what I discovered in my interviews. If we are brave enough to explore the darkness of the human condition, this perspective allows us to see the beauty of the rising sun that brings the new possibility of the eternal into time, and time into the eternal. My contention is that this very attention to human experience and divine action makes justification a significant framework for practical theology.

---

7. Douglas John Hall's quote, I believe, staves off the critique that my perspective is melodramatic, or too dark. It no doubt is a danger, but embedding it in Christopraxis frees it from nihilism. "Every theological posture has its danger, and no doubt the danger peculiar to the theology of the cross is that it readily lends itself to a religious expression of pessimism, melancholia, and despair. However, something altogether disruptive must happen to this theology before it can become the vehicle of a religious pessimism, namely, it must cease to be a Christology." *Lighten Our Darkness: Toward an Indigenous Theology of the Cross* (Lima, OH: Academic Renewal, 2001), 150.

Justification and Ex Nihilo

These last paragraphs may lead some to scratch their heads. It appears that to move justification off the legal platform and onto the existential stage is to lock it into a perspective outside of revelation itself (into some opaque philosophy). This argument for the experiential depth of justification may seem to take attention off God's ministry as God's being as becoming. But this need not be the case; it is rather the legal that is an artificial philosophical conception, adopting Platonic and Aristotelian notions of perfection. The existential justification perspective that Jüngel is working is animated by revelation itself because it claims justification as the very shape of God's ministry—but, again, justification as existential/experiential and not legal.

And this existential/experiential dynamic of justification runs so deeply for Jüngel that it is bound in creation itself. Justification is not animated solely by human offense but rests at the core of God's own being (as love), forged as the shape of God's ministry to concrete human beings as those bound to God through nothingness. Justification is not just a legal occurrence but is the fullness of God's ministry of becoming (of revealing Godself) through ex nihilo.

So Jüngel creatively binds the (doctrinal) hermeneutics of justification with creation ex nihilo, asserting that justification and creation, so often standing in opposition or seen as distinct in theological systems, are fused. Justification rests on the lived and the existential/experiential because it is bound to ex nihilo.[8] For Jüngel, to understand even creation (as ministry) is to see it through the concrete experience of justification.

This makes justification the continuation and culmination of God's very being as becoming.[9] Justification is the continuation of God's coming through ex nihilo, with the culmination found in the turning of death into life by

8. Paul Tillich says, "The formula creatio ex nihilo is not the title of a story. It is the classical formula which expresses the relation between God and the world." *Systematic Theology: Reason and Revelation. Being and God* (Chicago: University of Chicago Press, 1951), 254.

9. Graham Watts explains the Trinitarian form of Jüngel's justification perspective: "This distinctively ontological approach to the doctrine of justification coheres when explaining the situation of humanity in union with Christ. In the event of justification, God approaches us in the addressing word; in the Spirit God interrupts our existence and redefines it. In this event we are made new, we have a new experience of our being; in Jüngel's view we become authentically human. It is the work of the Spirit to actualize the particular and unique mediation between man and God realized in Jesus Christ. As justified, the human individual is set free in order to act in obedience to God. Human activity no longer seeks to be self-justifying but responds to the grace of God revealed in Christ through the Spirit. Hence Jüngel applauds Barth for grounding ethics in Christology." *Revelation and the Spirit: A Comparative Study of the Relationship between the Doctrine of Revelation and Pneumatology in the Theology of Eberhard Jüngel and of Wolfhart Pannenberg* (Milton Keynes, UK: Paternoster, 2005), 50.

God's Word (Christopraxis), which creates ex nihilo, perishing *in nihlio*, so that through the perishing, through nothingness, we might be born into new possibility (1 Pet. 3:18).[10] This is God's very ministry, to speak possibility out of nothingness, starting in creation and culminating in justification. It is to create being from nonbeing, in and through God's giving of God's own being of love (John 3:16) through becoming in the Word (Chrstopraxis).[11]

POSSIBILITY AND NOTHINGNESS

Creation ex nihilo itself is revelation; God comes to what is not God to bring it into being. God unveils Godself by entering nothingness with a Word of new possibility, by creating something out of nothing for the purpose that this something, as an ontological reality, might share in God's being through God's continued act of ministerial coming.[12]

Nothingness stands as the opposition to God's ministry; it threatens the very creation God unveils Godself to create. Nothingness haunts a child and swallows his friend, striking him with cancer. And nothingness can threaten creation because God chooses to create and act continually within creation as *possibility*, as a minister who brings the event of God's Word and not as a hard deity of *actuality* that imposes a will outside the being of God's very self, which is the ministerial indwelling of the love of the Trinity. *Nothingness can threaten God's creation because God chooses to be with creation as minister (person) and not as static force.*[13]

---

10. Jüngel provides an explanation in this dense passage: "This abstract formulation immediately becomes concrete when we think back to the event of justification. For this event makes it clear that the divine distinction between the possible and the impossible is an event of the Word of God which leads the world back to nothingness and makes it anew out of nothingness. Making the possible to be possible and the impossible to be impossible is the business of the Word; in the event of the Word, God both distinguishes himself from and relates himself to the world. In the face of the actuality which perpetuates that which is real and which, even in 'making the future' only changes what is actual, the event of the Word of God lets the possible become possible and hands over to perish that which has become impossible. This means: by distinguishing between the possible and the impossible. The Word of God occurs as a word of promise and judgment." *Theological Essays I* (Edinburgh: T&T Clark, 1989), 113.

11. This commitment is why my perspective is a practical theology of the cross. As Hall says about the *theoloiga crucis*, "What is most significant for our present concerns in all of this is that the theology of the cross as Luther elaborates it is a theology that determines to take its stand within the experience of negation." *Lighten Our Darkness*, 114.

12. While I am deeply committed to this justification perspective, I am also leaning here on John Zizioulas and his dialogue with the patristic fathers. His chapter "Created and Uncreated" is particularly formative here. See *Communion and Otherness* (Edinburgh: T&T Clark, 2006).

13. Zizioulas pushes this point hard and convincingly. See "Created and Uncreated."

But while this nothingness stands as a threat to all that is, haunting children in their sleep and taking babies from their mothers, nothingness cannot impose itself on God.[14] This nothingness that is not God has become the doorway into which God breaks in as event (revelation). God's act is an act of possibility, and this possibility is seen only against the backdrop of nothingness. It is out of nothingness (ex nihilo) that God ministers. The nothingness is bound to God, by God acting and ministering through it, by God bringing possibility out of nothingness. The confession of creation ex nihilo is the claim that God's ministry is God's being as becoming out of nothing that acts through nothingness itself.

So while God's Word stands over and against nothingness, the unbinding creativity of God's Word makes nothingness serve God, using it as the doorway into the possibility of God's act, *making it the entrance of the eternal into time*. Through nothingness, God's ministering Spirit of love comes to me in the hole. Nothingness becomes the doorway for the entrance of the Word that creatively prevents the eternal and time from being confused or conflated. For time is only as the possibility of the creative Word of God next to nothingness (ex nihilo). God comes to the world; God creates the world out of nothingness, and for this God's act comes always as possibility, always as the mission of ministry.

And for this act of God to remain always possibility, it must come out of nothingness, out of impossibility—this is why Christopraxis as the ministry of God has the ex nihilo always at the center, as Anderson has said. The Word always speaks of possibility: The Word speaks over the void of nothingness and creates (Gen. 1:1-6). The Word speaks of a dead womb bringing forth the promise (Genesis 21). The Word speaks of an old man leading a people from slavery (Exodus). The Word speaks of a poor nobody virgin bearing the Word itself (Luke 1:30). Because God's being is in the becoming of ministry, God's ministry is always the Word of possibility.

Ron experiences God's Word coming to him in grief in the loss of his wife, saying with a Word of possibility that "Martha is home," now get up

14. Jüngel defines what he means by nothingness, "We shall take up this thought, but interpret the facts which it points to according to the knowledge we have gained so far. Thus the void, the Nothing, from which God created the world is not considered evil or even empty. The Nothing is nothing other than nothing. It has no merits and no demerits. It is quite simply meaningless. The void gains meaning only in the context of being. This is what gives the void its character of evil: the Nothing which is called into being within the framework of creation and dominates creation. It is the possibility of being annihilated which threatens existing things within creation. Only the void which is called into being, only the Nothing which is called into being over the created fellowship, only that determines the dreadful aspect of Non-existence. And this is exactly what sin does: it calls that void into being, and that is all. That is what makes up all of its wretchedness as well as its perilous depths." *Justification*, 112.

and live. Rachel experiences nothingness in the blame she places on herself for her husband's death, and then the Word comes to her through a newspaper article, telling her to live, for it was not her fault. In the hole of despair as my own being bears the loss of Benjamin to the nothingness, the Word comes to me, and through the nothingness it says "run, run, run, and fear no more, live!" Possibility appears as an event next to, in, and through nothingness. Possibility can only shine with the force of a million suns against the backdrop of nothingness.

CREATION AND THE EX NIHILO

Even in the perfection of the garden, before the fall, the ex nihilo remains; the nothingness out of which humans were created continues in their being, for they are creatures given the possibility of life from the very Word (Christopraxis) that creates in and through nothingness. They have come from nothingness and to nothingness they shall return if they should dare unlatch themselves from God who comes to them "out of nothingness," *if they should dare deny that God is their minister and that they received God's ministering act of possibility out of nothingness.*

The tree at the center of the garden of which they should *not* partake is metaphorically the doorway back into nothingness; to enter it is to seek to reverse God's Word, to be outside of this Word that has formed them out of nothingness as possibility. They stand as the fullness of God's possibility; they are what is possible for the love of the God who is the one essence of three hypostases (persons) in relationship.

But taking the fruit of the tree (Genesis 3), they seek an *actuality* of their own, an actuality made from human action that needs not God's possibility, choosing to live in the actuality of their own power rather than in and through the possibility of God's act of ministry, which comes out of nothingness. They are tempted (and succumb to that temptation) to cut the lines from the God of the Word of possibility to create for themselves an actuality, to allow their own action, their human word, to justify themselves. They no longer want God's ministry, instead desiring the power to be outside it, no longer being weak and susceptible to nothingness. They want to be God's equal.

They choose their own actuality over the possibility of God's ministry, and they do this because the possibility is always set within the event of God's being as becoming; it is always a happening in and through God's Word of ex nihilo. The first humans choose the absurdity of making themselves (actualizing themselves) as "like God," as their own ministers, because they curse the nothingness, because they seek to be beyond ex nihilo. But to be beyond ex nihilo is to be beyond, or opposed, to God's ministry. And being without God's ministry is losing God's being, which leads to the horrible separation and haunting release of nothingness outside the Word itself. Seeing this nothingness in them, no longer clothed in the direct ministry of God, the first humans know they are naked to nothingness and now shall surely die, for they are separated from the creative Word that uses nothingness to bring forth ministry (Gen. 3:7).

They wanted knowledge of good and evil, to be like God and therefore to escape the nothingness that is inseparable from their own being, for it is nothingness from which they came (Kierkegaard). The original sin can be interpreted as the human act to deny that they are the ministry of God, that God is their minister, whose ministry is possibility out of the nothingness that exists within them. This nothingness, the very reality that they are created ex nihilo, disturbs them and makes them susceptible to the serpent's temptation to be like God, by being beyond nothingness, by being their own ministers. Our concrete and lived existence is the struggle with this nothingness; it is the temptation to believe we need no minister, that we need no other (human neighbor or ultimately God) to be with and for us. This is why Luther defines sin as *incurvatus in se*, turning in on oneself.

Adam and Eve never try to deny God as much as to become "like God." They seek to be God by being outside of nothingness, to be like God by being in actuality, no longer having to face the ex nihilo. But, to deny the ex nihilo is to deny God's act and is an attempt to be as the creator, which is to have one's existence outside of nothingness; to be outside nothingness is to be God.[15]

CREATION AND JUSTIFICATION

Through opposition to the ex nihilo, sin enters into the world. The deception that human action can create for itself an *actuality* leads to the fall of creation.

---

15. Paul DeHart explains Jüngel's point, "The meaning of the death and resurrection of Jesus as a process of divine self-identification and self-determination is this: 'God is one who involves himself with nothingness.' The two events together, the fact that it is the dead man who is resurrected, help explicate God's self-involvement in the struggle. For Jesus' death and resurrection as divine events mean that God does not simply reject nothingness or destroy it, but rather God incorporates (literally, in the corpus of Jesus) nothingness into the divine life and history. Jüngel points out that the annihilation of nothingness would be meaningless. Since nothingness is defined by him as 'sheer indeterminacy' or, more metaphorically, as 'lack of place,' then God's victory in the struggle with nothingness must be seen as a 'neutralization' of it by determining it, by giving it a place. And that place for him must be God's own being." *Beyond the Necessary: Trinitarian Faith and Philosophy in the Thought of Eberhard Jüngel* (Atlanta: Scholars Press, 1999), 122.

It is the sin of believing that the human being can create an actuality outside the threat of nonbeing, that the creature can be like the creator. It is the hubris that we are in no need of ministry, that we are beyond nothingness because we have actualized ourselves. Impossibility is the concrete experience of needing a minister. And in such moments, many of the people I interviewed experienced an encounter with divine action.

This desire to create an actuality in which the creature is made into the creator is sin because it denies the ex nihilo, the location of possibility, choosing instead an actuality created by human action. But actuality has no need for God's ministry, and, having no need for God's ministry, it has no possibility of encountering God's being, which is the ministry of God's coming to humanity through nothingness itself. Thus, to pave over ex nihilo with human action is to be without God because it is to be God and therefore to have no need for God's Word to continue to minister to us by continually creating possibility in our nothingness.

Sin is the existential reality of denying nothingness by giving loyalty to the deception that human action can create an actuality for itself that eliminates nothingness.[16] However, to strive to eliminate nothingness through human actualities is to serve nothingness. This is sin's deception: to trust in human action to save itself, to need no minister. It is to turn in on ourselves, to turn in on our human actualities, and therefore to lose God's possibility that comes out of nothingness. It is to lose God's being as becoming, which is God's ministry. This is why God's act must first kill before it makes alive (Luther). This is why justification is the continuation and culmination of God's ministry, for all human actualities must be shown for what they are—death—so that from the nothingness of the barren womb, the ministry of God might bring new possibility, so that Sarah's boy might be born as the promise (as the ministry) because he comes ex nihilo.

So to seek actuality outside of ex nihilo is to deny the Word of God. The Word, which is God's very being as becoming, is God's ministry as Christopraxis.[17] Therefore, original sin is not the moral "doing bad" of eating

16. This has some connection to Reinhold Niebuhr conception of sin as developed in his Gifford Lectures. *The Nature and Destiny of Man* (New York: Charles Scribner's Sons, 1942).

17. Here I am following headlong Athanasius and other patristic fathers who contend that the Word is the eternal Son who is the Christ, eternally with the Father, begotten but *not* made. This allows for the potential of thinking of the Word, which will have an important place in this chapter, as connected to Christopraxis. I believe there is a link between justification and *theosis* for which this project does not allow further discussion. But, for instance, Veli-Matti Karkkainen says, "This view, traditionally called 'justification,' can also be called theosis according to the ancient doctrine of the fathers with whom Luther agreed. Justification and deification, then, mean the 'participation' of the believer in Christ which,

forbidden fruit but the very denying of God's ministry, and to deny God's ministry is to lose God's being which is in becoming. That is, sin separates us from God (Rom. 3:23), leading to the need for reconciliation through the action of justification, which can only be taken by God as the ministry of possibility, revealing the impossibility of human actualities so that from nothingness God's creative Word might spring, bringing life to our concrete experience of death.

REVELATION AND JUSTIFICATION

So God's very revelation, like strands of rope woven together, is justification and creation; these two intertwined events are the core of God's continued ministry. Justification is an existentially dynamic act bound in God's being as becoming, not simply a legal manifesto. And this is so because to justify is to reinstate the sharing relationship of God in humanity and humanity in God. It is to existentially/experientially reveal the nothingness within us so that we might turn from human actualities to the possibility of experiencing God's being as becoming in and through nothingness.[18] To justify is to forgive the sin that leads to denying God's possibility and cleaving to human actualities, which in the end can produce no salvation in themselves but can lead only to demonic death, only to the return to nothingness without the Word of possibility.

When human actualities, which have sought to eliminate the ex nihilo and therefore deny God's possibility, have failed, turning to death, there is a complete absence of hope, for human actuality has cashed in its chips for the now and lost the horizon of possibility. So when death comes to actuality it is demonic, for it is the complete end to what is, the end with no possibility of life. It is a nothingness freed by human action from the creative Word of God, a nothingness freed to actualize itself in human systems and forms, to kill and destroy what the Word has created as good and for life.

So justification itself becomes God's being as becoming in ministry. Justification exposes the impossibility of all human actualities, showing them to be only human constructs that in the end seek to eliminate nothingness by serving it. Sin enters the world through the denial of ex nihilo by propping up human action as an actuality. Justification is the return to possibility by the

---

because Christ is God, is also a participation in God himself." *One with God: Salvation as Deification and Justification* (Collegeville, MN: Liturgical Press, 2004), 46.

18. "Sin and evil are, so to speak, the negation of a relationship between creature and Creator. Sin and evil affect the creature's relationship to God in the form of an aversion to relationships." Jüngel, *Justification*, 94.

existential reinstating of the ex nihilo, reinstated by and through God's own act of ministry.

Justification connects time with eternity by judging human action as impossibility, restating the ex nihilo that binds human impossibility with the divine act of ministry. Justification is more than the legal imposition of Jesus's righteousness on guilty sin; rather, it fully reopens the ex nihilo that allows the human to be in union with God through the possibility of God's ministry. It then is no coincidence that every person I asked to speak of an experience of God's presence began with a concrete occurrence of ex nihilo (I never specifically asked for this; nevertheless, they always started here). As they articulated the ex nihilo, they witnessed to the concrete and lived encounter with the creative Word that came to them to minister life out of the experience of ex nihilo.

God's Word of possibility takes on flesh to perish, bearing the actuality of all forms of human action, perishing under them, so that through the Son's death, perishing might lead to an all-new possibility. Through perishing, possibility is bound, for through the perishing of Jesus death is fully embraced and encircled by the possibility of God. Through the perishing of Jesus, the perishing of Benjamin is given new possibility; Benjamin's being is found with Jesus and Marlen witnesses in joy to its possibility, "Elizabeth has seen Benjamin with Jesus; he is OK."[19]

FROM PERISHING TO POSSIBILITY, FROM THE CROSS TO JUSTIFICATION

Nothingness, as in the beginning, is the stage set for eternity to break further into time (this breaking of eternity into time is what I see as the heart of practical theology). Justification is the protohermeneutical doctrine of divine and human encounter because it reinstates, in as dynamic a fashion as creation itself, the understanding that nothingness, that death and sin, must serve God by becoming the concrete place of God's ministry, the space where nothingness is turned into something, turned into the all-new possibility of sharing in God's being as the becoming of ministry.

The cross stands arm in arm with creation ex nihilo; they are the two profound acts of God's ministry to give Godself to humanity through nothingness. In creation God gives God's Word to the nothingness so that the possibility of something might spring from nothingness. And in the incarnation and crucifixion God's Word becomes flesh, reversing original sin, for as creation fell when the creature tried to be the creator, so now the Word that

---

19. This is where Jüngel and Moltmann, colleagues at Tubingen, are similar.

is God, the Word that creates out of nothing, the Word that is the Creator, becomes creature.

And as creature, the Word, the Christ, Jesus, perishes. And this perishing is the fullness of ministry itself; it is ministry as justification, for the Word that is God perishes into nothingness, descending into the demonic nothingness that sin freed to exist outside the ministry of God, outside the creative Word itself. So in perishing, the Word descends into death to envelop it again, to bind nothingness once more to the creative Word, to make nothingness again serve the ministry of God's being as becoming, to make the nothingness part of God's being because the Word comes into it.[20]

In the beginning the Word created ex nihilo and the ministry of God came out of nothingness; in contrast, in the cross the ministry of God as the Word itself goes into nothingness. God's ministry as being as becoming (Christopraxis) is framed by the twin movements of creation ex nihilo and cross *in nihilo*.

Now that the Word has both come out of and come into nothingness, nothingness is surrounded (in resurrection); it is forced again to serve God by being as it was in the beginning, the stage of eternity breaking into time, the location of God's giving of Godself in ministry. And this happens at the ontological level as God gives God's being to create being out of nothingness. Now in the cross God gives God's being again so that the estranged being of humanity might again share in God's own being (Athanasius).

We are justified through the cross, for the cross turns our nothingness into possibility, our death into life, for our nothingness and *not* our action binds us to God (Athanasius). The cross shows all human actuality to be an impossibility for encountering God, for it is not God's ministry and God can only be encountered through God's ministry, not through human action.

And God's ministry is to love creation; God's ministry is for the creature to share in God's very being but to share in it through nothingness (again at the ontological level).[21] We share in God by being ministered to by God, by God coming to us ex nihilo and *in nihilo*. This was true in my own story and with

---

20. The reader should be able to see how this perspective is a *theologia crucis*; for instance, Anna Madsen says, "What, then, is the theology of the cross? The theology of the cross announces that God is found in death, for it is there that boundaries disappear. In the death of sin of suffering, of uncertainty, and marked by service, Christians are assured that God is present. The theology of the cross is therefore a theology of grace, a theology of freedom, and a theology of trust. These are words of hope and promise that are vital and indispensable regardless of history or context." *The Theology of the Cross in Historical Perspective* (Eugene, OR: Pickwick, 2007), 241.

21. This is the very argument, I believe, of Athanasius and the Cappadocian fathers.

nearly all the people I interviewed. Justification, then, is not a response to God's just anger for being wronged; it is the fullness of God's love. *God justifies because God loves.* This makes justification inseparable from ministry itself and not some metaphysical legal operation.

Love is always in the motion of ministry; it is always the act of going to others to embrace their nothingness. Matt, whose experience is described in chapter 3, goes to the homeless, bearing their nothingness as the ministry of love. Love embraces nothingness so that love can be with its beloved; love binds one to another, to share in each other, because it enters the life of the other through brokenness, through nothingness. Love is the ministry of being together by becoming, by coming to one another through nothingness. God is love (1 John 4:8) because God is on the move, because God is in ministry, becoming, seeking to give Godself to us, to be with us.[22] Only love is on the move because only love creates possibility out of nothingness. Justification is God's love on the move; it is Jesus Christ moving into death so that we might share in God's life, so that God might again be our minister.

INTO LIFE

Love is on the move no more fully than when the Word who is the Creator becomes the creature and moves into nothingness for us, perishing so that we might live.

But this creature on the cross *is* the Creator, and nothingness cannot hold God. Though Jesus perishes, nothingness cannot possess this eternal Word, the creative Word that turns nothingness into life. Because this Jesus is the Word and the Word is crucified, perishing (nothingness) is turned into possibility—nothingness is again bound in the creative act of God's ministry.

The resurrection turns perishing into possibility; *it makes all concrete lived experiences of perishing the location of God's being as becoming* and therefore paradigmatic to practical theology (again, this is what I saw in the interviews in chapter 3).[23] The human experience of perishing becomes the locale to explore the breaking in of the divine into the human. Joining Erin's experience of the perishing of her parents' marriage, Sarah concretely encounters God's action

22. "Only in God is there the ontological freedom to put one's own being totally at stake, to freely enact that being. But God's creative involvement in nothingness for the sake of the otherness of creation therefore means that God not only has love but is love. God is paradoxically a totally free act of total love; freedom as a 'constituent moment of love' means that no conflict exists between this utter freedom and this utter being-for-another." DeHart, *Beyond the Necessary God*, 124.

23. This is the resurrection perspective that is inspired by Athanasius, who beautifully connects cross and resurrection at the ontological level of sharing (participating) in God's being. See *On the Incarnation.*

leading her into a ministry of listening. And this exploration of experience can be done with many different frames, such as through ethnography or in conversation with psychology. (As long as these disciplines' observations are conditioned by the examination of concrete human experience as *impossibility* and not as actualities, such descriptions of reality are opened to us. But more detail regarding how this works will need to wait until the final chapter.)[24]

In creation ex nihilo God's Word brings the event of divine encounter out of nothingness. But when human beings despise the nothingness, trying themselves to be the Creator, to actualize their own existence beyond nothingness, sin is released and nothingness is unlatched from God's ministry. Now, they shall surely die (Gen. 2:17), for there is no life outside the ministry of God, which is the place of God's being. Because of sin, nothingness becomes death; nothingness is turned from the locale of God's ministry, from the *event* of God's becoming, into the nonevent, into separation and isolation.

But when Jesus perishes, nothingness is placed back into the fullness of the ministry of God because death is recast, transformed from nonevent into an event of eternity breaking into time.[25] Nothingness is transformed from the place of God's absence to the place of God's presence through absence. God's ministry is fulfilled in Jesus' death and resurrection; God's ministry, the place where the divine and human encounter each other, is shown to be the place where perishing turns into possibility—by the act of the Word itself (by Christopraxis).[26]

24. I'm trying in this chapter to make a case from within practical theology and with rich theological argument for Roslene Bradbury's statement. In the final chapter I'll try to show how to do interdisciplinary work within this perspective. But, overall, my project is to construct a view of practical theology that honors this tradition she is raising in the *theologia crucis*. "The classical crucicentric theologians reject all anthropocentric starting points for the knowledge of God, including starting points in human experience, the law, a self-engendered mysticism, and the several strands of natural theology." *Cross Theology: The Classical Theologia Crucis and Karl Barth's Modern Theology of the Cross* (Eugene, OR: Pickwick, 2011), 40.

25. Luis Pedraja explains Jüngel's position beautifully, "Jüngel understands God as actualizing the possibility of becoming finite in the incarnation. It is through the incarnation that God establishes the relationship between the finite and the infinite God. This possibility also brings forth a new possibility. Through God's identification with the death of Jesus, God establishes a relationship with the 'relationlessness' of the death that defines our finitude. This results in a new relationship between humanity and God that restores the relationship broken by our finite nature. The perishing of finite beings in time is not their annihilation. The inclusion of finite beings into the relational nature of God's infinity allows them to become a new possibility for becoming. In a manner that is strikingly similar to the function of God's consequent nature, God's being also mediates this relationship that allows what has perished to become a new possibility for becoming." "The Infinity of God: A New Possibility in the Thoughts of Whitehead and Jungel," *Encounter* 58, no. 2 (Spring 1997): 168.

So now, where God should not be found, in death (in experiences of human impossibility), God is found. God should not be found in a morgue, but, according to Rachel, God is—in and through the act of ministry itself as a cabbie rests his hand on her shoulder. Jüngel says, "The death of God, in that it defines the being of God, changes death. In the event of God's death, God allows death to define his being, and thereby disposes of death. In the event of God's death, death is ordained to become a divine phenomenon."[27] Concrete and lived places of God's absence are the very places where ministry begins, for in these places of God's absence, places of nothingness and impossibility, the creative Word that has entered cross and resurrection moves, bringing new possibility. Jüngel states, "The cross reveals not just the fact that God is creator, but also the pattern or mode of God's creative activity."[28]

Practical theology as the articulation of the practice of ministry attends to the places of God's absence, the places where God should not be found. When we speak of the *experience* of God's absence, when we attend to impossibility, when we invite those bearing impossibility to articulate their impossibilities, we put away the delusion of human actualities and trust again, together, in the possibility of God's becoming among us. And when such impossibilities are spoken, they become shared, and when nothingness is shared, ministry occurs. The divine shares in the human and new possibility spills forth with the chorus of new life.

For us to share in God's being is to share God's form, but the sharing of this form is not the direct transcendental entering of the actuality of God's being. This is not open to us (not yet at least); rather, we participate in God's being by taking God's form of ministry, by being ministers. But as ministers, our concrete actions are directed not toward the actualities we can create but toward the sharing of concrete persons' experiences of nothingness (in their homelessness, in the divorce of their parents). We invite them to speak of

26. "Jesus' resurrection from the dead promises that we shall be made anew out of the nothingness of relationlessness, remade ex nihilo, if through faith in the creative Word of God we allow ourselves to participate in the love of God which occurs as the death of Jesus Christ. In this sense, Christian existence is existence out of nothingness, because it is all along the line existence out of the creative power of God who justifies. The Christian is accompanied by this nothingness in the double form revealed in Jesus' death and resurrection: as the end of the old and the beginning of the new, as a reminder of the judgment enacted in the sinner, and as the promise which surpasses judgment in the same way that grace has surpassed sin (Rom 5.20). *Media vita in morte sumus*, in the midst of life we are in death; but even more *media morte in vita sumus*, in the midst of death we are in life." Jüngel, *Theological Essays* I, 109.

27. Quoted in J. B. Webster, *Eberhard Jüngel: An Introduction to His Theology* (London: Cambridge University Press, 1986), 84.

28. DeHart, *Beyond the Necessary God*, 122.

nothingness, trusting that when the event of concrete nothingness is shared, the practice of ministry, the practice of "sharing-in" is ignited, and so ignited that it connects the eternal with time (it is so powerful that even my interviews became experiences of ministry). When the suffering mother speaks of her son's mental illness, when a wife speaks of the death of her husband, or when the young man speaks of the stress of a dehumanizing job, the event of sharing is born as new possibility in and through nothingness (I will say more about this in the next chapter).

JUSTIFICATION AS TURNING DEATH INTO LIFE

Justification, as we said at the beginning of this chapter, is the turning of death into life; though we are bound in sin, though we are inclined to trust our own action and seek for actualities for ourselves, though we fear ex nihilo, Jesus has turned our perishing into possibility, showing the futility of all human actuality to save itself.

We are justified; we are invited to live from the honest place of our nothingness, given the gift of God's love in it. We are set free from our own need to create an actuality for ourselves and set free to live in God's possibility. We are called to embrace our nothingness as the place where eternity enters time. We are justified because, after cross and resurrection, it is impossible for us again to imagine (though we do) that our works can create anything, that our formed actualities are better than God's loving possibility. For God's possibility is born from death, born from what we've been running from, our impossibility.

We are justified to participate in God's being by joining God's ministry of witnessing to God's turning of perishing into possibility, death into life. We are freed to be ministered to by God through our nothingness and therefore to minister to others through their own nothingness.

We participate in God's being by being ourselves ministers, by joining our neighbor's nothingness, embracing it in love as the possibility of God's act. We join in God's being by joining God's ministry by sharing in the nothingness of the creation, participating in others' lives as the participation in the divine act to turn what is broken and dead into new life.

The human minister participates in God by participating in the life of her neighbor, by being a minister, but this participation is not in itself a human act that can create an actuality. Justification claims the impotence of all human action, even human ministry. Rather, this human action even as ministry cannot create but can only share in nothingness, proclaiming in its shared concrete humanity that the possibility of God's own act is on its way.

In the love of one to another, in a love that seeks only the possibility of the other, the divine moves. From shared nothingness new possibility is born, as shared nothingness is the form of God's own ministry, a form our own broken, impossible humanity can join and can join because shared nothingness is not a work toward an actuality but a prayer for God's being to come as a new possibility. It is the act of a mother praying for her young boy. Human ministry is deep sharing in the life of our neighbor, not as a work but as a prayer for God's possibility to come in and through our shared nothingness. Greg shares so deeply in his friend's grief, embracing the nothingness before God, that in prayer he receives a word from God that promises a new possibility through the act of God's own ministry.

Practical theology and ministry are inseparably linked: practical theology is attention to the concrete and lived, and there can be no more concrete and lived experience than wrestling with nothingness.

PRACTICAL THEOLOGY UNLATCHED FROM ARISTOTLE

Through significant theological discussion, I have tried to articulate how justification is itself an existential experience with nothingness (and with God in that nothingness). From here, following Jüngel, I linked creation ex nihilo with justification, showing God's ministry as the bringing out of and going into nothingness. This allowed me to place experiential nothingness as the locale for divine and human action, interpreting experiences like Rachel's, Ron's, and Stanik's as encounters with this reality. This has kept an experiential core that is central to practical theology, an experiential core that stands as concrete and yet transcendent, lived and yet mystical. In other words, the central experiential core of nothingness becomes an essential zone to imagine (or better, to experience) divine encounter and to do so christocentrically, to do so as Christopraxis. And this rich articulation of divine action opens wide doors to human participation. We participate in divine action. We participate in God's very being by being in ministry, by sharing in nothingness as possibility. Ministry is linked from both the divine and human side as the sharing in nothingness as possibility.

This allows practical theological perspectives to be deeply theological while also gripping human experience as central. In turn, it allows for human practice to be essential, but to be essential as the ministry of shared nothingness in anticipation of divine encounter (possibility).

With the rest of this chapter we must come back to a major issue I introduced at its beginning, picking up a perspective I have been spinning and contrasting but have yet to explicate fully. I asserted earlier that my justification approach would move practical theology away from Aristotelian actualities and toward possibility as framed by creation ex nihilo and justification. In the earlier sections of the chapter I often contrasted actuality and possibility, but I did this without articulating the depth of contrast I'm seeking. Therefore, I will next show more fully not only how a Christopraxis practical theology differs from the other dominant perspectives of practical theology that are constructed on Aristotelian actuality but also how justification is the lifeblood of Christopraxis as practical theology.

ACTUALITY VS. POSSIBILITY

Aristotle contended that actuality preceded possibility, that from actuality, possibility dawns. What is a priori for Aristotle is the actuality of human action itself, the contention that human action has the potential to create a possibility for itself from itself—from its own actions. We create actualities through our repeated action; for instance, through righteous acts a human being becomes righteous as an actuality because she has taken enough actions to do so.[29]

These actions have the power to create a new actuality because they are direct; they are done for a telos, for a possibility. The human being wants to be good—this is the possibility she seeks—so having this telos, her actions are directed toward this possibility. They are done with a form of virtuous excellence because they seek a telos that her own action, if molded by the possibility, can actualize. She is able to create what she desires through her actions.[30]

The great advantage of this Aristotelian perspective is that it makes human action fundamentally productive. Human actions need not be arbitrary, but they can be powerful, creating in themselves new possibilities. These unarbitrary human actions that possess such power to create new possibilities

29. "Attempts at such a revision as a rule came to grief because with Aristotle they still presupposed that 'the possible' is a category formed by reference to the category of 'the actual.' The Aristotelian doctrine of the priority of actuality over possibility was not really called into question. Yet it is just this doctrine which made the possible into a 'half-being over against that which is,' in the sense of a 'not-yet-being' which is still to be; 'in the Aristotelian world, the possible is a kind of ghostly being.'" Jüngel, *Theological Essays I*, 101.

30. Here Jüngel explains, "Aristotle shaped this idea into a metaphysical first principle. His declaration that it is clear and obvious that 'actuality is prior to potentiality' was of incalculable significance for the history of thought (and here, indeed, it would be appropriate to say: for the history of being). This affirmation of the ontological priority of actuality over possibility . . . pushed thinking, that which is thought and that which was made therefrom in a direction which has come to determine the world. Aristotle's decision was one with consequences such as few other events have had. It is, therefore, appropriate to make it a matter for reflection." Ibid., 98.

must be thought of as praxis, as reflective actions done with a telos toward a new actuality in mind. So praxis itself is the power to create actualities out of human action. Marx retrieves praxis from Aristotle, giving it a bite, by asserting that the job of the philosopher is not simply to describe human actuality but to take action to change the actuality by creating a new possibility from the force of human action itself.

ARISTOTLE IN PRACTICAL THEOLOGY

This Aristotelian perspective has been paradigmatic to contemporary practical theology. Many, as I said, make Aristotle a core dialogue partner or at least a foundational source. Some have done this with a liberatory edge. Others, through a focus on practice, have seen the potential of human action, especially human action done in or as community. They have asserted that communal human action, embedded in the actuality of its virtues created through its practice, holds the potential to reverse the sad possibility of church decline, for instance, to create an actuality of vibrancy for the church through human practice itself.

In a connected way, practical theology has seen potential in Aristotle as it relates to the performative nature of pastoral practice. So, needing to train pastors, for instance, practical theologians have used Aristotle to recognize the depth of performance itself, showing how pastoral practice operates in the logic of other practices, like learning a musical instrument: "by skillful playing of the lyre, one becomes a lyre-player, an artist on the lyre, who then has the possibility of playing the lyre skillfully; bad lyre playing, by contrast, makes one a bungler."[31] In the same manner, excellent pastoral performance possesses within it the potential of creating an actuality of excellent churches. Excellent practice seems to hold the potential for creating an actuality out of human performative practice itself, claiming that ministry is contingent on the actuality that human practice creates.

This cleaving of practical theology to Aristotelian actuality makes sense, I suppose, for a field centered on practice and action as its central text. And it is true that Aristotle's perspective of human action could not show the potential and potency of human action more strongly. Practical theology has undoubtedly created rich projects from within this actuality-to-possibility framework that Aristotle has given us. But, because practical theology has succumbed to this actuality-to-possibility framework, it has been much harder

---

31. Ibid., 106.

for its significant projects to attend to divine action, to articulate with as much depth the act of God as it does the act of the human agent.

And this is so, I believe, because the Aristotelian actuality-to-possibility framework stands in opposition to the biblical form of divine action itself. This actuality-to-possibility framework binds reality so tightly within human praxis that it leaves little space to articulate divine action. It does not allow for the reordering of praxis itself, unteasing praxis from actuality and placing it instead on the possibility of God's own being as becoming (Christopraxis). And this praxis of God stands in direct opposition to human praxis as conceived by Aristotle, for we never experience divine action (divine praxis) as an actuality, but only as a possibility.[32]

To Possibility

As I have said, we experience God's ministry only as that which comes to us through nothingness, judging all human action and its yearning for its own created actuality as the primal sin, as the desire for the creature to be the Creator. Actuality is the sin to live without the need of God, to be our own minister. It is a sin in which our own actions create an actuality where we do not need God because we do not need a minister. Aristotelian actuality is the denial of nothingness. And without nothingness we do not need a minister because we are god; we possess the power to create actualities. God becomes in Aristotelian flavor an unmoving, unministering force that *may* metaphysically exist but, when push comes to shove, is unneeded.[33]

Aristotelian actuality can make human praxis significant, but by giving human praxis this power, it eliminates God's being as becoming, making divine praxis an impossibility because God can no longer move outside of human praxis itself; God can only move within the actuality that the human creates. Aristotelian actuality then becomes the completion of original sin. Humans attempt to become the creator to such an extent that God can only exist as creature, as one who supports and affirms the actualities of human praxis

---

32. "Jüngel maintains that while perishing is synonymous with a tendency toward nothingness, it cannot adequately be defined solely in these terms; there is a positive aspect to the concept. This he expresses in terms of the possible: 'that which is ontologically positive about perishability is the possibility.' On the basis of the theological appreciation of the ontological priority of the possible over the actual, there can be an 'ontological plus' in that which perishes: the power of the possible which inheres in the perished past. Jüngel draws upon the philosophy of Kierkegaard to express this further." Watts, *Revelation and the Spirit*, 59.

33. I daresay that this view of God has filtered into practical theology through the overattention to Aristotelian actuality.

(this has become the paradigmatic form of discussing divine action in practical theology, in my opinion).

Following Jüngel, I claim that actuality is a delusion. It is the illusion of sin; it is the teeth of deception, for God is absent in actuality but present as the event of God's being as becoming as possibility.[34] While God in Godself is an actuality (an actuality of three persons in one substance), the act of God comes to humanity not in actuality but as solely possibility (as the event of revelation). God's being as becoming out of nothingness means God encounters humanity always through possibility. The human creature has no access to God's own actuality but is given Godself through God's ministry of possibility through nothingness (ex nihilo and *in nihilo*). This was true for all ten people I interviewed.

The praxis of God, Christopraxis, stands in opposition to the actuality-to-possibility framework by asserting that all divine action encounters humanity not in the actuality of human actions or structures but in the possibility of God's ministry as being as becoming. Then, because God's being is in becoming, we encounter God never as frozen actuality but as possibility, as the one who transforms our nothingness into life, who takes what is dead and makes it alive, who comes at 2:35 a.m. to give new life out of the death of a dehumanizing job.

Praxis as action toward an actuality then can only be something that God does as the culmination of God's own ministry, in the full actualization of creation participating in God, unencumbered by sin in the *eschatos*. Praxis is Christopraxis because it is transformed from human actuality to the possibility of God's ministry through nothingness. *Only God can have praxis because only God possesses an actuality, an actuality of Godself as Trinity.* All human forms of praxis that are not transformed by the ministry of God, as participation in death for the sake of the possibility of life, are illusions because they seek to eliminate nothingness in the power of human praxis as actuality.

---

34. Jüngel explains his position, "As future possibility is the concrete way in which the world is determined by nothingness, out of which God's creative love lets being become. What can be made of the future on the basis of past and present does not belong to the dimension of possibility; rather, as that which is not-yet actual, it belongs to the dimension of actuality. What can be made does not become, in the strict sense of 'becoming ex nihilo.' We make actuality out of that which is actual. We change, we transform. In this way, we make the future. God, however, is not one who transforms; he is the creator, who allows possibility to move towards actuality. But this possibility arises from the divine distinction between the possible and the impossible, arises, that is, ex nihilo. The world's possibility is not within but external to its actuality. And its being is external to its futurity." *Theological Essays I*, 117.

"The Devilish Fellow"

Luther stood in opposition to Aristotle, saying pointedly (and humorously) as only Luther could, that while all the Greek philosophers are a problem for a biblical theology (and I would add for a practical theology that attends to God's ministry), Aristotle was a "particularly devilish fellow."[35]

And Aristotle was particularly devilish because of this very framework of actuality to possibility—that is, Aristotle's belief that human action could create for itself, that human action (works) could create the actuality of the human agent's righteousness and virtue. This perspective was devilish for Luther because, from the location of God's ministry as God's being as becoming, human actuality is impossible; there is no such thing as actuality between the divine and human.[36] God comes to us never as an actuality but always as possibility, as promise (which is why I said above that ministry is sharing the other's nothingness as prayer).

This means that if we are to be righteous, for Luther, it is never through human action but through divine gift; it is through transformation of what is not righteous that righteousness is given.[37] It is through justification! This is why Jüngel believes justification is the doctrine above all doctrines and why I am pushing so hard to make it central to practical theology. Justification is not simply a framework of God's abstract and cosmic legal state but is rather the assertion that God is a minister and that we encounter God only in possibility

---

35. Quoted in Jurgen Moltmann, *Theology of Play* (New York: Harper and Row, 1972).

36. Jüngel explains, "Luther objected on more than one occasion to the Aristotelian thesis that a person becomes righteous by doing right (i.e. by doing that which is righteous). 'We do not become righteous by doing righteous deeds but, having been made righteous, we do righteous deeds.' Or: 'We are not, as Aristotle believes, made righteous by the doing of just deeds, unless we deceive ourselves; but rather—if I may say so—in becoming and being righteous people we do just deeds. First it is necessary that the person be changed, then the deeds (will follow).' Already in his lectures on Romans of 1515/16, Luther insisted on drawing a distinction between the philosophical or juridical and the biblical use of the concept of *iustitia* (righteousness). Whilst philosophers and lawyers understand righteousness as a quality of the soul, in biblical usage righteousness depends more upon the imputation which God effects than upon actuality." *Theological Essays I*, 105.

37. Jüngel explains, "Even in Luther's early works we find the rejection of this opinion, which went back as far as Aristotle. Luther expressed this contradiction most clearly in his Disputation Against Scholastic Theology: 'We do not become righteous by doing righteous deeds but, having been made righteous, we do righteous deeds.' In the previous year, in a letter to Spalatin, Luther had given a name to the authority he was combatting: 'For we are not, as Aristotle believes, made righteous by the doing of just deeds, unless we deceive ourselves; but rather—if I may say so—in becoming and being righteous people we do just deeds. First it is necessary that the person be changed, then the deeds [will follow].'" *Justification*, 247.

through nothingness.[38] Justification is the articulation of the reality of divine and human encounter.

While Aristotle asserts that human beings can be righteous by actualizing the possibility of righteousness through their actions, Luther claims this as ridiculous, as devilish, for it makes divine action unneeded (or needed only as an example for human actualization).[39] The great gift of the gospel, of Jesus' own ministry (Christopraxis), is to give to humanity what humanity is not, to give us through the Spirit the gift of being children of God, to give humanity a new possibility born from what humanity is not, making humanity righteous while it is still sinful, giving life while yet we die.

For Luther and Jüngel, the human being is made righteous by being its opposite.[40] Human beings are righteous because God has encountered them,

38. Roland Spjuth explains, "Jüngel claims that justification implies a powerful attack on Western ontology which, since Aristotle, has celebrated the primacy of actuality and works. Such an understanding of being means a world enclosed within its present actuality and potential. In contrast, Jüngel emphasizes that justification by faith implies that the world lives by possibilities which actuality does not possess and which it can only receive as an external gift. From this perspective, the fundamental horizon of being is not actuality and human making but divine creativity that brings new possibilities into being *ex nihilo*. Jüngel strongly reinforces the disruption between present actuality and divine possibility by stressing that justification always happens as a divine judgment or annihilation of previous attempts to enclose being in actuality and production." "Redemption without Actuality: A Critical Interrelation between Eberhard Jüngel's and John Milbank's Ontological Endeavours." *Modern Theology* 14, no. 4 (October 1998): 507.

39. Jüngel discusses Luther, saying, "'*Prius necesse est personam esse mutatam*,' it is first necessary that the person be changed. The necessity of a change of being which is asserted here presupposes that Luther does not regard the unrighteous person as one who can equally determine him or herself to be righteous or unrighteouss for then it would be the *liberumorbitrium* (free will) which determined itself to act righteously or unrighteously. For Luther, however, the unrighteous person is one who is already unrighteous, that is, a sinner who, lacking the freewill which belongs to God alone, cannot make him or herself righteous through any human act. As a sinner, this already unrighteous person is one whose being is the radical negation of the being of the righteous person, not simply logically but ontologically." *Theological Essays I*, 106.

40. Watts further articulates Jüngel's position in relation to Luther and their shared aversion to Aristotle. "For Luther, the justification of the sinner comes through faith in the justifying, creative Word of God. Jüngel acutely perceives that this runs counter to the Aristotelian view of the priority of the actual; 'how can a person become righteous prior to that persons deeds?' Luther's doctrine speaks of a change of being prior to change of act. The being of an unrighteous person is unable to become righteous through any human act. There is 'the most radical antithesis between the unrighteous and the righteous person.' Thus the righteous, changed person can only be understood 'ex nihilo creata (created out of nothing).' This new creation is grounded in the creative Word of God. If the life of the unrighteous person is understood ontologically as a negation of being, then apart from the life giving Word of God, 'nothingness holds sway between the homo peccator (sinner) and the homo iustus (justified person).' It is through the event of the cross and the resurrection of Christ that the sin of

giving God's being as becoming, giving God's being by being their minister, ministering through their impossibility, so that they might have an all-new possibility born from divine action itself. Human beings are righteous because God's act has made them so (hiding them in Christ; Col. 3:3), and it has done this concretely, by meeting them in and through their nothingness (the cross) and turning it into life. Humans are justified, and therefore made righteous, not through human action but through the ministering act of God that again and again creates ex nihilo, giving us life in God's own being as God in the action of Jesus (Christopraxis) goes into nothingness.

So a Christopraxis practical theology of cross makes a broad leap away from Aristotelianism, *moving its perspective of practical theology from a framework of actuality to possibility to one of possibility through nothingness.*[41] "To think God in unity with perishability in the event of the cross is to think God in the midst of the struggle between possibility and nothingness, being and non-being. To speak of the death of God . . . is to proclaim that God has his being in the midst of the struggle and that even in the midst of perishing he is the living one."[42] It claims that a practical theology constructed on Aristotelianism, while appearing concrete and lived (because of its attention to the actuality of human action), is in the end an abstraction, and a deeply (devilishly) deceptive one at that.[43]

This is because Aristotle's perspective takes no account of the depth of sin and death that hangs so heavily on human action, keeping it from ever meeting

humanity is revealed; at the cross Jesus became sin for us. He thus manifests the true nature of sin yet also speaks the word of the Gospel to us. Jesus' resurrection from the dead promises a newness of life out of death and nothingness; we are created ex nihilo through faith in the Word of God. Thus 'Christian existence is existence out of nothingness, because it is along the line existence out of the creative power of God who justifies.'" *Revelation and the Spirit*, 55–56.

41. DeHart explains these contrasting frameworks, "But if possibility is the ultimate horizon of actuality, then according to Jüngel a new dichotomy is seen to surpass in ultimacy the old one: the distinction possible/impossible. Impossibility here must mean that nothingness or utter lack of relation out of which God creates and redeems. If the cross and resurrection of Jesus Christ are the keys to our knowledge of both the justifying God and the creator, then these events are also the keys to conceiving of possibilities which come to the world and to human beings 'from outside,' in other words, from God. The world cannot actualize itself in its totality, nor can the person actualize his or her own justification on the basis of previous actualizations. Ultimate possibility comes from God." *Beyond the Necessary God*, 112.

42. Watts, *Revelation and Spirit*, 60.

43. "Transitory being as the site of the struggle between possibility and nothingness—this is the locus of God's being. With this statement the ultimate foundation has been reached of Jüngel's ontological doctrine of God the creator and redeemer of creation. This is the result of a radical understanding of a theology of the crucified one, a theology which takes seriously 'God's self-identification with the dead man Jesus,' as Jüngel likes to phrase it." DeHart, *Beyond the Necessary God*, 121.

a telos that could save it, making human actualities ever tragic, for no matter how excellent they may be, they cannot turn death into life. They can't heal the wounds of Ron, Rachel, and Margo, who find the strength and love of God not in their own activity but in the care of the Spirit that comes to them as new possibility out of their concrete and lived experiences of nothingness.

So in the end, actuality ignores the concrete reality that we are not God, that we have no power to create actualities, and that this is the very deception of the garden itself. Ironically, this Aristotelian starting point is incongruent with the heart of practical theology itself. Practical theology has been deceived into thinking the abstract is concrete and the concrete abstract. Aristotlianism has pulled a devilish trick on practical theology. It has put practical theology in a cul-de-sac of seeking to articulate human actualities, keeping it so busy trying to do so that it has ignored the concrete realities of human impossibility and the wrestling with human nothingness. Aristotle has therefore kept practical theology's vision low to the ground where it fails to imagine concretely how the eternal moves into time, how reality is stratified and mysterious.

This also means that Aristotelian actuality lacks the depth of the lived because it takes no account of death, of the many experiences of nothingness that we live. It cannot bear the realities of broken marriages, lost children, grieving friends, and depressed states, for it looks not within these realities for new possibility (for redemption) but instead builds towers in Babel (Genesis 11), trying to reach heaven by its own action.

Conclusion

Only by turning to the framework of possibility through nothingness can we truly articulate the concrete and lived experience of human beings, and do so in such a way that divine encounter is a full-blown possibility (this is what I desired to do in chapter 3). It is here, in this framework of possibility and nothingness embedded in creation ex nihilo and justification *in nihilo*, that practical theology can attend to the depth of human and divine action, of time and eternity.

7

The Concurring of the Divine with the Human

Participation, Personhood, and the Concursus Dei in a Christopraxis Practical Theology

The last chapter concluded by recalibrating practical theology so that it might run not on the Aristotelian framework of human actuality to possibility but rather on the biblical and theological rails of possibility through nothingness—it is possibility through nothingness that embeds my Christopraxis perspective in the *theologia crucis*. On these rails, I argued, practical theology is not only allowed to move deeply into human experience (through *nihilo*) but also into divine encounter. In the framework of possibility through nothingness, eternity and time are joined while remaining differentiated. This joining of the divine and human is the act of ministry itself. God acts, eternity breaking into time, for the sake of ministry. God's being comes to humanity as God's ministry, as redemption from Egypt. God's name is "I am who is becoming" (Exod. 3:14), who is in ministry, grasping nothingness with both hands so that a new possibility, a promised land, might break forth.

God's being is given in the act of ministry in and through the possibility-through-nothingness framework: the Israelites have no potential or potency in their human action to create an actuality for themselves of freedom (Deut. 7:7). However, the eternal remains distinct from time—divine encounter as ministry cannot be conflated with human action in time, for all human action needs the justifying act of Godself given in ministry, most fully seen in the perishing of the cross (again, the *theologia crucis*).

This differentiation remains: God is minister and humanity remains always in need of justification, needing again and again for the ex nihilo to be reinstated so that God's ministerial act might come in and out of it. Nevertheless, there remains a sense, an invitation, a gift, of human participation in the divine, and this participation is shaped by God's being as becoming in ministry itself. It is shaped by Christopraxis; in and through the ministry of God through the humanity of the perishing Jesus we participate in God's being—that is, we experience redemption—as God participates in our own being.

PARTICIPATION AND PRACTICE THROUGH MINISTRY

We have pointed in the direction of participation a number of times in the last two chapters. I have asserted in both chapters that we share in God's being not by taking on God's actualized form (this is to confuse the Creator and creature) but by taking on the form of God's action, by sharing in it, by ourselves entering into ministry. Ministry itself opens up the possibility of the divine and human encounter. Christopraxis asserts that concrete and lived communities encounter the living Christ not as ideology or doctrine but as minister, as the one who comes to them as the event of new possibility in and through nothingness, ministering to them through the Spirit so that they might live in and with God. This is what Shirley, Lynn, and Margo describe when they state their sense of being "cared for" by God's presence.

Practical theology is fundamentally, at its disciplinary core, a field that studies living human documents. It must do so for the sake of ministry, yes, for the sake of health, revitalization, and justice, but these possibilities must be imagined not through the actuality of human effort but in dispositions of prayerful petition.[1] This means that practical theology studies living human documents first and foremost for the sake of articulating divine encounter, to confess and proclaim how human beings experience and participate in the event of God's becoming among concrete people like Ken, Ron, and Rachel.

Practical theology constructs and examines practices, but these practices must be formed around the possibility-through-nothingness framework, freeing them from human actuality (we'll see how Archer does this in part

---

1. Karl Barth shows how prayer is the linking of divine and human action but, as such, through ex nihilo. "Therefore Christian prayer is inevitably a confession of his own weakness and inability and unworthiness, of the whole lost condition in which he is discovered in the sight of God. It is an indication that his utterly empty hands are the only offering which he can bring before God and spread out before Him. . . . To pray in the Christian sense means to renounce all illusions about ourselves, and openly to admit to ourselves our utter need. The man who will not do this will never pray. The Pharisee in the temple had a heart which seemed to be full of praise and thanksgiving. But he did not do this and therefore he did not pray. We must necessarily pass through this humiliation if our worship of God is not to be self-deception." *Church Dogmatics* III.3 (Edinburgh: T&T Clark, 1960), 267.

3). Practices, from a Christopraxis perspective, are transformed by the act of ministry itself. In the possibility-through-nothingness framework, practices become profoundly the acts of ministry, and as the acts of ministry, they become participation in the being of God's becoming. So practical theology may study practices, but practices must be dislodged from the Aristotelian actuality-to-possibility framework that so quickly makes practices into social constructions used by human beings to justify themselves in religious acts, as a way for human action to create excellence as a human actuality.[2] Instead, practices must be seen as emotive actions that are for feeling our way into reality. Ministry consists in practices that provide the possibility of encountering the act and being of God's becoming. Ministry is thereby event.

Rather, for practice to be central to a Christopraxis practical theology of the cross, it must be placed in the service of ministry. Only by subordinating practice under ministry can it rest in the possibility-through-nothingness framework. Here, practices like prayer and baptism are first and foremost encounters with the divine being, with God's being as minister.[3] And because they are this, prayer and baptism inextricably rest in the possibility-through-nothingness framework, for this is the only way to encounter God's being as minister. Under the water you go into nothingness and out of it you come into new possibility. Prayer and baptism, to name just two, are *not* simply practices but are the concrete actions of God's becoming to us in ministry, and as concrete actions of ministry they invite us to participate in them. Our participation is not only as the one receiving but also as one giving, sharing "in" God by doing ministry in and through the possibility-through-nothingness framework, taking actions to join people's nothingness as a witness

---

2. This bears some resemblance to James Loder's understanding of practices needing to be negated so that the void can be negated and they can move us from two-dimensional reality to the four-dimensional reality.

3. Paul Nimmo explains that for Barth prayer is the shape of human action that joins divine action. "Barth explains that 'prayer is the most intimate and effective form of Christian action. All other work comes far behind, and it is Christian work …only to the extent that it derives from prayer, and that it has in prayer its true and original form. When the Christian wishes to act obediently, what else can he do but that which he does in prayer.'" *Being in Action: The Theological Shape of Barth's Ethical Vision* (Edinburgh: T&T Clark, 2007), 147-148. Nimmo continues, "For Barth, this act of petitionary prayer is 'man's modest participation in the work of Jesus Christ, in which it has indeed come to pass that this man has made God's cause utterly His own.' In this act, then, the ethical agent responds to her own election in Jesus Christ by herself electing to be in and for Jesus Christ. Barth writes that in this active invocation of God, the individual 'aims at the renewal, or rather, the dynamic actualization, of what has become a static, stagnant, and frozen relationship with God. While the relationship is never less than actualized from the divine side, it is in the act of invocation that it is actualized from the human side.'" Ibid.

and sacrament (true ministry) of the coming possibility through God's own being. This was the ministerial act of the cabbie to Rachel. He took on distinct practices of hospitality and care (giving her water and a hand on her shoulder), but these practices served the larger reality of ministry.

This all means that practical theology is not first and foremost a discipline that studies practice (as many leading scholars argue) but a discipline that reflects on ministry, seeing ministry, first, as divine action in concrete experiential communities, which leads, second, to seeing ministry as human actions (like preaching, caregiving, and youth ministry) that participate in the unfolding possibility of God's own ministerial action.[4] And this ministry is *not* just clerical but the very participatory action of all who experience divine encounter through nothingness.[5]

To understand the depth of ministry (from the divine and human sides) we may need to examine (sometimes empirically) practice. But to define practical theology as solely the study of practice is to succumb to a great temptation, and it is a temptation because practice has become a rich construct of discussion in philosophy and the social sciences.[6] Practical theology with its interdisciplinary origins should no doubt be in dialogue with these perspectives. But practice cannot be practical theology's heart, for such a view of practice takes no account of God's becoming and rests too squarely on the actuality-to-possibility framework.

---

4. Among those arguing that practical theology is foremost a discipline that studies practice, see Elaine Graham, *Transforming Practice: Pastoral Theology in an Age of Uncertainty* (London: Mowbray, 1996). Keith Johnson articulates wonderfully Barth's concern for the centrality of ecclesial practice. My concern with practice is very similar. Johnson explains, "The ecclesiological cost of this type of solution, however, proves to be too high, and this is especially evident when we consider this solution's effect on the form of the church's vocation. To see the nature of this problem, we turn to Barth's worry that an ecclesiology which focuses upon the mediation of God's grace through church practices inevitably makes the reception and possession of this grace the primary end of human action in the church. In his view, when the telos of the church is the facilitation of the ongoing reception, preservation, and cultivation of Christ's benefits in our lives, then the distribution of the benefits through ecclesial practices becomes the church's primary vocation. This is the action that "counts" in the church. The task of witnessing and proclaiming God's Word to those outside the church becomes secondary to the task of cultivating God's grace in the lives of those inside the church." "The Being and Act of the Church: Barth and the Future of Evangelical Ecclesiology," in *Karl Barth and American Evangelicalism*, ed. Bruce McCormack and Clifford Anderson (Grand Rapids, MI: Eerdmans, 2011), 224.

5. To see more concretely how prayer particularly allows for divine and human encounter as the shape of pastoral ministry, see chapters 13 and 14 of my book, *The Relational Pastor* (Downers Grove: IL: InterVarsity, 2013).

6. See Bourdieu, Certeau, and MacIntyre to name a few.

The heart of practical theology must be its concern for ministry; ministry is the rudder of the field, for it is ministry that allows for rich discourse of divine and human action in the concrete and lived. Ministry allows us to speak deeply of human action (even using the social sciences) but always within view of divine encounter. Ministry allows practical theology to center its attention on the participation of human action in the divine being, which is given to us as the one acting in ministry (Christopraxis).

MOVING FORWARD

Participation, then, must be the theme for the remainder of this chapter. If the last chapter focused on was justification as the heralding of human impossibility, then this chapter explores how impossibility becomes the counterintuitive doorway into participation in God's being. If the last chapter emphasized justification as the reinstating of nothingness, then this chapter underscores the possibility of life and redemption bound in participation in the being of God. For justification to be the core hermeneutic of Christian life, as I argued in the last chapter, and not simply a frozen doctrine, it must move us into the discussion of participation in and with God—that is, into the fullness of ministry.[7]

Therefore, this chapter will explore what has often been called in the tradition the *concursus Dei*, examining particularly Karl Barth's understanding of this perspective with the hope of showing more deeply how divine and human action can be imagined to come together as both act and being.[8] I will presume that because God is a minister, we participate in God's *being* through joining

---

7. The inability to connect justification with participation and its ramification can be seen in certain Lutheran confessional theological perspectives. Many of these perspectives have richly articulated justification. But because they do not connect this perspective in any way to participating in the divine being, their discussion of justification feels as welcoming as embracing a cold pole on a twenty-below day. Here I'm seeking, following Jüngel, to connect justification to participation, or one might say to connect justification to sanctification. Yet, too often sanctification has been seen as an outward, pietistic sign of justification. Rather, I'm replacing sanctification with participation because I'm contending that the response to justification is to participate in ministry as sanctification. The Lutheran tradition has called this vocation, yet I'm also avoiding this term because too often vocation has been understood as a way of acting that is unconnected in any dynamic way to participating in the divine being itself (and becomes functional as opposed to ontological). Participation in ministry of being as becoming through nothingness then seems the most helpful way of affirming in a new way sanctification and vocation.

8. There is a more than a little nod here to Dietrich Bonhoeffer's text *Act and Being*, in which he affirms and critiques the early Barth. I lack the space here to go into this critique but hope in this chapter to honor Barth's perspective while doing something constructive with it that moves beyond it.

God's *action*. But this process is circular: this action, because God's *being* is in becoming, means that joining God's action is *participating* in God's *being*.

I will work to bring act and being together in practical theology. Practical theology has done well in speaking of action (though most often human action because of its being trapped in the Aristotelian actuality-to-possibility framework), but it has done less well in speaking of being (whether divine or human). It would be an overstatement, but not by much, to claim that the formative projects in practical theology have been allergic to ontological conceptions.[9] The field's heavy dependence on philosophies of practice, Aristotelian *phronesis*, American pragmatism, forms of Marxism, and postmodern deconstruction has drawn it away from ontological conceptions, keeping it, in my mind, from attention to the *concursus Dei* and therefore making any talk of divine action thin and lacking an evangelical spirit (because in the end it cannot speak of the depth of being, of being toward death and nevertheless being made new; Col. 3:3).

Centering practical theology on ministry may avoid the problem of thin talk around divine action, but only if we will contend that ministry is the shape of divine and human encounter (the *concursus*), that ministry holds together and propels us deep into both act and being (full participation). Practical theology must assert, then, that human ministry is not simply functional, but revelatory (it reveals and leads to participation in the divine act and being); it is the movement into being (of neighbor and God) through act. This was Matt's experience: he feels God come to him, like never before, through the action of ministry for the least of these homeless men. Matt understands himself as participating in God's life as he shares in the being of these men—looking into their eyes. Human ministry moves into being as revelatory because human ministry's concrete actions in time *for persons* join God's own Trinitarian life—it is an event of concurrence. For God is ontologically a minister, first ministering to Godself as three hypostases in one *ousia*, and from this covenant of ministry (grace) within Godself, God gives Godself through action (called revelation) as the one *ousia* that is three hypostases ministers to creation as the event of becoming. Through encountering this action of revelation, we are given the gift of participating in the Trinitarian covenant of grace that is God's very being (*ousia*) as the act of love for three persons (*hypostasis*).

9. The allergy I believe has something to do with its disdain for "realism." As I already mentioned at the beginning of this project, I have no such allergy. In the next chapter I'll drive headlong into pushing practical theology in a "critical realist" direction. This form of realism not only connects nicely to the revelatory realism of my neo-Barthian perspective, but also makes ontology a central focus. The great exception to practical theology's allergy to ontology is John Swinton's work.

As human hypostasis, as persons in the imago of this ontological ministering God, we share in God's being by sharing in God's ministerial act of coming to, of being with, and of acting for persons, as Matt does with the homeless men and Sarah does with Erin.[10] As we will see through the Cappadocians and Zizioulas, personhood (hypostasis) as a differentiated and yet shared ontological reality allows for the dynamic participation of the human in the divine, for a deep and rich *concursus*.[11] Through human ministerial action both the one ministered to and the one ministering are taken up into the being of God (Matthew 25), finding themselves "in Christ," in Christopraxis as act and being. There is therefore at the heart of practical theology bound in ministry an attention to divine and human action, or the *concursus Dei*.

The Concursus Dei

The *concursus Dei* has incredibly important implications for the shape of practical theology. And yet in North America there appears to be no practical theological perspective that explores it. The *concursus Dei* is the Christian tradition's wrestling with how to relate "two seemingly incompatible notions: 'the lordship of God' and the 'free and autonomous activity of the creature.'"[12] In other words, the *concursus Dei* explores how human action can participate in divine action and yet to be considered free and autonomous—that is, truly human action.

This is not an easy association to tease out. Yet, if we retreat to the Aristotelian actuality-to-possibility framework, we are freed from any conundrum, for the divine being may be a reality, but divine agency itself becomes wrapped in synergism. Because human action knows no ex nihilo and

10. John Zizioulas explains, "The spirit of this image is precisely that in the Church a birth is brought about; man is born as 'hypostasis,' as person. This new hypostasis of man has all the basic characteristics of what I have called authentic personhood, characteristics which distinguish the ecclesial hypostasis from the first hypostasis, the biological one." *Being as Communion* (Crestwood, NY: St Vladimir's Seminary Press, 1985), 56.

11. I'm walking a thin line that moves me very close to the orthodox conception of *theosis*. I'll try to nuance this below, but in the end I'm not concerned to avoid it. This may lead some to think my heavy contention for justification through the Lutheran tradition is inconsistent. But this need not be so. Rather, here I'm tipping my hat to the Finnish interpretation of Luther and, in particular, to the work of Karkkainen. I am with many of my Lutheran colleagues in seeing the Finnish interpretation as a problematic historical argument—I'm doubtful that the historical Luther can be seen as *some* Finnish interpreters propose. But, I *do* think that the Finnish interpretation is an interesting and helpful constructive theological move that can be formative—for me it is formative in drawing practical theology more deeply into both justification à la Luther and participation à la Athanasius and the Cappadocians.

12. Johnson, "Being and Act of the Church," 209.

ontological language is bracketed out, deceiving us into believing that human action can create for itself its own actualities, God's act need not be discussed. Divine action associates with our own free action so fully that they are nearly inextricable. In the end this makes all human action, at least human action that appears to be excellent, as God's own. There is little need to talk about divine action in our churches or in practical theology because God concurs with the potency and potential of our own action. The *concursus Dei*, then, is the synergism of divine action with the power of the free human act.

If synergism is an ugly ditch to imagine the *concursus*, but one that practical theology has tended to construct its models within, there is another ugly ditch and one that practical theology has avoided intensely. Another way to imagine the *concursus Dei* is as determinism.[13]

If synergism claims, through Aristotelian actuality, that excellent human action is divine action, thus keeping divine action from having any "cause" of its own (a problem, as we will see below), then determinism does the reverse, stripping "cause" from human action, which is just as problematic. Synergism asserts that human action is the engine of any association between the divine and human, making divine action only the "amen" to the constructions of human-formed actualities. Determinism claims no (or incredibly limited) freedom or cause for the human agent; human forms of action are predetermined by the very script of God's heavy sovereignty. The human being concurs with God and therefore God with humanity by God simply determining all occurrences. The human being then may have the perception of freedom, but it is only an illusion because everything done concurs with God, for God determines it all.[14]

---

13. Barth has often been accused by practical theologians of destroying the freedom of human action in his bold statements of the divine. Yet, this is a misreading. For instance, Barth says, "God accompanies the creature. This means that He affirms and approves and recognizes and respects the autonomous actuality and therefore the autonomous activity of the creature as such. He does not play the part of a tyrant towards it. He no more wills to act alone than as the Creator He willed to be alone or as the Sustainer of the creature He affirms that He does not will to continue alone. Alongside Him there is a place for the creature. Alongside His activity there is a place for that of the creature. We even dare and indeed have to make the dangerous assertion that He co-operates with the creature, meaning that as He Himself works He allows the creature to work." *Church Dogmatics* III.3, 92.

14. There are ways that I'm stepping out of certain Lutheran commitments here and more into Reformed perspectives. My work has often been the balancing of these two significant traditions. It is a common Lutheran perspective to claim that "free will" is an impossibility. This assertion is made not because of rigid determinism and fetishing of God's sovereignty, but for anthropological reasons. There can be no free will because sin is a determinative power that traps the human being. My own anthropology, as indicated in the last chapter, is sensitive to this perspective. But even with this

The irony of determinism is that while it eliminates the possibility of human freedom in action, it can never truly live out concretely this perspective, for human existence is nearly impossible without some sense that one's actions are freely one's own. But the irony is doubled because, though it seeks to determine human action through the divine, asserting that human action is not free, in so doing it loses the agency and freedom of the divine as well. In "*concursus* determinism" God cannot move, God's being is not in becoming, for God is frozen by a determined script that God has created; God becomes the tragic, silly deity that cannot love because God is trapped by God's own determinism. Practical theology has rightly avoided this trap, but this avoidance has only pushed it further into the ditch of synergism.

The possibility-through-nothingness frame that shapes God's being as becoming is not attended to by either synergism or determinism. In synergism there is no need for justification because there is no ex nihilo, so if God exists at all, God's job is to concur with humanity (at times, this is wrongly called "incarnational").[15] But determinism, too, has no need for the ex nihilo reinstated by justification. For in determinism the Word is not creative; the Word itself cannot speak in and through the ex nihilo of human freedom, working life out of death. Rather, the Word is only a looped recording repeating a script that humanity cannot but concur with. The possibility-through-nothingness frame is lost, for the love that sends God out and *in nihilo* is not. Determinism has no place for Christopraxis because the living Christ's praxis in the world is too stiffly determined.

Because both synergism and determinism undercut justification, they allow for no possibility of participation. Synergism cannot participate in God because it has no need for the ontological otherness of God; it has little interest in being. And determinism cannot move into frameworks of participation because it has no sense of true act. God is not one that acts with and for, but a rigid computer programmer. So in neither synergism nor determinism can one participate with and in God, for one cannot encounter the being of God through the act of God. Neither synergism nor determinism can be a possibility for divine and human action—neither takes into account the centrality of hypostasis (personhood),

---

sensitivity, I believe it is necessary to have some conception of human freedom. Lutheranism may have had a hard time constructing its own rich methodologies of practical theology in part because of this inability to have room for human freedom. I hope in a small way to correct this, and to do so in conversation with Karl Barth.

15. See Bonnie Miller-McLemore, *Christian Theology in Practice: Discovering a Discipline* (Grand Rapids, MI: Eerdmans, 2012).

where, as we will see, act and being are held together as participation through justification.

BARTH AND THE CONCURSUS DEI

In *Church Dogmatics* III.3 Karl Barth takes up the discussion of *concursus*.[16] Continuing our move away from Aristotle, here Barth too stands in opposition to the "devilish" perspective of the philosopher.[17] Yet, while Barth will seek a path for divine and human action beyond the Aristotelian influence, he begins by affirming that Aristotle, and through him Thomas Aquinas, was right to explore divine and human action through the concept of "cause."[18]

To affirm "activity," for God to be a dynamic agent, as Christopraxis asserts, is to affirm cause. To speak of the action of God is to be moved to give account of the cause and impact of this action in encounter with free human agents, who also can take action that "causes" effects in the world (Exodus 32). To imagine God as minister is to speak of cause. Ministry encompasses cause because ministry is an action, and what it causes through its action is a participation in being through hypostasis. Nearly all the people I interviewed spoke of cause in relation to divine action. Greg heard God speak and it caused him to go to his friend, Sarah was caused to keep listening, and God's coming to Stanik caused him to leave his job. All the people spoke of divine action as real because it left the mark of cause, and because it did, it led them to see it as a real experience of God's ministry coming to them.

---

16. I am not interested here in simply repeating Barth's position but will take the audacious step to actually construct a perspective with Barth now as a direct dialogue partner. This means that the frameworks and even rhetorical movements I've made with Anderson and Jüngel come into play here as well. Therefore, the careful reader will notice that I'm speaking of Barth in a kind of Jüngelian way. I make no apologies for this. Most often Barth is the monolithic theologian (and for good reason) that sets the rhetorical flow for others. I've reversed that here.

17. Echoing again Luther's quote from the previous chapter.

18. "Face to face with the difficulty both schools, the Reformed no less than the Lutheran, made a formal borrowing at this point from a philosophy and theology which had been re-discovered and re-asserted at the end of the 16th to the beginning of the 17th centuries—the philosophy of Aristotle and the theology of Aquinas. The borrowing consisted in the adoption and introduction of a specific terminology to describe the two partners whose activities are understood and represented in the doctrine of the concursus in terms of a co-operation, the activity of God on the one side and that of the creature on the other. The concept which was adopted and introduced was that of 'cause.' For it was by developing the dialectic of this concept that they both effected the definition of themselves on the one side and the other, and also decided the difference which already existed at this point within the Evangelical faith itself. This, then, is the controlling concept for the form assumed by Evangelical dogmatics in this and in all kindred topics." *Church Dogmatics* III.3, 98.

If practical theology is to speak of the eternal breaking into time and if justification as the reinstating of the ex nihilo is central, then we must affirm that divine action itself has "cause." It causes life to spring from death; it causes a participation of human being in the divine being; it causes mothers to find comfort and children peace. When eternity breaks into time, it leaves a mark! It causes dead wombs to bring forth life and stutterers to lead and liberate—it gives new (baptismal) being (2 Cor. 5:17). The *concursus Dei* is the wrestling with the "cause" of the eternal in time; there can be little more central to practical theology, for this cause impacts the concrete and lived.[19]

Yet, as we said earlier, it appears that practical theology has avoided the *concursus Dei*, steering clear of "cause" by wrapping itself in the blanket of synergism. Wanting to appear scientific, practical theology has embraced synergism's wish not to speak of God's free action, for it fears the ambiguity (and university disdain) of divine cause. Ignoring Aristotle's discussion of "cause," established practical theology sticks to the excellence of human action toward a telos. Practical theology has tended through its focus on practice and empirical studies to move past conversations surrounding divine "cause" unless that cause is locked within socially constructed realities of human action. Human action but not divine can have "cause." Evangelical communities (again, defined either broadly or narrowly) cannot affirm this, for they, in lived and concrete ways, desire to speak and live from the *experienced* action of God in their lives as true "cause." Jesus has come to them and "caused" transformation.

On the other extreme, determinism, while appearing to have no fear of divine cause or any need to appear scientific, fears the "cause" of human action contaminating its dogmatic models of sovereignty and perfection of deity. Both perspectives, then, violate the *concursus Dei* by eliminating "cause," which in turn opposes either the freedom of God or the freedom of the human being. It is my contention that practical theology, as attention to the concrete and lived,

---

19. Barth explains "cause": "It is ostensibly a question of the relation between the divine activity and the creaturely. But activity means *causare*. Activity is movement or action has as its aim or object a specific effect. To act means to bring about an effect. The subject of such *causare* is a *causa*, in English, a 'cause,' something without which another and second thing either would not be at all, or would not at this particular point or in this particular way. A *causa* is something by which another thing is directly posited, or conditioned, or perhaps only partly conditioned, that is, by which it is to some extent and in some sense redirect and therefore altered. Now if we are speaking of the activity, and therefore the *causare*, of God and the creature, then wittingly and willingly or not, we are describing and thinking of both of them in terms of *causa*. And at once we have to begin our manipulation of the dialectic of the concept, and it was in this process that the older dogmaticians found inspiration and guidance in Aristotle and Thomas. For quite obviously God is a *causa* in one sense, and the creature in quite another." *Church Dogmatics* III.3, 98.

must affirm "cause" both in the realm of human experience (agency/structure) and divine action (revelation).

DANGERS OF "CAUSE"

Barth is willing to affirm the Aristotelian conception that the discussion of *concursus Dei* must not turn from "cause." However, Barth explains that, once affirming this point, we can go no further with the philosopher, for in so doing we risk three misunderstandings: (1) causality, (2) things, and (3) genus being.

(1) *Causality.* The first misunderstanding is to lock "cause" and therefore the *concursus Dei* into causality, into a sense of natural inevitability. Nature, it appears, is made up of principles of causality. Objects fall from a table because of the causality of gravity; people die and get sick because of the causality of germs, atrophy, and time. Causality is the principle of cause as determined by nature.

Divine action in this misunderstanding is reduced to the principles of the natural. To confuse "cause" in the *concursus Dei* as causality is to peer at natural phenomena and expect divine action to concur with the laws and precepts of time itself. To lock "cause" into causality is to make divine action subject to nature. God, then, exists under the domain of the natural. Human action and divine action *can* concur because both are subject to the natural causality.[20] Aristotle's gods can tragically be pinned by the same natural forces that upend human beings; these pagan gods of the Greek tradition no doubt cause things, but nature also pins its cause on them.

Such a perspective needs almost no discussion to be seen as problematic. It may be possible in this perspective to contend that God is still above the natural, that God remains the creator but has nevertheless chosen to succumb to its principles so that God might concur with humanity.[21] But we cannot follow this perspective in a Christopraxis practical theology of the cross because

---

20. Barth explains, "If we had no choice but to think of *causa* or cause as the term is applied in modern science, or rather natural philosophy, with all its talk about causality, causal nexus, causal law, causal necessity and the like, then clearly it is a concept which we could not apply either to God or to the creature of God, but could only reject. That was how A. Ritschl understood the term, and in consequence he conceded that the whole doctrine of the *concursus* has to be dismissed, as though it stood or fell with this particular understanding of cause. As he saw it, the idea of God cannot be squared with the scientific explanation of nature. And therefore we should be doing violence to God if 'under the concept cause we compared Him with natural causes which can be understood by observation.' . . . The *causa prima* as they envisaged it cannot easily be identified with a natural cause which can be understood by observation." Ibid., 101.

21. Some process theology makes similar claims, and this is the position of panentheism.

we have already claimed that justification is the central hermeneutic of divine action that seeks participation as an all-new possibility, holding to a distinction between the creature and Creator.

Therefore, divine action is God's being as becoming through the framework of possibility through nothingness.[22] Possibility through nothingness is an event (of God's becoming) that penetrates the natural, throwing its determinative power into question. In the framework of possibility through nothingness, the "cause" of God is to give to human beings the impossible—to give to Sarah a child though her womb is dead (Genesis 21), to give new life through participation in the divine being itself. God's very ministry comes from eternity and therefore moves over and against the causality of the natural. God's being is given in the act of a bush that burns but is not consumed. When the act of God's coming is witnessed, the natural is reversed, the dead live. God's ministry is to overcome the determinative power of the causality of the natural.

(2) *Things.* This very perspective also moves us away from the second misunderstanding or danger of exploring "cause" in relation to divine and human action. This second danger, Barth explains, is to lock God and the creature into "things" or "objects." This misunderstanding of the *concursus Dei* as the concurring of "things" is constructive for us. Barth explains that if divine and human action truly do associate, and associate with the depth of true cause, then this relation of cause must *not* be between objects but rather between distinctive (asymmetrical) and yet bound subjects.

Here Barth asserts that any talk of the *concursus Dei*, any way to explore divine and human action, must affirm the hypostatic character of the divine and human. Any *concursus* must not be imagined as objects in association, but as persons in relationship.[23] *Personhood itself allows for freedom in union.* It allows

22. It is interesting that in the volume of *Church Dogmatics* (III.3) in which Barth discusses the *concursus Dei*, he also ends the volume by discussing nothingness, which is a kind of picture of our movement between justification and participation. "Why is it that the being of the creature is menaced by nothingness, menaced in such a way that it needs the divine preservation and sustaining and indeed deliverance if it is not to fall victim to it and perish? Obviously it is menaced by something far more serious than mere non-being as opposed to being, although it is of course menaced by non-being too. But what makes non-being a menace, an enemy which is superior to created being, a threatened destroyer, is obviously not its mere character as non-being, but the fact that it is not elected and willed by God the Creator but rather rejected and excluded. It is that to which God said No when He said Yes to the creature. And that is chaos according to the biblical term and concept." *Church Dogmatics* III.3, 76.

23. "But the concept *causa* does not merely describe activities, but acting subjects. And between the two subjects as such there is neither likeness nor similarity but utter unlikeness. We cannot deduce from the fact that both subjects are *causa* the further fact that they both fall under the one master-concept

for freedom and yet participation—essentials for the *concursus Dei*—and freedom and participation that stretch to the ontological level.[24]

Personhood is the very transformation of freedom from the framework of actuality to possibility to the framework of possibility through nothingness. Freedom in the framework of actuality to possibility is, to follow Zizioulas, the freedom to negate. It is to imagine freedom as the ability to actualize oneself, to be free from *all* constraints to do and be what one wants (to meet the telos one aims for), to create for oneself the actuality one wishes.[25] One is free to take actions to actualize the excellence one desires. One is free to do this as an individual free thing, seeking individual freedom, making all in the world also objects or things, making God the object, the idol, which magically helps one get the things one wants.

To follow the Aristotelian actuality-to-possibility framework comes with the great danger of turning everything into objects and things.[26] Because the human being can actualize a possibility through excellent action (goals), a telos becomes the objectified end that need not take account of personhood, making everything a thing in the world attainable through excellent action.[27] This is why Barth cannot go with Aristotle and why we have advocated for imagining God's action through the framework of possibility through nothingness. This framework, as I will show below, makes hypostasis, personhood, central and the very heart of the concurrence of the divine with the human.

causa; that they may both be reduced to that one common denominator; that they are both species belonging to the one genus. On the contrary. They cannot even be compared." Ibid., 103.

24. Zizioulas adds texture to this perspective, "The fact that causation in God has nothing to do with divine substance or nature, but only with his personhood, shows that true personhood in humans as 'images of God' must be free from the necessity of nature if it is to achieve otherness. Freedom from nature and dependence on the person is a lesson learnt from divine causality." *Communion and Otherness*, 142.

25. "All this means that personhood creates for human existence the following dilemma: either freedom as love, or freedom as negation." Ibid., 46. Zizioulas discusses this further on 46ff.

26. "If the term *causa* is to be applied legitimately, care must be taken lest the idea should creep in that in God and the creature we have to do with two 'things.' The German word for cause . . . might easily suggest this. A 'thing' or 'object' is something which in part at least is perceptible and accessible to man. If we have to do with a 'thing' then this means that even if only defectively we believe that we are capable of examining, recognising, analysing and defining, in short of 'realising' it, and in some degree we know how to control it. But neither God nor the creature is a *causa* in this sense." Barth, *Church Dogmatics* III.3, 101.

27. "All theology is a meditation about God and the creature. But since it meditates and speaks about them they are always in danger of becoming things. . . . Now when the Aristotelian dialectic of the causal concept was applied to the operations of God and the creature, did it not to some extent involve thinking and speaking about them in that way?" Ibid., 102.

Yet the trap of objects through the actuality-to-possibility framework, as Zizioulas has shown, leads to only one end, which stands in radical opposition to participation, the affirming of personhood, and God's ministry of giving life through impossibility. To imagine freedom as to be "free from" (to pick up Luther's language) is, at its extreme, to negate any subject, even yourself, that stands in opposition to you. And the human being as creature can only negate that which it has made into an object, into a thing, and it is negated because as thing it is a threat to freedom. When freedom is bound in objects, then objects that oppose freedom need to be negated, for whatever stands in opposition to me being free must be eliminated.

Zizioulas states that this perspective of freedom through things leads finally, if one is ever brave enough to follow it all the way down, to suicide. For there is no way to truly actualize the fullness of freedom in the lived concrete world until one chooses to truly become god for oneself by negating oneself so that one is no longer contingent or constrained by others. One's very life, Zizioulas shows, is gift, but one is not free to choose it; no one freely decides to be born or to even breathe. Thus, to be truly free from contingency and free from others (to lock freedom in the realm of objects and things) is finally to negate oneself. This is why Sartre is quite right, that if freedom is to be free from (if it is bound in the world of objects—something unchristian), then "other people are hell," for other people always remind us that we are not free, that we are not God. And the only way to truly be free in a world of things, in a world not made up of persons, is to negate oneself or live always in opposition and competition with others—to never do ministry as participation.

Yet, the freedom of *concursus Dei*, Barth asserts, is not one of objects and things but of persons (hypostasis); it is the cause of human person to divine Person, of divine Person to human person. Freedom is not to be free from, but to be free for. This is the heart of *concursus Dei*; it is the mutual but distinct (asymmetrical) freedom of divine and human agents to be for each other, to participate in and with each other.

To follow Zizioulas again, freedom rests not on negation but on *love*, where one is given life and true freedom through participating in the personhood of another.[28] Love asserts that we are subject, hypostasis, and that God is too. Objects cannot love; only self-revealing subjects can concur with

---

28. "Freedom in this sense is ontological, not moral, that is, it springs from the very way the hypostases are constituted, with the person of the Father being the initiator at once both of personal being and of freedom, that is, of ontological otherness in the Trinity, if freedom is to be understood ontologically, that is, as the freedom to be oneself, uniquely particular, and not as a freedom of 'choice,' which would in any case be inappropriate for the Trinity." Zizioulas, *Communion and Otherness*, 122.

each other's lives, can participate in each other's being through acts of love, can accompany a woman into a morgue. To think of cause in the *concursus Dei* is to think of the loving action (the ministry) done with and for persons, the kind of actions that invite, that cause, the beloved to participate and to share in the being of the other. "As a person," Zizioulas says, "you exist as long as you love and are loved. When you are treated as nature, as a thing, you die as a particular identity."[29]

The *concursus Dei*, divine and human action, is bound in the love of persons—Greg goes to his grieving friend with a word from God because he loves him. Love reveals that true freedom is found in binding one to another, but this binding is freedom, not jail, because it is the binding of free subjects in the joy of being free for each other, of participating deeply in each other's very being through the actions of ministry, through the action of joining nothingness for the sake of the new possibility that love can bring.[30] This is why Jüngel claims so forcefully that God is love—God is found between possibility and nothingness, giving Godself to nothingness as the act of love. Love births new possibility in the realm of human-to-human ministry, and this is so because God's ontological state is love (1 John 4), a love that goes out from and into nothingness so that we might participate in the love that is the divine being, that is the three hypostases in one *ousia*.[31]

In the light of a Christopraxis practical theology of the cross this is essential, for God's being is in the becoming of ministry; God is, as Anderson asserts, first and foremost a minister. And as minister, God reveals Godself not as thing but as self-revealed subject of love, who is ontologically constituted as love, whose being and act are fused in the ministry of giving Godself to humanity for the sake of love, for the sake of true participation. And God's revealing of Godself comes as the ministry of the giving of Godself to human subjects; the Word that is God in pure subjectivity, encountering the human being that is no thing, but also a subject, though different from the Word. When Greg, Sarah, Matt, and Ken experience divine action in ministry, they are led to see those they are called to as persons to love. When encountering their person—"looking into their eyes," as Matt says—they know the ministry of God to be coming to them.

29. Ibid., 167.

30. "Since something can come out of nothing, ex nihilo, it can be both real and other in the absolute sense. The doctrine of creation out of nothing was about otherness and freedom in ontology." Ibid., 18.

31. Zizioulas too claims this, stating, "It thus becomes evident that the only exercise of freedom in an ontological manner is love. The expression 'God is love' (1 John 4:16) signifies that God . . . subsists . . . as Trinity, that is as person and not as substance. . . . Therefore, as a result of love, the ontology of God is not subject to the necessity of the substance. Love is identified with ontological freedom." Ibid., 46.

Matt understands himself as participating in God's ministerial action when he shares in the life of the homeless.

The *concursus Dei*, then, must not only avoid natural causality but must also affirm subjectivity. God concurs with us not as impersonal force (of synergism or determinism) but as subject, as person. The cause of divine action must take the form of subject encountering subject, of sharing, of participating in the subjectivity, in the personhood, of the other. It then is no surprise that those Luhrmann (see *When God Talks Back*) and I interviewed spoke of God in very practical ways.

We are not talking about a disconnected conception of activity but the movement of active subjects, of persons in relation—pushing us into the lived and concrete of practical theology. Ministry becomes central because ministry is the action of active subjects, sharing in the life of another, not to bring in a cause from outside the subjects but for new possibility to be birthed (to be caused) from the loving sharing of nothingness—from communicating to a nine-year-old Shirley that she is cared for as she faces the nothingness of illness.

(3) *Genus Being.* This then leads to the final of the three misunderstandings and one that helps to balance the discussion above. In the second misunderstanding I made a strong claim that both the divine and human must be seen as subjects, that hypostasis, personhood, is central to both human being and divine being, that "cause" in *concursus Dei* is experienced within personhood itself. This perspective will have to be teased out more below as we explore a Cappadocian anthropology for practical theology, locating personhood as the place of divine and human encounter and further infusing ontological language into a Christopraxis practical theology of the cross.

Yet, in this third misunderstanding we must safeguard against any overstatements regarding those ideas. Barth calls this third understanding the mistake of "genus" being.[32] To assert that both the divine and human are impacted by "cause," that as free persons they mutually (but not symmetrically) impact each other, runs the risk of assuming that both the divine and the human actually exist under the same genus—in other words, that the divine and human are two beings under the same species, two beings equally impacted by cause. This, Barth contends, makes "cause" the sovereign power in the world.

Rather, it is important to assert that cause itself is distinct, that "cause" exists under the free subjectivity of both divine and human persons. This then

32. Barth explains, "But if this was so, then necessarily they would come under a single master-concept, they would form part of a single genus, they would be reducible to a single common denominator. And we could only conclude that we are not really dealing with God and the creature and their mutual co-operation." *Church Dogmatics* III.3, 104.

forces us to see the divine and human as two distinct (unlike) subjects, one whose cause is bound in time and another's whose cause is the event of eternity breaking into time.[33]

So for Barth there is no one kind of "cause" but rather differentiated "causes." That is to say, there is divine cause and human cause. Both exist as true cause, having true impact on the subjectivity of God or humanity, but their cause is not of the same species. Divine cause is not the same as human cause in *concursus Dei* because just as human beings share the image of the divine as hypostasis, this sharing of image reveals that they are not equal. They correspond but not in the same way.[34]

This is the ultimate problem that Barth sees with Aristotle, moving Barth, like Luther, to see him as "devilish." What makes him "devilish" is that the "absolute unlikeness [of divine and human being and act] was not safeguarded."[35] Barth makes such a strong assertion of unlikeness not to backtrack from the assertion surrounding subjects but to fortify it. The unlikeness allows both (distinctly) to be self-revealing subjects. To speak of "cause" is not simply to describe generic activities but acting subjects, and these subjects have their being in the qualitatively different realms of time and eternity.[36]

---

33. Zizioulas explains, showing a strong connection between his position and Barth's at this level, "What divine causality teaches us is that personal otherness is not symmetrical but a-symmetrical. There is always in this otherness a 'greater' one, not morally or functionally but ontologically. Otherness is, by definition, 'hierarchical,' since it involves absolute specificity emerging not from qualities—as is the way with natural otherness—but from the gift of love as being and being other: we are not 'other' by ourselves but by someone else, who in this way is, 'higher,' that is, onto logically 'prior' to us, the giver of our otherness." *Communion and Otherness*, 143.

34. "Hierarchical ordering is inherent in personhood, all personal relations being onto logically a-symmetrical, since persons are never self-existent or self-explicable, but in some sense 'caused' by some 'other,' by a 'giver' who is ontologically 'prior' and, in this sense, 'greater' than the recipient." Ibid., 144.

35. Ibid., 103.

36. Barth states, "If the term *causa* is to be applied legitimately, it must be clearly understood that it is not a master-concept to which both God and the creature are subject, nor is it a common denominator to which they may both be reduced. *Causa* is not a genus. Of which the divine and creaturely *causa* can then be described as species. When we speak about the being of God and that of the creature, we are not dealing with two species of the one genus being. When we speak about the divine nature and the human nature of Christ, we are not dealing with two species of the one genus nature. And so, too, in this case, to put it rather differently, it must be clearly understood that when the word *causa* is applied to God on the one side and the creature on the other, the concept does not describe the activity but the active subjects. And it does not signify subject, which are not merely not alike, or not similar, but subjects which in their absolute antithesis cannot even be compared." Ibid., 102.

Within these two realms of time and eternity we see "cause" as qualitatively distinct. What is shared by divine and human act and being is that all "cause" is the result of acting subjects (it is real). What is distinct is that the act and being of God and humanity are not equal (they exist in different strata of reality). As we've said, humanity, as the image of God, is hypostasis as God is hypostasis, but God's very being as constituted as the hypostases of Father, Son, and Spirit means that all "cause" within Godself that therefore breaks into the world comes as event of personal encounter (ministry) but is grounded in itself. It is still fully relational, affirming subjectivity, for Godself is the relationship of three in one, but divine action is also "self-grounded, self-positing, self-conditioning, and self-causing," for unlike human subjects who can have their being only in and through others (through friendship as John Swinton has asserted), God's being has no contingency because God in Godself is the relationship of pure subject.[37]

Because the human being is made subject by what is constituted outside the self, any human action that has "cause" *cannot* be self-actualizing; to act, the human being must find an ontologically distinct counterpart. Bound in time, the human being needs ontologically what it is not for it to be. Any human cause is contingent on the otherness of distinct subjects to have its being (this is the difference between the creature and Creator and why ex nihilo is gift, for it reminds the creature of the need for others, of being made to be free for others to need a minister).[38]

Divine "cause" is free from this contingence, for God has no ontological need outside Godself; God needs no ontological other to give God being, for God is Trinity. And as Trinity, God remains subject. The very subject relation that constitutes hypostasis for humanity exists outside it, but for God this relation exists in the same *ousia*. Humanity is only the image of God and not God, for the ontological constitution of being in relations exists outside of humanity's *ousia*, but God is fully and unequivocally a being who is relation, whose hypostasis is not bound in distinct *ousia* but rather is in the same *ousia*. This makes divine "cause" distinct. It makes divine cause the breaking in of eternity into time, for eternity is the being of God as the hypostasis of three in one *ousia* acting within time. The very divine cause is the act of God's

---

37. Ibid., p. 103. See John Swinton, *Resurrecting the Person: Friendship and the Care of People with Mental Health Problems* (Nashville: Abingdon, 2000).

38. "Now, for the [church] Fathers, the world's being was fully and truly being, but it was, of its nature, a perishable being: having come out of nothing, it could return to nothing and perish. Such a position would be scandalous to the ancient Greeks, who could never conceive of being as ultimately perishable; even in the Platonic idea of non-being, there is eternal survival of being thanks to participation in the being of the One." Zizioulas, *Communion and Otherness*, 18.

hypostatic being becoming to humanity. Revelation as divine act is revealing, distinct causing, of the event of divine hypostasis unleashed in time, showing the distinct causing of a participation of the human hypostasis in the divine being through the shared hypostasis of Jesus Christ, through Christopraxis.

Toward the Second Article to Get to Cause

Practical theology focuses on the concrete and lived; it attends deeply to experience. Yet, it has not attended enough, in my opinion, to people's concrete and lived experiences of divine cause, of the impact of divine action. I have tried to move in this direction and to do so by turning to the *concursus Dei*, exploring misunderstandings and shortcomings of practical theology in imagining (or neglecting to imagine) the relation of divine and human act and being. We have followed Karl Barth in this conversation but only so far as to see the problems of the *concursus Dei*. It is now time to turn more directly into construction, which will move us through justification into participation and connect us with the experiences of those in chapter 3.

If "cause" remains a significant piece of the *concursus Dei*, and the *concursus Dei* an important element of practical theology, then how does Barth imagine it outside the "misunderstandings" he has identified?

Not surprising for the reader of Karl Barth, he begins tackling this issue by exploring the act and being of Jesus Christ.[39] In other words, Barth begins, to take him into my own project, with Christopraxis. Barth explains that to understand divine cause, to explore how the divine and human act and being relate, is to turn from the first article of the creed to the second.[40] It is to explore

39. Keith Johnson draws out this focus of Barth on the second article, but beautifully shows how Barth's perspective is similar to the Christopraxis perspective I've articulated above. Johnson states, "The picture Barth paints is this: Jesus Christ, the one who was crucified at Golgotha there and then, lives and reigns as the resurrected one here and now. As the living one, Christ is not idle in the world but active. By the power of the Holy Spirit, he is active in proclaiming here and now the work of reconciliation accomplished there and then, Jesus Christ alone is 'authorized and competent' to proclaim this Word of God, but 'he does not will to be alone' in this proclamation. Through the power of the Spirit, he summons Christians to serve as heralds who proclaim this Word of God alongside him." "The Being and Act of the Church," 222.

40. "As the doctrine of the *concursus* and indeed the whole doctrine of providence is expounded there must be a clear connexion between the first article of the creed and the second. If the causal concept is to be applied legitimately, its content and interpretation must be determined by the fact that what it describes is the operation of the Father of Jesus Christ in relation to that of the creature. Basically, the doctrine of the *concursus* must be as follows. God, the only true God, so loved the world in His election of grace that in fulfillment of the covenant of grace instituted at the creation He willed to become a creature, and did in fact become a creature, in order to be its Saviour. And this same God accepts the

the Father who creates ex nihilo, by giving attention to the Son who goes *in nihilo*, by making the incarnate move of the Creator (the Word) becoming the creature (the perishing Jesus). This, Barth contends, keeps us from rigid forms of determinism or soft forms of synergism, pushing us to explore all forms of concurrence through participation of time and eternity that nevertheless allow for their distinction.

This move of Christopraxis, to give Barth my language, is for the divine to bear the human; *it is for the divine to enter into ministry, the divine act to be ministry*. The divine cause remains distinct, but because it fully shares with humanity in Jesus Christ (as distinct subject), it moves the "totally other" God to be minister. Christopraxis reveals unequivocally that God's being is in the becoming of ministry.

Barth's perspective of God may be as "totally other," but this totally other God radically encounters us as subject because this God is subject, "causing" concrete and lived experiences of participation (reconciliation). These experiences are events of encounter, encounter with the very ministering love of God. God is love because God is minister, revealing Godself in events of the Subject encountering subject, of divine hypostasis encountering human hypostasis through ex nihilo (justification). But this encounter that goes through nothingness (that justifies) is for the purpose of participation, for the human to be ministered to by God that he or she might share in the life of God (Col. 3:3).[41] I experience the personhood of Jesus come to my scared person in the hole, loving me and telling me to run and then to go and tell that God has ministered to my person through the person of Jesus that met me in nothingness to give me God's very self.

This participation is bound in act and being. As we will see in the next few paragraphs. we participate in God by joining God's action, by becoming ministers as God's *being* is in the becoming of ministering *action*. But this ministering act is always through the possibility-through-nothingness framework (justification), keeping participation from being constituted in

---

creature even apart from the history of the covenant and its fulfillment. He takes it to Himself as such and in general in such sort that He co-operates with it, preceding accompanying and following all its being and activity. So that all the activity of the creature is primarily and simultaneously and subsequently His own activity, and therefore a part of the actualization of His own will revealed and triumphant in Jesus Christ." *Church Dogmatics* III.3, 105.

41. Zizioulas says beautifully, "For God constitutes the affirmation of being as life 'eternal life,' and is not 'God of the dead, but of the living!' (Matt. 22:32). And this means that theology, unlike philosophy, teaches an ontology which transcends the tragic aspect of death without in the least accepting death as an ontological reality, death being the 'last enemy' of existence (I Cor. 15:26)." *Being as Communion*, 48.

human agency (works righteousness). Human ministry is true ministry; it participates in the being of God, for God has invited us to join God's being through the act of ministry itself, through being ministered to and therefore joining (participating) in ministry—this was the case for Matt, Sarah, and Greg. "As the creature works in time, the eternal God works simultaneously in all the supremacy and sovereignty of His working. The *concursus divinus* is a *concursus* simultaneous."[42] And this simultaneous work is that of ministry itself.

But, as Barth's words point out, all human forms of ministry, while true invitations to join in God's being by sharing in the being of the one ministered to, cannot be confused as the same species as God's ministry. Human forms of ministry are done in time and therefore must always stand under and be locked within the possibility-through-nothingness frame—Greg goes to the nothingness of his grieving friend, Sarah to the nothingness of Erin's experience of her parents' divorce, and Matt to the nothingness of the men's homelessness.

But divine action, God's own ministry, comes from eternity, and though it comes through justifying action of possibility through nothingness, it constitutes a reconciliation that ontologically takes those ministered to through the nothingness of their own hypostasis and into the divine hypostasis, into the very being of God. Human actions of ministry cannot perform at this ontological level of participation in themselves. Human actions of ministry can only witness to God's own action, which is to join all human forms of ministry so that such actions might have ontological impact, but ontological impact only because the divine cause joins them (those I interviewed spoke of their action being taken up into God's own action—Sarah hears God directing her in her acts of ministry to just listen). Through the Spirit, the divine cause joins human actions of ministry taking those ministering and being ministered to through justification (possibility through nothingness) into participation with the being of God, to hide human being in the Trinitarian being of Godself.

This no doubt is to move Barth into deeper conversation with the patristic fathers (particularly Athanasius and the Cappadocians).[43] I will have more to say

---

42. Barth, *Church Dogmatics* III.3, 132.

43. Peter Leithart gives a definition of participation through Athanasius. This is a perspective I'm following: "For Athanasius, participation has a number of additional implications. Participation always involves a share in something external. Participation and externality go together; the participated (original) and the participant (i.e., the derived) are divided from each other and are usually divided ontologically. That which participates and that which is participated are not just different beings but different sorts of beings. Athanasius does little with the Platonic doctrine of ideas and makes little use of the technicalities of the modified Platonisms with which he was glancingly familiar. But he uses the concept from Plato and plugs it into a biblical worldview, that is, a worldview that distinguishes Creator and creature. In place of participated forms, then, Athanasius has a Creator. Creatures exist by

in this regard below. For now it is enough to point to the linking of act and being in the concrete and lived experiences of ministry. And this linking of act and being is seen as love. Love is the ontological constitution of God (1 John 4:8) that binds act and being; love moves to subjects as act but through act opens being to the other. Love is an ontological reality that we participate in only and always through action. Love is a cause that acts for participation—to not say anything but just be with another as ministry, as Erin speaks of the pain of divorce.[44]

So, the divine cause enters time and space for the sake of loving accompaniment, so that human subjects might participate in the divine subject but do so through the action of ministry. Because God's being is in the action of ministry, we participate in the divine being by sharing in divine action, by entering into ministry as the fellowship of action. This fellowship of action holds to the asymmetry (distinction) of "cause." Human action is bound in impossibility; it sits in the framework of possibility through nothingness. But because the divine is the action of ministry, which comes out and goes into *nihilo*, human action that does the same—that is, *confesses its nihilo* for the sake of participating in the hypostasis, participating in subjects as persons—is bound in the fellowship of ministerial act with God. This is what we saw with Matt; participating in the homeless ministry, sharing in the person of those on the streets, drew him into deep experience of God's presence.

LOVING ENCOUNTER OF SUBJECTS

The *concursus Dei* then takes the shape of loving encounter of distinct subjects because God is love (ontologically; 1 John 4:16). Divine cause is itself the ministry of love and as such is primary. Human action is response to divine love. As love it is free and truly independent (it is free for God and humanity), but as love it is inconceivable outside of response (it is free-for). And though God remains the primary source of action because, unlike us, God *is* love, our very

participation in God because creation is not part of God's existence nor internal to him." *Athanasius* (Grand Rapids, MI: Baker, 2011), 66.

44. Zizioulas's perspective here will be informative as I continue to develop this argument. "So, the Christian God does not create because he loves the beautiful and wants to give form and beauty to the world. He creates because he wills something else to exist other than himself, 'something' with which to have dialogue and communion. He creates because he wants to give existence to something which in no way existed before (hence, creation from ontologically absolute nothingness). The creative act of the Christian God is essentially an ontological act, properly constituting another existence. The creative act of Plato's god is essentially an aesthetic act, the giving of form to preexistent matter." *Communion and Otherness*, 252.

responses to God's love have true "cause," truly impacting the divine being as our responses deeply impact the hypostasis of our neighbor, loving them as we love ourselves (Matt. 7:12).[45]

In the actions of ministry the concurrence of divine and human action occurs because ministry is bound in the love of subjects, of persons. This love draws such action as deep as being, making ministry the sharing in hypostasis, making participation simultaneously in neighbor and God through the possibility-out-of-nothingness framework. "Barth contends that, where the Christian serves God [i.e., is in ministry], there is a 'fellowship of action . . .' between Christ and Christians."[46] We concur with the divine through the fellowship of action, through joining the divine action of ministry, by responding to the divine love of ministry, by ourselves becoming ministers and entering or confessing ex nihilo for the sake of participation (with God and neighbor), by going to the homeless and brokenhearted, as Matt, Sarah, and Greg do.

This then makes human action of incredible worth. It is *not* of the same kind as God's own action but is true response to God's action. Human action has significant importance, for as response, human action is not simply passive or lacking concretion; rather, human action is ministry to concrete and lived persons. We concur with divine action by embracing our neighbor, by being his or her minister. So this view of the qualitative distinction of time and eternity and the radical turn to divine action in practical theology need *not* eliminate the significance of human action. Rather, it does the opposite, making human action more significant, for it is not solely a political or pragmatic function but a fellowship of concrete subjects in the being of God in and through human action, participating in the divine being through the act of ministry itself.

This means, as we said above, that practical theology should reflect deeply on human action, but it should do so as ministry, exploring empirically the shape of human ministry as encounter with distinct human subjects that witness to participation through action in the divine being itself. Practical theology,

---

45. "For anyone to love God, then, is a matter of relationship (of personhood) and not of nature. . . . Thus God loves us not through our nature (or through His nature) but through a person ([that of] Christ) and only in this way—through this person—can we love him in turn. If anyone should say that personhood has nature within it and therefore the love of God becomes a natural property of man, he not only overlooks the difference between nature and person, but also confuses the natures, the properties of which naturally remain unconfused and are only united in a communication idiomatum hypostatically (i.e., personally). If the uncreated properties could have become part of the nature of the creature (and especially, as some say, in creation), then we would not have needed the person of Christ." Ibid., 278.

46. Nimmo, *Being in Action*, 154.

then, can study deeply human action, but never outside the vision of ministry. This keeps practical theology theological and not a stepchild of the sociology of religion. The sociology of religion studies societal religious conceptions and forms. Practical theology may glean from this, but *its ultimate purpose is to study the practice, action, and conceptions of ministry.* And ministry itself can only be conceived as a practical reality because it is first a theological one; it is the practical (concrete and lived) theological conception of God's being as the becoming of ministering subject to human subjects called to respond to God's action of ministry by becoming ministers themselves. Greg is called to go and tell his friend, Sarah is called to listen, and I was called to run and testify to God's act that came out of nothingness. Ministry becomes the hermeneutic for many types of human action, which, as we will see below, can frame interdisciplinary conversations.

The Electing Covenant of Grace

Barth has grounded the *consursus Dei* in the fellowship of action that takes the shape of loving subjects of divine call and human response—of what I have called the fellowship of shared ministry.[47] Though Barth has grounded this in Christopraxis (again giving him my language), this grounding should not lead us to assume that before the incarnation God concurred with creation other than as minister. We have already used too many Old Testament narratives for such a perspective to be assumed. Rather, for Barth the incarnation of the Word becomes dynamically the fullness of God's being as the becoming of ministry, for it is from the very beginning, through the covenant of grace, that God is revealed as minister.

Grace itself is the fellowship of action that moves into participation in being. Grace, as the ontological reality of God's own being, constitutes God as minister. God acts as minister because God is love, and when this love goes out to what is not God, calling what is not God to have "cause" on God's being, it is grace.[48] Grace is God's calling out, God's seeking and openness to response.

---

47. Nimmo explains where I'm standing when he says, "Barth operated with an actualistic ontology, in which . . . the [human] agent as a being in action is called to corresponded to the Being in action of God." Ibid., 2. Terry Wright adds further depth to Nimmo's points, "We have rejected already the possibilities that God either causes creaturely activity or steers it towards correspondence with his own activity. Instead we have proposed that God acts and invites us to act with him, that he calls and we respond obediently and willingly. Although this does not mean that God does not or will not work without us, it does mean that in the freedom of his grace, he asks us to share or participate in all that he does—not because he needs to do so, but because he wants to do so. It is simply a matter of grace." "Reconsidering Concursus," *International Journal of Systematic Theology* 4, no. 2 (July 2002): 214.

Grace, Barth explains, is the only way to conceive of *concursus Dei*. Grace enters into nothingness, bringing life out of it for the sake of participating in the divine hypostasis. If grace is the heart of God's own being as love, a heart that as grace seeks to share in what God is not, then covenant is the movement of grace into time. It is the shape of God's ministry; it is participating in distinct (asymmetrical) subjects. It is the shape of the *Concursus*; it is the proclaiming of the fellowship of action as true grace.

But as the covenant of grace, it is forged in election. Election is a perspective that allows us to hold both justification and participation together.[49] Election is always constituted out of nothingness. God elects to create what is not God out of nothing (Genesis 1); God elects Israel to be God's people because they are nothing (Deut. 7:7), and David to be God's king because he too is nothing (1 Samuel 16). God acts, as election shows, through the framework of possibility through nothingness (justification) for the sake of the elect sharing in God's being by participating in God's becoming, in God's action of ministry (which in its fullness is Jesus Christ—Christopraxis).

Humanity is invited to participate in the divine being by being elect by God to join God's action, by being elect to be ministers through the humanity of Jesus Christ. At times and for purposes God elects particular people(s),

---

48. Keith Johnson explains, "This covenant of grace provides the specific framework from which the relationship of divine and human action must be considered. It cannot be regarded from any other basis." "The Being and Act of the Church," 210. "The first assertion is that while we cannot consider human action apart from its relation to divine action, this relation does not undermine the integrity of this action as a human action. How are we to understand this idea? From Barth's doctrine of election, we know he understands the relationship between God and humanity in terms of 'two distinct aspects': God's election to be Lord and Helper of humanity and, included in this election, the corresponding election of humanity to be 'witnesses of God's glory.' This, Barth argues, means that 'the being and essence and activity of God as the Lord of the covenant between Himself and man includes a relationship to the being and essence and activity of man'—the one demands the other." Ibid., 212.

49. Nimmo explains further, "The actualistic way in which Barth construes the grace of God also has immediate consequences for his doctrine of justification. For Barth, the relationship between God and the ethical agent is never static but is rather always dynamic. Barth writes that 'There is no present in which the justification of man is not still this beginning of justification' for, even in her best works, the ethical agent 'still stands in continual need of justification before God.' Barth therefore asserts of the individual that 'Every morning and every evening his situation is one of departure in the very midst of sin.' Indeed, the Church as a whole is engaged in the same movement: 'the Christian community both as a whole and individually will always be somewhere on the way in the movement from yesterday to tomorrow, and therefore *Deo bene volente* from the worse to the better. Consequently, Barth writes of the new individual created by the call of Jesus Christ that 'although his sin and guilt are indeed behind him, they are behind him in such a way that they are still a potent factor in the present, so that he must continually receive afresh his freedom from them.'" *Being in Action*, 162.

like Israel, but always for the purpose of ministry, to be a blessing to the world. All humanity is elect to be ministered to and therefore to participate in ministry through the humanity of Jesus Christ, who remains always in ministry (Christopraxis). Election can never be imagined as favoritism (or clericalism), but only as the calling to join God's ministry. The elect are *not* "better" than others, just particular subjects (hypostasis) called to participate in a particular way, at a particular time, in God's ministry (which is for all creation to participate in the act and being of God through Jesus Christ).

So any conception of the particularity of (ministerial) election is only so against the backdrop of universal election—that all humanity is elect to receive and participate in the ministry of God. Humanity's very ontological state as subject (hypostasis) qualified all to universally be ministered to by God and therefore to join God's being by ministering to other human subjects.[50]

The very image of God in us, which I have defined as hypostasis, as personhood, as being the relationships that are us, means that the divine vocation of humanity is to be God's partner (*concursus Dei*). Unlike all other creatures, we are hypostatic creatures, and as hypostatic creatures we are given the divine, ontological call to participate in God's being by joining God's action, by ministering to creation. We do so never as creation's dominating lord but as hypostases, as subjects elect to embrace fellow hypostatic creatures, loving all creation as the gift of God given to us as the concrete and lived environment in which to minister to our fellow hypostatic creatures, to listen and not talk, for instance. And we act to minister to them by sharing (participating) in their life by giving a friend a word in grief. The image of God is the universal election of all humanity to be ministered to as subjects and therefore to participate in ministry as subjects.

THE CAUSE OF THE COVENANT OF GRACE

The universality of election is essential because election is always for participation in the covenant of grace, for creation, Israel, and David to participate in the divine being by joining God's ministerial action.[51] Israel and

50. I'm taking a distinct position in opposition to Kathleen Cahalan's definition of ministry. And one that I believe in a very different way moves past the clerical paradigm—or perhaps does not so much move past as radically reconceive the paradigm itself. I'm trying to do this reconceiving through articulation of divine being and act.

51. "If this is so, How does God work through creaturely activity so that at once the activity remains that of both God and the creature? This, says Barth, is 'the mystery of grace in the confrontation and encounter of two subjects who cannot be compared and do not fall under anyone master-concept.' God's action simply has 'no parallel in the creaturely sphere.' For Barth, concursus is to be understood first by

David are graced with the invitation to join their own being with the divine being by becoming ministers, sharing God's form through action that is bound in being. To be ministers that find fellowship (at the ontological level) with God's own action, they must always remember that they are justified for this ministry only by the action of God that elects them out of nothingness, giving them a possibility that they could never possess in themselves, a possibility that can only be the result of God's own ministerial action.[52]

God's action (election) "causes" them to be ministers, but as subjects (hypostasis) being ministered to, and therefore called into ministry, human subjects bring "cause" to God. Human action counts for much, for as response in ministry, human beings take the form of the divine being, moving the divine being (the eternal) to participate, to be affected by the "cause" of concrete and lived subjects. God gives "cause" to humanity by calling us into ministry, and in ministry we are promised that divine action will impact our being and action, as our being and action will impact God's own.

Israel and David have no actuality in themselves—to be a chosen people or king—all concrete actuality points in the opposite direction. But they are elect, for from their nothingness the "cause" of an all-new possibility breaks forth as God's being as becoming among them. Israel is the people of God and David a man after God's own heart (Acts 13:22) not because their own action possesses possibility but because God encounters them in nothingness, which leads them to become ministers, participating in God's divine being through the possibility-through-nothingness framework.[53] Creation reveals that God elects another to be with God (to participate in God) by being ministered to by God, by being given God's being through the ministerial action of God, which is the election of grace out of nothingness.[54]

recognizing that God's ultimate action towards creation is in Jesus Christ; the rest of the divine activity may be known only through this particular action." Terry Wright, "Reconsidering the Concursus," 210.

52. "Barth observes simply: 'If God comes to man in His divine Word, He does not do so because He needs man. . . . If man goes to God in responsibility before Him, he does so because he needs God.' Herein lies the continued affirmation in the Church Dogmatics of the 'infinite qualitative difference' between God and humanity." Nimmo, *Being in Action*, 102.

53. Of course both David and Israel fall into sin in the biblical story. And this falling into sin is the forgetting that they are elected out of nothingness, that they are in need of God's act. Israel wants a king for itself, seeking to live in the framework of actuality to possibility and denying the framework of possibility out of nothingness.

54. "Athanasius can rely precisely on his ontology to make the point that whereas our whole being is a participation in God, our nature is still absolutely distinct and 'external' to God, not because we have any 'structure' which is 'of itself' independent of God, but because we participate in God 'from nothing.'" Khaled Anatolios, *Athanasius: The Coherence of His Thought* (London: Routledge, 1998), 209.

So the "cause" of God is bound to the language of election, making "cause" then take on the space of ministry itself. And it does this from the very beginning. Any divine cause, any articulation of divine and human act and being, cannot be articulated outside of or in opposition to the shape of ministry itself. Therefore, natural causalities like hurricanes and earthquakes, while needing articulations of theodicy, are not "caused" by the ministry of God, as pundits like Pat Robertson have argued. For Jesus Christ, Christopraxis, is the hermeneutic of God's ministry (John 9).

The divine cause impacts humanity as loving encounter of ministry since the divine cause that is bound in Jesus Christ (in Christopraxis) is the very covenant of grace that constitutes the inner hypostatic relation of the Trinity and therefore is the impetus for creation itself. This may be why Shirley says, "God did not so much rescue me as care for me." This highlights that God comes to us not as a mammoth force but as a minister. God, out of the flowing ministerial love of the Trinity, in and through the covenant of grace, "causes" to be that which is not God, that which has no ontological connection to the Trinity, by speaking it out of the communion of grace into being ex nihilo. Creation is not God, but creation through the "cause" of the covenant of grace is invited to be with God, for God is so *with* creation that God honors and responds to human action, to human cause. This human cause cannot determine divine cause, for divine cause is ultimately the very covenant of grace, is the very ontological shape of God's being as minister. But because this is so, God freely responds to human action, allowing human cause to exist within the covenant of grace, within the ministerial act and being of Godself.[55]

Human action then is significant; it possesses the power, given it to by the act and being of God, to join (or oppose) the covenant of grace. This is how the concurrence of the divine and human act and being occurs—it can happen only within the realm of the covenant of grace, which is the very ministry of God.

This means, then, that *concursus* is not so much God accompanying our actions to bring about his purposes, but of God inviting us by his Spirit to participate in his own sovereign activity. In doing

---

55. "Barth's doctrine of the concursus is thus explicitly Trinitarian: he posits that the concursus 'is an operation in the Word and therefore by the Spirit, in the Spirit and therefore by the Word.' In this Trinitarian sphere, writes Barth, even under the lordship of God, 'the rights and honour and dignity and freedom of the creature are not suppressed and extinguished but vindicated and revealed.' Ultimately, then, the very fact of the *concursus Dei* itself indicates that God 'affirms and approves and recognizes and respects the autonomous actuality and therefore the autonomous activity of the creature as such.' There thus remains alongside the activity of God a place for that of the creature." Nimmo, *Being in Action*, 122.

so, God does not commandeer our actions but instead acts himself whilst giving us the opportunity to accompany him; but our accompaniment of his activity cannot in any way be said to restrict it. For it is an accompaniment that follows rather than leads.[56]

So human acts of ministry that uphold and participate in the hypostasis of others as grace, that meet others ex nihilo and *in nihilo*, take on the cause of ministry and therefore are joined and taken into the divine cause. This is why giving a neighbor bread, shelter, or hospitality (Matthew 25) is to encounter the presence of Christ, for these are human actions of cause that join the divine being and act of becoming in ministry. They are the hypostatic action of the covenant of grace.

This allows us to move beyond the connection Barth makes between the first and second articles of the creed and to turn now to the third article and the work of the Spirit. *Concursus* may find its full association by connecting divine and human act and being through the very work of the Spirit. *It is the Spirit's work to lead us into participation, as it is the Son's work to reinstate the ex nihilo for the sake of justification.*[57]

Spirit, Participation, Personhood, and Practical Theology

As I said in chapter 5, at the heart of a Christopraxis practical theology of the cross is what Anderson calls a Pentecostal experience. What he means is that a Christopraxis perspective needs the working of the Spirit, as Christopraxis claims God's being is the becoming of ministry, and the hermeneutic of this continued ministry is Jesus Christ himself, who is active in the world.

---

56. Terry Wright, *Reconsidering the Concursus*, 213.

57. Moving into the last third of this chapter, the reader will observe that I am trying to combine Barth's perspective with Athanasius and other patristic perspectives. Thinkers like Anatolios believe Barth and Athanasius are in opposition. But, Anatolios, I believe, has missed Barth's *concursus Dei* perspective. Any of the critiques he levels against Barth here, Nimmo shows to not be the case. "The difference in tone between Barth's emphasis on the dialectical opposition of God and world, and that of Athanasius, is signaled by the fact that Barth refuses to speak of humanity's cooperating with God, whereas Athanasius can draw a theological portrait of Antony as a co-worker with Christ. . . . If we can consider Athanasius as a dialogue partner in contemporary theological discussion, we thus gain a theological model that provides a corrective counterpoint to both the Schleiermacherian danger of an anthropocentric monism and the Barthian danger of incipient dualism. Or, more positively, Athanasius's model succeeds in affirming both the ineffable, sovereignly free and transcendent being of God (with Barth) and the nearness of this ineffable presence within the human realm (with Schleiermacher)." Anatolios, *Athanasius*, 209.

Therefore, it is the Spirit that leads us into concrete and lived experiences of this reality of God's continued ministry in Christ.

The Spirit does this because it is the Spirit's work to bring forth participation—at the level of act and being, at the level of Father and Son, Creator and creature, human neighbor and human neighbor.[58] By the Spirit the human being is made minister; through the Spirit human action *can* participate in the divine. The Spirit is the fellowship of action that allows for the mutual but distinct "cause" of divine and human ministry. The Spirit allows for the possibility of *concursus*.

So if practical theology attends to ministry as divine and human action, then practical theology is fundamentally a theological perspective that attends to the Spirit, for the Spirit leads us into the concrete and lived experience of God's being as becoming through Jesus who reinstates the ex nihilo by going *in nihilo*.

Practical theology is a theology of the Spirit because the very work of the Spirit is concrete and lived participation in God and one another, bringing the eternal into time. The Spirit raises Jesus, bringing the perishing Jesus back to life so that the perishing Jesus might again, through *nihilo*, participate in the being of God as God. The Spirit allows for participation at the level of action, allowing our action to participate in the action of God—and thus permitting us to be ministers by taking on the actions of God's own ministry, which is the revealing of God's own being. Sarah hears the Spirit telling her not to speak but to listen as the act of ministry.

But this Spirit that cleaves divine and human action has its being in the relational life of three hypostases in one *ousia*. This Spirit is God, and therefore, while moving in time to bind human action to divine ministry, the Spirit (simultaneously) cleaves action in both participation and being. The Spirit creates life by going into and moving out of *nihilo*.[59] The Spirit goes into death to find the perishing Jesus, resurrecting and giving Jesus life out of nothingness. This work of giving life is the ontological work of the Spirit, for the Spirit is the Spirit of life, leading what is bound in death into participation with God who

---

58. This is similar to Latini's levels of *Koinonia*. See *The Church and the Crisis of Community: A Practical Theology of Small-Group Ministry* (Grand Rapids, MI: Eerdmans, 2011).

59. Barth here shows how the focus of his second article moves into the third and is fully Trinitarian. "Every time that God shows forth His power to the men of His choosing, and through them to others, every time, then, that He acts, He does so in the following way: His Word goes forth to these men. To be received by them in the power of His Spirit; His Spirit is given to these men, to receive His Word of power." *Church Dogmatics* III.3, 142.

is eternal life as Trinity.[60] It is the Spirit that moves through justification into participation. The Spirit works to bind not only action but being.

THE SPIRIT'S CALL TO MINISTRY

A practical theology that attends to the Spirit (a Christopraxis perspective) is moved into ontological language. Through the action of ministry the human being is made minister, and as minister, she concurs with the divine being by being led by the Spirit into divine action—given a word while gardening to minister to a friend, such as what happened with Greg in chapter 3.

Yet, this is not a return to clericalism or the ontological priority of the professional minister, for it works in the reverse. Clericalism and professionalism claim that one is ontologically transformed by ordination (calling) and then takes action out of that ontological transformation—an ontological transformation bound in the elitism of being only for a few special, powerful *men*, generally speaking. This Christopraxis perspective claims something different: it reverses the order of being to action. One is a minister not by ontological transfer but by joining God's action.[61] The Levite is bureaucratically ordained but no minister because, by ignoring and leaving the beaten person (Luke 10), he refuses to join God's action. But the Samaritan is made minister by joining his action with God's own. By entering into ex nihilo, by joining the beaten man's suffering, his action turns ontological because he shares his being with the beaten man, bandaging his wounds. In so doing, these actions of ministry participate in God's own being, for God is ontologically a minister whose being is in becoming, in the event of bringing life out of death.

60. For the Spirit as the Spirit of life, see Jurgen Moltmann, *The Source of Life: The Holy Spirit and the Theology of Life* (Minneapolis: Fortress Press, 1997). "Likewise the Spirit is 'life-giving' because He is communion' (II Cor. 13:14). The life of God is eternal because it is personal, that is to say, it is realized as an expression of free communion, as love. Life and love are identified in the person: the person does not die only because it is loved and loves; outside the communion of love the person loses its uniqueness and becomes a being like other beings, a 'thing' without absolute 'identity' and 'name,' without a face. Death for a person means ceasing to love and to be loved, ceasing. To be unique and unrepeatable, whereas, life for the person means the survival of the uniqueness of its hypostasis; which is affirmed and maintained by love." Zizioulas, *Being as Communion*, 49.

61. Nimmo pushes deeper in this perspective, "Throughout the Church Dogmatics, however, Barth steadfastly declares the reality of human correspondence. The objective reality of what has happened to the ethical agent in Jesus Christ is not without its effects in her life as a being in action. As Christians know Jesus, so too they know 'themselves' as men reconciled, justified and sanctified in Him, and may thus make use of the freedom indicated to them in Him.' And more than this, Barth insists that 'the love of the children of God does become an event in the act or acts of human self-determination: it is a creaturely reality.'" *Being as Action*, 157.

The Samaritan participates in God's being because his own action joins God's ministry of bringing life out of death. But he can only join this action concretely and practically by sharing in the personhood (hypostasis) of his human neighbor.[62] He joins God's being by taking on the action of ministry to his neighbor, which is to join his being (to be with him) through nothingness. For in and through nothingness God's act moves to bring forth possibility—true participation.[63]

Action leads into being a minister, and all who are hypostases, all subjects, all people are invited (called) into ministry. This does not take place through a special ontological state; we *all* already possess the ontological state of ministry that is hypostasis, which is being a subject through action to and for others.[64] And this universal ontological state that makes us ministers, that connects act and being, is bound in the possibility-through-nothingness framework. Through our nothingness, through our need for justification, divine action comes to us as an ontological reality, giving us life out of death. Through ex nihilo we are hypostases, our hypostasis is revealed: we need others to ontologically be.

This bringing of life out of death that is God's ministry *is* the very hypostatic nature of Godself; it is to participate through our subjectivity in God's own hypostasis through the Spirit. We continue to participate in this ontological reality of being given life out of death by joining God's ministry, by ministering to our hypostatic neighbor as a witness to the participation

---

62. Here Barth reveals what we saw earlier, that there is a deep hypostatic impulse in his work on the *Concursus*. "Rather remarkably, a true theological realism consists primarily in a constant awareness of the fact that neither God nor the creature is a thing. That on the contrary to those who really want to think and speak about them. To theologians—if they are not to thresh empty straw—they must always be self-revealed." *Church Dogmatics* III.3, 102.

63. Zizioulas relates this perspective on personhood to soteriology. "The eternal survival of the person as a unique, unrepeatable and free 'hypostasis,' as loving and being loved, constitutes the quintessence of salvation, the bringing of the gospel to man. In the language of the Fathers this is called 'divinization' (theosis), which means participation not in the nature or substance of God, but in His personal existence. The goal of salvation is that the personal life which is realized in God should also be realized on the level of human existence." *Being as Communion*, 50.

64. Nimmo points to the personal dynamics in Barth's perspective. "The command of God as the Word of God comes to the ethical agent in a profoundly personal way. On the one side, the Word of God is for Barth 'the truth as it is in God's speaking person, *Dei loquentis persona*.' On the other side, the command of God has the character of 'an act of God which takes place *specialissime*, in this way and not another, to this or that particular man.' Barth asserts that 'God confronts man in an individual and solitary relationship when He gives him His command and prohibition, and again man stands before God in an individual and solitary relationship when he has to receive this command and prohibition.'" *Being in Action*, 20.

(reconciliation) of our being with the divine through justification, through ex nihilo.

THE PERSONAL

But this means we must spin down deeper into what we have just said. I insinuated earlier that when the Spirit unites, the Spirit unites not substances but persons.[65] The divine and human can only concur at all, as we have said, because the human is in the image of the divine and this image is of a hypostatic kind—a kind that is ontologically constituted in relationships of action, of loving and being loved.[66] Hypostasis is the confession of the uniting of the personal as an ontological reality in and through the action of shared life, of being with and for, of being in union.[67]

The Spirit unites the Father and Son, the divine and human natures in Jesus (the hypostatic union), and human cause and divine cause through shared personhood (concursus Dei), through the participation in the being (the

---

65. Zizioulas's analysis is informative: "Among the Greek Fathers, the unity of God, the one God, and the ontological 'principle' or 'cause' of the being and life of God does not consist in the one substance of God but in the hypostasis, that is, the person of the Father. The one God is not the one substance but the Father, who is the 'cause' both of the generation of the Son and of the procession of the Spirit, Consequently, the ontological 'principle' of God is traced back, once again, to the person. Thus when we say that God 'is,' we do not bind the personal freedom of God—the being of God is not an ontological 'necessity' or a simple 'reality' for God—but we ascribe the being of God to His personal freedom. In a more analytical way this means that God, as Father and not as substance, perpetually confirms through 'being' His free will to exist. And it is precisely His Trinitarian existence that constitutes this confirmation: the Father out of love—that is, freely—begets the Son and brings forth the Spirit. If God exists, He exists because the Father exists, that is, He who out of love freely begets the Son and brings forth the Spirit. Thus God as person—as the hypostasis of the Father, God. This point is absolutely crucial. For it is precisely with this point that the new philosophical position of the Cappadocian Fathers, and of St Basil in particular, is directly connected. That is to say, the substance never exists in a 'naked' state, that is, without hypostasis, without 'a mode of existence.' And the one divine substance is consequently the being of God only because it has these three modes of existence, which it owes not to the substance but to one person, the Father. Outside the Trinity there is no God, that is, no divine substance, because the ontological 'principle' of God is the Father. The personal existence of God (the Father) constitutes His substance, makes it hypostases. The being of God is identified with the person." *Being as Communion*, 41.

66. This focus on hypostasis has deep and historical pastoral implications. Zizioulas explains, "By contrast, the bishops of this period, pastoral theologians such as St Ignatius of Antioch and above all St Irenaeus and later St Athanasius, approached the being of God through the experience of the ecclesial community, of ecclesial being. This experience revealed something very important: the being of God could be known only through personal relationships and personal love. Being means life, and life means communion." Ibid., 16.

67. For much more on this see my book *The Relational Pastor* (Downers Grove: IL: InterVarsity, 2013).

personhood) of the other through action. In the same way, the Spirit unites time and eternity, divine and human action, in and through human action of ministry that shares in the being of neighbor (Matthew 25). Jesus Christ is present in such encounters of two or three ministering to each other (Matt. 18:20) because the Spirit of Christ, the Holy Spirit, unites in participation the divine with the human through the act and being (the ministry) of sharing in personhood—of joining the other's person through ex nihilo.

As image of God, as hypostatic creatures who have our being, as Zizioulas argues through the Cappadocians, in the relationship of persons, humanity is ontologically conditioned to be ministered to and therefore holds the ontological potential to be ministers.[68] The potentiality is turned into reality when the Spirit joins the human being, empowering her for participation in divine act and being, leading the minister into ex nihilo of the other person for the sake of sharing in the other's person, just as the cabbie does with Rachel. For shared hypostasis is the act of ministry that leads into shared being at both the divine and human level. We share in the being of our neighbor by acting in ministry for her. And as the Spirit joins these actions, we are taken into the being of God. In sharing in the other's hypostasis in ministry we are sharing in the hypostasis of Jesus through the Spirit (Matthew 25), and to share in Jesus' hypostasis is to be taken into the divine life.

To be a person is to be our relationships, and we can only have relationships by acting with and for others. The Spirit, too, is a relationship,

---

68. "The essence, therefore, of the anthropology which results from the Trinitarian theology of the Cappadocian Fathers lies in the significance of personhood in human existence. The Cappadocian Fathers gave to the world the most precious concept it possesses: the concept of the person, as an ontological concept in the ultimate sense. Since this concept has become, at least in principle, not only part of our Christian heritage but also an ideal of our culture in general, it may be useful to remind ourselves of its exact content and significance as it emerges from a study of the theology of the Cappadocians." Zizioulas, *Communion and Otherness*, 166. "Personhood, as I have argued, is the mode in which nature exists in its ecstatic movement of communion in which it is hypostasized in its catholicity. This, I have also said, is what has been realized in Christ as the man par excellence through the hypostatic union. This, I must now add, is what should happen to every man in order that he himself may become Christ (according to the Fathers) or 'put on Christ' (according to Paul). And this is what makes Christ the head of a new humanity (or creation) in that he is the first one both chronologically and ontologically to open up this possibility of personhood in which the distance of individuals is turned into the communion of persons." Ibid., 245. Zizioulas continues, "For the Cappadocians, 'being' is a notion we apply to God simultaneously in two senses. It denotes (a) the . . . (what he is) of God's being, and this the Cappadocians call the ousia or substance or nature of God; and (b) it refers to the (how he is), which they identify with his personhood. In both cases, the verb is to be . . . , that is, being." Ibid., 125.

the relationship of the Father to the Son.[69] It then is the Spirit's work to unite humanity with humanity and humanity with God through hypostasis.[70]

The Spirit moves into time, binding human action with divine encounter of God's own being. The Spirit calls our person into participation in the person of Jesus, both as ontological reality (we are hidden with God in Christ; Colossians 3:3) and as a fellowship of action. We join Christ's continued ministry (Christopraxis). This hypostatic reality moves us to call this perspective Christopraxis, for it claims that practical theology is divine and human encounter and that divine and human encounter only happens in and through personhood, through Jesus' own person given to us by the Spirit as God's being as becoming.

Because this ministry is God's being as the act of becoming in the personhood of Jesus, the Spirit too takes us, those who participate in this fellowship of action through our nothingness, into a *hidden* participation in eternity itself—we are made children of God (Gal. 4:1-7), born anew (1 Pet. 1:23) as new creations (2 Cor. 5:17). Thus, a Christopraxis practical theology of the cross constituted in hypostasis not only claims that the eternal enters time through hypostatic creatures' experiences of ex nihilo but also claims that time is taken into eternity, that encountering the divine act and being through ex nihilo of the cross of Christ, the human being is taken into the divine life (this is the fullness of soteriology). When I asked people to tell of an experience of God, many told of a concrete and lived experience of ministering to another person. As Athanasius has asserted, the Spirit works to move us through the death of Christ (justification) into participation with the Trinity itself—to share in God's very being.[71]

PRACTICAL THEOLOGY AS HYPOSTATIC

Divine and human actions are a hypostatic reality, and this reality drives deep into the concrete and lived. As hypostatic human beings, we have our being in and through others. Being ministered to and being in ministry are grounded at the anthropological level, connecting anthropology, justification, and reconciliation/participation.

69. Here I'm following Karl Barth; see *Church Dogmatics* I.1 (Edinburgh: T&T Clark, 1936).

70. Again, for more on this see my book *The Relational Pastor*.

71. "Divinization, the coming to dwell and to abide within the life of the Trinity, is possible only if the divine Holy Spirit is the initial source and ceaseless vitality of that communion of Trinitarian life, a life that finds its summit and completion when the indwelling Spirit raises up human beings' mortal bodies, as he did Jesus', so as to share in the incorruptible and immortal life of the eternal Father." Anatolios, *Athanasius*, 119.

We are, anthropologically, the hypostatic creatures that are our relationships. This means all forms of human action take on significance for practical theology, as they either stand for or against this hypostatic reality. Practical theology studies childbearing practices, object relations psychology, urban planning, and so much more in order to understand their effect on the hypostatic nature of humanity, helping us see or know for the sake of ministry with concrete persons. And practical theology studies the church for how it faithfully or unfaithfully witnesses in its life to this hypostatic nature—how the church is the community of persons in ministry for one another and the world.[72] Because practical theology is grounded in hypostasis, claiming that the human being is hypostatic, we can never ignore the possibility of divine action within these perspectives.

The hypostatic nature makes dialogue worthwhile with all forms of thought that attend to personhood. But practical theology in this dialogue also has something to add because, in claiming personhood, the open doors to discussing divine encounter and the need for Spirit are clear (as we will see, for instance, in the next chapter on critical realism).

Nevertheless, practical theology in this dialogue can never dilute its claim that divine action comes through nothingness, through human need, which leads us to participate in the being of the one in need—to be with and for our neighbor as minister, as friend. Practical theology actually can draw the social sciences, especially professional ones like medicine, law, and therapy, toward the significance of human action taking the form of ministry.[73] This has happened, but most often in a way that is disconnected from practical theology itself. For instance, Rogerian psychological practice has shaped itself more as something *like* the encounter of persons in ministry than has Freudian practice, with its conception of the expert doctor treating the sick.[74] And many other perspectives are claiming the need for communal, relational encounters that find interesting connections to ministry itself.

72. This is the heart of Zizioulas's project. It is the claim that the church is a community of persons that live to witness to the world of this hypostatic nature. There are many more implication for this in relation to practical theology.

73. Zizioulas adds to this, "Thus, the empirical man does not represent the reality of the human being in its fullness even for a purely humanistic approach to man. Whether one speaks, in terms of natural sciences, about the evolution of man, or, in terms of social sciences, about the man of the evolving society, it remains true that the empirical man is essentially 'the raw material' for the conception or creation of the real man. Only by setting up the empirical man against a certain vision do we make him a real man." *Communion and Otherness*, 207.

74. John Swinton in his book *Resurrecting the Person* does something very similar. He calls for health care providers to see personhood, to be drawn into friendship—ministry—as a way of giving care.

Practical theology claims that the shared but distinct hypostatic natures are what gives divine and human action its concurrence. Eternity breaks into time through and in hypostasis, for both divine and human act and being are subjects. The concrete place of divine encounter is in and through hypostasis itself. But this shared hypostasis is not "a point of contact," is not an *analogia entis*, for the hypostasis of the divine and human are unalike. The divine hypostasis is an actuality while human hypostasis is always bound in nothingness and the need for possibility outside itself; it is always in need of justification.

Both the divine and human are hypostases in the sense that God *is* the relationship of three in one; God's being is bound in hypostasis. But because this is so, this God is in *no* need of a relationship outside God to be. But humanity *is* in need; we are unlike God in that we cannot constitute our own hypostasis within ourselves, for we are never plural hypostases in one *ousia*, which means we are always in need of others to give us our being—to be our minister.

It is better to think of the shared hypostatic nature of the divine and human as the ontological reality of the *analogia relationis*. And this relation becomes the locale of divine encounter in concrete human existence. The eternal breaks into time in the concrete and lived reality of sharing in hypostasis, and this sharing of hypostasis, of participating in personhood, is ministry (as act and being). We ontologically need a minister, need another hypostasis to be with us. And when these others are with us, it is an act of ministry that connects the divine with the human.

CONCLUSION

Practical theology is concrete as both act and being because practical theology attends to concrete and lived personhood. It explores, studies, and leads forms of human action deep into the relational encounter with persons; it uses the social sciences and arts to help it see personhood, to help it understand the personal, trusting that when it does, when it moves into the ministry of persons through the Spirit, it enters into divine and human encounter and becomes Christopraxis. Therefore, all interdisciplinary perspectives, all pragmatic initiatives must attend to this hypostatic nature. Practical theology then is concrete and lived because it attends to persons, exploring the cultural, political, liberatory, psychological, and social impact of the relationships that are us. This hypostatic nature allows practical theology to attend deeply to human action (as being) and yet explore how, through this hypostatic nature of humanity, through the fellowship of action (ministry), we are taken through the Spirit into participation (union) with God.

PART III

8

Critical Realism and Practical Theology

In the last two chapters the theological lifting has been heavy. I have sought to drag practical theology onto significant theological ground, making a case for a Christopraxis practical theology of the cross. I've left open the critique that my discourse is more theological than social scientific, empirical, or even philosophical. These have often been the more comfortable tongues of practical theology, especially post–Seward Hiltner, leaving open the possibility that I have left the demarcation zone of practical theology itself.

Yet, I would disagree. I have sought to stay consistently within the field by focusing on the concrete and lived, by giving central attention to experiences of God's coming like those in chapter 3. I have focused on the concrete and lived by thrusting ministry into the center, and the experiential by claiming the event of encounter with divine being. Therefore, I have turned from the common tongues of practical theology to explore the theological depths of experience. And while the tongues practical theology has used have been severally critiqued, most directly by Purves—with his effort to evacuate such discourse and return to classical doctrine—I do not share his sentiment. I've shown my own unease with Purves's path, a single minded emphasis on doctrine is just as disconcerting as the absence of attention to divine action in much of established practical theology.

My own immersion in theological language in the last two chapters has little to do with disdain for the practical theological "common tongue" and its turning from classic theological language. Rather, my own turning to the theological is to keep with the heart of practical theology itself! I have turned to the theological to attend more fully to experience, to the very foolish experience of divine love for us! Where the likes of Purves have turned to (a rigid Barthian) theology to escape what is perceived as the cul-de-sac of the experiential, I have aimed to show that a Christopraxis perspective embraces experience as central for practical theology.

Yet, unlike those scholars in established practical theology, I have claimed that this experience is the encounter with the divine being itself. I have claimed that persons have concrete experiences of the divine breaking into time, of *feeling* the Spirit ministering to their person, of being swept up into the participation in the divine being by ministering to others, by feeding the hungry and embracing the weeping, and by listening and not talking, as Sarah did with Erin.

I turned from the social-scientific, empirical, and philosophical tongue of practical theology not because such discourse is vapid but because it has not helped us articulate the depth of experience, especially the evangelical experience that so often stands outside the aesthetic or political commitments of established practical theology.

This means that my theological turn in the last three chapters is not for the sake of theology but for the sake of articulating experience as richly as possible. I have used theology in an ad hoc way (Hans Frei); I have used it because it most helpfully allows me to speak of the depth of experience, to make sense of experiences like those that Paul had on the road to Damascus (Acts 9) and those in our own lives that, though they may not be as dramatic, are nevertheless real. I have said that practical theology's heart is *not* theology, but ministry. *But ministry (as opposed to practice alone) needs the discourse of the theological to attend to the fullness of its subject.* It is true that I would prioritize theology above the other tongues practical theology has most often used, but not because theology is superior—theology, like all other forms of discourse, is a human project. I would do so because theology possesses within itself the ability to speak of these experiences we have of God's becoming to us, of God's ministering to our person. Theology helps us make sense of the experience of hearing God speak to or meet us, as almost all the people I interviewed witnessed to. Theological discourse gives us the best epistemological tools to express and reflect on the reality of God's act in our concrete lives (I will say much more about this below).

Therefore, in the last three chapters I have spoken (theologically) of how the divine being encounters the human being as an experienced *reality* (I am claiming this as an essential heart of the field of practical theology). But this attention to how the divine being encounters the human being and how the human being acts in response to the experience of divine being risks the critique of theological hegemony and the loss of the practical. Practical theology has sought to do its work from the ground, using social-scientific, empirical, and philosophical perspectives to do so (for they are *perceived* to be more grounded—which I'm not sure is true). Yet, I am claiming that experiences with the divine are real. And theology is more helpful because it attends to this realism, which the social sciences *often* ignore.

It is now time to justify this assertion. Therefore, keeping the evangelical experience central (the experience of divine encounter with the human), we will turn in this chapter from the theological to the philosophical and social scientific. Picking up a philosophical/social-scientific perspective that allows us to attend to divine encounter, we will connect it with the claims that divine action is in itself a reality. Turning to this position places my deeply theological perspective squarely within the zone of practical theology. While my Christopraxis perspective has drawn deeply from theology, it nevertheless *also* roots itself in a philosophical/social-scientific perspective that allows for (certain) empirical examinations, but never in a reductionistic way that denies concrete experience itself—even concrete experience with the divine.

The perspective I'll explore is critical realism. My assertion is that a Christopraxis practical theology of cross is embedded in a critical realist personalism that not only allows for the statements I have made above, statements I admit can only be confessed, but also allows for these confessional statements the possibility of truly being real, and real from the level of scientific discourse (that is, the language to which established practical theology has wanted to attend).[1]

The objective of this chapter, then, is to explicate how my Christopraxis practical theology is embedded within critical realism, making it possible for us to speak of divine action not as only a foreign confessional statement outside of or disconnected from reality, but as confession of reality, as the experience of something real—dare we even say, true.

CRITICAL REALISM

Critical realism is a philosophical/social-scientific perspective that has its origins (at least in the vein I'm working) in the thought of Roy Bhaskar, Margaret Archer, and Andrew Collier, to name just a few. It is a secular scientific perspective inasmuch as it does not seek to provide an apologetic for theism, and many atheists work from a critical realist perspective in the sciences.[2] Yet, as we'll see, because of its realist attention, there are deep convergences with some of the theological perspectives we've explored above.[3]

---

1. Critical realist personalism is a perspective that Christian Smith has articulated in his important book *What Is a Person?* (Chicago: University of Chicago Press, 2010).

2. Yet, all three of the thinkers named above have made the assertion, from within this philosophical/social-scientific perspective, that transcendence or God is worth exploring from within critical realism.

As a scientific perspective, critical realism rests on three overarching commitments. These three commitments will be explored in turn (though there will be large chunks of dialogue between each of the three) and connected to practical theology. We'll see how they deepen the Christopraxis perspective I've been constructing, placing Christopraxis within the scientific purviews that practical theology seeks to attend to.

1. Ontology over Epistemology

The first commitment of critical realism is to reverse the priority of epistemology over ontology that has been *en vogue* since the Enlightenment and the work of Kant.[4] Critical realism is a *realism*; it claims that there are entities that are real in the world that exist outside what can be known. Reality itself exists independent of any epistemological structure. Philosopher John Searle says it this way, "Realism is the view that there is a way that things are that is logically independent of all human representations. Realism does not say how things are but only that there is a way that they are."[5]

Epistemology, the realist asserts, is always a representation and an imperfect one at that. Epistemology is a model of reality and should not be confused with reality itself. Reality always overspills our epistemological conceptions of it. All forms of science, critical realism asserts, are epistemological representations

3. Margaret Archer, Andrew Collier, and Douglas Porpora assert, "Critical realism is a philosophy of science that stands midway between a positivism that has failed and a more current postmodernism, which, from a critical realist perspective, is equally flawed. Indeed, from the standpoint of critical realism, postmodernism is much more akin to positivism than its proponents allow, for example, in both positivism and postmodernism the question of God's existence is not legitimately admissible to rational debate." *Transcendence: Critical Realism and God* (London: Routledge, 2004), 1.

4. Christian Smith explains, "This belief in our inescapably alienated condition was set up for us in part by Immanuel Kant's key distinction between 'noumenal' reality and 'phenomenal' reality—a disastrous move driven by a desire to preserve morality in a world of Newtonian determinism—that is, between things 'as they really are in themselves' and things as they merely appear to us. Noumenal reality no doubt exists out there, this account supposes, but we humans have no good access to it because all of our knowledge is limited by our restricted capacities of empirical perceptions. The only world we can ever reside in is the world of appearances. We are separated from the world as it really is by an unbridgeable epistemic chasm. Thus we are locked off in the prison of our own perceptual disconnections from the real. Saussure's contribution to this line of thinking is also evident. These assumptions are what lead constructionists to believe that we humans have no reliable access to reality, that whatever is reality 'for us' must be a product of our active minds constructing it out of our cultural categories and through social interactions for our own pragmatic purposes." *What Is a Person?* (Chicago: University of Chicago Press, 2010), 170.

5. John Searle, *The Construction of Social Reality* (New York: Free Press, 1995), 155.

of reality. Reality is always more than any science (including theology) can measure or know. This doesn't make science futile, but it does direct it toward humble articulations of reality. It does this rigorously and critically but always under confession of its limit. Science's rigorously formed epistemologies are always in the end "believed" or trusted or confessed or taken in faith (all ministerial language) because no scientific epistemology can get its arms *completely* around reality.

Though science can never possess reality in its scientific representation (in its epistemologies), though what *is* (ontologically) is always more than these representations, science nevertheless seeks to say something true about reality. Thus, the objective of science is never to possess reality but "to conform the shape of our minds to the nature of the reality that exists beyond (but also including) our minds."[6]

From a realist perspective, then, there are things that exist in the world that we cannot know. Reality itself is stratified in such a way that human consciousness cannot completely capture reality; reality exists independent of the human mind. Reality includes the human mind but is (ontologically) more than what the human mind can know (epistemologically). While to some this seems like a truism, it has not been the trajectory of philosophy—or of the social sciences, here following philosophy—since the Enlightenment. This has moved humans to often contend that only what can be epistemologically known (or even proven) can be real. Critical realism, however, calls into question this conflation of epistemology that swallows ontology. It does not hold to the equation that what can be known is real but rather asserts that there are brute realities (again following Searle) that *are*, whether they are ever cognitively conceived by epistemological frameworks or not.

From a realist perspective, we as human knowers and our sciences as human constructs do not possess the equipment to know reality completely and finally. There are real things in the world that we cannot know as a totality. For instance, we cannot know for certain the expanse of the universe; its mass is not only not measurable but also existentially crushing—it transcends our consciousness. We believe the universe is real (really massive), though we cannot fully epistemologically conceive of it. We contend that the universe is massive because, though we cannot know it in toto, we have experienced it in part through the epistemologies of science. But because we have experienced it in part, we understand that there is much we cannot know about it.

---

6. Smith, *What Is a Person?*, 94. This statement by Smith sounds must like discipleship, as the conforming to what is real.

In similar ways, God in Godself is not a reality that humanity is able to conceive. God in Godself is hidden to us. This does not mean God doesn't exist, as that would be to subordinate ontology to epistemology. But it does mean that we have no access to this reality and in the end, then, cannot say if there is a God or not.[7] At the same time, we cannot say that we know there is no God on the basis of not being able to epistemologically conceive of this God beyond a doubt (this very perspective is why the revelatory realism of God's being as becoming is central to my perspective).[8] Archer, Collier, and Porpora state: "We thus arrive at the critical realist affirmation of ontological realism. Does God exist? From the standpoint of ontological realism, the question is legitimate. The question has both sense and possible answers. From the standpoint of ontological realism, reality in general exists quite apart from our knowledge of it. There is, then, nothing inappropriate about asking whether or not that reality includes God."[9]

Critical realism moves fully into a postpositivist position in the sense that it does not concede to the epistemological hubris of contending that what is real is only what can be proven. Critical realism is a perspective that reminds scientists that they are creatures and, as creatures, are epistemologically fallible.

THE EPISTEMIC FALLACY

To deny this realist perspective (to yield to Hegelian idealism or Humean empiricism, for instance) and contend that epistemology constitutes reality, that reality itself is only what can be known or constructed by knowers, is to enter what critical realists call "the epistemic fallacy."[10]

---

7. "From a critical realist perspective, what is real is real even if it does not act or otherwise manifest itself in a way that is observed. That applies to God. God remains independently real even without a world to act on or a humanity to experience God's manifestations." Archer, Collier, and Porpora, "What Do We Mean by God?," in Archer, Collier, and Porpora, *Transcendence*, 25.

8. Archer, Collier, and Porpora restate my point, "For many today, it will already be startling for us to assert that God may exist even if we cannot know for certain that God exists. Yet, one of the premises of critical realism is ontological realism. Ontological realism asserts the ontologically objective consists of reality, independent of our beliefs about it. It follows that something may belong to reality even if we remain mistaken about it or even completely ignorant of it. The existence or non-existence of God is a paradigm case." *Transcendence*, 1.

9. Ibid., 10.

10. Practical theology, most especially in some European forms, has taken a strong turn toward the empirical, almost making a case that practical theology can only be an empirical form of theology. My realist commitments see this move as a negative reduction of the field by supporting a downward conflation of the human being. An overly (or solely) empirical view falls headlong into the epistemic fallacy. As Smith says, "Reality has a deep dimension often operating below the surface of empirical

The epistemic fallacy is the belief that human knowers construct reality through their epistemological operations. But this, again, is for epistemology to swallow up ontology. This swallowing up starts with scientific positivism, where what is real can only be so if it can be proven in a laboratory—if it cannot be proven, it is not real. But it continues into Wittgensteinian language games, where it is assumed that only epistemologically constituted language games are real (or can be accessed as real). All we perceive as real is made so by language (Saussure). What is real is *formed* by language itself. But then, pushed to the extreme, when the language is deconstructed there is actually no reality under it at all; so, for instance, Derrida can assert that "that there is nothing outside the

experience. To think otherwise is to commit what critical realists call the 'epistemic fallacy,' namely, to reduce what is to what we can empirically observe. That is a debilitating move." *What Is a Person?*, 14. And it is a debilitating move for practical theology, for while it gives the field the sense of scientific rigor, it is a reduction of reality that keeps it from speaking of divine action. But it does more, because an overempiricism is a downward conflation that keeps the field of practical theology from speaking of reality and leads it to settle for measuring the regularity of events rather than exploring the layered and emergent meanings of the events. Smith says that "social science should seek to generalize. But its generalizations should focus on the structured and causal nature of the real, not so much on the regularity of events." Ibid., 97. Practical theology has followed the social sciences into this cul-de-sac. This doesn't eliminate the empirical from practical theology but does push it to be grounded in realism. Smith explains what this looks like: "The first thing realism always wants to know is: what actually exists? The foremost task, therefore, is to describe what is. Quantitative social science is, as Stanley Lieberson reminds us, generally much better at telling us what exists and is happening in the social world than explaining why and how it exists and is happening. As I have said above, social science generally wants to move beyond simple description to causal explanation. That is a legitimate aspiration. But it can only do us good to acknowledge that variables analysis is particularly limited in its ability to explain." Ibid., 305. Smith writes further, drawing a distinction between the real, the actual, and the empirical. Practical theology would do well to acknowledge these distinctions, seeking for its projects not only to be empirical (as has become en vogue) but also to say something about realities and actualities. Doing so allows it to keep theology in the conversation. Smith states, "According to critical realism, the real is not conterminal with the empirical. So, we must distinguish among the three aspects of the real, the actual, and the empirical. The real is what exists—material, nonmaterial, and social entities that have structures and capacities. The real exists whether we know or understand it. The real possesses objective being apart from human awareness of it. The actual, by contrast, is what happens as events in the world, when objects that belong to the real activate their powers and capacities. The actual happens in time and space, whether we experience it or not. The empirical, by contrast, consists of what we experience, either directly or indirectly. Thus, what we observe (the empirical) is not identical to all that happens (the actual), and neither is identical to that which is (the real). The three must not be conflated." Ibid., 93.

text."[11] What is real is only a socially constructed reality, made real by human epistemological assent.

The epistemic fallacy is the belief that all that is real can be known, that there is actually no reality outside the constructs of the human knower and what the human knower can empirically prove. It is true that all knowledge is value laden and theory laden, that there is no human knowledge from nowhere (Gadamer). Critical realism affirms this and is therefore sympathetic to hermeneutical theory (I'll say more on this below). But this assertion that all knowledge is value and theory laden does not mean there is no ontologically objective world.[12] There may be distinct epistemological worldviews, distinct interpretations of the world, but this does not mean "we inhabit objectively different worlds" or that "there is no objective world."[13]

Browning's own hermeneutical practical theology is of immense help from an epistemological perspective, but it is flawed in its inability (or unwillingness) to attend to an ontological reality. Browning lacks significant theological articulation of divine action because when epistemology absorbs ontology and reality is *only* hermeneutical, God cannot move because God cannot be real; there is no reality for God that is independent of the epistemological

11. Here Archer, Collier, and Porpora expound on Derrida's position and in so doing highlight why I have critiqued Miller-McLemore and Fulkerson for equating everything to the cultural in their postmodern theory. "Whatever Derrida meant by this claim, and he has since equivocated on what he did mean, there is no question about how this pronouncement was heard by many within the academic community—who subsequently went on to become heralds of the new postmodernist movement. It was heard as a declaration that there is no objective reality beyond our own, individual, cultural interpretations. If reality exists anywhere, it exists only in our cultural texts and discourses. As these vary, so does reality itself. Thus, once again, it becomes illicit to ask about God's existence in itself, apart from any cultural context. As with post-Wittgensteinian philosophy with which it is closely aligned, with postmodernism too we can only ask whether God exists in this or that discourse or social text." *Transcendence*, 10.

12. Archer, Collier, and Porpora explain, "It may be that, epistemically, we can only know the world through concepts of our own making, but within our own concepts, we must always make an ontological distinction between what we believe exists independently of us, and what does not. Otherwise, we simply conclude that the universe is coterminous with our knowledge of it. To avoid this conflation, critical realism insists on an epistemological distinction between what it calls the transitive dimension (our beliefs or knowledge claims about the world), and the intransitive dimension (what the world is actually like apart from us)." Ibid., 2.

13. "Critical realism does not deny the value and theory ladenness of knowledge. What it does is to counter the epistemic fallacy. The epistemic fallacy involves the fallacious inference that because there is no epistemologically objective view of the world, there is also no objective world ontologically. Such an inference leads to the extravagant and relativist claim that, to the extent that we embrace different world-views, we inhabit objectively different worlds." Ibid.

constitutions of human creatures. This was not how the people I interviewed experienced God. They experienced God as really coming to them or, as people in Luhrmann's study said, "as realer than real."

Critical realism affirms both the need for hermeneutical theory and empirical study, but it refused, as some theorists call it, the "suicide pact" of contending that only what can be empirically proven without doubt is real or, that there is no reality at all because everything can be deconstructed.

When falling into the epistemic fallacy without the priority of ontology over epistemology, the creature becomes fully the creator. The human creature is so fully the creator that it is through human knowledge that there is reality. The human epistemological agent is creator, for there is nothing real outside of human knowledge. This is why in chapter 5 I placed justification as central to practical theology: justification restates ontology over epistemology by reconstituting the ontological ex nihilo.

The ex nihilo is an objective reality that cannot be epistemologically wiped away. Nothingness is an ontological realism, a reality to which all of us are bound. We may have our own hermeneutical interpretation and worldviews, but nothingness is a stark, shared truth—shouting against our hubris that our epistemological words can create for ourselves no salvation. Justification states that the realism of sin and death cannot be washed away by any human epistemological forms or systems (any human actuality); nothingness is a real experience of loss of a child, like Benjamin. Only the realism of the ontological act of God could save us from the reality in which we find ourselves. Sin comes into the world as the attempt to eliminate the ex nihilo, as the desire for the creature to become the creator. We could say that human beings cannot stand their epistemological fallibility and seek to know all (have knowledge of good and evil; Genesis 2) by standing above reality. Sin and death are realities to which practical theology has not attended enough because to do so would be to reverse the field from the epistemic fallacy in which it has become comfortable.

My justification perspective, then, is not solely a confessional dogmatic statement but one that correlates with the scientific perspective of realism. Justification is the reinstating of the real. It is judgment against epistemological hubris and a return to the priority of ontology. It is the assertion that human beings are not creators of reality, but rather reality as sin and death impinges on us, confusing and so easily making opaque our epistemological conceptions of reality. Justification reminds us that what is truly real is beyond us—for we are on earth and God is in heaven. We are not God and cannot escape our ex nihilo—we are stuck in epistemological relativity (which is to foreshadow the second commitment of critical realism).

BELIEF AND FAITH

Positivism, then, is a dream (and a theologically corrupt one at that). Any scientific perspective is centered, as we said earlier, on belief because it is a representation of reality and cannot possess it fully. Even the most epistemologically observable phenomena must be examined through faith. To avoid reductionism (which positivism always leads to), we must recognize that even the simplest of phenomenon are emergent realities, made up of combinations of realities, stretching all the way to the subatomic level, which we believe is real but cannot be observed in itself, so must be trusted in faith to be. There is much in the sciences that we *believe* that our minds cannot conceive. Just because we cannot prove it completely does not mean it is not. Porpora states, "Whether or not science often actually invokes the word truth, it is indispensable to its practice. If scientists are not to remain rehearsing the same issues, they must build on something. What they build on is what they—either collectively or individually—consider to be true or in correspondence with objective reality."[14]

Critical realism then asserts that what we can know we know as an imperfect encounter with at least part of reality. As Smith says, "reality exists with its own objective structures and dynamics independently of human cognition of it—people do not construct reality but only construct more or less well their meaningful beliefs about and interpretations and understandings of reality."[15] What we say we know (epistemology) is actually the confession of what we *believe* to be so about reality (ontology).

This is why theological epistemologies are no less scientific than other scientific epistemologies (and I make no apologies for chapters 5 and 6). They all share the desire to articulate a piece of reality, to say something true of reality that always spills over any of science's conceptions. Theology too must be engaged critically—it is not master discipline of reality (as it was believed in medieval Europe)—but theology is also not, from a realist perspective, to be eliminated from saying something true about reality, something true about the experience of Rachel and Stanik. Giving epistemological shape through theological discourse to Rachel and Stanik's experience becomes an act of ministry itself. Some in the hard or social sciences claim that they avoid speculation by attending to concrete, measurable phenomenon, which they assume theology cannot do. This is where practical theology, and practical theology as ministry (Christopraxis), makes a contribution.

14. Douglas Porpora, "Judgemental Rationality and Jesus," in Archer, Collier, and Porpora, *Transcendence*, 55.

15. Smith, *What Is a Person?*, 94.

Practical theology claims that speculative theological epistemologies (for instance, systematics) are problematic because they cannot attend to the concrete and, as my Christopraxis perspective would add, have little room for articulating how concrete experiences connect to reality. In addition, practical theology as Christopraxis makes a contribution by claiming, just as the other sciences do, that people have concrete and lived "experiences" of reality and that many people claim (make sense of) these distinct lived experiences as the event of encounter with divine being. Experience (of reality) leads one into epistemological conceptions of what is real and true.

Practical theology as Christopraxis, like other sciences, asserts that *through our concrete experience* we begin to make epistemological assertions about reality that can be rationally judged as true.[16] Practical theology, then, can return theology to a science by helping to connect (again) experience and reality by means of critical discourse (this was my objective with people in chapter 3, taking them into the theological work of part 2).

This is also the explanation for the essential interdisciplinary nature of practical theology: it turns to other epistemologies to help articulate reality, but it comes to these other scientific epistemologies knowing that they too provide only provisional knowledge of a reality greater than the scientific epistemology can know. It may be that the only way to create a locale for true interdisciplinary discourse is by setting it on the stage of realism. Without the realist humility to check the disciplines (to remind them that they are always provisional), one scientific epistemology will always threaten to swallow the other, claiming that it alone knows reality (theology did the swallowing in the Middle Ages, and the hard sciences since the Copernican revolution). From a realist perspective, practical theology (as I will show in the chapter 10) enters discourse with other disciplines' epistemologies of reality, using their epistemologies ad hoc next to concrete experiences of ministry to help do ministry in a form that connects to reality, which we believe is God's being as becoming.[17] My own interdisciplinary method will follow Archer in asserting that "ontology [realism] . . . acts as both gatekeeper and bouncer for methodology."[18]

---

16. Smith says it this way, "Further, scientific knowledge is fallible but is not all equally fallible. Contra empirical realism, scientific knowledge never perfectly corresponds to reality. Contra strong constructivism, scientific knowledge is not hopelessly relativistic in merit. We must live with the fact that we never have perfect human knowledge of the real. Still, some accounts of the real are identifiably better than other accounts. Again, it is the job of human knowing generally and science specifically to engage the process of sorting through the merits of different accounts." Ibid., 94.

17. This is my interdisciplinary method in short.

So just as other sciences, theology attends to a reality that is more than it can know by examining experience. Practical theology becomes essential to all theological science not because it is pragmatic but because it attends most rigorously to experience itself. We must now turn to critical realism's conception of experience.

EXPERIENCE

From a critical realist perspective our epistemological conceptions of reality are actually experiences with the event of imperfectly encountering reality. As we pointed to above, we formulate our epistemologies because we have experiences with reality. From a realist perspective, we can assert that people have experiences of divine action. All experiences of divine action as reality, from a realist perspective, are revelatory: they are event-filled encounters of cause. Philosophical/social-scientific realism claims that all epistemological knowledge is born from the encounter with part of reality through our experience. From a realist perspective my attention to divine action in this project is merited, and from a critical realist perspective this allows us to see the revelatory in concrete and lived experience, claiming that it is through experience of cause that we experience any reality at all.[19] Stanik calls his experience real because it caused him to feel heard and then reorder his life, leaving a prestigious job to cook for campers.

Practical theology has lacked an ability to talk about divine action because it has minimized ontology by conflating it with epistemology. Often, it has done this so it could more directly speak of practical experience. But it has then fallen into the epistemic fallacy and either dips its toes or dives headlong into antirealist conceptions. By so doing practical theology has eliminated evangelical experiences of encountering divine action as real or even true (or, at the very least, worth studying as true), distracting it further from attending to the heart of ministry, which is to witness, testify, and proclaim the real event of divine and human encounter (Christopraxis). So how then do realism and experience connect? Exploring their connection is essential to a Christopraxis practical theology.

---

18. Margaret Archer, *Realist Social Theory: The Morphogenetic Approach* (London: Cambridge University Press, 1995), 22.

19. Very similar to what we argued in chapter 7 through the *concursus Dei*.

EXPERIENCE AS CAUSE

I have already pointed in the direction of this connection. Realism and experience connect through cause. In other words, we experience something as real because we are impacted by its cause. Ron says God really spoke to him because the encounter caused him to get out of bed and live again after the death of his wife. We call something real because we encounter it or, better, it encounters us. Jesus came to Elizabeth with a word for Marlen that Benjamin was safe, causing Marlen to experience peace. And when that something encounters us, it must possess cause for us to call it real, for it to shape our epistemology.[20] For an experience to be real there must be a collision of sorts between ontological realities. As Matt said, "Now I know what Jesus was all about." Something is real because our own being has come up against something else that is (possibly) ontologically real, leading us to make sense of the encounter. We give epistemological shape to what has delivered a cause to our being, revealing a new reality to us.[21]

When we experience a cause (something that impacts our being), we say, "That experience was real" (or as people in Luhrmann's study said, "realer than real"). We even assert that through the experience we have encountered something true. We believe it is true (truth) that our spouse loves us because we have experienced it as a cause on our being (if your partner cheats on you it will *cause* you to doubt the truth that he loves you and doubt whether it was ever true that he did, whether your love was ever real). Cause makes an experience a revelatory experience of reality. If something happens that leaves no cause on me (like pumping gas), it may still be a fleeting generic "experience." It might be real enough, but I quickly forget it because it lacks the revelatory power of epistemologically shifting, even in just a degree, my conception of reality ("I did not know the Lord was in this place"; Gen. 28:16). The very experiences that become transformative to my person are those that have cause that forces me to see reality differently—they are experiences of the real.

Such an encounter could be a transformationally horrible experience of abuse that causes a child to perceive reality as hostile or a profound experience

---

20. Smith explains, "The real may consist of material things, such as chemicals and hurricanes, or of nonmaterial entities, such as structures of memory or identity or personhood. What matters in establishing their reality, in most cases, is their possessing or being endowed with some properties, mechanisms, forces, characteristics, powers, tendencies, or interactive relations capable of producing causal effects in the world. Entities that do are real; they are the things that constitute the intransitive objects of scientific inquiry." *What Is a Person?*, 15.

21. It is hard *not* to see Paul's own conversion in Acts 9 in this light.

of another person sharing in your person as the act of ministry that causes you to see the reality (truth) that you are loved.[22]

I believe in gravity as real because I feel the cause of a fall or I believe in ghosts because I have experienced a supernatural reality. I may later be convinced that my experience was not of a ghost but of a loose shutter, but at least for a time my practical experience in reality leads me to believe something about reality. Others may think I'm crazy because they have no experience of ghosts, but their interpretation of my craziness is based on nearly the same logic as my belief in ghosts—it is based on our opposed or opposite *experience*. I believe ghosts are real (as part of reality) because I have causal experience; my friend sees them as not real because his own experience is absent of ghostly realities, therefore, never delivering a cause that would lead him to call them real.[23]

We often call such experiences with reality that have the causal effect of bringing epistemological change "conversions." We are converted into a new epistemological conception of reality because we have been taken into an event of seeing reality differently. This conversion is an experience, as all religious conversions are. There is no way for it to be other than concretely experienced. People are converted when they see what is true about their reality (that they are in need of justification, that they are dead in sin) in light of a new reality (that Jesus perishes so that they might have life). For instance, Rachel is converted to a changed epistemology: she opens the newspaper and feels God say to her, "It isn't your fault your husband died." She feels the cause of ministry that changes her epistemology through a concrete experience with a reality she believes is God. But this evangelical experience of conversion, as Michael Polanyi has shown, is not only about religious experience. He shows

22. In the last chapter (as well as in my other work) I have pushed hard for the encounter of hypostatic person to hypostatic person as central (as ministry), because such personal relationships are encounters that have deep experiential cause on our being—they possess the power to reveal a new (true) reality (the reality of God's own being are becoming in ministry).

23. As we'll see below, there are also structural, societal, and cultural realities that lead him to think the ghostly stuff crazy. He actually has what I'll call "dependent objective reality" on his side, making the burden of proof on me. But even with this burden of proof, my experience is still affirmed enough to assume that maybe, just maybe, it is true. It may be a long shot, but it is not completely dismissed. This shows how deeply rooted experience is to our engagement with reality as human beings. By the way, it is worth stating, for my own sake, that all this first-person talk of believing in ghosts is only an analogy. I personally don't; I have had many weird experiences that lead me to be open to this reality, to think reality is more stratified in a spiritual direction than we are socialized to believe, but my believing in ghosts has not passed a threshold of congruence with the rest of my life. This is something like Chaves's religious incongruence theory.

that scientific discovery is most definitely the experience of conversion into new epistemological conceptions of what is real; it is a conversion because it is an event of encountering (part of) reality differently. It is a conversion because it is the experience of reality that encounters us at the level of cause—it causes us to see something (God, ourselves, physics, economics) differently. This is why Polanyi asserts that all knowledge (all epistemology) is personal knowledge; it is only knowledge because it is the conversion into *experiencing* the real differently.[24] It is personal because one experientially is caused to convert their epistemological perception of reality through the event of the cause that shatters the epistemological conception of the real with the weight of realities transcending ontology.

When I am caused to epistemologically convert, I say that I have fallen into truth, that I have seen the truth and it has set me free. Truth is possible from a realist perspective because truth is the experience of what is real. Because it is experienced by fallible human agents, there is always the possibility and need for epistemological relativism (which, again, is the second component of critical realism that we'll discuss below), but this does not eliminate that human beings can have partial but true experiences of reality—and when we do, we are compelled to call them truth, as all the people I interviewed did.

In postmodern discourse it has become paradigmatic to claim no possibility for truth, and rightly this has been asserted to point to the epistemological relativity of experience itself. But this epistemological relativity can only lead to the conclusion that truth is an impossibility if we conflate epistemology with ontology. If we claim that there is no reality but only competing experiential epistemologies, then truth is an impossibility. But if there is a real world

24. Mark Mitchell explains Polanyi's position, "Polanyi's use of St. Augustine as a model for his post-critical epistemology makes it especially appropriate to speak in the idiom of conversion. While Augustine's famous conversion was a religious one and the type of conversion Polanyi discusses is primarily epistemological, the two are essentially the same. Whether in the religious or in the epistemological sense (and at times they may be one and the same), a conversion produces an alteration in one's fundamental interpretive framework. Such a 'change' necessarily alters how one views the world. Conversions entail a radical shift in one's interpretive framework or they may produce only a modest modification; the depth of the cognitive commitment may be measured in either case by the ensuing change of our outlook." *Michael Polanyi* (Wilmington, DE: ISI Books, 2006), 93. He continues, "Conversion occurs when one's interpretive framework is challenged by that of another. In such cases, one encounters a new conceptual language that produces a different interpretive framework, which in turn implies a 'new way of reasoning.' When opposing frameworks are so different that adherents of one cannot even speak intelligibly to adherents of the other, the possibility of one partisan convincing another of the superiority of his position is slight. But even when persuasion becomes impossible, conversion remains viable." Ibid., 94.

that exists beyond the human mind, if there is a shared objective reality (like oxygen, matter, and finitude), then there is the humble and always contested but nevertheless possible ability to say something true, for to say something true is to say something that is real.

To uphold the integrity of critical realism it must be restated, at the risk of redundancy, that what is experienced as real, as true, does not foreclose on the totality of reality. You may have experiences that leave a cause, but this does not mean there is not more to reality itself. Your experience is a way (the only way for the human being) into reality, but reality can never be captured by subjective experience—it always overspills every epistemological position.

I may have an experience—a real experience, like having my best friend die of cancer when I was a child—that might cause me to epistemologically conceive that God doesn't exist. While this experience is subjectively real, that does not mean it is objectively the case. As a matter of fact, I may later have a new experience (a conversion experience) that causes me to question my epistemological commitment. I will question it because I have had a new practical experience with the causal effect on my being reordering my subjective reality.

And my subjective reality, even in its openness to transition, is always engagement with an objective reality. Realism asserts that there is an objectivity to reality but concedes that the way we experience this objective reality, in significant part, is subjective—it is through experience. This means that one's subjective experience has the potential to imperfectly witness to (part of) reality. Archer, Collier, and Porpora make a strong case that the subjective experience of transcendence (of experiencing divine action) is no less legitimate than the atheistic presumptions of the university.[25] They contend that the atheistic so-called scientific commitment can be interpreted as held by those who simply have not had an experience of the transcendent. They no doubt will, without this experience of reality, deny that this reality exists (that it is true). This is

25. "Throughout their history the social sciences have privileged atheism. . . . Indeed, social science bears much responsibility for enabling atheism to be presented as an epistemologically neutral position, instead of what it is, a commitment to a belief in the absence of religious phenomena. In part, this derived from the personal irreligiosity of the founding fathers; Durkheim and Marx were prominent 'masters of suspicion,' whilst Weber declared himself 'religiously unmusical.' In equal part, it can be attributed to the pervasive methodological endorsement of empiricism, which illegitimately confines investigation to observables. At best, empiricists consigned non-observables to the metaphysical realm; at worst, the non-observable was deemed 'nonsense' in logical positivism. In sum, empiricism confirmed the hegemony of sense data over everything that can be known. Since realism has mounted such a remorseless critique upon empiricism, a parallel critique of its bedfellow, atheism, is now overdue." Margaret Archer, "Models of Man," in Archer, Collier, and Porpora, *Transcendence*, 63.

more than reasonable. But it is just as valid to assume, because of *experience*, that this reality is true, as Shirley, Lynn, and Margo do. The experience of the divine has had cause on their being. So it is legitimate for some to say that they have had an experience of divine action; it is even legitimate for them to see this experience as having such cause on them that it was revealed to them as truth. This is not illogical, but it will always have to be defended by placing such experiences called "truth" back into conversation with other experiences that are also claimed to be true and bound to the real.

This is why ministry, from my perspective, *is* practical theology. Even from the human side, looking from the ground up, ministry is encompassed in testimony and witness. The human agent does practical theology as ministry because ministry attends to these experiences, opening space for people to articulate their experience of reality through testimony of their experience and witness to divine action through their experience. Ministry is giving them space to *interpret* their experience.

Critical realism does not say that divine action is truth, only that it could be. Such experiences have had causal impact on persons and reality is always more than we can know, but we can know it (provisionally) through our experiences. Critical realism says divine action is possible but does not say this in a dismissive way (like, it may be possible for pigs to fly). Rather, because our epistemologies are conversions into perceived realities through experience, people's experience of what they call real must be deeply respected (my approach to practical theology is based on the desire to respect the evangelical experience).

Critical realism says not only that divine action is possible but that, though it may be possible, it may not be true. Many people have *no* experience of divine cause, and with no cause there is no reality. So critical realism does not prove my articulation of divine action in my Christopraxis approach, but it does allow space for its possibility and creates this space by attending to experience (an essential for practical theology). Moving practical theology into realism gives us many openings to discuss divine encounter because it raises the importance of practical experience (as we'll explore more below) and it does so through cause. And as we saw in the last chapter, cause is the central component in the *concursus Dei*. Philosophical/social-scientific realism allows us to speak of the experience of cause that is beyond, or interrupts, our epistemological preconceptions. It allows us to have experiences that we confess (believe) as real, as true.

Realism is no apologetic for divine action, but it reinstates ontology over epistemology, which from a philosophical/social-scientific perspective allows space for discussion of divine act and being. However, this view of reality as cause, which is so tied to subjective experience, needs to be extended.

LAYERS OF REALITY

We should be careful here because we experience reality in layers. I have described how experience, cause, and reality are connected, but I did this mostly by attending to the subjective layer of reality. This will remain significant for my perspective because, as experiential human beings, our subjectivity is central to our epistemologies of reality. But there are other forces (material and nonmaterial) that exist outside our subjectivity that have cause on our being and therefore must be called real.

THE DEPENDENT SUBJECTIVE LAYER

Smith, drawing from Searle, explores three layers to reality. First, reality can be perceived as subjective. What is real here is one's personal experience, and Archer and others believe, as I have said above, that people's personal experience is a legitimate (though always unsettled) resource for interpreting reality.[26] This is so because such personal subjective experiences have cause; even the delusions of the individual at the very least leave cause on him. He sweats with anxiety because he is sure the large yellow bunny will get him. There is no correlation between his subjective experience and what all others experience (no one else experiences the yellow bunny so it has no cause on them; its reality is questioned and therefore only exists as real in what Smith calls the dependent subjectivity of the anxious man). But it is real to this anxious man, leaving a cause on him—as much as others try to talk him out of his delusional conceptions, he cannot escape them because they *feel* (they are experienced as) so real.

At the layer of dependent subjective reality, the yellow bunny may be called real, but reality is not solely constituted in the dependent subjective. Subjective reality can be individually dependent (as in the case of our anxious man) or relationally shared. Relationally shared subjectivity is like the shared subjective experience of children feeling the love of their mother. The

---

26. I mean "personal" here in the full weight of its ambiguity. "Personal" could be read as "singularly"; this is part of the subjective layer of reality. But "personal" could also be read (as is my theological commitment) in a relational way that asserts that we have our being in shared connection with others. Therefore, the subjective layer of reality is subjective in a singularly dependent way, but also in a shared way. Subjective experience can be seen as either dependent or shared. Here too I'm following Polanyi, who asserts that the scientist must move into experimentation and discovery through passion. Polanyi contends that the rational, pure objective researcher is a fallacy and that all true discovery comes through the subjective (personal) passions of the scientist.

experience of their mother's love is subjective—most confess that they feel it, that they share a subjective experience that they witness to as real because of the experience's effect on their being. Thus their experience is subjective but not solely dependent on (not locked in) one individual's consciousness like the yellow bunny is (I'll wait to say more about shared subjectivity until I get to the third layer of reality).

From a critical realist perspective, subjective experience is not to be scorned but embraced (and my Christopraxis perspective has made it central). But this embracing does not mean that reality is only and completely subjective (whether in its dependent or shared form). *This reduction of reality to only the subjective has been a major mistake of American Evangelicalism that has led to many cultural, societal, and theological problems* (I'll explain more below). So, to advance us into the second layer of reality we could say that for the yellow bunny to move beyond the dependent subjective layer of reality, beyond the delusions of the anxious man, it must (eventually) produce a shared subjective experience, and this shared subjective experience needs to connect (emerge) to the second layer of reality, which Smith calls "dependent objective reality."

DEPENDENT OBJECTIVE LAYER

By dependent objective reality Smith means material and nonmaterial realities that are constituted in larger social systems or perspectives (Searle calls them "institutional facts"). These dependent objective realities are often socially constructed, as in Smith's own example of recycling. But once constructed, they take on a reality that has the force of organizing people's action (delivering cause). "We do not socially construct reality," Smith explains, "but we do out of reality creatively construct the social and refabricate the material. And the social in turn becomes for us a part of reality."[27]

Recycling is real (though a hundred years ago it was not) because it brings cause as social realities. Recycling does not simply exist in people's subjective experience (though it does) but also powerfully in their shared social experience (reality) of separating cardboard from plastic and placing it on the curb as a practical action. These realities are dependent because they exist only through human construction and participation, but they are objective because they exist (are made real) beyond the subjective willing or experiencing of any single person or group.

I could subjectively claim to my neighbor that recycling isn't real, that because I subjectively refuse to or cannot experience it, recycling does not

27. Smith, *What Is a Person?*, 197.

exist. But this subjective commitment will not stop the recycling truck from roaring past my house at 7:00 a.m. These dependent objective realities are social constructions and therefore are dependent on human assent and perpetuation, but once they are socially solidified, they exist beyond the subjective will of individuals or groups.[28] As an objective reality, recycling takes no concern for my solely independent subjective experience. As a dependent objective reality, recycling is only real through human social construction, but as constructed it becomes real through its significant cause on me (and the society of which I am part).[29]

Michael Emerson's study of Evangelicals' conception of race provides another example.[30] Emerson discovered that a growing number of Evangelicals had an epistemological conversion experience toward racial reconciliation, subjectively seeing a new reality in which people of color were befriended and treated as equals. Yet, he shows that while this subjective experience led to a new subjective reality, it did not move up the layers of reality into the dependent objective. Evangelicalism can be critiqued, and Emerson does so, for ignoring (or denying) dependent objective reality, keeping its feet only in the subjective and leaving the structures and forces of dependent objective reality as they are. Therefore, in Emerson's study Evangelicals refused to acknowledge racism's institutional forms, committing themselves to racial reconciliation only on the subjective plane of reality. This was a plane that people of color appreciated enough but in the end missed the painful (dehumanizing) realities of racial profiling, economic conditions, and incarceration that exist on the dependent objective plane of reality. Dependent objective realities include nonmaterial realities like democracy, conceptions of race, and family systems, and of course material realities like freeways, capital cities, family size, ghettos, and so much more.[31]

For the yellow bunny to be real (beyond the dependent subjective), it needs not only to have shared subjective experiential impact but also to become objective in social realities. If hundreds (or thousands or millions) of people also

28. Unless groups can fight to change them through political and cultural engagement. Because dependent objective realities are socially constructed, they can also be deconstructed. But what is often missed is that the motivation for this engagement is often born in the shared subjective.

29. This is what Smith calls soft social constructionism as opposed to hard social constructionism, which falls into the epistemic fallacy of believing that all that is real is only a social construction.

30. Michael Emerson and Christian Smith, *Divided by Faith: Evangelical Religion and the Problem of Race in America* (Oxford: Oxford University Press, 2000).

31. For a discussion of the imaginations of race, see Willie Jennings, *The Christian Imagination: Theology and the Origins of Race* (New Haven, CT: Yale University Press, 2010).

have a subjective experience of the yellow bunny and then meet to discuss it, learn about it, or even commune together with it, the yellow bunny would remain in the layer of the subjective reality but would also move into the layer of dependent objective reality. One could still deny that yellow bunny is real, but one could not deny that there are a number of people whom claim to have experienced the yellow bunny and now own real buildings in which to worship the yellow bunny and offer real ideas that impact society. Not only would numbers of other people experiencing the yellow bunny give credence to the subjective experience (showing again how cause and reality are connected—we concede that yellow bunny *might* be real because of its impactful cause through shared subjectivity), but these shared subjective experiences would take on socially constructed forms of agency and structure that would lodge the experience in more than simply the subjective, moving it into (dependent) objective realities.

The yellow bunny is real in the layer of the subjective—no one doubts that it has an effect on the anxious man; his paranoia and racing heart witness to its cause. But its realness must be left in the subjective realm, real to the individual delusional person (hence its dependent subjectivity) but real no further. The yellow bunny emerges from lower subjective experience to the higher dependent objective reality as shared subjective experiences take on uniting forms of agency and structures within our social environments.

This does not minimize or illegitimate subjective experience, for through subjective experience that becomes shared, new dependent objective realities have the potential to emerge (be constructed, and constructed as real). Luther had a profound subjective experience of the justifying action of the divine being, which he called real. This subjective experience led him to challenge the dependent objective reality of the Roman church. This, in turn, led to the reform of the dependent objective reality of the church in and through the shared subjective experience of many who also experienced the divine being this way, claiming it as real.[32]

A Christopraxis perspective, then, does not ignore or minimize dependent objective realities of church, tradition, and society. It claims them as real and therefore as locales for ministry. It is opposed, because of its critical realist veins, to the Evangelical mistake of conflating all reality to the subjective, ignoring material and nonmaterial structural realities in society, for instance. A

---

32. Of course the history is more complicated than just this. Some princes and barons had no subjective experience of divine action but did see an opportunity for structural change in dependent objective reality, so they backed the reformer. But to say that the Reformation was only about structural societal change is to be more than a little reductionistic.

Christopraxis perspective claims that reality is more than subjective. But also because of its same critical realist veins, it claims that the evangelical subjective experience can witness to reality.[33] That reality cannot be reduced to only the dependent objective existence of ideologies, structures, and cultural formations. *A Christopraxis perspective claims that these dependent objective realities do not stand alone but exist in stratified (emergent) layers of reality and that dependent objective realities need both to be critiqued by and to critique subjective reality.*

It is my contention that the methodologies of established practical theology have often reduced reality to only the dependent objective (as Evangelicals have conflated all reality into the subjective).[34] This reduction has allowed practical theology to give rich attention to human forms of action, studying liberation, congregational practice, and much more. But this reduction of reality has also had the effect of both disparaging the evangelical subjective experience and eliminating the possibility that these experiences are more than (*more real* than) socially constructed epistemologies.

Established practical theology has often followed the university in contending that all reality is epistemologically (socially) constructed. While this has allowed for rich and significant articulations of practice, socialization, and empirical analysis, it has hamstrung practical theology from attending to the depth of *shared* subjective encounter with the divine being. Thus, practical theology has not embraced the emergent layers of reality (or realism at all), foreclosing on dependent objective reality, which, when stripped from the others, lacks any ability to be real outside of the epistemological constructions of human minds and agents.[35]

---

33. Notice that I have made a distinction between "Evangelical" with a capital *E* and "evangelical" with a lowercase *e*. With the capital letter I denote the sociological Evangelical movement (as in the claim that American Evangelicalism voted for Bush), and with the lowercase letter I denote a broad theological perspective that claims the realism of the act of God as it encounters subjective persons.

34. Archer, Collier, and Porpora's words about the social sciences I think could also be leveled against practical theology. "Admittedly, in anthropology and sociology today, social scientists approach religion with caution. They do not want to embroil themselves in theological issues. That, they think, would compromise their status as scientists. It is partly for this reason that social scientists prefer the post-Wittgensteinian and postmodern approaches to religion. An exclusive focus on religious practices, discourses and texts allows social scientists to bracket methodologically any question about the truth of the putative realities to which they refer. Instead, social scientists can examine the exclusively social contribution to religion." *Transcendence*, 13.

35. "Emergent properties are relational, arising out of combination (e.g. the division of labour from which high productivity emerges), where the latter is capable of reacting back on the former (e.g. producing monotonous work), has its own causal powers (e.g. the differential wealth of nations), which

This is why, in my opinion, the Aristotelian framework of possibility to actuality has been so intriguing to practical theology, for it has been the most potent way to speak of the recasting, reworking, and reordering of the dependent objective reality. But it has done this at the peril of the stratified nature of reality itself, moving away from imaginative conceptions of divine encounter because divine action cannot exist within a reality that is *only* dependent objective.[36] *And it cannot exist here, for when dependent objective reality is all there is, then all reality is epistemologically constructed and there is no possibility for any ontological reality beyond epistemological constructions of dependent objective reality that human beings construct.* When all reality is reduced to the dependent objective, the creature has become the creator: all that is, is because human beings have socially constructed it from the power of human epistemology. Human epistemology is so powerful that it is its own creator and lord and therefore has no need for the divine reality that acts to justify us so that we might participate in the highest level of reality—God's very Trinitarian self (Athanasius).

It is no wonder, then, that liberal mainline congregations and schools have often been accused of lacking the willingness to talk about divine action and people's concrete experience of it. It is no wonder because reality has been reduced to only the dependent objective, making societal or cultural engagement all there is. Established practical theology's allergy to realism (and its stratified nature) has led it to overdose on the pills of dependent objective reality, claiming in its drugged state that all reality is dependent objective. Archer, Collier, and Porpora say directly, "Mainline Protestantism and Reform Judaism may each have heroically demythologized their religious content to an extent that no other religion has dared. It is no accident, however, that these are each also denominational forms in decline."[37]

But, of course, part of this contention is a result of Evangelicalism's own conflation of all reality (even God) to subjective experience. If mainline liberalism has reduced reality to the dependent objective, then Evangelicalism

---

are causally irreducible to the powers of its components (individual workers)." Archer, *Realist Social Theory*, 9.

36. "Objective reality is by nature not flat but stratified, existing on multiple, though connected, levels, each of which operates according to its own characteristic dynamics and processes." Ibid., 95. Smith continues, "In a critical realist world—the world I believe we actually inhabit—reality is stratified; higher levels are emergent from lower; and different causal properties, mechanisms, and dynamics exist and operate at varying levels according to concerns appropriate to their own levels and not to others." Ibid., 203.

37. *Transcendence*, 9.

has conflated all reality to the subjective. It is no wonder, then, that neither established practical theology nor practice-directed Evangelicalism can speak theologically of divine action. In established practical theology divine action has been reduced to structures, traditions, or ideologies in dependent objective reality, whereas in Evangelicalism divine action has been conflated with aesthetic or moral feelings in the subjective. My Christopraxis perspective, resting on critical realism, seeks to avoid both the reduction and conflation that have hampered practical theology.

INDEPENDENT OBJECTIVE LAYER

The third and final layer of reality is what Smith calls "independent objective reality" and what Searle calls "brute facts." While a layer of reality is no doubt socially constructed and therefore called dependent because it is dependent on human minds and action, critical realism asserts that there is also *independent objective reality* that exists independent of whether the human mind can or ever will conceive of it. Searle explains that there are brute facts that exist beyond any social construction. For instance, while we can socially construct many reasons for and practices within the experience of death, we cannot change the brute fact that all human being is toward death. This is a brute fact!

This independent objective reality is not outside (or elsewhere) than the real, just other or beyond what the human being is capable of knowing completely (again, the realist contention that ontology precedes epistemology). In critical realism God is not transreal or suprareal, somehow only existing beyond reality. God *does* exist beyond and other than subjective or dependent objective realities but nevertheless is a part of reality, the part Smith calls the independent objective layer. [38] We can declare (believe) that God exists in reality because some people in shared subjective ways point to cause (we can even point to cause in the dependent objective layer). In connection to the

---

38. This is why Barth's theology is better understood as (critical) realist than as neoorthodox; see Bruce McCormick's *Karl Barth's Critically Realistic Dialectical Theology* (New York: Oxford University Press, 1997) and Paul La Montagne's *Barth and Rationality: Critical Realism in Theology* (Eugene, OR: Cascade Books, 2012). This is so because Barth is not placing God in a metaphysical nether world, but as a reality that the human being doesn't possess the equipment to know. God may be real as a brute fact, but we can only know this by experiencing an encounter with God. We can have no knowledge of God outside of God's free act to make Godself known. God is an independent objective reality in Godself, and there is no way for the human being to know God in any other way. The human being can only know this God by experiencing the action of this God and experiencing this action as a subjective reality that is **critiqued by and also critiques** dependent objective realities (theologically we might call these tradition or community or creed).

concursus Dei, realism asserts that cause points to the possibility that something is real. This does not free theism from doubt; *any* reality in the independent objective layer can be doubted because fallible human epistemology cannot possess it.

So in this third layer, that which is real, whether it is material or nonmaterial, natural or spiritual, always spills over and cracks open human epistemology with the force of encounter with an ontological reality that exists in the independent objective layer. This could be God or the size of the super black holes that are *believed* to exist at the center of the universe. People can just as easily say, "I don't believe it," to God or to black holes, for both are independent objective realities that cannot be proven by human epistemologies that exist on the lower plane of stratified reality.[39]

Of course, God and the black holes are distinct (even ontologically), but in the layers of realism both are independent objective realities that are independent of human epistemology, both as ontological facts and as realities too large or deep for human consciousness to fully comprehend. But this does not mean that we can *never* know independent objective reality. It does, however, mean that we can never know independent objective reality in itself—we can know it only as we personally encounter it, for, again, all human epistemology is located on a lower plane of reality itself.[40] We can only know independent objective reality by experiencing it in part, through an encounter that happens in and through our own (and shared) subjective reality in cultural and social locales.

That the earth is round is an independent objective reality; it would be and remain round if no human being or society ever conceived it as such. As

39. "Emergence theories such as Bhaskar's are fighting on fronts against dualist or pluralist theories which assert the complete independence of higher strata on lower, and against reductionists who assert the ultimate unreality of the higher strata." Andrew Collier, *Critical Realism: An Introduction to Roy Bhaskar's Philosophy* (London: Verso, 1994), 112.

40. Smith explains how and why independent objective reality exists outside of the human mind. "In other words, independently objective reality consists of the material elements, forces, energies, and their innumerable emergent products existing and operating at multiple levels—but not including human mentally and socially constructed dependent subjective and objective realities. The key qualities that distinguish independently objective reality from the first two kinds of reality are its mind-independent ontology, mind-affecting causal capacity, and bounded practical performance. First, independently objective realities possess existence in reality independent of human mental activity. Second, given normal human perceptual equipment and participation in reality, they possess the natural ability to impinge upon human bodies and minds from their position of objective ontology in ways that can influence the perceptions and conceptions that human minds make and hold of reality. In short, they possess epistemically relevant construction-directive capacities." *What Is a Person?*, 187.

a matter of fact, even when the earth was believed to be flat it was (really) round. This conception of a flat earth was passed on as real through dependent objective ideologies and structures. The earth's independent objective reality as round would only become known through a personal encounter in which Magellan had the subjective experience (the revelation) of watching ships return to port, witnessing their masts first against the background of the horizon. Magellan had an event of ontological encounter with independent objective reality, which transformed (epistemologically converted) him. This encounter was not outside the reality of his subjective experience, which put him in tension with the reality of dependent objective ideologies and power structures of his society. Magellan dealt with the very stratified nature of reality itself.[41]

I have used the distinction between time and eternity throughout my argument, seeking a practical theology that speaks of eternity moving into time. But this moving of eternity into time is not simply the mixing of metaphysical containers; time and eternity are not ontotheological buckets but stratified layers of reality. The very commitment to the qualitative distinction between time and eternity (Kierkegaard) is the prophetic assertion that reality cannot be captured in toto by human epistemological forms. "God is in heaven and you

41. Andrew Collier says further, "The relation in religious contexts between the two verbs 'to reveal' and 'to experience' is this: revelation is always revelation by someone of something to someone; for the present context, revelation by God, of some aspect of himself, to human beings. Experience is always someone experiencing something: in this context, a person experiencing aspects of God. Where genuine revelation has taken place, the two verbs denote the same process from two sides. But it is possible to experience some quality as belonging to God when it does not. In this case, no revelation has taken place, and the experience is illusory." "Natural Theology, Revealed Theology and Religious Experience," in Archer, Collier, and Porpora, *Transcendence,* 134. Collier continues, articulating how I see revelation and religious experience as connected in my critical realist Christopraxis practical theology: "However, from the fact that all revelation is known through religious experience, it does not follow that what is known is simply the experience and not revelation at all. To focus on the experience rather than the revelation (except for special, limited purposes) is to falsify the experience, for the experience is focused not upon itself but on the revelation. *A theology that takes as its subject matter religious experience rather than revelation goes astray in the same way that Berkeley led empiricism astray about human knowledge in general.* However, theology cannot bypass religious experience in its rightful focus on revelation, because there is no access to revelation aside from religious experience. We need to hold to two truths here, in order to avoid the epistemic fallacy: (l) our only access to revelation is through religious experience, and (2) religious experience can be false, can present as revealed what God has never revealed and what contradicts what God has revealed. Hence, two errors are possible which arguably Schleiermacher and Barth respectively are at least prone to, if not always guilty of: one can take all religious experience at face value and obliterate the distinction between that which is true and that which is false; or one can take for granted what the content of revelation is (a particular book or creed or the confessions of a particular Church) and refuse to answer the legitimate questions 'How do we know? Why this putative revelation and not that one?'" Ibid., 135; emphasis added.

are on earth," as Kierkegaard said. But heaven and earth are not to be confused as metaphysical places, necessarily, but as stratifications of reality. Kierkegaard's assertion is that reality is ontologically more than what the human being can know and that if there is a God, this God acts and moves outside of or beyond our epistemological assumptions.[42] God's very act and being—like the Hegelian movement of *Geist*—cannot be constituted in human epistemological systems. Reality is always ontologically more than epistemological systems can possess.

Polanyi contends that all (hard) scientific discovery functions in the way of revelation.[43] Scientific experiments are not the possessing of reality but the personal experiential encounter with part of reality, which leads us to confession through our subjective experience with this part of what independent objective reality is like.[44] All scientific discoveries are much like the ministerial actions of witness and testimony. They give witness to their personal (subjective) experience of independent objective reality in discourse and debate with dependent objective communities, seeking to understand, much like Anselm, what this personal encounter means (how it is real).

42. This is what I think Barth means by the wholly otherness of God—not that God is metaphysically cordoned off from humanity, but that God is the reality that cannot be made into the idol of human systems of epistemology.

43. Paul La Montagne explains Barth's position on revelation, a position that finds congruence with my project overall and Polanyi's personal knowledge and critical realism in general. "This means that there is a God to be known and we do have real knowledge of God in revelation. None of the questions to be addressed in theology can even be raised as questions about God apart from the reality of revelation. Barth is not beginning with an inquiry into whether there is any such thing as revelation, and what revelation must be if we encounter it. Rather, he takes it for granted that we have been encountered by God in revelation and that all theology is a post hoc investigation of what we encountered in revelation and who we must be because we have encountered it. This does not mean that Barth denies the question as to whether or not revelation does occur. As we will see later, Barth recognizes that all theology is done in the face of this question, and cannot wish it otherwise. But theology, and in particular church dogmatics, does not even begin until we have given, at least provisionally and hypothetically, a positive answer to this question." *Barth and Rationality: Critical Realism in Theology* (Eugene, OR: Cascade Books, 2012), 114.

44. Smith, quoting Polanyi, explains, "Pure objectivity and personal detachment are thus not only not possible in the search for knowledge but also totally undesirable. 'As human beings, we must inevitably see the universe from a center lying within ourselves and speak about it in terms of a human language shaped by the exigencies of human intercourse. Any attempt to rigorously eliminate our human perspective from our picture of the world must lead to absurdity.' The quest for objectivity, we can see in retrospect, meant well, but it was misguided. The true good that objectivity sought to accomplish was not really about objectivity as detached neutrality. Rather, it was about personal commitment to seeking the truth about reality instead of forcing reality to fit into our interests and biases—and that inescapably entails personal dedication, involvement, judgment, and responsibility." *What Is a Person?*, 182.

As we personally wrestle with reality, our faith seeking understanding, we can know part of independent objective reality because it is reality, and as knowers we exist (indwell) reality in all its layers. We cannot epistemologically master the layers that are above us (independent objective reality), but even this layer comes to us as parts of reality. To continue to follow Polanyi, we can know (or, better, experience) independent objective reality, not because we can climb to a perch where we can observe this independent objective reality but because we indwell it (it encounters us) in a personal way. We cannot epistemologically possess it, but we do live in and through all the stratified layers of reality itself. And because we rub up against them personally, all our knowledge of reality is personal.

It is a personal encounter, but not because all independent objective reality is personal, much of it is just brute fact, like gravity, death, and round planets revolving around the sun. It is personal because we personally experience it; we experience it in relation to our personal being. Just as all epistemological transformation is similar to religious conversion, so all discovery is similar to the evangelical experience of encounter with higher levels of reality (with independent objective realities). And this personal experience is ontological. It is deeper than epistemology, for we have experiences with independent objective reality that escape all epistemological language games; they are greater, more real, existing on a higher plane of reality because they encounter us as real even outside of the ability to describe them. This again demonstrates that we experience—indwell—all the layers of reality but can never possess those above us; this is why James Loder always told a student struggling with a paper, "You know more than you can say."

The infant indwells the independent objective reality of gravity by personally living in it, soon (within months) knowing how it works by experiencing it personally—by dropping her cup dozens of times from her highchair at mealtime to *experience* gravity's cause. The child can't describe this knowledge, the child cannot describe anything, but even without the ability of language she is experiencing reality and has knowledge of it through encountering its cause. This knowledge is what Polanyi calls "tacit knowledge"; it is knowing more about reality than we can say. And, in turn, our inability to say it, or say it for certain, does not mean it is not real. We can only say anything at all through our personal encounter with reality (which has limits). Many who have had encounters with the divine being will say that it was just so real (see Luhrmann) and so real because they can feel cause. Nevertheless, though they can feel it so strongly, they cannot describe it; it escapes description because it was a personal encounter with the real—with an ontological reality that is above them.

From the level of tacit knowledge, it is possible that people's subjective experience of the divine being is real. Just because they passionately and subjectively believe in their experience doesn't illegitimate it as real but actually, according to Polanyi, positions them, because of their encounter, to know the real.[45] People's assertions of their subjective experience that they have encountered God as an independent objective reality *can be* perceived as personal knowledge. And this form of divine encounter wears marks similar to those of scientific realism.

It is not illogical (though always said in faith, as is belief in black holes) to say that we experience God's being as becoming to us as minister. God's being is an independent objective reality, but we can know God (that is, we can have epistemological knowledge of this independent objective reality) only because God's being comes to us (this is why I've said over and over that God's being is in becoming). And it is my contention, as my Christopraxis approach affirms, that this reality comes to us as a *shared subjective reality*, as an experience of personal knowledge. And in contrast to our beliefs about gravity or black holes, we confess because of our personal knowledge that this God who comes to us as an independent objective reality is in Godself a cause that moves to us as subject and as subject can be experienced in our own personal subjectivity.[46] La Montagne, making a case for critical realism in Karl Barth's perspective, says, "'God's being revealed' means that 'God becomes an object of our experience.' Revelation makes God accessible to experience. Experience means the 'process of perceiving ourselves, our world, and the two in indissoluble correlation.'"[47]

This subjective experience is not an experience with a dependent subjective reality (not a delusion, not the yellow bunny). It is a shared subjective experience, for it is personal, as it comes through our own ministerial action in the dependent objective reality that shares in another's person. Through ministry, subjective experience is shared, and, confessed in its sharing, it

45. "The very best of science, Polanyi shows, involves not the detachment of scientists but precisely the opposite: their deep personal involvement. The generation and comprehension of knowledge entails not simply the following of formal rules and procedures. More importantly, Polanyi observed, it requires of knowers personal commitment to truth, capacities to perceive the value of potential discoveries, active engagement in inquiry, the exercise of artful skills, reliance on tacit understanding, the making of judgments of belief, the discernment of patterns and meanings in holistic gestalts of data, appreciation for the beauty of the known world, provisional and wise trust in other knowledgeable authorities, passion for and joy in discovery, and the taking of responsibility for reporting knowledge well." Ibid., 181.

46. As we saw in the *concursus Dei*.

47. La Montagne, *Barth and Rationality*, 140.

witnesses to being an experience of the independent objective reality. *Ministry embraces all layers of reality!*

I would call this shared experience of ministry a hypostatic subjective reality. Just as subjective experiments in science have the humble potential to encounter reality at the level of its independent objectivity, so theology uses the experiential action of ministry to encounter the independent objective reality that is God. This makes practical theology of central importance in the full theological endeavor. Just as scientific experiment gives us framed experiences of reality, so too, we confess, does ministry.[48] In and through experiencing one's person shared in as the act of ministry one experiences (with another) the independent objective reality. *In the act of ministry, independent objective reality is experienced as subjective reality that is lived out in dependent objective realities in the church and world.* Therefore, we can experience independent objective reality, but we experience it through our subjective reality that seeks verification and continuity or finds conflict in the dependent objective layer of reality.[49] What is clear is that these three layers of reality are linked, and all realities are experienced.

EXPERIENCE AS PRACTICAL ACTION

What I hope can be spotted, even through the dense, layered canopy of reality that we have discussed, is that through *practical experience* we engage, and therefore can know (in part), reality. Through experience framed by practical action we engage all the layers of reality. The child in the highchair can engage reality, but not because she is a well-oiled epistemological machine. She is anything but. Though she is still so epistemologically nascent, she is

---

48. "In any field of study, the nature of what exists cannot be unrelated to how it is studied. This is a strong realist statement." Archer, *Realist Social Theory*, 16.

49. Or it does not find continuity. Mark Chaves has argued that there is actually a religious incongruence that often happens. I do not have time or space to deal adequately with Chaves's important point. I'll only point to the possibility that finding consistency or even unity between these three layers of reality is easier said than done. It may be that most people do not seek or care to have congruence between these layers. Chaves explains, "Some religious leaders and people strive for religious congruence, but not all do. Striving for congruence is not an essential feature of religion—unless we declare it such by definition." "SSSR Presidential Address Rain Dances in the Dry Season: Overcoming the Religious Congruence Fallacy," *Journal for the Scientific Study of Religion* 49, no. 1 (2010): 9. He continues, "How might we overcome the religious congruence fallacy? Obviously, we should hesitate to treat religious beliefs as stable dispositions, we should hesitate to explain behavior by connecting it to religious affiliations, practices, or beliefs from which the behavior seems to follow, and we should try to better understand the conditions under which religious congruence really does emerge. But I want to go beyond these obvious implications." Ibid., 10.

able to experience reality, even the layer of independent objective reality. She can do so because she is capable of taking on practical action; she experiences the parts of reality through practice done by her body.[50] The very practical action of picking up and dropping a cup draws her into the experience of reality. It draws her in because she indwells reality as embodied; through her practical action she tests reality. It is *not* language (epistemology) that allows her to know reality; rather, her practical engagement with reality itself (engaged prelanguage) allows her eventually to take on epistemology.[51] She encounters first the ontological reality of her own being; through the embodied experience of her earliest practices she engages reality.

Archer makes a case that reality is not the social construction solely of human epistemological agents who create what is real through language.[52] Rather, she shows that the infant, long before possessing language, learns through emotive practice to encounter reality.[53] The infant uses practice to experience the reality of his own self-consciousness. In the practice of feeding and grabbing he encounters reality through cause. The child's practice, even in the first few weeks, relays the ontological reality to the child that it is in a world. But the objects in the world are not the child because the child is other than the objects.[54] This is an essential truth to learn of reality, and

---

50. Erik Erickson even contends that infants through practice can feel whether their caregiver is trustworthy, even to the point of feeling the larger communal interpretation of the caregiver.

51. Archer talks further of language in relation to realism. "Language shares intentionality with practice: they are both 'about' something. Thus Merleau-Ponty ends in accord with realism, for as Collier puts it, 'language can only be learnt by reference to reality. Not only is there no one privileged access to reality, language is not even the first runner. Linguistic interaction presupposes practical interaction, in which the pre-linguistic child engages, through play and the satisfaction of its physical and emotional needs.'" Margaret Archer, *Being Human: The Problem of Agency* (London: Cambridge University Press, 2000), 136.

52. Archer says, "Realism is thus 'concerned with actions which are practical, not just symbolic: with making (poesis), not just doing (praxis), or rather with doing which is not, or not only *saying*'" Ibid., 310.

53. Archer states further, "Pre-verbal practical action is the source of basic principles of logical reasoning which are prior to and necessary for discursive socialisation. There is no reason to believe that such practical activity ceases with the acquisition of language. The primacy of practice has therefore been defended as prior to participation in society's conversation, and also necessary to our acquisition of the logical canon which is quintessential to our rationality." Ibid., 153.

54. "We must all have transactions with an undifferentiated reality from our first day of life. At first we cannot know reality as subdivided into the inanimate and animate, animate and human etc. before we begin our practical dealings with it. Hunger, thirst and discomfort are our initial physiological prompts to such exchanges, but their imperiousness serves to reinforce Marx's important insight that we are committed to continuous practical activity in a material world, where subsistence is dependent upon the working relationship between us and things, which cannot be reduced to the relations 'between the ideas

Archer explains that it happens through practical action far before language is a possibility. Archer states directly, "Such popular views [of practice], in the Wittgensteinian tradition, necessarily make epistemology prior to ontology. Social realism reverses this relationship, and can do so because it sees practice as pivotal. It is our doings in the world which secure meanings, and not vice versa."[55]

These prelinguistic practical actions are engendered or avoided not because of rationality, Archer explains, but because of the emotive.[56] The child drops her cup, testing reality, because it feels good to do so; it allows her to participate in a cause, to therefore *feel* herself as real. It signals an ontological fact to her; it signals that gravity exists and that she is not the cup, that she is real outside or beyond the cup. Even when the object disappears, she still experiences herself; she *feels* the emotive pull to drop the cup again or feels sadness because it has disappeared.

The infant feeds and grabs, making eye contact with his mother because these practices feel good, they make him real by being bound to another that is his mother. The emotion that leads into practical action shows the importance of our embodiment. We are not just epistemological brains but full bodies that experience reality.[57] But it also shows that reality is fundamentally

of men.' Our practical work in the world does not and cannot await social instruction, but depends upon a learning process through which the continuous sense of self emerges." Ibid., 122.

55. Ibid., 189. Archer explains further: "As Piaget's experiments showed, the acquisition of thought and mastery of the principles of identity and non-contradiction, which are indispensable for any communication at all, are acquired in practice. This being the case, language can only be learnt after unmediated practice in the world, and it gains its meaning from its relation to this same independent reality. To consider language to be dependent upon reality, rather than reality upon language, is to lift the linguistic portcullis; what we experience reality to be will determine what we talk about in the public medium, and not vice versa, contra Society's Being." "Models of Man," 68.

56. "It is, of course, a straightforwardly realist definition which presumes that emotions are about something in the world (they are intentional or, as some would prefer, intentional in nature)." Archer, *Being Human*, 195. Archer explains further why emotion is important, "The central assumption made here is that our emotions are among the main constituents of our inner lives. They are the fuel of our internal conversation and this is why they matter. Thus there is no difficulty in going along with Elster . . . and arguing that quite 'simply, emotions matter because if we did not have them nothing else would matter. Creatures without emotion would have no reason for living nor, for that matter, for committing suicide. Emotions are the stuff of life.' In exactly the same vein, St Augustine asked rhetorically if we would not consider a general *apatheia* to be the worst of human and moral defects. The importance of the emotions is central to the things we care about and to the act of caring itself." Ibid., 194.

57. Archer's theory here is much deeper than I have space to articulate, but this quote points to its depth: "What it does mean is that the theoretical work involved is performed and recorded in ways which are non-linguistic. The modality is practice and the medium of inscription is the body.

relational; emotion is experienced in a relational environment of cause. We feel deep experiences because the reality we encounter is ontologically relational (reflection on independent objective reality through both theology and physics points to this—both a hypostatic theology and Einsteinian relativity make this case).[58] Emotion, practice, and experience then are tightly woven as a relational ontology in a critical realist perspective.

To turn to realism in practical theology is not to delete the importance of practice, but it is to shift it from under the domain of epistemology (where it has so often rested), placing it instead in the orbit of ontology. In critical realism, *practices (practical action) are the very forms that mold our experiences of reality*. Realism then is fundamentally practical, not only because it is essentially experiential but because these experiences are housed in practical action. Reality is always more than our practical actions, but through our practical actions we encounter reality itself. *Through dropping the cup, nursing at the breast, ministering to our neighbor are we drawn into the real.*

Critical realism heightens the importance of practical experience and yet does so by opening avenues for practical experiences to actually be true experiences of divine encounter. All we can know about reality is what we confess about it through our embodied emotive experience, and many of us have confessed an evangelical experience of divine encounter. Lynn even explains that she felt like she was floating, asserting "that this must be what true love feels like." This experience has often come to us practically; it has come through a minister, another who stands with us in our nothingness, ministering to us in and through the most practical of actions (crying with us, feeding us, listening to us—all emotive and embodied practices we call ministry). These ministerial actions, in a realist frame, are not merely socializing practices but experiences of reality itself, delivered to us in the casing of practical action. Ministry is the practical action (the practice) that allows for the experiencing of the reality of God (this is why Anderson is quite right that ministry precedes theology). Being cared for from nothingness to new possibility through practical actions of ministry reveals experientially (as an event) that God (as

---

Importantly this retains our continuity with the animal kingdom, whose higher forms are also held to manifest this embodied sense of self, and it is what unites all members into the community of humanity (for this sense is a necessary part of our developed species-being)." Ibid., 124.

58. "In defining emotions as relational, that is as emerging from situations to signal their import for our concerns, there is less preoccupation here than usual with the occurrence of 'an' emotion, its nomenclature or classification. Because of their situational and relational character as imports, our emotionality is regarded as a continuous running commentary (that is something we are never without) and therefore it is only in sudden or urgent contexts that we are aware of a specific emotion." Ibid., 197.

independent objective reality) is real and really loves us, drawing us through ontological realism of practical action to ontological communion of Godself.

Of course, these practical experiences are always open to misunderstanding; they are epistemologically fallible, but, nevertheless, they are believed to be experiences of the real (at least in part). We know reality not through epistemological assent but through our practical experiences that deliver revelations of the stratified nature of reality. Through the practical action of ministry itself, experiential space is opened for us to have an ontological encounter with God as independent objective reality. These experiences, because they are bound in the practical action of ministry, are concrete and lived and therefore bound in relational networks, but they nevertheless possess the possibility of being true encounters with the divine being. Practical actions that prioritize ontology over epistemology possess this power!

So a critical realist perspective attends to the practicality of experience—something deeply important to practical theology. Practical experience is central because ontology has priority over epistemology. We cannot know reality through disconnected epistemological assent, for reality must be experienced as an ontological encounter (event). But this ontological encounter happens as practical experience (as ministry). We experience the reality of God most often not through reading systematic theology, as if it were an epistemological blood transfusion, but through the practical experiences of worship and prayer, through the practical actions of another ministering to us. Through these practical experiences we encounter reality; in ministry Matt feels he has a true and real encounter with God.[59] Practical theology is ministry (Christopraxis) because it can attend to the practical experiential while not swallowing ontology into epistemology; it is ministry that allows practical experience to be the encounter with God from a realist perspective.

2. Epistemological Relativism

I have spent a considerable amount of space articulating the first commitment of critical realism—that ontology stands over epistemology—showing how this philosophical/social-scientific perspective has great resonance with a Christopraxis practical theology of God's being as becoming in ministry.[60] I

59. This is what Michael Polanyi means by personal knowledge. See *Personal Knowledge: Toward a Post-Critical Philosophy* (Chicago: University of Chicago Press, 1962).

60. Collier contrasts a bankrupt cultural form of relativism with the form of realism that I, and other critical realists, mean, "'Relativism' is presented as respecting people's freedom, but what it actually is, is treating that freedom as a matter of arbitrary taste rather than rational deliberation which requires grounds for decisions." Andrew Collier, "Realism, Relativism and Reason," in Archer, Collier, and

will not match the space used with the second two points, but I saw the need to make a strong case for realism in practical theology. I wanted to show how realism opens up significant conversations on human experience and how it might be that this experience is connected to a higher stratum of reality that might even be called God. This allows us to see that attention to divine action is not abstract (disconnected from reality) but can connect to human experience. This turn to realism also allows us to move practical theology beyond its overattention to dependent objective realities of church, tradition, and ethics (an overattention that has wrongly viewed them as the sole domain of what counts as practical). When practical theology focuses too completely on such dependent objective realities, it contends with antirealist perspectives (like postmodern deconstruction, positivism, or Wittgensteinian language games) that argue for hermeneutics, empirical analysis, or public praxis bound in the language of past tradition as the beginning and end of practical theology.[61] The philosophical/social-scientific realism I've presented allows for articulations of the stratified nature of reality itself, asking practical theology to at least consider that to truly attend to the concrete and lived is to explore people's experience of the stratified nature of reality, allowing for the possibility that they do experience the ministerial action of God's being. This allows for open space to discuss God's being as becoming in ministry as the central thrust of practical theology itself. My overall objective thus far has been to focus on the *realism* in critical realism. But now it is time to turn to the *critical* element of the perspective.

REALITY, EXPERIENCE, AND EPISTEMOLOGY

The realism on which I'm resting my Christopraxis practical theology of the cross is a *critical* realism. It asserts that there is no conclusive epistemological foundation that can know reality fully.[62] There is a reality, but knowledge

Porpora, *Transcendence*, 44. He continues, "But there is another kind of relativism, if indeed we want to call it that, which does not insult the various contending beliefs, and is compatible both with ontological realism and judgemental rationalism. This is the recognition that any body of beliefs, including one's own, is likely to contain its quota of false beliefs. This applies to all beliefs, not just religious ones, but it applies to these too." Ibid., 45.

61. "True enough, language does help to constitute a part of reality, but not the whole of reality. Much that is real is nonlinguistic and nonconceptual. Thus, rather than understanding reality as created by and enclosed or trapped within the all-pervading presence of language, we should understand language as one crucial but subsidiary part of the all-pervasive existence of reality." Smith, *What Is a Person?*, 160.

62. Archer, Collier, and Porpora explain epistemic relativism, "What epistemic relativism does mean is that all our judgements are socially and historically situated. Our judgements are conditioned by our circumstances, by what we know at the time and by the prevailing criteria of evaluation. For this reason

of this reality is always contested. Assertions or confessions of reality must be critically defended, for reality itself is always greater than what the articulator of reality can know. Critical realism asserts that there is a real world that exists outside the human mind but believes that human minds are relativized in their seeking to grasp this stratified reality.[63] Smith states, "Critical realist personalism entails a fallibilist theory of human knowledge, [it asserts] that our knowledge is always incomplete, endemically subject to error, and never certain."[64]

As creatures we are socially and historically situated; this idea critical realism holds in common with postmodern theory and its hermeneutical focus. Critical realism too is hermeneutical—not because it believes reality is created by interpretive human minds, but because it believes that reality is more than what human minds can possess. Human minds are always grounded in social and historical locales that color their experience, and reality itself transcends the human capacities to know it fully. Critical realism is hermeneutical, but only as hermeneutics are thrust into service of realism. Epistemology is relativized because the human knower cannot stand at the top stratum of reality and know it from a god's-eye point of view.[65] Searle says, "We do not make 'worlds'; we make descriptions that the actual world may fit or fail to fit. But all this

among others, our judgements are always fallible. Epistemic relativism further means that we are each positioned to see the world somewhat differently. Our experiences of the world vary." *Transcendence*, 4. They continue, expanding this concept into the purview of atheism, "The quality of epistemic relativism extends even to atheists and agnostics. Their absence of religious experience is itself a kind of experience. The absence of religious experience is epistemically relative too, subject to prevailing norms, circumstances and conceptual schemes. It is subject even to such factors of personal biography as resistances, prejudices and preferences. Perhaps, for whatever reason, atheists and agnostics are just not situated so as to experience transcendent reality. Perhaps they experience it but fail to attend to it. Perhaps they experience transcendent reality and attend to it but interpret it in more mundane ways. In any case, the purported experience of absence is no less corrigible than the experience of presence." Ibid.

63. "Because knowledge is by its nature something in our human minds. It is a product of our human subjectivity. Knowledge is a pattern in the mind that refers to external reality, but knowledge itself is internal to the mind and to subjectivity. It is the external or physical world to which knowledge refers that is independent, not the knowledge itself. Critical realism accepts that knowledge is a psychical structure in our own minds, and thereby not identical with the known, wherever the known is something other than the mind itself. This means that knowledge, realistic knowledge, is never independent or apodictically certain." La Montagne, *Barth and Rationality*, 59.

64. Smith, *What Is a Person?*, 304.

65. "Epistemic relativism means that our knowledge or beliefs about reality are always socially and historically conditioned. The criteria we use to decide upon the truth, and the concepts by which we express it, are all fallible. Moreover, we arrive at truth—when we arrive at all—without foundations, without fail-safe methods that can be determined in advance of enquiry." Archer, Collier, and Porpora, *Transcendence*, 11.

implies that there is a reality that exists independently of our system of concepts. Without such a reality, there is nothing to apply the concept to."[66]

This second perspective of critical realism, like the first, has deep congruencies with the justification perspective I presented above. Here too the human being is reminded that she is a creature and not the creator; she is informed that her epistemology is a human epistemology and that reality is greater than what she can know.

All knowledge of reality is experienced in reality. Like with all other forms of hermeneutical theory, critical realism contends that what we know we know in and through our situated locale (as creatures).[67] But this situated locale is real, and there are realities that exist above it. I claim that my experience with the divine being, for instance, is real, but I claim it and therefore it is open to the possibility that I am wrong about my interpretation of it. I must continue to place the knowledge of reality I have experienced into dialogue and discourse with other epistemological conceptions of reality. Not only do I have to, but I am compelled to by the very shape of human personhood.

Human beings are fundamentally persons (hypostatic beings) that seek to make sense of reality through experience, most often through shared experience. Unlike other animals, we are animals that must share our experience, giving epistemological shape to our experiences with reality. Our experiences of reality move us to construct epistemological conceptions of reality born from those experiences. This circle from reality to experience to epistemology is broken open because of our hypostatic nature, because we not only construct epistemologies but feel the necessity to share them with others (as a way to share in others). And we feel compelled to do so because we take

---

66. Searle, *Construction of Social Reality*, 166.

67. Smith explains that there is a place for social constructionism in critical realism. He states, "I want to restate from the perspective of critical realist personalism what is valuable and important in social constructionism, what constructionism can and cannot do and say, and how we might adjust some of the most promising versions of its approach to be more truthful and useful. Social constructionism properly understood is not only perfectly compatible with but also indispensable to critical realist personalism. How then should we appropriately approach social constructionism?" *What Is a Person?*, 157. Smith continues, "First, let us affirm what in social constructionism is good, right, insightful, and necessary for understanding reality. Social constructionism is right that positivism is a dead-end approach to social science, which fails to produce adequate understandings of human social reality. It is also correct in claiming that foundationalist epistemologies are discredited and that impersonally objective forms of human knowledge are impossible. No human knowledge is indubitable and there is for humans no 'God's eye' view 'from nowhere' from which to study reality. All perceptions require active human interpretation, and language plays a huge role in human thought. Moreover, the constructionist perspective is right that many different kinds of observable physical and social 'texts' underdetermine their own interpretations, making 'correct' interpretations difficult and sometimes impossible." Ibid.

as brute fact that others too exist in reality, that they too experience reality. We share our epistemology with others because we assume that our epistemology is relevant to them because we both exist together in an objective world that is real and not just the interpretation or social construction of discursive minds. This is, I believe, why all the people I interviewed were willing to share their stories. After a short connection the stories between us flowed with ease.

But when we share these epistemological conceptions of our experiences in reality, we quickly discover that others have had different experiences (often because of their own social and historical locale, but not only because of this), and these experiences lead to different or opposed epistemologies.[68] So whether or not we agree about the epistemology of our experience(s) of reality, it is never self-evident, for reality's stratified nature makes reality always in part mysterious, independent as it is of our consciousness. But both our need to share these experiences through epistemology and reality's essentially mysterious nature then relativize epistemology. In the need to share our experience, we find other persons do not find congruence with our interpretation of our experience of reality. So our epistemology of our experience of reality is always contested. This philosophical/social-scientific perspective is *critical* realism because it contends that our epistemologies, as a result of the depth of our experiences with reality, are multivalent and must be critically assessed and debated.

Because of this reality-to-experience-to-epistemology framework, critical realism will not allow us to assume that our (or any) epistemology is a priori true, possessing authority because it is religious or confessional, for example. There is no foundational authority in which our epistemologies can rest. To find such an authority is to violate the "realism" of critical realism, it is to place some human epistemology above the ontology of reality (which is exactly what Christian fundamentalism does). If any epistemology is to exist outside of the subordination of epistemology to ontology, then reality is thrown into question and the human being is conflated with the Creator.[69]

---

68. The differing experiences of others are often a result of their own social and historical locale, but some would say that they have a different experience with high strata of reality, like an experience of Buddhist nirvana. Of course, this is partly based on social and historical locale, but it is reductionistic to assume it is only this. Those having the experience would claim a real experience with a higher form of reality.

69. "Critical realism accepts 'epistemic relativism,' that is the view that the world can only be known in terms of available descriptions or discourses, but it rejects 'judgemental relativism'—the view that one cannot judge between different discourses and decide that some accounts are better than others (Bhaskar, 1986, p. 72)." Andrew Sayer, *Realism and Social Science* (Los Angeles: Sage, 2000), 47.

BIBLE, TRADITION, AND EPISTEMOLOGY

Just such danger has occurred, in my mind, in fundamentalism's attention to an inerrant Bible. The Bible becomes an authority that exists above the reality of human minds; though it is a human book, it is somehow freed from epistemological questions to exist on a separate plane of existence (the Bible must become divine and its human origin ignored). And when this is assumed, when the Bible becomes such a divine epistemological magnet, it sucks all ontology into it, smothering it. So now God as free actor, as a living ontological reality, as Christopraxis, is swallowed by the epistemology of the authority of the Bible.[70] The Bible as epistemological foundation, not the ontological act and being of God, sets all the terms for fundamentalists.

The fundamentalist problem is not with their belief in the Bible but their belief that the Bible exists outside human minds and is a priori on a higher layer of reality. As opposed to Islam, Christianity has always held that Scripture was birthed from human minds and that tradition is human minds in reflection. Scripture's authority then is not as an ontological reality but in its epistemological operations that function under the ontology of God's own act and being. Scripture, for instance, is given authority only because it has been trusted to reveal (to witness to) a higher level of reality, to help us make sense of our experience through Scripture's epistemological narration of the being and act of the living God. In fundamentalism the Bible then becomes a god (or oddly, more important than God) instead of an epistemological account made by human minds that witnesses (even reveals) their experience with the ontological act and being of God, with an experience of the reality of God's being that encounters us from a higher (highest) layer of reality.

A critical realist perspective will not allow us to turn the Bible into an ontological reality that exists outside human minds. Nevertheless, it will allow us to give *authority* to Scripture and the Christian tradition but only as we place Scripture and tradition under the actuality (the realism) of God's own being. Scripture and tradition are not independent objective realities; they do not exist independent of human minds (as we said). Scripture and tradition exist on a lower plane of reality than, say, the Trinity. The Bible and Christian tradition are only real as communities use them. The Bible is powerful and holds authority as an epistemological frame that we confess (believe) mediates a higher layer of reality to us, not as a purely ontological reality. Many people through the centuries have *experienced* higher levels of reality (the very act

---

70. This is why Ray Anderson prioritizes Christopraxis over the Bible, placing the Bible as an essential epistemological case for the reality of God's ministry.

and being of God) through reading and meditating on the Bible; they have experienced (or made sense of their experience of) the act and being of God through epistemological articulations of the Scriptures.

Critical realism will not allow us to turn the Bible or tradition into God, but it *will* allow us to assert that God's being as the becoming in ministry does (possibly) exist as independent objective reality and one that we can experience. We *need* the Bible then as an epistemological framework for understanding the experiences we've had with reality (with God). So Scripture and tradition are trusted epistemological assertions about the ontological realism of God's being as becoming. Scripture, the church claims, is unique (authoritative) not because it is an independent objective reality but because it faithfully witnesses in its epistemological operation to the being and act of God, who, it asserts, is an independent objective reality.[71] Scripture and tradition do not smother human experience in a Christopraxis perspective based in critical realism, as they have in Purves's work. Rather, Scripture and tradition become epistemological lenses that help us make sense of our experiences of the living God, whose being is in becoming, who comes to us in our reality (experience) from a higher stratum of reality.[72]

Christopraxis is a biblical practical theology, but only as it sees the Bible as an epistemological best account of the ontological reality of God's being as becoming. Christopraxis is first and foremost centered on the ontological state of Godself that human beings experience as ministry. It uses (needs) the Bible to give epistemological shape to the experience of this ontological reality. It is a practical theology because it attends first and foremost to experiences of reality, but it confesses that we have experiences of God, using the Bible's epistemologies to articulate the depth of these experiences with reality—with God's being. Matt, in my interview with him, discussed the reality of God coming to him through the eyes of the homeless men. He then used Matthew 25 as a way to understand and describe this experience.

71. Collier explains how tradition fits into a critical realist perspective and how it too is epistemologically reasonable in discourse with science. "For the Catholic, the Church is a rational authority on matters of religious belief, just as the scientific community is a rational authority on beliefs about the mechanisms of nature. So believing that Christ is of one substance with the Father because a council of the Church has said so is not a leap in the dark, any more than believing that there are quarks because my Penguin Dictionary encyclopedia says so, and I assume that it represents the consensus of the scientific community." "Realism, Relativism and Reason," 42.

72. Porpora explains helpfully, "What Biblical criticism produces is always what critical realism calls a transitive object of knowledge. It is in other words not the reality itself but only a description of that reality. As such, it is always a human product. If we want, we might refer to it as a social construction." Douglas Porpora, "Judgemental Rationality and Jesus," in Archer, Collier, and Porpora, *Transcendence*, 49.

While Purves runs the risk of placing the epistemology of doctrine (tradition) over ontology, Christopraxis will not allow for this conflation. Like Purves, Christopraxis turns to doctrine, but it sees doctrine as only (but powerfully) epistemological best accounts given throughout the history of the church to help it make sense of, and therefore imagine, the *experiences* of ontological encounter (realism) it has had with God's being as becoming.

RELATIVITY AND POSTFOUNDATIONALISM

Critical realism says that all we can say of reality is what we (or others before us) have experienced and then shared in epistemologies, and these epistemologies can say something true of reality but can never possess the fullness of the stratified nature of reality. This means our experiences of reality are never conclusive, for there are many who have views of reality that are different from and opposed to our own. *This does not mean there is no reality.* Postmodernism has seen the relativism of epistemology as proof that there is no reality at all, that all that *is* just is competing epistemological conceptions. Pluralism of epistemology is proof that there is no ontology, the postmodernist believes. It is as if the epistemological relativity has been such a bad dream to the postmodernist that it leads him to assume there is nothing real but the epistemological pluralistic nightmare. A critical realist is not threatened by the pluralism of epistemology; critical realism affirms the relativity, seeing it not as a reason to question reality but as a witness to the stratified nature of reality, to the truth that reality is more than our minds can possess.

This means, like postmodernism, critical realism *is* postfoundational. It claims no foundational methodology that will lead to truth.[73] But unlike postmodernism, it believes there is a truth; it just must be discovered humbly by those in lower strata of reality. No foundational method can free the human mind from its locale in lower strata and move us to some foundational peak of observable (undoubted or uncontested) truth. This foundation does not exist. Truth must be discovered personally (again following Polanyi) by (hypostatically) articulating our experiences of reality in discourse with other

---

73. Smith explains how critical realism is critical by being postfoundational. "What 'critical' intends to communicate about this realism is its antifoundationalist character, its fallibilist understanding of science as a socially situated human practice, its resistance to modernity's absolute separation of fact from value, and its readiness to engage in normative critical theory without (because of its ontological realism) collapsing into ideology and crass academic political activism." *What Is a Person?*, 98. He continues, defining foundationalism, "Foundationalism here being the epistemological project of identifying some fundamental belief or principle to serve as the basic and universal foundation of inquiry that will introduce indubitable knowledge." Ibid., 207.

people's experiences. Truth is not foundational, but hypostatic; it is bound and therefore discovered in shared experiences of persons who share their epistemologies.[74] But we share them not, I would argue, just at the level of intellectual discourse; more profoundly, we share them at the level of ministry, for in ministry (not intellectual wrestling matches) our experiences are indwelled as our persons are shared in. Ministry allows us to deeply connect experience, reality, and personhood with epistemology. It is ministry that upholds the personal (hypostatic) nature of the other as we are drawn to their epistemologies not as a language game but as the articulations of their (deepest) experiences with reality.[75]

Truth can be discovered, the critical realists assert, but only through debate, dialogue, and evaluation with distinct epistemologies shaped from people's distinctive experiences. But these debates, dialogues, and evaluations must not be zero-sum games of rightness, I would argue, for there is no foundation to free us completely from doubt. I would add that dialogue must take the shape of hypostatic encounters, where the other is embraced so their experience cannot only be heard but shared in. *Truth, as experiences with the multistrata of reality, can be discovered best through ministry, for ministry takes the personal shape, the hypostatic shape, that makes us open to sharing in others' experiences as a way of hearing their epistemologies and therefore together experiencing something true of reality.* Ministry makes room for the hypostatic sharing of epistemologies that move into ontological encounters with reality—ontological encounters with neighbor and God. Ministry, then, embraces epistemology in its fully hermeneutical nature but orders it under ontology.

Truth, itself, if it is to be encountered, is always discovered, to follow Polanyi. And a Christopraxis critical realist position asserts that it is discovered through the act of ministry. It is through dialogue as hypostatic beings where

74. Archer, Collier, and Porpora explain, "The only methodological a priori is continued openness to dialogue, dialogue especially with those with whom we disagree. In contrast with postmodernism, the critical realist stance towards oppositional others is neither respectful silence, nor the uncritical eclecticism of pastiche, but a Socratic openness that takes the other's viewpoint seriously enough to allow it the possibility of altering our own." *Transcendence*, 11.

75. Archer, Collier, and Porpora use a story of Mary and Thomas to explain the conversation between epistemologies, "As the two discuss further, they become for each other what the Jewish tradition calls Haverim. Haverim are study partners who inspire each other's intellectual growth by lovingly challenging each other's claims to the truth. From a critical realist perspective, it is Haverim that we all ought to be to each other." Ibid., 19. Here I'm saying something similar, but also deeper. I'm saying that ministry is Haverim, but also deeply spiritual because it operates out of the hypostatic nature. It is not just intellectual, but deeply relational. But as such it does as much, and I would argue more, than Archer, Collier, and Porpora want Haverim to.

we see, hear, act, and take joy in each other that we are most prepared to be drawn into the higher levels of reality (my interviews themselves took this shape).[76] We assert that ministry is hypostatic; it leads us into sharing in other persons in and through their experience, leading us to minister to them by embracing and dialoguing with their epistemologies of their experience. This hypostatic sharing (place-sharing), we discover, moves us into higher strata of reality. In the acts of sharing in others ontologically through their epistemologies (their stories), we experience a higher level of reality, we feel taken up or empowered by the Spirit. The Spirit comes to us in ministry where we shared as hypostatic beings, taking us into the hypostatic nature of the independent objective reality of God's own hypostatic nature. But we can only know God exists as hypostatic nature because we, like Paul, have experienced this God call us, saying, "It is I, Jesus, whom you persecute" (Acts 9). In and through sharing in others' experiences and hearing their epistemologies (in and as ministry), placing them in discourse with our own, we can move into saying something true of reality.[77]

This *critical* element of critical realism is not like the dirty looks of the high school cool kids, critically belittling, but the ministering act of "faith seeking understanding" with our neighbor, confessing our conception of our experience one to another, making such confessions the avenue to share in each other's lives. The epistemic relativism of critical realism is much like the ministry of confession and testimony.

Thus, a Christopraxis perspective is not a foundational confessionalism, fencing itself off from other epistemologies, ruling them *wrong* because of its own foundational commitments. It is postfoundational, for it claims no guarded locale that is beyond relativized experience of reality itself. And critical realism admits that reality is confusing, for parts of reality (whether of God or super black holes) transcend the equipment of human epistemology. A Christopraxis perspective based on critical realism is not a foundational confessionalism but a postfoundational confessionalism bound in the action of ministry itself.

It is a postfoundational confessionalism because critical realism claims only that we have experiences of reality and that these experiences of reality must be narrated and then shared (confessed in dialogue). There is nothing that

---

76. The idea of taking joy is an echo of Barth's presentation of the shape of the action of relational being in *Church Dogmatics* III.2 (Edinburgh: T&T Clark, 1960).

77. The ministry I mention takes the shape of place-sharing, I would argue. My conception of ministry at its height is what I call place-sharing. For more on this concept see my books *The Relational Pastor* (Downers Grove, IL: InterVarsity, 2013) and *Revisiting Relational Youth Ministry* (Downers Grove, IL: InterVarsity, 2007).

a priori rules them in bounds or out. But as we'll see below in the final of the three elements of critical realism, some epistemologies may be better than others—not because they are based on some foundation but because they make a case through dialogue that resonates with our being as true, leading us deeper into the ministry of God in and through ministry with and for our neighbor.

3. Judgmental Rationality

The third movement of critical realism is judgmental rationality.[78] Not only does critical realism contend that there is a real world, a stratified real world that we experience, but these experiences of reality that we forge into epistemologies are not all equal. How could they be if our epistemologies of reality are fallible? This third layer of critical realism highlights the *critical* element of the perspective, for it asserts that some epistemological perspectives may be better than others and that we are forced within reality to make decisions about the epistemologies of reality. We are "forced" because we exist in reality and seek to explain our experiences of reality. Because of the plurality of epistemologies, many conflict or are diametrically opposed in their views of reality. Because we have experiences with reality, we are positioned to make judgments about reality. But we are positioned in such a way that we are propelled to judge epistemologies yet never from a safe place outside the mysterious confusion of being in reality. Nevertheless, in reality we judge some epistemological perspectives to be more concurrent with reality.[79]

78. "Judgemental rationality means that we can publicly discuss our claims about reality, as we think it is, and marshal better or worse arguments on behalf of those claims. By comparatively evaluating the existing arguments, we can arrive at reasoned, though provisional, judgements about what reality is objectively like, about what belongs to that reality and what does not." Archer, Collier, and Porpora, *Transcendence*, 2.

79. Smith adds, "People every day and everywhere unselfconsciously evaluate alternative interpretations and explanations about what is real, how reality works, which factors cause what outcomes, and what truth claims can be trusted. And human persons have the natural capacities to evaluate such interpretations and explanations sufficiently well so as normally to be able to cope with the numberless demands, challenges, needs, and problems of life. Fixing a broken car, deciding what to plant and when, knowing what to do about stomach pains, choosing a financial investment, deciding whether to confront a friend about a problem, packing for a long vacation—all of these require complex processes of collecting information, assigning causation, projecting possible futures, estimating probabilities, evaluating claims, and committing to decisions. Nothing says that people's judgments are always smart, accurate, or reliable. People make mistakes. Reality can be hard to sort out. Things go wrong. Yet no living person can opt out of making such judgments. Nobody can transcend the requirement of engaging in practical activity and learning truth about reality as well as they are able. We do it all the time. If we did not, human personal and social life would collapse. This means that normal people have a

Of course, such judgments are postfoundational; they are not judged for not assimilating to some foundational knowledge but judged as better up against concrete experiences with reality and in conversation with other (trusted) epistemologies.[80] We say things all the time like, "I just don't believe it," which more often than not is related to our experience of reality. I don't believe in aliens, finding such epistemologies of their existence and government cover-ups irrational because I have no experience, no phenomenological encounter with such a reality, and I have heard no compelling epistemology that converts me to see through my own experience the possibility of alien activity. However, when I'm told of the size of the universe and its millions of suns, my epistemology of no aliens is placed in discourse with the epistemology of the mass of space, and I wonder. I still hold to no aliens, but I know that reality is bigger than what I can know, and it is possible that enough experiential evidence and more convincing epistemologies could be found to make me change my judgment.

I don't believe the alien epistemology, not because I have conclusive, foundational facts demonstrating it is not true but because it doesn't square with my experience and the epistemologies I have embraced to help me make sense of my experiences in and with reality.[81] For instance, I have trusted the biblical text as an epistemology that gives witness to my experience in reality, and it says nothing in word or spirit of aliens. This doesn't mean there are no aliens (for the Bible says nothing of cars and I believe in them); it just means that until I have such experiences of them, my trusted epistemologies lead me to rationally judge them as unreal.

REASON, RATIONALITY, AND THEORY

What does critical realism mean by rationality? Because human beings are hypostatic creatures that experience reality, form epistemologies of their experience, and then share these epistemologies, creating a plurality of epistemologies, and because there is an objective world, some epistemologies are better than others (as we said). But this better-ness is judged next to and within experience, so this better-ness is evaluated not outside reality, in some space created by reason, but in practical experience with reality. "Rationality" is

great deal of reality-based experience making judgments about what is real and how things work. It also means that normal humans are well practiced at making sense of how linguistic representations of the world relate to real processes and events in the World." *What Is a Person?*, 168.

80. Like Scripture or tradition.

81. And of course "my" experience is important, but "my" experience is also a shared experience in communities whom I impact and who impacted my epistemology.

not assumed to be the foundations of natural laws, for instance, in which reason takes apart the universe piece by piece, asserting that something is "nothing but" its natural components. Critical realism opposes this Humean rationality because it assumes that only what human reason and rationality can know *is*.[82]

82. I quote Smith at length here because I cannot say it better than he does, explaining how human experience is a legitimate path to follow in exploring reality: "We have long been taught by a particular view of science to doubt the reliability of our lived experience as human persons to tell us true things about reality. This view of science has taught us that personal perception and experience are subjective, biased, and idiosyncratic and often produce misleading appearances, particularistic perspectives, and false models of reality. We see the sun moving, for example, but science tells us that really the sun is standing still—it is the earth that is moving. We think we have freely chosen our political attitudes, but then we are told that most of the variance in our attitudes can be explained by ten demographic variables in multiple regression analyses that are driving them. Therefore we ought to not trust our personal, subjective, phenomenological experiences to tell us truth about reality. Rather, we should trust the methods and findings of naturalistic sciences, or perhaps social sciences that are modeled on the natural sciences, as the final authority explaining reality. There background assumptions inform naturalistic scientism's view of science. The first is the ontological assumption of materialism, that what exists consists of physical matter, the forces of energy that animate matter, and the natural laws inherent in matter and energy that govern them. Everything is material nature. Immaterial entities that are not examinable by physics and chemistry—such as meanings, values, moral facts, and certainly things 'spiritual'—do not exist. The second assumption concerns perspective and authority, namely, the premise that the natural sciences are neutral and objective, which is good and reliable, compared to personal human perception and experience, which are biased and subjective, and so problematic and untrustworthy. The third assumption built into naturalistic scientism's claims concerns right method—namely, that the best way to understand and explain anything is through reductionist analysis. The true properties and dynamics of any subject are best revealed by breaking the subject down into its component parts existing at lower levels to disclose the more primary elements constituting the subject. This reductionistic move points downward to explain, shifting toward increasingly elementary levels of reality. . . . These three background assumptions—materialism, objectivity, and reductionism—justify naturalistic scientism's discounting of people's phenomenological experience as a guide to valid and reliable knowledge about reality, including about human life." *What Is a Person?*, 105. Smith continues, "Following Charles Taylor and others, however, I believe that when it comes to understanding the human world, naturalistic scientism's frame work is inadequate. We have good reasons to doubt its picture of human persons and the knowledge of them it generates. We also have good reason to think that there is much important to learn about ourselves as human from our own best perceptions and experiences, even those that are personal and subjective. I rely in part on Taylor's phenomenological epistemology . . . to build my argument about the nature of human personhood in this book. . . . The starting point of this phenomenological approach that opposes naturalistic scientism is that terms of our experience that we cannot live without to best 'make sense' of our lives provide legitimate and important clues about what is real. To be clear, the 'terms' that Taylor is specifically defending in his argument are morality and value, though his argument can easily be extended to make sense of other aspects of human experience, such as personhood, to which naturalistic scientism is often blind. So, when it comes to explaining human life, even social scientifically, the unavoidably personal experience of living life cannot be radically separated off as providing untrustworthy knowledge. As persons, all we have is our best personal knowledge about

The rationality of critical realism moves past a naturalistic phenomenology that enthrones reason as king or as the wrench that takes reality apart, denying that reality is itself stratified with layers that transcend human reason.[83] Rather, critical realism contends that a phenomenon is almost never to be seen as "nothing but," that reality as a whole is not its components but its emergence.

Critical realism follows something similar to Charles Taylor's antinaturalistic phenomenology, contending that we have experiences that cannot be deconstructed to their "natural" components through the use of reason. Our experience of reality leads us to give epistemological best accounts of reality, and these best accounts are judged in discourse, debate, or, as I would add, ministry with other's best accounts. Rationality allows us to construct best accounts, but these best accounts are only that, our epistemologically relative "best accounts" of a reality that is more than we can know. We must humbly assert that our rationality cannot disclose *all of* reality; we must also take faith that our rationality, because it is born from our experience, can say something true of reality.

Because there is a reality and as hypostatic creatures we construct epistemologies that seek to understand this reality, we can judge if one perspective is more helpful than another. But to avoid foundationalism or the use of reason to stand outside reality, we make these judgments phenomenologically; we feel our way into asserting one epistemology is better than the other (as I did above with aliens). We can judge in this way because as human beings in reality we know more than we can say (we have tacit knowledge). From a critical realist perspective, it is not rationality that conditions experience but experience that must be rationally explored. Experience leads the way because we encounter reality only through experience.[84] *Rationality itself is that which is congruent with our experience in*

the world we live in, gained through a variety of methods, including but not limited to naturalistic science. Since reality is a unity, terms we need to make sense of our own experiences cannot automatically be cordoned off from informing the narrower task of scientific inquiry and explanation." Ibid., 106.

83. "By definition and mission statement, naturalistic scientism cannot recognize, much less adequately understand and account for, immaterial realities, like value, meaning, morality, and personhood. So it is stuck with the misguided task of denying, reducing, eliminating, and explaining away, with terms alien to the realities themselves, that which is often most important in human life." Ibid., 114.

84. "All this means is that when we first come together for discussion, we each will assign the burden of proof to perspectives counter to our own experience. . . . The epistemic privilege here is personal or individual rather than public. We each personally accord the privilege to our own standpoint, and it is epistemically rational for us to do so. Just as in science as a whole it would not be epistemically rational to

reality. It is called rational because it makes sense next to our multivalent experiences in reality.[85]

This means encounter with reality must be theorized about because it is fundamentally mysterious, because it is more than, overspilling human epistemologies. Critical realism's judgmental rationality that is built on epistemologies of an ontological realism means that our experiences must be theorized. That theory is not counter to experience but the outworking of experience that seeks understanding.

THEORY AND NORMATIVITY IN PRACTICAL THEOLOGY

Practical theology from a critical realist perspective starts in experience; it starts with phenomena in practice, seeing practice as an emotive (not hegemonically language-based) engagement with reality.[86] But it does not stay here—it moves headlong into theory construction. A Christopraxis practical theology does

abandon a paradigm at the first anomaly or problem, so, too, is there a rational, inertial tendency associated with our own personal paradigms." Archer, Collier, and Porpora, *Transcendence*, 20.

85. Thinking this way, rationality can be called such even in seeming contradictions. It seems irrational for a lover to forgive her cheating boyfriend, for this is his second strike, but she has an experience of his love that is deeper than the seeming contradiction of forgiving him, so in seeming incongruent she return to him. But because of her deep experience she sees her return not as irrational, but done for good reason. Christianity, too, is a seemingly contradictory faith, holding to bread and wine being just bread and wine and yet the real presence of Christ, of Jesus being just human, but at the same time fully divine. These realities seem opposed to reason, but only from a foundational conception of reason. From an experiential phenomenological locale these commitments are reasonable, for we (and millions of others) have encountered this bread and wine as the presence of Christ.

86. Earlier I critiqued forcefully the focus of practical theology on practice, yet following Archer I have also shifted to what I call emotive practice. The cutting edge of this distinction is to see practice not as a language-based reality, as most practical theologians have done. I oppose such an understanding of practice because, as Archer, Collier, and Porpora say, it attacks the personal experiential and does not attend to the hypostatic nature of the human being. Only seeing practice as an emotive encounter (event) with reality that precedes language can avoid this and uphold the experiential nature of the human being. "It is not only any independent reality that is lost or bracketed out of analysis by an exclusive focus on practices, discourses and texts. The individual subject is bracketed out of existence as well. As a result, what is lost is the very category of experience. Practices, discourses and texts do not experience. Only individual subjects do; and what individual subjects experience, when they experience, is reality. Individuals and reality are the twin end-points connected by practices, discourses and texts. It is through practices, discourses and texts that individuals experience reality and express the reality they experience. Thus, to try to understand practices, discourses and texts, without their end-points, is like trying to understand the institution of marriage while bracketing out husbands and wives. To the extent that the plurality of stances toward the transcendent originates in the plural ways that the transcendent is experienced (or not), our approach to the transcendent must readmit the category of experience." *Transcendence*, 13.

not shy away from theory nor believe practical theology can do its work by only describing or attending to the pragmatic without moving into theory construction.[87] Because theory is born in experience, it is not disconnected from practice but rather stands as the judgmental rationality of experience. A Christopraxis practical theology believes, with James Loder, that sometimes the most practical thing is good theory, for "good" theory is an imaginative and well-thought-out (though admittedly relativistic) articulation of what has been experienced as real.

Critical realism shows us that theory being practical is not just the clever defense of the ivory tower academic to her hungry students starving for some ministerial bread. Rather, critical realism shows us that theory is the rational laying out of our phenomenological experiential encounter with reality. Theology is the theory of divine action, but theory here is not to be interpreted as disconnected from reality; rather, theology entails the deeply connected epistemologies that make rational judgment of reality, a reality experienced through divine (ministerial) encounter. Practical theology can and should empirically examine how people are experiencing reality, giving that experience epistemological shape as they make judgmental rational decisions about it. This theorizing, critical realism claims, is not done just by professionals but by all people, for all people encounter the stratified nature of reality through their experience. Theology is grounded in critical realism and is always practical because of its emotive experiential immersion in reality.

Earlier I used the theology of Jüngel, for instance, to move into theory construction. I have chosen Jüngel as a dialogue partner because his theory helps me to see (understand) my experience of reality. I have done this not to subvert the practice-to-theory-to-practice loop that mobilizes practical theology (through I have questioned the centrality of human praxis). Rather, I have used Jüngel's theology as an epistemological account for my own experience of God's being as becoming (and the experience of the communities in which I have worshipped). I have moved past Browning, Miller-McLemore, Fulkerson, Bass and Dykstra, and Purves not because I see an inconsistency in their use of theory; in many ways I see great depth and veracity in their projects. Rather, I have personally judged them, because of my own experience with reality, contending that each scholar's theory does not attend enough to the phenomenological experience of divine action that I (and those in chapter 3) have experienced as real.

---

87. Miller-McLemore raised such perspectives as a potential growing edge of practical theology in her presidential address at the Academy of Practical Theology meeting 2012 in Amsterdam.

My own Christopraxis perspective will also come under the same judgment by others who either have not had this experience with reality (of divine encounter) I have articulated or feel that I have not constructed a sound enough epistemology of this experience, that my theory does not correlate enough with reality. But as I have done, they will judge this perspective next to their own experience with reality, seeing my theory as not connected enough to reality as they experience it. They will reason that my theory does not say enough that is true of reality.

Judgment of my work, and my judgment of the work of others, has nearly everything to do with *normativity*. As hypostatic animals bound in a stratified reality of competing epistemologically rationalized interpretations of reality, we are propelled to turn our best accounts into normative commitments. These commitments norm the way we see reality and how we act within it. When our epistemologies have been forged in the fire of judgmental rationality they become our norms, stories we tell ourselves about ourselves and reality that direct our action and self-definition.[88]

Critical realism believes it is disingenuous to do theoretical work outside admitted normativity, as even the "theory" of antinormativity is a norm that directs one's action. My Christopraxis perspective is a deeply normative practical theology, and it makes no apologies for this, stating its interpretation of reality boldly but also humbly, for while it confesses deep norms, it holds to these norms because of experience, recognizing that others have other experiences that give them other norms. And because there is an objective reality, these distinct normative commitments can be respected, shared, and rationally judged next to my own humble experience of the real.

This doesn't make all theory equal; all theory could only be equal if there were no objective reality. But because there is an objective reality that is obscured by our place in its lower strata, we can judge the epistemological theories of others, though only from a place of humble recognition that reality exists independent of theorizing human minds.

I will not be surprised that my project will taste bitter in some people's mouths, for my theorizing of my experience will be judged by them as unreal, and their own normative commitments will keep them from partially or fully converting to my epistemology. Their own normative commitments are born in and through their own experiences and epistemologies (stories) they've been told or told themselves about reality. But my normative position is also born in experience, experience that I, along with those I interviewed, claim is real.

88. I'm leaning here on Christian Smith's *Moral Believing Animals: Human Personhood and Culture* (Oxford: Oxford University Press, 2003). I will focus much more on this text in the following chapter.

So while we may continue to disagree, my deeply committed theological normativity should not mar my project, for my deeply held theological norms are bound in my phenomenological experience with reality and must be rationally judged as such. My Christopraxis practical theology is a kind of normative practical theology that sees divine action as a norming reality; it holds to this commitment not as foundational but as experiential encounter. But it does not shy away from claiming its normative starting point. My Christopraxis practical theology sees this not as a retreat from attention to experience (as I hope I've shown) or, importantly, from human action. It starts with experience of divine action that norms epistemologies of reality but also *contends that normativity is the motivation for human action*, that we as human being are always seeking to make sense of the mysterious stratified reality we are bound in, theorizing and norming our experiences of reality.

And it may be that admitting and affirming normativity, as opposed to diminishing it (and trying to be nonnormative), even allows for something like rich interreligious dialogue.

Conclusion: Christopraxis and Interreligious Dialogue

Interreligious dialogue from a critical realist perspective is just that: dialogue. It is the placing of trusted epistemology in discourse with other people's trusted epistemologies, respecting that we both trust and believe our own epistemologies but recognize that our trusted epistemologies see reality in distinctly different ways. Critical realism doesn't minimize the possibility that we hold to importantly distinct conceptions of reality, but it does remind us that we are similar in the inability of our deeply held epistemologies to possess all of reality. Critical realism differs from nonrealist perspectives of interreligious dialogue found in liberal positions that seek to use poststructuralism, Wittgensteinian anthropologies, or Durkheimian social theory to claim that "different religions no longer need to be opposed by their mutually exclusive claims of truth. [For] in reality, none of them is making truth claims at all. They are all just expressing the different stories by which their respective communities live. As such, the stories are just sources for different social identities."[89] In contrast to such a position, critical realism holds that each

89. "The post-Wittgensteinian approach to religion has been particularly well received by anthropologists and sociologists. In his classic work, *The Elementary Forms of the Religious Life*, Emile Durkheim suggested that the experience of God is the experience of group feeling and that in worshipping God, society essentially is worshipping itself. Ever since, anthropologists and sociologists have been inclined to approach religion as an expression of community. The theological question—whether or not God actually exists—is considered to be beyond the compass of social science.

religious perspective is making rational epistemological assertions about its adherents' experience of reality. The distinct faiths are not simply and finally social constructions, but sophisticated dependent objective realities created for and because of their experience with an independent objective reality.[90]

Interreligious dialogue from a critical realist perspective leads us to the highest level of respect, for we believe that our Muslim or Hindu friend is not simply doing practices to form a social identity but takes on these actions and epistemological conceptions because she has experienced something she believes is real, because these actions and epistemologies help her articulate an ontological experience.[91] Our own experiences with reality may be different; in dialogue I may confess only Christ and Him crucified (1 Cor. 2:2), and my own confession must be respected as well, for I too claim it as an experience with reality. We now are moved into discourse where we share our experiences and through that process (and the epistemological shape we've given to our experiences or have had given to them), we judge our friend's experience while always respecting that she holds it to be real.

Consequently, the post-Wittgensteinian perspective offers anthropology and sociology a way of studying religion that does not require their taking any stand on the reality of the referents of religious language. Does God exist? Well, in some religious language games, God does exist, and in non-religious and even some religious language games, God does not exist. That is all there is to the matter." Archer, Collier, and Porpora, *Transcendence*, 8. The quote in the text is from ibid.

90. Collier adds texture to my thoughts of interreligious dialogue, opposing the form of relativism that says that religious believing is "nothing but" the personal commitments of individuals. "The first position that I have been criticizing—groundless 'personal belief'—is certainly relativism of a kind. However, if it is the kind that licenses phrases like 'time for me,' it is a kind which is incompatible with both ontological realism and judgemental rationalism. It is worth speculating why this relativism has become the 'common sense' of the present time. I suspect that it is to do with the teaching of controversial subjects like religion in schools. Obviously the teachers cannot tell a multi-cultural class which religion is right. What they could do is examine the truth claims of several religions, and try to get a tolerant, respectful argument going between the adherents of these different claims. That would be difficult. What is much easier is to present all religious beliefs as, so to speak, cordoned off by quotation marks: this is what Buddhists have as their 'personal beliefs,' this is what Muslims have, this is what Christians have, and so on. All the beliefs can be inspected, but since none is taken seriously as a truth claim, but is seen rather as the mark of identity of a different group, no discussion gets going between them. I even suspect that this is part of the spontaneous ideology of the teaching profession, and goes beyond matters of religious beliefs." "Realism, Relativism and Reason," 44.

91. Porpora explains how religious perspectives are no doubt bound in traditions but are also more than traditions. "Religious experience normally occurs within a tradition of religious teaching and practice (in this too it is like other experience). Yet, in the end, religious experience constitutes the only ground we can have for giving credence to such traditions, or indeed for developing and transforming them." Douglas Porpora, "What Do We Mean by God?," in Archer, Collier, and Porpora, *Transcendence*, 26.

This points to the possibility that even this discourse of judgmental rationality might be framed as ministry. For in respecting our friend's epistemology as real, we must enter her experience and share in it, placing our own next to it. In ministry with her, in being ministered to by her, we can continue to explore our distinctive and important epistemologies of reality. For her to understand my epistemology of reality she must experience it, allowing me to minister to her, so that she might experience the depth of epistemology that gives an account of reality. The Christian faith, I would contend, following my Christopraxis position, makes the best epistemological case to another for the judgmental rationality of Jesus' divinity, not through logical or analytical apologetics but through experiential, hypostatic acts of ministry—for this is where we encounter the living Christ. Christopraxis claims that even interreligious dialogue happens in ministering to the other.

9

Human Action

Throughout this project I have sought to offer an "about face" to practical theology, calling it to give direct attention to the mystery of divine action as the core of its disciplinary focus on the lived and experiential. I have tried to make a case for the lived and experiential encounter of divine action as coming to us in the shape of ministry itself. I have asserted that ministry is first and foremost God's own action that comes to us in experiences *ex nihilo* and *in nihilo* (justification) for the sake of the love of giving us God's very being (participation). So God's being is in the becoming of ministry, and we experience the divine being in the lived act of ministering to us. We take the divine being's form (being conformed to Christ—Christopraxis) by taking on ourselves, through the Spirit, the actions of ministry, by sharing in the hypostatic personal being of our neighbor.

So practical theology is a theological discipline that gives its primary attention to the lived and experiential by making ministry its central focus (and text). By doing so, it seeks to articulate the character of divine ministry by giving practical theology a distinctive theological voice, making it a dialogue partner with all other forms of theology, and making it inextricably *theological*. In addition, it attempts to convey the shape of human ministerial actions by keeping practical theology focused on lived and experiential—and even performative—human actions, seeking to explore how teaching a class, preaching a sermon, leading worship, or running a youth program participate in the divine being by joining the divine action of ministry through the framework of possibility through nothingness.

INTO HUMAN ACTION

This very framework of human action joining divine action in and through ministry compels us to reflect deeply on human action itself. As I have mentioned in previous chapters, established practical theology has done rich and excellent work on human action, exploring it through hermeneutical theory, habitus of practice, feminist theory, postmodern place theory, and neo-Aristotelian conceptions of *phronesis* and praxis. Such work has secured practical theology on solid academic ground, giving it the footing to build past its bastardized state in the basement of the theological enterprise.

Yet, because this rich work has been done primarily with attention to human action, practical theology has gained its confident structure by linking up to the social sciences, as pointed to in the theories of human action provided earlier. In the last chapter and in this one as well, I too will turn to the social sciences. However, I have tried in my chapters on justification and participation to make space for an understanding of anthropology (and therefore human agency) that is constructed from conceptions born from the experience of divine encounter itself. I have turned to critical realism and its scientific conceptions because, while it is not an apologetic for divine action, it refuses the reductions that eliminate it from most social-scientific conversations, reductions that have drawn practical theologians' attention away from transcendence or divine encounter. Following this theological commitment in dialogue with realism, I have asserted that human action is always bound in the framework of possibility out of nothingness and cannot, because of sin and brokenness, create a possibility for itself. In the language of realism, human epistemological constructions have no ultimate power in themselves to create or possess the fullness of reality.

Therefore, human act and being are always in need of the negating and resurrecting work of Christ crucified (Christopraxis), always in the need of independent objective reality to encounter them as a personal event (as revelation). This realist conception of human impossibility also points to the human being's possibility (given to it as the ministerial gift of personal encounter). As hypostatic creatures, as persons, we are open to encounter. We are the relationships that make us; we have our being in and through relationships that place us into reality, and therefore we are open ontologically to the possibility of encounter. All our knowing is conditioned by our hypostatic nature of belonging, to paraphrase Polanyi.[1] And through this

---

1. Smith adds a social-scientific element to my theological assertion that we are our relationships, helping us to define what kind of relationships do indeed make us—deeply spiritual relationships of love, or, as I would say, of ministerial action, for ministry is engendered from and for the sake of love. "But note that I am not merely suggesting that any kind of social relationship or communication defines human personhood. Particular kinds of relationships, especially those involving love, are what matter. By 'love' I do not mean feelings of attraction—which tend to be oriented to the gratification of the self. Instead, by 'loving,' I mean relating to other persons and things beyond the self in a way that involves the

hypostatic encounter (which I have called ministry) we are given personal knowledge of the multistrata of reality—even *experiencing* the independent objective reality of God's own being as it becomes to us. We have our being through experienced, concrete, and lived relationships of encounter that take the shape of ministry (like the ministerial act of a mother holding her newborn child, which, object relations psychology has claimed, the child needs to be ontologically secure and therefore know reality). "Meeting, sharing, engagement, fellowship, and communion are constituting activities of personhood—not functional means or afterthoughts."[2]

Through such encounters we discover and experience the layers of reality itself, recognizing, for instance, that we as (nascent) conscious beings (gaining our consciousness not primarily through language but emotive practice) exist on a higher layer of reality than a sippy cup. We also discover that our mother is not us. As she leaves and returns in response to our own need (impossibility), we learn that she is more than us, responding to us and loving us as a mystery of ministry. And we learn through this ministerial action that reality is also more than us, that things exist on higher strata that we cannot possess.[3] Smith states from a social-scientific perspective, "By virtue of their personhood, persons are quite able to climb past themselves to attend to and devote themselves to that which is beyond themselves. According to personalist theory, the ultimate form of self-transcendence is love for and communion with other persons."[4] This is what I mean by ministry.

Made in the image of this independent objective reality that is hypostatic (God), we are hypostatic and therefore made to receive ministerial action, to be ministered to as the Father ministers to the Son and the Son to the Father, all through the Spirit that binds the hypostases of the three into one, being made one by the complete unity of their indwelling ministry one to another. So, made in this image, we are made to receive the ministerial action of others (our very being cannot be without this ministerial action, to return to object relations psychology). But this also means that we are made (motivated) to *give*

---

purposive action of extending and expending of oneself for the genuine good of others—whether in friendships, families, communities, among strangers, or otherwise. Human persons are such that their very selves are centered in and grow out of relationships of genuine care for each other that are not purely instrumental but require genuine giving of the self in love in various ways for the good of others." Christian Smith, *What Is a Person?* (Chicago: University of Chicago Press, 2010), 73.

2. Ibid., 73.

3. James Loder makes a similar argument in *The Logic of the Spirit: Human Development in Theological Perspective* (San Francisco: Jossey-Bass, 1998).

4. Smith, *What Is a Person?*, 65.

such ministerial action, to embrace the brokenness in love of another in and through their impossibility. It is only when we give into sin—the sin of acting as though we are creator and not creature, therefore seeking to eliminate, deny, or rage against the ex nihilo—that our hypostatic impulse to minister to our neighbor is thwarted by our fear of death and all its friends.

Justification reinstates the ex nihilo of creation, putting to death the misconception that we are our own creator and giving us the gift of being creatures again, creatures that need the hypostatic ministerial action of God's own self. As Adam is "put to sleep" when no counterpart can be found for him to receive or give ministerial action to (Genesis 2), so justification puts to death the illusion that we can live without a minister, that we exist somewhere other than between possibility and nothingness, a concrete and lived place that becomes the very stage for received and given ministerial action, received and given at both the divine and human level. Justification claims that we are hypostatic creatures standing in need of a minister, given our being through the ministry of God, embracing it in and through concrete and lived forms by ministering to and being ministered to by our neighbor.

In earlier chapters, summarized here, we have gone so far in explication of human action as to say that human action must be understood as taking the shape of ministry, upholding our anthropological state as hypostatic creatures caught between possibility and nothingness, existing in a real world that exists independent of our minds, which are bound in lower strata of reality itself. It is true that these commitments around human action are born from my conceptions of divine action; I have done my best to articulate divine action and nature as God's being as the becoming of ministry, arguing that this opens avenues for us to see how ministry itself becomes the sharing of the divine in the human.

But we must now press our conceptions of human action deeper, seeing if my commitments to human action born from reflection on divine action can move from solely theological conceptions to any social-scientific perspectives. I will contend that they can and that ministry is the connecting tissue. Yet, any social-scientific perspective will have to find congruence with the philosophical/social-scientific viewpoints of (critical) realism I explored above.

SOCIAL-SCIENTIFIC MODELS OF HUMANITY

William Alston has argued that the human sciences are "major adversaries of religion, precisely because of their conception of humanity."[5] And this conception, Archer has argued, is an elimination or deconstruction of transcendence, or as we might frame it in this project, a loss of the possibility of the experience of divine encounter. Archer has explained, through her critical realist perspective, that divine encounter *cannot* be assumed or even proven. And therefore, the social sciences are right to have a level of skepticism about such experiences. But, it is also true that people (millions of them) claim to have had such experiences, and these experiences *may be* encounters with higher strata of reality; just as they may not be true, they also may be true. The social sciences have often been blind to this possibility, not because these experiences are necessarily unscientific but because the social sciences' *theories* of humanity rule it out. Archer believes that the social sciences have two operative anthropologies that de facto rule divine encounter as out-of-bounds.

These two theories of humanity are what Archer calls "modernity's man" and "society's being." These two perspectives stand in opposition to each other, warring over their conception of humanity so vigorously that they have distracted us from seeing that both may be erroneous.[6] The war is so ferocious, dominating all discourse about humanity and human action, because these two conceptions are essentially "mirror images of each other . . . one stress[ing] complete human self-sufficiency, whilst the other emphasiz[ing] utter social dependency."[7]

MODERNITY'S MAN

It is "modernity's man" that asserts humanity's self-sufficiency. Modernity's man builds the human being up, seeing him as glorious because of his one essential component—instrumental rationality. His instrumental rationality defines him: he *is* "the capacity [to] maximize his preferences through means-ends relationships and so to optimize his utility."[8] So the human is build up through

5. Margaret Archer, "Models of Man," in *Transcendence: Critical Realism and God*, by Margaret S. Archer, Andrew Collier, and Douglas V. Porpora (London: Routledge, 2004), 63.

6. Archer contends that the human being is an emergent reality that cannot be reduced to "nothing but" society, nor understood as emerging from the lower strata of reality, existing beyond reality, or existing on the peak of reality. It is her commitment to emergent scientific theory in part that leads into the anthropology she holds. I too have leaned on emergent theory throughout the last chapter. I have not had the time or space to articulate this perspective directly, but it rests deeply in the background of my realism. Archer explains this all in relation to anthropology: "Realism construes our humanity as the crucial emergent property of our species, which develops through practical action in the world. Our continuous sense of self, or self-consciousness, is advanced as emerging from the ways in which we are biologically constituted, the way the world is, and from the necessity of our human interaction with our external environment." *Being Human: The Problem of Agency* (London: Cambridge University Press, 2000), 50.

7. Archer, "Models of Man," 64.

8. Ibid., 65.

his rational capacity, and this rational capacity is so glorious that it constitutes the human as center of all existence, giving him the hubris to think that he stands at the peak of reality, determining through instrumental rationality what can exist and be true at all (rationality becomes, or at least reveals, foundations). His instrumental desire determines reality. Modernity's man exists squarely in the hubris of the Aristotelian framework of actuality to possibility: the actuality of human instrumental rationality gives shape to reality. Archer has called the misstep of modernity's man in the social sciences "upward conflation." While this perspective recognizes that we live in a real world, it conflates human instrumental rationality with reality so fully that it sends human consciousness to the top as ruler of reality and, as I would add, falling into the primal sin of upwardly conflating the creature as the creator.

This perspective is born in the Enlightenment and its desire to displace God from the peak of reality with human consciousness, so now standing at the top, the human being might be emancipated to seek his own future. Believing he has the instrumental rational capacity to do just that, modernity's man is free from metaphysics, nature, and even history. With man placed at the peak and man's rational conceptions as glorious, reality becomes a disenchanted place, for only what logical rationality can prove is real.[9] Existence can then *only* be natural and social and is therefore "ontologically purged of transcendence," for reality is surrounded and pinned by human instrumental reason.[10] What is natural or social is proven to be only by the rational capacity of the modern man. These very rational capacities, especially right after the Enlightenment, become foundational, or rather it was instrumental rationality that could unearth the foundations of reality itself.

We have already, following Archer, critiqued this perspective in the previous chapter, placing Christopraxis on a postfoundational conception of reality. Yet, we have not yet wrestled with the very ramification of modernity's man for the conception of human agency itself. Because instrumental rationality is glorified and the human defined as the capacity to maximize his preferences through the optimizing of utility, it is asserted that all human action follows from that rationality. The human being acts to maximize his own survival, for this is the most instrumentally rational possibility. While high Enlightenment foundationalism has come under the friction of critique, dulling its once glorious shine, the conception of human agency born from this perspective

9. See Charles Taylor's *A Secular Age* (Cambridge, MA: Belknap Press of Harvard University Press, 2007), in which he discusses richly the move toward a disenchanted age, following the thought of Max Weber.

10. Archer, "Models of Man," 65.

has not received the same critical appraisal. Rather, rational choice theory, embedded in an anthropology of modernity's man, has stood strong as a paradigmatic explication of the motivation of human agency in the social sciences.

In the rational choice theory born from modernity's man, the human being is *homo economicus*, and desire to enrich his *individual* worth explains the motivation for all his actions. He acts to enrich himself, to solidify his survival, and to glorify himself. After all, he has claimed the peak of reality: he is the proprietor of what is, he is the creator of reality through his instrumental rationality, and his actions in this reality are motivated by his desire to rule this reality, to instrumentally get what he wants, which at its core is survival. Modernity's man as *homo economicus* is a calculator and all his action is calculating. He rationally calculates all costs, taking only the actions that enrich him or get him his wants. And this individualized perspective also explains his social actions; he does what he does to survive or win, rationally choosing one action over another because he has, through rational instrumental means, calculated the costs, whether implicitly or explicitly. So the human being does everything because it is good for his bottom line.

While in contemporary social science, Enlightenment hubris of modernity's man has been blunted some, its explanation for the motivation for human action has not. Rational choice theory is a dominant perspective, one that quickly bleeds into pastoral practice and our conception that people calculate which church enriches their own or their family's life, leading us to believe that program offerings and funny preaching will win membership and church vitality in a competitive religious marketplace.[11]

Rational choice theory has taken on an even stronger assertion about human motivation through the use of evolutionary theory. It is assumed that our genes have rationality of their own, leading us to act in certain ways that uphold and perpetuate them. So, rational choice theory says we love our children not because they are hypostatic persons and in ministering to them we are taken into deeper and higher levels of reality, that love itself exists in a higher stratum of reality (which is why John says "God is love" [1 John 4]), but rather because our genes want their own survival. We love our own children because they share our DNA and we want our DNA to survive. In loving them we really love ourselves. Rational choice theory as a fundamental anthropology

---

11. For more on this conception see chapter 3 of *The Relational Pastor* (Downers Grove: IL: InterVarsity, 2013). There I don't mention rational choice theory directly, but it is the driving theory beyond the individualism that I'm critiquing.

sees as good this fallen sinful nature of humanity, Luther's *incurvatus in se*, the actuality of human being and action.[12]

Modernity's man takes no account and finds no congruence with the articulations we have made about human act and being through the lens of divine action. Modernity's man can never be a minister, for modernity's man is in no need of a minister. He stands at the peak of reality, able through his instrumental rationality to get all he wants; he can rationalize his way beyond *nihilo*. And because he is constituted as a calculator of cost, all his interactions with others are stripped of ministry, for ministry is always too costly, calling us like the good Samaritan (Luke 10) to risk our purity, safety, and resources for the good of another called stranger—another with no shared DNA that might motivate our action. We act for the beaten other, ministering to his need, because we are hypostatic beings, and as such we are given our being through the action of sharing in another's hypostasis. Seeing the beaten man's impossibility, witnessing his beaten person (hypostasis), I'm propelled (by the Spirit), over and against the cost, to minister to his person from my own person, to stand with him in his impossibility. Through our shared hypostasis we might be taken into a new possibility, into a higher stratum of reality, joining (participating) in God's own hypostatic being as the three who minister so deeply to each other that they are one.[13]

12. I am not trying to assert here that rational choice theory is the heart of the theological conception of sin; for instance, Smith states, and I agree, that there are many ways to be self-centered. He explains, "It is not obvious that human selfishness is conceptually identical to the rational pursuit of self-interest. Being a selfishly oriented person does not automatically make one an economics textbook model of the rationally calculating, strategic, ends-oriented, maximizing actor. There are many ways to live a self-centered life, not all of which embody Homo economicus." Christian Smith, *Moral, Believing Animals: Human Personhood and Culture* (Oxford: Oxford University Press, 2003), 31. Though I agree with Smith and see sin as more than just rational choice theory, I nevertheless think it touches on a theological reality of being curved in on ourselves so that the other is never one to minister to, but instead one to compete with.

13. This following quote by Archer articulates how "modernity's man" and rational choice theory destroy the hypostatic nature of humanity, making ministry impossible by making our relationships for exchange: "'Economic man' has already entered the scene, endowed with an instrumental rationality which will strive to drive the best bargain, such that he never pays more than he needs and never settles for less satisfaction than he can get. The world through which he moves is the global market place in which everything, unless it be a desire itself, is open to negotiated exchange. To the bargain-hunter this includes our relationships, for nothing intrinsic to them precludes them from exchange, if market prices make their exchange part of the best bargain. Thus, instead of the traditional picture in which people are partly constituted by their relationships, it is now only in the case of personal attachments that any relationship can be saved from commodification, i.e. because someone's individual emotion has chosen it as an end—and while ever his tastes do not change. Hence the picture of the lonely stranger of modernity

Therefore, rational choice theory (*homo economicus*) is not a possibility for exploring human action in a Christopraxis practical theology because it stands in opposition to ministry, undercutting the hypostatic nature of humanity in rational choice theory's desire to upwardly conflate humanity. A hypostatic nature is essential for ministry as encounter with higher strata of reality through experience and action in concrete lived realities. *And rational choice theory seems to oppose the lived and concrete experience of many who love not for gain, but because it pulls them into what is real.* We act the way we do because we have experienced higher strata of reality that call us through our own action into them; encounter (revelation) with reality motivates human action. And this revelation, I am arguing, comes through the lived and concrete experience of the hypostatic nature of our neighbor—through a man beaten by the side of the road. We say in such concrete lived experiences that it was just the right thing to do, that it was right, the Samaritan might say, to bandage the wounds of the beaten man. It is right, not next to some foundational moral law but because we have a personal experiential encounter with a higher stratum of reality, making our action a normative act, *normative because we confess it takes us into a higher stratum of reality.* We desire to place our own action in congruence with a reality greater than us. We act as we do for normative reasons (I will say more about this in what follows).[14]

Even from a social-scientific perspective, Archer has shown that rational choice theory can take no account of normativity, of how people through emotive experiences with reality are converted to truths that set the direction for their action. As Archer says,

who selects his relationships in the same manner as his other purchases and who can know no loyalties because all his loyalty is vested in his own internal desires. This makes him selfish even when his behavior appears otherwise, for such 'altruism' as he displays merely corresponds to his inner desire to behave benevolently. Homo economicus can have a taste for philanthropy, in which case it is the task of his reason to make him a well satisfied philanthropist, a cost-benefit effective benefactor and a philanthropic maximiser. If his high ranking preferences run to charity, then let the cats' home or the refugee agency be the best run of charities." *Being Human*, 54. For more on this in connection to pastoral ministry see *Relational Pastor*.

14. I have been quite hard on rational choice theory because I do not believe it encompasses the whole of human action, but such a perspective could be *one* reason for human action within a normative perspective. Smith explains, "In which case, rational choice theory does not trump a normative theory of culture by reducing and reinterpreting the variety and complexity of human motivations into the singular motive of rational self-interest. Rather, if anything, a normative or moral theory of culture, such as the one suggested here, reinterprets rational choice theory as describing one particular mode of human motivation and action that reflects and embodies a specific moral order situated in a particular place in history and culture." *Moral, Believing Animals*, 33.

> One of the most important things with which this model [modernity's man] cannot cope is the human capacity to transcend instrumental rationality and to have "ultimate concerns." These are concerns that are not a means to anything beyond them, but are commitments that are constitutive of who we are—the expression of our identities. Who we are is a matter of what we care about most. This is what makes us moral beings. It is only in the light of our "ultimate concerns" that our actions are ultimately intelligible. None of this caring can be impoverished by reducing it to an instrumental means–ends relationship.[15]

Because rational choice theory cannot take account of a normative realism, it also cannot handle what I would call the core hypostatic ministerial realities found in human action. Rational choice theory and modernity's man have little answer for things like voluntary collective behavior, human dependence on others, and most profoundly within this project, the expressive solidarity and willingness to share with others, even to share in others (to love and be with).[16] Love is never cost-effective, but it is the most beautiful of realities because it takes us into new and higher forms of reality. In other words, rational choice theory as a model for human action cannot take account of ministry, and because it cannot take account of ministry (why one human being would love another human being), it has no room for the possibility of divine action (and especially divine action as God's being as becoming in ministry). To put it in the language of the social sciences, *modernity's man and rational choice theory are blind to the experience of transcendence that gives human beings an ultimate concern and motivates their action.*[17]

Society's Being

If modernity's man pushes humanity into complete self-sufficiency, then society's being emphasizes utter social dependence. It looks at the theory of modernity's man up and down and shakes its head in disbelief, claiming that emancipation into instrumental reason is an illusion. We cannot climb to the peak of reality, possessing and knowing it completely, society's being asserts. Rather, any climbing at all is a delusion, for we can never escape socializing

---

15. Archer, "Models of Man," 65.

16. These three are taken from ibid.

17. We'll have to watch out here for the religious congruency fallacy that Chaves points to. I'll try to take consideration of this as I articulate my interdisciplinary perspective below.

forces that impinge on us. As Richard Rorty says, "socialization . . . goes all the way down." Society's being rightly counters the hubris of modernity's man but, while knocking him off his ledge, tears down all of reality with him. When socialization goes all the way down (or up), there is no reality other than that which is socially constructed, and independent objective reality is lost. Where modernity's man upwardly conflates humanity, Archer explains, society's being boldly downwardly conflates humanity, "improvising humanity, by subtracting from our human powers and accrediting all of them—selfhood, reflexivity, thought, memory, emotionality and belief—to society's discourse."[18] This downward conflation, as we saw in the last chapter, attacks reality, following aggressive postmodernity in claiming that there is no reality outside the text (Derrida) of society's discourse. We are only what society makes us through its ideologies.[19]

When reality is lost in socialization, so too is the human self. In postmodern theory there is no self, for the self is nothing more than the composition of society's ideological discourses. Freedom is only an illusion; we are what the discourses of our society say we are. The self is no hypostatic being, created in and through the realities of ministerial action that take us into higher strata of reality (transcendence); there is nothing essential about personhood at all. We simply are what society makes us. And because we are, there is no room in such a social-scientific perspective for any sense of transcendence, as metaphysics receives a stake to the heart. Religion, faith, and theology become only locales of discourse and have no possibility of saying anything about what is true or real, for there is nothing true or real outside society's discourse.

Divine action is also lost. If it exists at all, it is bound so fully in the discourses and practices of a religious society that all transcendent realism is stripped from it. Normativity itself is no longer bound in the epistemological conceptions of real experiences with higher strata of reality. Instead, it can only produce faux norms, the socially constructed norms of religious discourses that are only relevant within those particular discourses. Normativity has nothing to do with reality itself, for there is no reality outside the discourses of society. The

---

18. Archer, "Models of Man," 60.

19. Andrew Sayer explains the difference between postmodern theory and critical realism: "Defeatist postmodernists tend to assume that because the world is so open, diverse and complex, nothing of lasting or universal application can be said about it, and because theory is so contestable and yet difficult to test, anything goes. Critical realists accept the premise but argue for a different conclusion: that notwithstanding the daunting complexity of the world and the fallible and situated character of knowledge, it is possible to develop reliable knowledge and for there to be progress in understanding." *Realism and Social Science* (Los Angeles: Sage, 2000), 30.

norms of discourse are not assumed to be provisional articulations of a higher (transcendent) stratum of reality, for there is no such thing—there is only the discourse of society's being.

This model, while radical in its interpretative deconstruction, has had a harder time as a social theory in articulating the motivation for human action. It can say much about the ideologies and power structures of society, and it can explain well why human beings function as they do, but it has a much harder time explaining why human beings are motivated to act at all, as the cabbie, Greg, Matt, and Rachel do. If we are only society's being, why act at all? Why care?

Hard postmodernity has a difficult time answering; if normativity is an illusion, a hall of mirrors given to us by the discourses of society, and if there is nothing outside these warped reflecting discourses, why act at all? It appears that we are motivated to act, or at least the shape of our action comes, through deconstruction itself: we swing at the mirrors because they are false, distorting us.[20] But again, why act? The model of society's being says we are distorted, but there is no way for us to exist beyond *some* distortion because there is no self outside society's discourse; in the end, there is no self at all. We act because we are stuck as society's being; we must act to subvert our socialization, to show that our being and action is only a construction given to us by society. In other words, human action is motivated to deconstruct the socialized forms given to humanity.

But why, if reality is *only* the text and socialization goes all the way down, would we be motivated to deconstruct at all? If there is no normative ultimate concern, where does the passion to subvert the ideologies come from? Seeing this problem, some postmodern theorists, following the likes of Levinas, have claimed that motivation is born in seeing the other and therefore motivation is always against power ideologies of socialization that harm the other.[21] But how do we judge what is harm? If reality is only socialization and people are only society's beings, is it not possible that even our action to care for the other is just deceptively engendered from the echo chamber of socialization?

---

20. The best of examples of this is John Caputo's *Weakness of God: A Theology of the Event* (Bloomington: Indiana University Press, 2006). Here Caputo use Derrida's deconstruction as a way of Christian living; it is deconstruction that shapes discipleship.

21. It is interesting that Levinas even moves into using at least pseudometaphysical language, calling the face of the other an infinite reality, a reality that cannot be totalized by the discourses of society. This seems to me to point to the cul-de-sac of postmodern theory. And it also shows a way forward in a kind of personalism that I too am pushing in this project, a personalism I'm calling our hypostatic nature.

We are caught in a vicious defeating circle: because there is no reality, once we subvert this socialization, once we deconstruct the ideologies, we are caught again in another net of socialization. The very tools for subverting socialization are shown to be made out of nothing more than further socialization. There is no answer for why human beings act, for even our action only gets us stuck in another socialized prison. Unless there is some conception of realism, some confession of a reality greater than human minds and therefore societal socialization, there is no motivation for human action. There is only nihilism, for there is nothing real and truly no reason to act at all. We are only society's being. This is the suicide pill, as Archer and Collier call it, that postmodernity must take.

And if one theoretically lack the nerve to take it, then as Smith says, most theorists in society's being fall back into a form of rational choice theory, ironically taking the motivational impulse for human action from a theory they otherwise completely oppose. If we are only society's being and if all we *are* is caught in socialized ideologies, then in the end we simply do what we do either in conformity to the social system or in the struggle to be emancipated from it. We do this not for normative realist reasons but because of what it gets us, because in opposing the discourses we recreate the discourse in a way that serves our own ideologies (this is why most postmodern theorists in the academy become ferociously political). We use instrumental reason to deconstruct the ideologies so that we can replace them with other ideologies that we like more. And because these ideologies have no realist normative locale, they can only in the end be brought forth for the reasons favored by *homo economicus* (if we are honest!).

Toward Normative, Believing Animals

If practical theology is to be in conversation with the social sciences (and I think such a conversation is essential to its disciplinary soul), then the anthropological models of modernity's man and society's being have significant problems. Archer explains these problems:

> Neither of these two models can capture the "man of faith" who is responsive to sacred revelation or tradition. Thus, "Modernity's Man" represents an anthropocentric being, incapable as an "outsider" of sufficient embedding in a sacred tradition such that this helps to constitute his being-in-the-world. He is also closed against revelation by his human self-sufficiency. This means that he will always reduce divinity to the anthropomorphic—ideal typically to

the Goddess of Supreme Reason. Conversely, Society's Being is so sociocentric that he is swamped by tradition (form of life, language game, etc.), and thus lacks the wherewithal to elaborate upon it, and is only open to revelation in so far as it is mediated to him by society. Anthropocentric "Modernity's Man" makes God and his society in his own image. Sociocentric "over-socialised" man is the product of society, as is his God.[22]

These are major problems against the backdrop of a Christopraxis practical theology of the cross, where divine action as God's being as becoming in ministry is central and where this attention to divine action leads us to ministry itself as the locale of divine and human encounter. This encounter of the divine and human is the heart of a Christopraxis practical theology, and its conversations with the social sciences find company in and through critical realism. So too, then, must our anthropological conceptions. From the locale of our experience and reflection on divine action we have claimed the human being as a hypostatic creature whose being and act is constituted in the giving and receiving of ministry at both the divine and human level. But additional questions are raised as we continue this conversation with the social sciences: How would such a perspective find association or convergence with a scientific perspective? And is it possible that if such a convergence could be found, and found in a realist vein, it might help us articulate the motivation for human action better than rational choice theory (which, as we argued, stands outside the ministerial core of both divine and human being and act)?

Christian Smith has offered just such a perspective of the human being in his book *Moral, Believing Animals*.[23] Here Smith articulates an anthropology in a realist frame that offers an alternative answer for human motivation than the one rational choice theory provides. And one I'll show opens up rich possibility for dialogue between the social sciences and a Christopraxis practical theology.

Smith makes a social-scientific assertion that human beings are norming (moral), believing animals that narrate their lives. This perspective stands in direct opposition to upward or downward conflation of modernity's man and society's being.

22. Archer, "Models of Man," 67.

23. In this book Smith's critical realism is nascent; it will not be developed more deeply until *What Is a Person?*. Though his critical realism is nascent in *Moral, Believing Animals* and Smith takes a few corrective steps in *What Is a Person?*, the larger infrastructure of realist social theory is here. I'll take some liberties to stretch his perspective in *Moral, Believing Animals* into a more fully formed realist perspective; I see this as consistent with Smith's work.

Believing

Smith asserts, in opposition to upward conflation, that we are all believers. There is no way for the human being to *be* in the world other than in a state of belief, and almost all of our actions, too, are born from our ontological state as believing animals.[24] We are the distinctive animals that must believe, for our consciousness transcends instinct and is able to contemplate the possibility of higher strata of reality. We are conscious animals, but not like my dog who is conscious that he has a bur caught in his tail. Instead, we are the kind of animals that are conscious about our consciousness, able to contemplate (imagine) realities beyond what our consciousness can completely conceive.

Because we are such animals that can be conscious of our consciousness, our most important action (our agency) is born from belief and not preprogrammed instinct. We do what we do for held reasons that connect to belief. They may be stupid reasons that reveal bad beliefs, but nevertheless we believe and therefore these beliefs direct our action. The fifteen-year-old girl starves herself, taking the motivated action to not eat, not because of instrumental-rational choice but because she has deeply held beliefs. She believes that she is fat and that being fat will thrust her into a nothingness where she will be left without the relationships her hypostatic being needs. She acts to starve herself, even knowing it is bad for her (too costly), because she believes being skinny, even if it costs her health, is an actuality she can create for herself that will save her from nothingness.

From the anthropological level of being always believers, we assert that instrumental reason cannot lead us to the peak of reality, for we exist in lower strata of reality. All our views of reality are relativized and clouded by our bounded locale in these lower strata of reality. Therefore, upward conflation is not a possibility because of the epistemic relativism of critical realism.[25] And

24. Here Smith articulates his movement past upward conflation. "Modernity—despite having often, because of its particular moral belief system, characterized 'mere beliefs' as subjective and emotion based and thus needing to be overridden by reason and knowledge—has in fact done little to change our human condition as fundamentally believing animals." *Moral, Believing Animals*, 50.

25. Here Smith articulates the postfoundational location of his position, showing how his understanding of the human being as moral, believing animals connects to the epistemic relativity that critical realism offers. "We see, then, that what any people, including ourselves, know about life and the world, about how life ought to be lived, is not founded on an indubitable, universal foundation of knowledge. These are not built on solid piles that have been driven down into a very bedrock of known reality that lies accessible beneath every human person. Rather all of our knowledge and life practices—however obvious and well-founded they may seem to us—are built like large rafts on beams of particular trusted assumptions and beliefs that themselves float freely in the shifting seas of culture and history." *Moral, Believing Animals*, 53.

our action in reality can never be outside of the need to believe. Through Polanyi, we made this same assertion in the last chapter, saying that because reality is stratified and human epistemologies exist somewhere in the middle of reality, we are stuck with always and forever being beings of belief. There is much about the ontological state of reality that human beings do not have the equipment to know unequivocally. We are creatures and not the creator, which means our actions are always engendered from beliefs. These beliefs may be held as a consistent whole, but more often they are like potentially contradictory arrows in a quiver that we grab to direct our action in world.[26]

To argue that human action is engendered from belief and not instrumental reason stands in opposition to the rational choice theory of modernity's man, for modernity's man is not a believer but a calculator. He need not trust or believe because his reason can secure for him an actuality in which he can act through the motivation of his own gain. Of course, at certain levels, even modernity's man must believe that he is a calculator that can achieve his gain. But, as Smith has argued, while this position ironically elevates the human being as lord, seated on a throne of instrumental reason, it also reduces him by limiting his agency to only the notes (the tapping fingers) of functional calculation, leaving little room for the possibility that he may act because he believes in things he calls sacred, holy, or transcendent—like being loved, an experience the fifteen-year-old believes only skinny people get.

For example, Matt talked about his experience of divine encounter in ministry among the poor, which was described in chapter 3. Matt acts to feed the poor not because such actions make him feel good about himself and therefore are worth the cost, but because in so doing he believes he is (that is, he concretely feels himself) participating in a higher reality through the ministerial action of sharing in another's hypostasis. Matt takes this action because he believes this; he has no foundational proof, just his experience, but his experience of being ministered to and ministering to others directs his action.

We are forced as human beings into a state of belief by reality itself. To put it in theological language, we are forced into belief by the reality that we are creatures and therefore our reality is always stuck between possibility and nothingness. The fifteen-year-old girl feels the nothingness of believing she is fat; she needs the ministerial action of another that holds her hypostatic being to provide the concrete witness of possibility in and through the nothingness, converting through shared nothingness her belief of relational loss into the

26. See above for Chaves's religious congruency fallacy.

communion of hypostatic love. If she does not receive this ministry, she will act to create her own actuality, only thrusting herself deeper into nothingness.

We are bound to always be in a state of belief because, though we may try, there is no way for us to escape our ex nihilo. We are animals who are embodied, encountering our world through our emotive experiences (and practices), not primarily our rational-instrumental minds. The action of the fifteen-year-old to stop starving herself can only occur if she is converted into a new belief system (this converting maybe done by a church or a therapist). And ministry, one to another, I argue, possesses this power of conversion, for ministry comes to us in and through our hypostatic being, binding us in the witness to higher reality, a reality in which we are loved, and therefore changing our beliefs in and through a normative experience of this reality. The fifteen-year-old my find strength in therapy, but to lead her to health the therapist will in no small way become her minister.

That our action is engendered by our belief means for Smith that human action cannot be animated simply by the engine of instrumental rationality that finds its fuel in the calculation of individual gain. Rather, all human functioning begins with "first committing ourselves to sets of assumptions and presupposed beliefs that make any functioning human life possible."[27]

We take action, such as believing that school will start tomorrow as it did today and that our child's teacher (or a substitute) will show up to teach her class.[28] We take great faith that the bus we put her on will constantly and consistently drop her off at the school.[29] We take actions, even bold ones like saying good-bye to vulnerable children, because we take *faith* we believe that the bus will get her there safely. If we could not trust this—if what we believed was true is shown not to be true—all our other actions for the day would be upended, and anxiety (or multiple other emotions) would fuse the gears of human action, potentially leading us to question even reality.

27. Smith, *Moral, Believing Animals*, 54.

28. "At the same time, precisely because human actors are constituted, developed, propelled, and guided by the social institutions in which their lives are embedded, the moral orders that animate social institutions also find imperfectly corresponding expression within human actors—in the assumptions, ideas, values, beliefs, volitions, emotions, and so on of human subjectivity, conscience, consciousness, and self-consciousness." Ibid., 149.

29. This analogy points to the fact that not only do institutions as dependent objective realities have beliefs but these beliefs get internalized inside us. Smith says helpfully, "Part of the reason why the moral orders internalized 'inside' of people do not entirely match the moral orders constituting and embedded in the institutions outside of and encompassing those people is that animals that are moral and believing actively participate in their own socialization. As discriminating agents who judge, embrace, reject, and modify." Ibid., 28.

"Only by believing in, committing to, placing faith in certain suppositions and propositions can we human animals ever be able to perceive, think, know, feel, will, choose, and act."[30] Human action is always belief. Smith says powerfully,

> We build up our lives from presuppositional starting points in which we (mostly unconsciously) place our trust and that are not derived from other justifying grounds. Thus what we know about life and the world, about how life ought to be lived, is not founded on an indubitable, universal foundation of knowledge [this is the problem of upward conflation]. Rather, we are all inescapably trusting, believing animals, creatures that must and do place our faith in beliefs that cannot themselves be verified except by means established by the presumed beliefs themselves.[31]

NORMING AND NARRATING

Following Smith, I've reimagined human agency beyond upward conflation by asserting that our action is always engendered from implicit or explicit beliefs: *we are believing animals*. To assert that we are believing animals is also, then, to argue that we believe in something, that there is an object or subject to which our belief is directed. And this object or subject is *real* (or why believe it!). This has led Smith to assert that we are not only believing animals, but *moral or normative* believing animals. Smith says, "Human culture and motivation to action are not at bottom instrumentally functional or practically rational matters but rather are very much normative concerns."[32] We take the actions we do because we have some normative commitment that calls some actions good or bad, deep or vapid, real or not.[33] We go to church, for instance, on Sunday not primarily because we calculate cost and recognize that it will be good for our social capital, but because we believe that it is something people like us do. Our normative commitment to who we are and what we are like *motivates* our action.[34] "Therefore humans are moral animals not primarily

---

30. Ibid., 55.

31. Ibid., 150.

32. Ibid., 80.

33. "What I mean by 'moral,' to be clear, is an orientation toward understandings about what is right and wrong, good and bad, worthy and unworthy, just and unjust, that are not established by our own actual desires, decisions, or preferences but instead believed to exist apart from them, providing standards by which our desires, decisions, and preferences can themselves be judged." Ibid., 8.

34. Wentzel van Huyssteen adds to this from the perspective of science and theology: "Human animals are moral animals in that we possess capacity and propensity unique among all animals: we have not only

because morality serves some instrumental interest. Rather, humans are moral animals because they experience, in part as a result of their self-consciousness, a particular relationship to themselves and the world that evokes a search for standards beyond themselves, by which they may evaluate themselves."[35]

The model of society's being, and its downward conflation, would agree that we act because of the normative ideologies of discourse to which we hold. But it would go further by claiming that such normative commitments are only socially constructed and therefore need to be subverted. We may do certain things, like go to church, because we believe the ideological socialization that people like us take such action. But society's being reminds us that while we may take such a normative stance, it is only normative for us (or our collective) because it is only a text of society's discourse. It is normative only in our consent; there is no realist core to it.[36] So we may believe things, society's being asserts, but all our beliefs are in the end beliefs in something unreal, something that is nothing other than the discourses of society.[37]

The problem is that once we recognize this, once we realize that there is no such thing as normativity because epistemological plurality will not allow for consensus of reality, we have no reason (or at least no motivation) to act. Why go to church if your normative commitment is hollow and you only go because the discourses you've been given determine it? There is no reason, yet people still go. They go, the model of society's being *wrongly* asserts, because they have

desires, beliefs, and feelings, but also the ability to form strong evaluations about our desires, beliefs, and feelings that hold the potential to actually transform them. Humans, for instance, have the ability not only to hate, but also to judge that our hatreds are wrong, and to decide that we do not want to be hateful anymore." *Alone in the World?: Human Uniqueness in Science and Theology* (Grand Rapids, MI: Eerdmans, 2006), 290.

35. Ibid., 291.

36. As we'll see below, this may be true at the dependent objective layer of reality, but it is not true, I contend, from the locale of all of reality.

37. Sayer provides a nice overview of downward conflation and its distain for normativity, "A still more radical rejection of normative questions comes from Nietzschean post-structuralism, which reduces normative problems of justice and morality in complex societies to simple patterns of interest and power camouflaging. . . . As Amy Gutmann points out, it is contradictory to argue that the content of all intellectual positions derives purely from a will-to-power, and to criticize them for doing just this, not least because it must undermine the critic's own arguments too. The reduction of all intellectual disagreements completely to conflicts of group interests is simply anti-intellectual and it is not clear why those who believe in the reduction bother to make a case at all when there are more direct routes to political power available. Such a radical reduction is not sustainable: those who sneer at values and morality get as upset as anyone else when someone treats them improperly. Moral discourse is indeed sometimes little more than a camouflage or legitimation of power, often hypocritical; but again, a bad use of such discourse need not drive out a good use." *Realism and Social Science*, 177.

either not deconstructed the discourses or because, even in knowing that church attendance is only a text, they've calculated the value of such participation. This is why Smith asserts that society's being and its downward conflation walks backward into rational choice theory. It ends up being no answer at all to why people are motivated to act and what shape human action takes (especially from the level of ministerial hypostatic love).

So, in opposition to downward conflation, Smith asserts that we must enter into norming processes and do so because reality is greater than our human minds can possess. Smith admits (as does a Christopraxis practical theology) that all our believing is relativized, and reality cannot be captured in the upward conflation of human rational foundational systems. Because of this, we are stuck with the valuative demand of living our lives by determining (believing) what is true or not. This believing can never be conclusive; nevertheless, to act in the world we must claim some normative assertions that direct our action—some faith in reality.[38] And these normative assertions come to us most often in narrative shape. All the people I interviewed in chapter 3 used deep and complicated narratives to articulate their claim of having a real experience with God.

Reality comes us to us *before* language.[39] Reality is not constituted through language (as downward conflation asserts); rather, we experience reality through emotive practice that precedes language—we know more than we can say (Polanyi and Loder). But these experiences with reality are given determinative normative shape through narration.[40] "People . . . most fundamentally understand what reality is, who they are, and how they ought

38. Here Smith articulates how normativity is bound within realism. "Humans are moral animals not primarily because morality serves some instrumental interest (even if in cases it may). Humans are moral animals, rather, because they experience, in part as a result of their self-consciousness relationship to themselves and the world that evokes a search for standards beyond themselves by which they may evaluate themselves. This is an account of morality that also takes human cognizance and intention seriously, as the sociobiological account does not." *Moral, Believing Animals*, 43.

39. I argued this point in the last chapter.

40. Smith here defines narrative very helpfully for us. "What then exactly is narrative? Narrative is a form of communication that arranges human actions and events into organized wholes in a way that bestows meaning on the actions and events by specifying their interactive or cause-and-effect relations to the whole. Narratives are much more than chronicles, which merely list discrete events by placing them on timelines. Narratives seek to convey the significance and meaning of events by situating their interaction with or influence on other events and actions in a single, interrelated account. Narratives, thus, always have a point, are always about the explanation and meaning of events and actions in human life, however simple these may be." *Moral, Believing Animals*, 65. Van Huyssteen, who will be a major dialogue partner in the second half of this chapter, continues, adding, "Narrative in this broader epistemic sense certainly not only implies the composition of stories, but much more involves our actions and

to live by locating themselves within the larger narratives that they hear and tell, which constitute what is real and significant for them."[41] The norms are *not solely* language games but shared experiences with reality, and these experiences that are shared, and shared as normative, are given to others through the language of narration, for narration possesses the hypostatic property of sharing in (of ministry). So it is through our sharing in stories of reality (through testimony) that we are given normative commitments that motivate our action.[42] Reality is more than language, but as persons (hypostatic beings) we are the animals that use language to articulate our lived experiences with reality (for again, reality is *experienced* before language). Experiences born from our actions in reality then become the norms that motivate our further action in the world.

But to say that narratives pass on norms that motivate our actions and that these norms are perceived as connecting to something real means that reflection on human action itself must attend to the stratified nature of reality. This gives us always the possibility that any normative commitment could be misguided and therefore lead to error or even the evil motivation of human action as a result of its narration corrupting and veiling reality—like the normative commitment held through the narration of propaganda in 1933 Germany that Jews were less than human, which motivated evil action against them.

Smith explains that human beings act the way they do because of the norms they perceive embedded within all the layers of reality itself. We feel these norms (through something other than instrumental rationality). Most of us do not pick our noses in public because we feel it normative to keep our fingers out of our nostrils. We have deep emotive reactions (feelings) when someone breaks this norm, calling it *gross*!

It is true that this normative commitment *is* socially constructed because its normativity is bound to the dependent objective layer of reality, and this layer is

---

discourses, as well as ourselves as engaged participants." *The Shaping of Rationality: Toward Interdisciplinarity in Theology and Science* (Grand Rapids, MI: Eerdmans, 1999), 210.

41. Smith, *Moral, Believing Animals*, 152.

42. Smith explains, "This is in part what it means to suggest that we not only are animals who make and tell narratives but also animals who are told and made by our narratives. The stories we tell are not mere entertainment. Nor do they simply suggest for us some general sense of our heritage. Our stories fully encompass and define our lives. They situate us in reality itself, by elaborating the contours of fundamental moral order, comprising sacred and profane, in narrative form, and placing us too as actors within the larger drama. Our individual and collective lives come to have meaning and purpose insofar as they join the larger cast of characters enacting, reenacting, and perpetuating the larger narrative. It is by finding ourselves placed within a particular drama that we come to know our role, our part, our lines in life—how we are to act, why, and what meaning that has in a larger scheme of reality." Ibid., 78.

always socially constructed. Nevertheless, it is constructed as objective, so even if we should decide it is not normative *for us* to not pick our noses in public, this will not change the disapproving looks we get from the people sitting next to us on the airplane. Our seatmates cannot help but gag when seeing our fingers in our noses, for their normative commitments are so deep and motivating to their own action that they feel this normative violation not in their heads but in their very bodies, in the revulsion that tightens their throats.

The dependent objective reality itself gives us norms that mold and direct our action. For instance, in Norway there is no normative commitment that says a small sleeping child in a stroller cannot be left outside a café while her mother sits with friends. In fact, it is believed that napping outdoors is the healthiest and preferred way for babies to sleep. Yet, in the United States, leaving a sleeping child outside a shop in a stroller is not only uncommon, it is experienced as *wrong*, as a danger, as immoral (leading to a 911 call and prosecution). Because of this normative commitment, an American parent, even in Norway, will feel deep motivation to refuse to leave her child outside and to be concerned even for *a stranger's child* left outdoors. The normativity of her dependent objective reality motivates her action. And it motivates it in such a way that it connects deeply to her being; if she goes against her normative commitments and leaves the child outside, even rationally assured that her baby is fine, she will feel (emotive) tension—worry—in her body. Though her child is not at risk, she has stepped beyond her normative commitments and feels herself lost in anxiety, unable to take other actions in the café; her worry is a toxin in her being, and it is so poisonous because she has violated something she holds (or something that was given to her to hold) as normative.

This normativity rests in dependent objective reality (and is therefore partly socially constructed), but it can also be found in the dependent subjective reality. Our actions are motivated by many things that have no instrumental rational or socialized base; they connect rather to some emotive lived feeling that nevertheless seems true, or at least helpful. A pitcher in a baseball game always jumps over the chalk foul line as he approaches the mound, motivated to take such action because he believes it normative, holding that when he does this action he pitches better, that he enters a reality (a zone) where his pitching is poetry. He does this action for normative reasons; it is what pitchers before him have done, and he has experienced, even over his better rationality, that not touching the chalk line connects him to a reality that makes him pitch well. He is motivated to take this weird action because he believes it true, even though he may admit that from a strictly instrumental-rationality perspective it is superstition, but nevertheless pitchers (even those playing for Harvard) take such actions. The pitcher claims that such action is not only normative for his performance, but, because it takes him into a reality, he also holds that jumping the chalk line (or wearing certain underwear) also norms the play behind him, helping his fielders and giving him good luck that hard-hit balls will find players' gloves. There is no rational benefit for this, as the pitcher expels energy jumping and keeping his pattern, but he does it because in the dependent subjective layer of reality it norms his action, giving some peace, or at least order, to his being.

This brings us back to the example of going to church. A man's action to go to church is motivated by normativity. He may go because the dependent objective community that he grew up in passed on a strict norm that says he must. He has not extracted this normative commitment from his being and therefore his action is motivated—even if he admits to himself that he hates it. He will only be motivated to not go when he has exorcised his normative commitment that is mediated to him through his dependent objective community and its stories (and it can only be exorcised by replacing it with another normative commitment, like the NFL). But it is also true that he may only go to church because he in the dependent subjective layer of reality and feels he must. He feels the norm, feels the pull of motivation that says to him that if he does not go to Mass this week, something bad may happen to him, and he tells himself this story to motivate his action on an early Sunday morning. He goes motivated by the dependent subjective norm.

It is also possible, then, that he is motivated to go because his norm is bound in another layer of reality. He may get up early for church, going every week, because in worship and liturgy he feels himself participating in the independent objective reality; he has a dynamic or quiet experience of transcendence (of communing with God) in and through the hypostatic life of this worshipping community. This is more than just socialized discourse or wealth-providing action; it is an experience with something real. He is motivated to act because he feels his being taken into a higher stratum of reality to encounter divine action. The cabbie goes with Rachel into the morgue at a cost—he loses the time to make another fare—but his action is motivated not by cost analysis ("maybe she'll tip me more") but by the normative pull of ministry, by the feeling that in being with her (hypostasis to hypostasis) he is doing what is right—that is, it takes him into a deeper reality.

The good Samaritan ministers to the beaten man over and against cost or socialized text, for normative reasons. But even these normative reasons transform other normative commitments that would keep him from acting. He reaches out to minister to the man over and against his dependent subjective reality, which speaks a norm of personal safety. He ministers to the man beyond also the dependent objective reality's norms, which shout that it is a trap for robbers, that no Jew would help a Samaritan, so why risk for this Jew? Yet, he acts because his very hypostatic being opens him to the hypostatic nature of God's own being as the becoming of an independent objective reality. The Samaritan is motivated to act for the man, to minister to him, because he confesses that it draws him into a higher stratum of reality, because in doing this ministerial act he touches something real, something transcendent. It is a normative commitment coming to him through ministerial action that he believes takes him into divine participation. He moves into direct action because he has witnessed the hypostatic nature of the beaten man, and the witnessing is a revelation, an encounter with a higher stratum of reality that calls him to participate, to take on the action of ministry itself.

Smith's assertion that we are norming, believing animals not only avoids upward conflation by asserting that we are always bound in locations of belief and never can escape them, but moves away from downward conflation as well. His perspective claims that our normative commitments are connected to our commitment to a genuine reality. These realities to which we commit, giving them normative power in our lives, may be wrong, like the normative commitment of the fifteen-year-old who believes that thin equals beautiful, but she commits to it with such force because she believes it to be true, because she holds as real that skinny is beautiful.

It is not simply her overcommitment to society's discourse that leads her to believe this. Even when she knows logically that skinny is unreal, that all models are airbrushed, she is not liberated because her action is latched not to rational choice but to perceived normative reality. She believes it is real, at least deeply real in a dependent objective way, which forces her action, even over against her rational knowledge. She cannot be liberated through knowledge but only through a ministry of hypostatic person to hypostatic person, through a ministry that takes her into a higher stratum of reality, linking her being to higher normative commitment, like the loving, justifying action of God. Entering into this new reality (possibility) cannot happen just through knowledge (which has been the Evangelical problem) but through the experience of this higher reality in and through our concrete lives.

Just as divine action is motivated by ministry, so too is human action. From the level of the social sciences, we would describe this as a movement toward the real. What motivates human action is the desire to experience higher strata of reality. We love our children not to continue their genes; we have children at all not because they offer value. Rather, studies now show that children cost us much in dollars, sleep, sex, and overall individual happiness. And yet we are motivated to have them over and against the cost because, in loving them, in sharing so deeply in their hypostatic being as they share in ours, we are pulled into higher strata of reality. Loving them is a transcendent experience of delight. Sarah listens to Erin and Matt drives every week to Portland to feed the homeless, not because of a motivation of gain but because in so doing each is taken into a higher reality—that is what motivates their action.

HUMAN ACTION IN A CHRISTOPRAXIS PRACTICAL THEOLOGY

So then to summarize, I have asserted, following this critical realist anthropology, that human action is directed toward or motivated by normativity. From a social-scientific perspective we might call this normative direction of human action "moral codes."[43] Following critical realism, I asserted that human action is propelled by normative experiences or perceptions of reality itself. We do what we do because we believe (whether explicitly or tacitly) it is real (making it normative), believing such actions correlate with or draw us into reality (we could be wrong, but we act at all because we believe).

Archer has helped us see that human action (even the prelinguistic action of dropping a sippy cup from a highchair) is bound in the desire to experience reality. Therefore, she says, it is an ultimate concern—a normative commitment, as Smith would say—that directs our action. The child is motivated to drop the cup not for any cost benefit, but because she is motivated to experience reality.

The movement toward an ultimate concern directs human action into an ontological reality; where rational choice theory can express reasons for action, these actions seem disconnected from human *being* (from ontology). Act and being in anthropology are braided in a social theory that sees the motivation for human action born from normativity, allowing us to speak of things like identity, purpose, and altruism in human action.[44] We believe our actions motivated *not* by cost evaluation (which reduces them) but by our lived experiences in reality itself, which provides us with normative commitments that further direct our action. As object relations psychology has said, once a child has experienced the reality of the love of her caretaker (a hypostatic personalism, I would add), she has the ontological security, the normative belief

43. For another example of this in sociology see *Code of the Street* by Elijah Anderson (New York: W. W. Norton, 1999). Both this book and parts of Smith's own work are also inspired by the thought of Ann Swidler. Smith is critical of her in the final chapter of *Moral, Believing Animals*, but nevertheless some of the nascent ideas of moral codes go back to her work.

44. Archer states, "In short, we are who we are because of what we care about: in delineating our ultimate concerns and accommodating our subordinate ones, we also define ourselves." *Being Human*, 10.

(experience) that allows her to act in the world. We give to or love others because we experience it (feel it) as right or holy to do so; we are motivated because of experiences of reality itself, calling it normative because such actions are felt to take us into higher strata of reality, opening up, Archer asserts, the possibility for the social sciences to discuss transcendence. And, this very perspective, following Archer and Smith, leaves open a space for practical theology to discuss divine action and yet stay committed to its interdisciplinary (social-scientific) soul.

To now engage this perspective of human action in conversation with our Christopraxis conception of divine action is to continue to follow the path of normativity. Practical theology has struggled with normativity (as we said in chapter 4) and struggled because it has linked itself far too tightly with anthropologies and theories of human action born from modernity's man or (more often) society's being.[45] This linking has resulted in practical theology's embarrassment with normativity and therefore with the flattening of its theological construction (keeping it from speaking of lived experiences of divine action itself). It has done this flattening because practical theology believed that to be in conversation with the social sciences left little room for normativity. Practical theology has assumed, because of blinders given to it by modernity's man and society's being, that normativity is unscientific, therefore making practical theology and its interdisciplinary soul wary of wedding itself to normativity.

Yet, following Archer and Smith, room has been created for practical theology to claim normativity within the interdisciplinary soul of the field itself.[46] Normativity does *not* imprison practical theology in a theological ghetto; rather, critical realism and its anthropologies open many roads for

45. One could argue that the history of practical theology is born in the Schleiermachian era's commitment to modernity's man, and the rebirth of practical theology since the 1970s has come on the wave of the rise of society's being. I think practical theology's commitment to (at different times) these two anthropologies has led those with evangelical sensibilities to look sideways at it. Therefore, I hope in this chapter I have placed practical theology on a social-scientific anthropology that may fit better the evangelical ethos (and pathos).

46. The social-scientific anthropology then that links itself to a hypostatic anthropology of divine action articulated in chapter 6 is a critical realist anthropology of norming, believing animals. This anthropology of norming, believing animals is critical realist because its normative commitments connect it to the ontological realism. And its *believing* fuses it with epistemic relativism, and, finally, its focus on narration draws us into conversations about rational, emotive judgment. An anthropology of norming, believing animals attends to all three commitments of critical realism, adding to it a rich articulation for the motivation of human action.

practical theology to hold to the normativity of divine action (as a reality), while explaining richly the very shape and motivation of human action itself.

These conversations open up for a Christopraxis practical theology of the cross the claiming of the normative heart of human action, leading a Christopraxis perspective to assert that human action that participates in divine action is *ministerial action*.

Understanding ourselves as norming, believing animals allows us to hold to the normativity of divine action as experiences of God's very being, as God's act of ministry to us (it allows this to be a ontological realism). It also allows us the space to move into this ontological realism while not succumbing to an antipersonalist rational choice theory which has no room for the care and love of the other *as for solely the care and love of the other*—as an experience that draws us into higher strata of reality (divine action). A critical realist anthropology of norming, believing animals allows a Christopraxis perspective to see human action as shaped (and motivated) by ministry itself, asserting that such (ministerial) human action moves into something real, leading us to confess such experiences as God's being that comes to us by acting with and for our hypostatic neighbor. Our action then can be for them as an experience of divine encounter, framed by love and transcendence, and need not degrade into cost analysis or political ideological deconstruction.

Ministerial action is human action that participates in divine action *as normative belief*. So ministerial action that draws the human into the divine is, from a social-scientific perspective, normative. But as normative it is also hypostatic; it is directed to the love of concrete persons and seeks to join the being of another through the action of sharing in the nothingness of another for the sake of new possibility (love). This concrete human action of ministry is confessed to take us experientially (and therefore normatively) into the very being of God in and through God's own hypostatic being that is given to us only through the action that moves from possibility through nothingness in ministry. Ministerial action then joins God (as an ontological realism) by sharing concretely in love of neighbor, by embracing the nothingness of the hypostatic other, giving to them our own hypostatic being as a new possibility (personalism).[47] This is why I said at the beginning of this project that a Christopraxis practical theology of the cross is a critical realist personalist

---

47. I have not spent space here articulating in depth a personalism; this is partly because of space but also because such a perspective can be spotted clearly in my other work (see especially *Relational Pastor*). For an articulation of how personalism is linked with critical realism and operationalized, particularly within sociology, see Smith's *What Is a Person?*

practical theology. This critical realist personalism is the social-scientific perspective that is congruent with a Christopraxis perspective.

So ministerial action, from a social-scientific perspective, is bound in a critical realist ontological realism (normativity) and a philosophical personalism (hypostasis). This commitment to normativity and hypostasis then is engendered from experience with divine action but finds significant correspondence with the theories of (some) social sciences. Therefore, from a Christopraxis perspective, all interdisciplinary conversations must see ontological realism (normativity) and personalism (hypostasis) as the gatekeepers and bouncers of those conversations. Normativity and hypostasis help order the social-scientific and theological epistemologies as they enter into constructive projects in practical theology.

Attending to this interdisciplinary process will be the objective of the final chapter. In this final chapter I will lay out an interdisciplinary method that sees ontological realism and personalism as gatekeeper and bouncer of the association of theories, perspectives, and epistemologies of practical theology and the social sciences.

But, because I have raised ministerial action as the shape of human action that deals most deeply with ontological realism and hypostatic personalism, I will need to take the bold step that has often been avoided in practical theology of making my interdisciplinary method pertinent to the concrete and lived practice of ministry itself. In other words, I will try (even through intricate intellectual conversation) to form an interdisciplinary method that might actually touch how it is that pastors and ministers enter into theological and social-scientific conversation in the field. After all, it is the action of ministry, I have argued, that constitutes both the being of God as well as the action of humanity that leads it into the event of God's own being.

10

Interdisciplinarity
Toward Ministerial Transveral Rationality

It seems fair, though possibly lacking nuance, to assert that practical theology's revitalization in the twentieth century has much to do with the evolution of the social sciences. Practical theology was locked only in application, having no dialogue partner and no task other than applying the work of big brother systematics, for instance, until psychology and sociology made their way onto the stage of academic life. Practical theology finds its own voice inside the theological enterprise by continuing to stay committed to the lived and concrete, but now doing so through the rigor of the theories and perspectives of the growing social sciences (which also seem committed to the lived and concrete and therefore are judged as helpful). One can see this in the work of George Albert Coe, Sophia Fahs, and Seward Hiltner. These are deep early works, whose depths are contingent on the cross-disciplinary method their authors take up. They boldly place the practice of Christian education or pastoral care, for instance, in conversation across disciplines, entering significant conversations with Deweyian educational theory and the newly arrived depth psychology.

Practical theology has led the way in the theological enterprise of asserting that we are always in need of a multidisciplinary approach to understanding complex phenomena, even (or maybe especially) those found in concrete and lived locales. Richard Osmer explains, "Multidisciplinary thinking is based on the assumption that many disciplines are needed to comprehend complex systems. It focuses on human knowledge as a whole and the role different disciplines play in understanding complex phenomena."[1] To truly understand the depth of an issue or perspective we are assisted by using multiple disciplines

---

1. Richard Osmer, "Cross-Disciplinary Thinking in Practical Theology" (unpublished article), 2.

in exploring it. Even the move in practical theology toward the empirical is bound in a multidisciplinary commitment that draws research methods from other disciplines, using them to shape practical theology's own empirical operations.

This multidisciplinary approach seems to me to be central to the field of practical theology. Both historically and performatively, I find it hard to call something practical theology that does not hold in some way to this multidisciplinary commitment. Church history or systematic theology, for instance, is not dependent on a multidisciplinary focus (though the most interesting projects of late have started to turn in this direction), but practical theology is. Without a multidisciplinary attention that moves into conversation with the social sciences, the lived and concrete is left vapid. This is why in this book I have focused so intently on critical realism, science, and human action.

But, this running from vapidness into the arms of another (social) scientific discipline runs a great risk. Other disciplines, as we explored earlier, are built on epistemologies (and therefore anthropologies) that take no concern with or even stand in opposition to divine action. Archer and Collier have pointed out that all the great fathers of the social sciences (Marx, Durkheim, and Freud) were atheists, and Weber himself said he was personally not wired for religious experience. These social-scientific fathers' experience with reality (or lack thereof) led them to construct theories bound in epistemologies that stood against, or had at least little patience for, a reality of transcendence. Archer and Collier have stated that this atheistic presumption has been such a deep rut that after these fathers, most theories in the social sciences fail to climb beyond the walls of their epistemological channel.

What this points to, if we presume (as I do) that practical theology is always multidisciplinary, is that this multidisciplinary engagement must be organized, and in such a way that one discipline is not imprisoned by the epistemology of another (which I would argue has happened to practical theology—it has given up its theological freedom to the social sciences and therefore since Coe and Fahs has had a hard time talking about divine action and the evangelical experience). This then means that presuming multidisciplinarity leads us to consider significantly our interdisciplinary approach.

Interdisciplinarity is the organized or conceptual articulation of how two or more distinctive disciplines enter into conversation so that the integrity of both is maintained and yet theory construction can be born from within their generative conversation.[2] I have called this interdisciplinary focus of practical

2. Osmer explains, "True interdisciplinary thinking operates in a manner that respects the integrity of different fields and coordinates their use in a methodologically explicit fashion. This is to be contrasted

theology its soul, for again I find it hard as a disciplinary marker to call something practical theology that does not enter the lived and concrete through such organized conversations with multiple disciplines. Van Huyssteen nicely explains what interdisciplinarity is and why it is important, "These differences are revealed in the epistemological focus, the experiential resources, and the heuristic structures of different disciplines. What this means for theology and the sciences is that the differences between them are far more complex and refined than just differences in objects of study, language, or methodology: the differences revealed in interdisciplinary discussion are often radical differences in epistemological focus and experiential resources."[3]

What then is an interdisciplinary approach that allows for ontological realism and hypostatic personalism (two core commitments born from both a Christopraxis conception of divine action and a critical realist social science)? Is there a way to put these perspectives into conversation in such a way that they may form a structure or method in which other interdisciplinary conversations might be organized? And in a way that places ministry as central?

MODELS OF INTERDISCIPLINARITY

Before we can draw out this interdisciplinary method, we must spend a short time looking at two dominant interdisciplinary methods, two perspectives that, despite their mutual depth, do not attend to the ontological realism and hypostatic personalism that I have raised as the gatekeeper and bouncer of method. I have made ontological realism my gatekeeper and hypostatic personalism my bouncer because of both the theological and scientific commitments that create space for the possibility of lived and concrete experience of divine action as ministry. And my commitments are set as they are because of my own experience and reflection within reality.

CORRELATION

The Lutheran Paul Tillich is the proprietor of the correlational method in theology. Tillich, inspired by a deep apologetic desire, constructed his systematic theology around a method of questions and answers. Tillich asserted that the theologian must attend to the explicit or nascent questions being asked

with a naive eclecticism in which concepts and research of another field are taken out their original disciplinary context and placed in a completely different theoretical framework in a haphazard manner." Ibid., 2.

3. Wenztel van Huyssteen, *The Shaping of Rationality: Toward Interdisciplinarity in Theology and Science* (Grand Rapids, MI: Eerdmans, 1999), 187.

in culture, using the social sciences or arts to surface the questions in all their significance. Tillich himself used depth psychology, existential philosophy, and visual art to bring to the surface these deep cultural questions. Once these questions bobbed on the surface, made buoyant by the social sciences and arts, Christian theology provided answers. So interdisciplinarity was organized around questions and answer. The social sciences were used, but only for the purpose of raising cultural questions, and theology was given direction to provide answers only *after* the questions have been stated.[4] This organization allowed for a rich and distinctive way to organize the divergent epistemologies of theology and the social sciences.

Many of the established practical theologians that we explored in chapter 3—most explicitly Browning and Miller-McLemore—have used a correlational method. Yet, in taking on this method they have not left it untouched. Rather, following the work of David Tracy, they have modified the perspective, not simply following Tillich but revising him.[5] The revision states that the job of the social sciences is not simply and only to surface the questions—it can also answer them. In the same way, theology not only answers surfaced questions but may also surface questions of its own. Theology becomes bound as tradition and symbols, just as the social sciences are themselves epistemological traditions.

All ontological commitments are voided from the original Tillichian perspective, and revised *critical* correlation is the commitment that reality is only the epistemological traditions that are placed in conversation, which might lead to human *phronesis*—to an actuality created from human epistemological correlation itself.[6] So now, Tillich's argument that the question of culture must

---

4. Tillich explains, "It is equally wrong to derive the question implied in human existence from the revelatory answer. This is impossible because the revelatory answer is meaningless if there is no question to which it is the answer. Man can not receive an answer to a question he has not asked." *Systematic Theology* (Chicago: University of Chicago Press, 1951), 2:13.

5. Tracy actually revises Tillich because of his Catholic commitments, seeing that culture because of natural law must not only be addressed but also held to provide some "good" in itself. Browning and Miller-McLemore similarly see culture as having "goods," but don't go necessarily in the direction of natural law. Both groups obscure Tillich by imagining that what he means by theology is a tradition that can be put into epistemological conversation. Tillich means this but also means more, means something ontological about God's own being.

6. Osmer adds some important depth to Browning's view that I simply do not have space for. Osmer says, "Both Browning and Groome deviate from Tracy's approach in *Blessed Rage for Order* by describing the correlational process as including contemporary praxis, both within the church and in culture generally. Interpretation, they argue, is embedded in praxis and commonly becomes self-conscious only as praxis becomes problematic or is subjected to critical reflection." "Cross-Disciplinary Thinking in Practical Theology," 8.

be correlated to the epistemology of divine (ultimate) being is revised, and the social sciences call the theological commitment to correlate (at least in part) to the epistemological visions of the social sciences; thus, the theological is stripped from its ontological correlation and reality becomes the discourse of traditions potentially cut loose from an ontological reality.[7]

This revised critical correlation has had deep impact in practical theology, and it is easy to see why. It allows for deep connection between theology and the social sciences, and a connection (conversation) that is organized. But this organization in its revised form has missed (or obscured) a deep commitment of Tillich's and therefore opens itself to a problem that eliminates the method from consideration for a Christopraxis practical theology.

Douglas John Hall has claimed that Tillich is no doubt an apologetic theologian, but one that has a deep kerygmatic moment in his theology.[8] And this kerygmatic moment, I would contend, must be seen against the backdrop of Tillich's ontological realism. The questions of culture are surfaced by the epistemologies of the social sciences, but, once surfaced, the kerygma, confession, of an ontological realism, expressed in the language of its epistemology (theology), addresses these questions. For Tillich, correlation is bringing the questions of culture into the ontological reality of God's own being. The answers are bound in human experiential encounter with the being of God, next to our own being.

Tillich's apologetic desires do direct him into significant and distinct epistemological conversations, and yet the revisionists' ignoring of his ontological realism has led them to avoid or ignore his ontology, entering into a discourse very close to the epistemic fallacy. When the correlational method is revised (and revised critically), it is revised so that it might be more flexible epistemologically. Browning finds it so helpful for epistemological reasons. But what is obscured is that for Tillich ontology is central. God is ultimate being, and for Tillich, as a Lutheran, the very crisis of reality itself, the crisis that God ontologically enters into the world through the cross (the *theologia crucis*), is what stands beneath his very correlational method. Tillich moves into epistemological correlation to make a case for the ontological realism (kerygma) of God's own being (this is, at least, a generous interpretation of Tillich).

---

7. Here one can't miss Tillich's ontology, an ontology that is similar to Archer's in ways. Tillich says, "Our ultimate concern is that which determines our being or not-being. Only those statements are theological which deal with their object in so far as it can become a matter of being or not-being for us." *Systematic Theology*, 2:14.

8. See *Confessing the Faith* (Minneapolis: Fortress Press, 1998).

So, critical correlationalist practical theologians have shown that a straightforward correlation like Tillich's is potentially epistemologically naive, and because it may be, they have made the move to deepen its epistemology. But in doing so, they have seen all reality as epistemological traditions and symbols; they have entered into an anthropology of society's being, claiming as it does that reality is only the discourses of socialization (this is highlighted in its understanding of "critical" in its updating of the correlational method). In so doing, revised critical correlation strips all ontology from the Tillichian correlation, leading the revised critical correlation method into an antirealist perspective, which is similar to society's being and its downward conflation.[9]

Moreover, such a revised critical correlation method has been critiqued, even within it own ranks, for being helpful only to those in universities and offering little direct help to those on the ground in ministry or those living in poverty, for instance.[10] And I would argue that those living in this concrete locale often have a sense of realism that frames their lives (through their experience), a sense of realism that makes a correlational method of deconstructing epistemologies, of asserting that everything is just traditions in discourse, unappealing.

So, at one critical end of practical theological interdisciplinary methods stands revised correlation, yet from the perspective of Christopraxis we have ruled it out, for it cannot link with the ontological realism that stands as gatekeeper for our interdisciplinary construction. If revised critical correlation stands at one extreme of interdisciplinary methods, then a Chalcedonian perspective stands at the other.

---

9. Hans Frei points to the core commitment to society's being in Tracy's work, "David Tracy, in his book *Blessed Rage for Order*, looks for a revisionist, post-liberal, and post-neo-orthodox theology, fit for people in a postmodern situation, and says that such a theological model may be formulated as follows: 'Contemporary Christian theology is best understood as philosophical reflection upon the meanings present in common human experience and the meanings present in the Christian tradition.'" *Types of Christian Theology* (New Haven: Yale University Press, 1992), 30.

10. See Matthew Lamb and Rebecca Chopp, as well as Tom Hastings's take in *Practical Theology and the One Body of Christ: Toward a Missional-Ecumenical Model* (Grand Rapids, MI: Eerdmans, 2007). Osmer says, "In this commitment to emancipatory praxis, Lamb and Chopp can be viewed as breaking with theological liberalism's preoccupation with questions of meaning posed by contemporary culture. Rather, they argue, theology must take its bearings from the reality of massive human suffering and the structures of domination that characterize our world." "Cross-Disciplinary Thinking in Practical Theology," 8.

CHALCEDONIAN

Much as we did in chapter 3, in which we tried to place Christopraxis somewhere between the extremes in practical theological approaches (somewhere between Browning on one end and Purves on the other), here too we seek an interdisciplinary method between extremes. So if revised critical correlation is on one end, then the Chalcedonian method is on the other.

The Chalcedonian method has its origin in Barthian and neo-Barthian perspectives. So earlier, where Tillich was led into correlation because of his deep apologetic interests, so here those working from a Chalecedonian perspective seek to attend to the central kerygmatic thrust of Barth's vision. And this is a tricky thrust to attend to, for Barth (especially the early Barth) appears to have no room for any foreign epistemologies to associate, yet alone cohabitate, with theology.[11]

Yet, two seminal Barth interpreters, T. F. Torrance and George Hunsinger, have asserted that though Barth's kergymatic commitments are strong and he argues against conflating foreign epistemologies with theology, Barth's thought does have significant room for the possibility of interdisciplinary discourse. As long as this conversation is organized, it is possible.[12]

While Barth himself never picks up this challenge, others have. Following the direction of Torrance and Hunsinger, Deborah van Duesen Hunsinger (hereafter referred to as VDH) has taken up this test in her book *Theology and Pastoral Counseling*. Here VDH places Jungian psychology and Barthian theology into interdisciplinary conversation. She begins by admitting the distinctive epistemologies represented in each theory. Following Barth, she contends that theology as epistemological reflection on God's revelation gives it priority over other epistemologies. Nevertheless, theology can learn from other lower epistemologies. To make sure that this learning holds to the difference in each perspective's epistemological subject, their conversation must be ordered

---

11. For an overplayed example see *Nein!* and Barth's conflict with Brunner over natural theology.

12. The two most significant Chalcedonian interdisciplinary practical theologians are Deborah van Deusen Hunsinger, who will take center stage here, and James Loder. Van Deusen Hunsinger (hereafter referred to as VDH) was greatly impacted by her husband George Hunsinger's read of Barth in constructing her own Chalcedonian method, and James Loder is impacted by the work of and his personal friendship with T. F. Torrance (they spent a good amount of time together at the Center for Theological Inquiry in Princeton, New Jersey). I will not discuss Loder here. I have made this decision mainly because of space but also because Loder's project of the Spirit offers a realism that simply needs more significant space to articulate.

by three rules drawn from the classical Christian conception of relating distinct realities

Following the fourth-century Council of Chalcedon's grammar of relating the divine and human natures of Jesus, VDH uses this structure (gleaned from George Hunsinger) to organize the conversation between Jungian psychology and theology. So just as the council asserted that Jesus' divine and human natures are related (1) without separation or division, (2) without confusion or change, and (3) with priority assigned to the divine over the human (in an asymmetrical relationship), so the epistemologies of the social sciences and theology must relate in turn.[13]

Psychology and theology enter into conversation without separation or division, recognizing that both are epistemological structures, having something to say to a shared phenomenon like the healing of an individual. But while they should not be separated, their conversation should not lead into a blending of one into the other, making what James Loder calls the *tertium quid*, a third thing that is neither psychology or theology (this is to violate interdisciplinarity).[14] To have such a conversation, each discipline must respect the other; particularly, VDH would argue, theology must be respected as a distinct and unique field that cannot be distracted from reflecting on God's act and being. And because theology does this, because it reflects on God, it should be given priority in conversation.

This third element of the grammar particularly chafes revised critical correlationalists and others in practical theology. It runs the risk (a risk that I believe VDH avoids) of infusing a kind of foundational rationality into interdisciplinarity.[15] It is clear that rationality itself must be considered and

---

13. Deborah van Deusen Hunsinger, *Theology and Pastoral Counseling: A New Interdisciplinary Approach* (Grand Rapids, MI: Eerdmans, 1995), 62.

14. Loder explains, "This tertium quid situation I consider to be the key problem common to interdisciplinary methodology in practical theology. It is problematic because, under the surface of the interdisciplinary discussion, it introduces an alternative reality that is not explicitly accountable to the terms of the theology-human science dialogue itself." "Normativity and Context in Practical Theology: 'The Interdisciplinary Issue,'" in *Practical Theology: International Perspectives*, ed. Friedrich Schweitzer and Johannes A. van der Ven (Berlin: Peter Lang, 1999), 362.

15. This long quote shows the thin line VDH walks to avoid this foundationalism—one can see a deep realist perspective within it: "The stipulation of asymmetry, however, implies that no such material equivalence exists between theology and psychology, for their essential subject matters are fundamentally different. Thus although the pastoral counselor who has acquired competency in both fields of discourse can move forth and back between them, he or she takes care not to translate theological into psychological categories or vice versa. Instead, theological and psychological modes of discourse are conceived as existing on different levels. Even when areas overlap (as in the theological doctrine of

central in interdisciplinarity, but, as we will see below, a foundational rationality is itself problematic. In relation to theology it can feel like a medieval trump card played at any needed point in the conversation. Theology can state that its epistemology is queen because it is about God, and God is the foundation of existence. Of course, the social sciences doubt such a foundation, and positing it risks denying the epistemic relativity of a postfoundationalism that critical realism holds to. So without the nimbleness of VDH, those working from a Chalcedonian perspective can easy trap themselves in or be accused of the mistaken steps of modernity's man and its upward conflation of the theologian.

But this is only part of the danger of a Chalcedonian perspective. Rather, from a Christopraxis position knitted together with a critical realist personalism, a Chalcedonian model seems to pass the gatekeeper of ontological realism, claiming God's revelation as a higher stratum of reality, asserting that reality exists outside the human mind and yet human minds can (in faith) reach or witnesses to higher strata.[16] Yet, the Chalceondian pattern runs into conflict around hypostatic personalism, therefore bouncing it from a Christopraxis perspective.

There is an irony here, for something like hypostatic personalism is central to Karl Barth's own anthropology (we saw this in chapter 6).[17] However, this personalist anthropology is somewhat obscured in the strict rules of the Chalcedonian grammar. Daniel Price, for instance, offers an interdisciplinary conversation between Barth and object relations psychology, yet for him these two distinct disciplines are not related through a Chalcedonian grammar but through the hypostatic nature of personhood itself. There is a transversal moment between the experienced *reality* of human personhood witnessed to by object relations psychology and a theological anthropology. This transversal moment, which is conditioned by and is for hypostatic personhood (one could say for ministry), leads to rich dialogue, which in the end is for the sake of

human nature vis-à-vis a psychological anthropology), only analogies not equivalences can be drawn between them. The Chalcedonian pattern is thus understood as the framework that governs the possibilities and limits of being 'bilingual.'" *Theology and Pastoral Counseling*, 64.

16. Here one can see how this perspective deeply passes the ontological realism gate; it in only at the level of personalism that I find it wanting. Therefore, I agree with VDH's statement here and find Barth's position captivating. "According to Barth, psychological concepts could not possibly exist on the same level as theological concepts because psychology by definition pertains only to a creaturely level of reality. For Barth there is a specificity to theological content which has no anthropological or psychological counterpart and to which psychological concepts as stich have no access." Ibid., 93.

17. See Barth's *Church Dogmatics* III.2 (Edinburgh: T&T Clark, 1960). See as well Daniel Price's *Karl Barth's Anthropology in Light of Modern Thought* (Grand Rapids, MI: Eerdmans, 2002) and Ray Anderson's *On Being Human* (Pasadena, CA: Fuller Seminary Press, 1982).

participating in a higher stratum of reality (which could be called divine action) through the personalist act of ministry itself.

While the Chalcedonian grammar is ingenious in helping us mark the rules of a conversation, it does not in the end lead us into hypostatic ministerial action (not in itself).[18] It helps us to keep the epistemologies of theology and social sciences clear but does not help us move into a form of ministry that attends to divine and human encounter. It is deeply methodological, but this method is not founded in the ministry of persons (whether divine to divine, divine to human, or human to human).[19] These are rules for language but in so being become obscured for use in ministry itself, for as we've seen both social scientifically (Archer) and theologically (concursus Dei), human and divine act and being are constituted not purely by language but by ontological encounter, hypostasis to hypostasis.

Fellow Barth scholar Paul Nimmo has made a similar point; Nimmo actually critiques George Hunsinger for overplaying the Chalcedonian pattern in the thought of Karl Barth. Nimmo not only thinks Barth is not as Chalcedonian as Hunsinger states but fears the use of Chalecondian logic actually may lock the divine action of encounter with human being (the concursus Dei) into a pattern that risks losing, as I would say, Christopraxis by focusing on methodological pattern rather than the experiential encounter of the incarnate one.[20] Nimmo states,

18. Here ministry itself is made linguistic and not hypostatic or personal (and only linguistic because it is first personal). "If pastoral counseling is essentially interdisciplinary, then in Lindbeck's sense pastoral counselors must learn to become 'bilingual.' They must learn to be as skilled in the language or symbol system of theology as they are in that of psychology. They must be equipped to interpret and experience themselves and their world in theological as well as in psychological terms. They must become as linguistically competent in the one discipline as in the other, interiorizing by practice and training two very different sets of skills. They must learn how to feel, act, and think in conformity with two different modes of thought." VDH, *Theology and Pastoral Counseling*, 5.

19. Though Theresa Latini has tried to rectify this by adding Barth's concept of *koinonia* to the pattern. But this only shows that the pattern needs a personalist add-on, like the one that Latini provides for in *koinonia*; see the appendix in *Church and the Crisis of Community: A Practical Theology of Small-Group Ministry* (Grand Rapids, MI: Eerdmans, 2011).

20. Paul Nimmo says powerfully, "The material problem with a 'Chalcedonian' interpretation of the concursus thus lies in jeopardizing the uniqueness and incomparability of the incarnation and therein undermining the identity and the fallibility of the creature. Use of the term 'Chalcedonian' brings with it a particular theological meaning which lies over and above the merely formal 'Chalcedonian' pattern of asymmetry, intimacy and integrity. In this respect, the problem with attaching it as a label is one of generalizing that which cannot be generalized." "Karl Barth and the Concursus Dei—A Chalcedonianism Too Far?" *International Journal of Systematic Theology* 9, no. 1 (January 2007): 68.

[George] Hunsinger propounds "the exegetical and hermeneutical premise that the terms of the Chalcedonian pattern are rooted in the biblical testimony regarding how divine and human agency are related." This statement contains the potential for bypassing the incarnation altogether in favour of a general model for this relation of divine agency and human agency. It leads Hunsinger to write—in apparent abstraction from the person of Jesus Christ—that there are "Chalcedonian stipulation[s]" which emerge from this premise, and that the "Chalcedonian" pattern "establishes" Barth's conception of double agency. However, it would seem preferable for the analogy between the being and activity of Jesus Christ and the being and activity of the creature to be proposed and defended directly, not by means of tertiary theological constructions.[21]

The pattern rather than hypostatic encounter is the driver; because the pattern itself is a "thing" (epistemological structure) and not a subject, this risks the loss of the core commitment of Barth's own perspective in the *concursus Dei*, as seen in chapter 6. Nimmo explains that there is a "danger that by abstracting a 'pattern' from the Symbol of Chalcedon and outlining its supposed three salient features, there occurs the sort of flattening and undesired systematization of theological material which is entirely contrary to Barth's actualism. Barth cautions that 'Who and what Jesus Christ is, is something which can only be told, not a system which can be considered and described.'"[22] As Barth has asserted, the *concursus Dei* happens only in and through subjects.[23] So while the Chalecondian pattern is significant (and helpful), in the end it is bounced because it obscures the hypostatic personalism central to my approach.[24]

21. Ibid., 71.

22. Ibid., 71.

23. VDH here talks much of the pattern, showing my concern that the personalist elements are missing, "After identifying a formal pattern of thought in Barth's theology, this book then goes on to use this pattern to bring theology and psychology into relationship. This formal conceptual device, which is referred to as the 'Chalccdonian pattern' and which involves elements of 'differentiation,' 'unity,' and 'order,' actually underlies a variety of different discussions in Barth's theology. In this book, however, the use of the pattern is extended beyond anything quite found in Barth in order to illumine theoretical and practical issues in pastoral counseling." *Theology and Pastoral Counseling*, 9.

24. Nimmo critiques George Hunsinger here to make space for a more personalist encounter, "It is therefore only in the event of revelation and in the corresponding event of faith that the two statements become simultaneously possible. But the point (contra Hunsinger) is that in this event, the creature can acknowledge and confess this. To argue that juxtaposition is the only way to express the 'Chalcedonian' nature of the incarnation (and by implication the concursus) seems not only to misrepresent the Symbol of Chalcedon itself but also to underestimate the significance of Barth's actualistic ontology of both God

REIMAGINING TRANSVERSAL RATIONALITY

With the above, I have stepped away from the dominant interdisciplinary perspective in established practical theology, asserting that revised critical correlation tends toward an antirealist perspective. I have also appreciatively, but nevertheless distinctively, walked away from the Chalcedonian grammar as an organizing approach for interdisciplinarity. Following Nimmo, I have critiqued it for moving into an abstract pattern that risks underplaying the hypostatic personalism of a Christopraxis perspective knit together with a critical realism. Both perspectives are eliminated because ontological realism will serve as my gatekeeper and hypostatic personalism my bouncer for interdisciplinary work in a Christopraxis perspective.

But I am using ontological realism as gatekeeper and hypostatic personalism as bouncer because ultimately I'm seeking to place ministry as the central shape of practical theology, for ministry itself attends to the concrete and lived as divine and human encounter. Therefore, if the soul of practical theology is interdisciplinarity, and ministry is the shape of a Christopraxis practical theology, then how does ministry provide direction for interdisciplinary interplay?

To move toward answering this question I will reimagine a unique interdisciplinary perspective called transversal rationality, seeking to affirm and yet shape it in new ways. I will call this reshaping "ministerial transversal rationality." I will explore each of its defining concepts, starting with transversal, moving to rationality, and ending with ministerial, which I hope to show nuances the perspective by contributing the motivation for transversality and therefore moves it beyond the purposes of solely intellectual projects and into the concrete actions of pastors and ministers in the field. This perspective rests on a view of divine action as God's being as becoming in ministry and of human action as the action of norming, believing animals that live in and through narration.

THE TRANSVERSAL

Transversal rationality is an interdisciplinary perspective that has its origins in the philosophical thought of Calvin Schrag and the theological work Wentzel van Huyssteen. It views fields or disciplines as discursive or even porous conceptions of reality. These discursive fields seek to articulate something true from their locations and approaches to thought, but such articulations

and the creature at this critical point and the role of faith and confession in the Christian life." "Karl Barth and Concursus Dei," 70.

always leads into overlapping or the transversing of other elements of other perspectives. So sociology cannot do its work in the depth it wishes without also at times transversing its so-called boundaries into anthropology, as economics must join the conceptions of mathematics. And yet, while these fields need to transverse each other, economics, for instance, moving into mathematics, we cannot say that economics *is* mathematics. While they transverse at points, they also depart.

But this only shows that there is simply no such thing as purely locked-away fields or disciplines. For instance, psychology and sociology are social sciences that have their origin in philosophy (and medicine); it is only after a period of discourse that leads to material like journals and conferences that a discipline inside a field is born, allowing it the independence to become, after a time, a field. Its birth is only because of the porous boundaries that exist in all disciplines, allowing them to transverse other perspectives.[25]

Because of this anatomy of these locales of thought and reflection, Schrag and van Huyssteen assert that interdisciplinarity can be imagined as the crossing of perspectives, and this crossing happens because perspectives (such as fields and disciplines) mutually enter each other's purview as they give attention to a phenomenon in reality itself. Schrag uses the analogy of pick-up sticks to make this point, claiming that disciplines and fields are actually strings or sticks of reflection on reality, but because reality is reflected on from within reality, there are multiple and crossing strings or sticks of reflection (for reality is always more than we can know—there is a surplus of epistemological constructions seeking to express or know parts of reality).[26]

25. Van Huyssteen explains, "In fact, different domains of human rationality, and therefore also different disciplines, while having their own integrity and specific identities, are in many ways connected and intertwined with one another precisely by the dynamic performative faculty of reason. This plurality is nonhierarchical and irreducible, and highlights important differences between various domains of rationality, and between disciplines. Even as it opens up the exploration of transversal spaces that allow for the connection of different domains of rationality. This also allows for the emergence of paradigmatic interdisciplinary networks and opens up the possibility that different disciplines in dialogue, although never fully integrated." Wenztel van Huyssteen, *Alone in the World?: Human Uniqueness in Science and Theology* (Grand Rapids, MI: Eerdmans, 2006), 20.

26. Van Huyssteen give in-depth attention to Schrag's perspective, "Schrag is proposing to use this metaphor in a new way and takes his cue from mathematicians (who take up the vocabulary of transversality when speaking of the transversality of a line as it intersects a system of other lines or surfaces), but also from physicists and physiologists: in the interdisciplinary and varied use of this concept a shared meaning emerges, having to do principally with the related senses of extending over, lying across, and intersecting. Schrag goes even further and follows Sartre in using the notion of transversality to indicate how human consciousness and self-awareness are unified by a play of intentionalities which includes concrete retentions of past consciousness. In this sense consciousness is unified by our

Interdisciplinarity happens at the accidental convergence and overlap of these locales of thought and reflection as they seek to make their best (epistemological) accounts of reality. "Accidental" may seem like an odd word to use, sounding arbitrary, but this is not necessarily the case, for each discipline or field is rigorously directed toward its experience with reality. It just so happens that in seeking to articulate reality there are others too that provide perspectives and insight surrounding their own experiences of reality—we bump up against these other epistemologies, finding that they bump us into conversation and therefore into interdisciplinarity or confusion and immediate evasion. We are bumping into these transversal conversations because disciplines and fields are, by nature, porous. The very surplus of epistemologies of reality (these epistemologies that are ordered to be called fields or disciplines) means there will be interactions and convergences. If there were no reality (other than the discourses of society's being and downward conflation), disciplines or fields could be created and remain independent or interact only for political or ideological reasons. But transversality sees the convergence of disciplines and fields as the natural outgrowth of reality itself; fields transverse because, as epistemological conceptions, they cannot possess reality but can only witness to parts of it, leading them in their partial confessions of reality to fall into overlap with other fields' or disciplines' own partial conceptions of reality.

As a result, there are points where one discipline lays over another, allowing for a generative convergence of discourse and mutual conversation. These conversations are done in reality for the purpose of experiencing and witnessing the *truth* of the very mysterious layers of reality (mysterious layers like how light can be both wave and particle, or how Jesus can be both divine and human, or how the human spirit can be healed through the ministerial care of another). Because reality is stratified and always more than can be possessed by epistemologies of any discipline, there are points where these convergences will lead to departure. Like following a pick-up stick, there are significant points of overlap (of transversality), but these moments or points of overlap, when followed, lead into divergence. *Reality itself pushes us into and out of such interdisciplinary conversations.*

experiences of self-awareness, emerging over time from a remembering consciousness in which diverse past experiences are transversally integrated. In using the notion of transversal rationality in this way, Schrag eventually wants to justify and urge an acknowledgment of multiple patterns of interpretation as one moves across the borders and boundaries of the different disciplinary matrices." *Shaping of Rationality*, 135.

Recognizing this, one can see interdisciplinarity as the transversal overlap, where a conversation is had, but the conversation is always organized by the very realization that at some point our fields' or disciplines' distinct approaches and attentions to reality will end the conversation (not necessarily in dispute, but in a vision or objective the other does not share or have interest in). I'm moved into conversation with a particular sociology (as I did in the last chapter) because it helps me articulate reality from within my experience of reality. I judge one sociological perspective over another because of the possibility for convergence, because its views overlap my experience (supporting or challenging my views) and therefore take me further in my conception of and experience with reality.

There are many points where psychology and practical theology transverse; both are concerned about the healing and shape of the human psyche, but psychology is not practical theology, nor practical theology psychology. While the two fields have significant places of transversal overlap, they also diverge, and they do so at the very point of their confession of the higher strata of reality. They overlap over agreements of reality: human beings have inner conscious lives and under stress these conscious lives of the human being can be damaged. But following this string or stick of overlap eventually leads to divergence, a divergence over reality, for practical theology (pastoral care) claims that the human being is made in the image of God and prayer is a spiritual reality (something real and more than psychic) that brings healing to the inner life. These commitments are made because of experiences and reflection in reality, because practical theology claims reality *is* this way. Psychology cannot do so, claiming the conversation must end because it either denies such a view of reality or simply wishes to say nothing about such things. To say it another way, practical theology (at least in a Christopraxis approach) holds that divine action itself can bring forth healing, while psychology has no experience of such a reality (or, even if it does, it chooses from within its string of disciplinary discourse to not attend to that layer of reality).[27]

Transversality allows for a clear organization of distinct disciplinary conversations, and it sets the table for such conversation by holding to an ontological realism. All disciplines and fields are porous, transversality claims, because reality is always *more* than one field, discipline, or perspective can possess in any thought experiment or position. So transversality as an interdisciplinary perspective holds to an ontological realism of the stratified

27. This element of my view has some similarity to Nancy Murphy's perspective in *Theology in the Age of Scientific Reasoning* (Ithaca, NY: Cornell University Press, 1990).

nature of reality itself. The boundaries between fields, disciplines, and perspectives are always porous because these areas of contemplation and action always exist in lower strata of reality, or at the very least they are themselves locked in the stratum of reality they seek to examine and therefore cannot stand outside it.

Transversality is, then, a realist perspective; it moves away from downward conflation by holding to an ontological realism, believing there are real things in the world that exist outside the human mind.[28] Interdisciplinary conversation is the overlapping conversation of relativized epistemologies in conversation about a reality that can be known, but only in part.[29] Therefore, the need for interdisciplinarity is not bound in the ideologies of culture (critical correlation) or the strict tradition of doctrine (Chalcedonian) but in reality itself, for reality is always more than any mind, system, discipline, or field can know *in itself.*

Transversality has often been called a postmodern perspective (van Huyssteen himself has called it such), but this label only fits because transversality is postfoundational.[30] It is not postmodern in the sense of believing there is no reality other than the texts of socialization.[31] In earlier

28. Here van Huyssteen articulates an appreciation for a critical realism similar to that upon which I have placed Christopraxis. "'Realism' in a pragmatic form of critical realism thus enables us to speak of disclosure, and refers to the attempt at reliable cognitive claims about domains of reality that may lie beyond our experience, but to which interpreted experience is our only epistemic access." *Shaping of Rationality*, 218.

29. Van Huyssteen explains his realism, which I would argue is very close to the critical realism I have presented above. "The 'realism' involved here is 'hypothetical' because, since we have embodied minds, it is a reasonable hypothesis that there must be a real world that, by a process of evolutionary selection, has produced our minds. This hypothetical realism is a realism without correspondence theories, and without the kind of empiricism that would claim only sense experience as a foundation of all knowledge." *Alone in the World?*, 101. One can see this similarity in Andrew Sayer's critical realist assertion: "I would argue that it is the evident fallibility of our knowledge—the experience of getting things wrong, of having our expectations confounded, and of crashing into things—that justifies us in believing that the world exists regard less of what we happen to think about it." *Realism and Social Science* (Los Angeles: Sage, 2000), 2.

30. Van Huyssteen explains his use of postmodernism and also how he is pushing against it, "In this move the postmodern problematization of the classical, modern claims for universality is embraced, but then postmodernism is used against itself by showing how the figure of transversality can more productively address the issues at hand. On this view, therefore, transversality replaces universality." *Shaping of Rationality*, 139.

31. Transversal rationality seeks to split the difference, as van Huyssteen says, between modernism and postmodernism, or as I would say, following Archer, between upward and downward conflation. "Transversal postfoundationalist rationality thus enables us to shuttle in the space between modernity and postmodernity: the space of interpreted experience and communicative praxis which enables paraxial critique. Articulation, and disclosure, here, finally, transcontextual, even transhistorical judgments and assessments can be made without gravitating into an empty universalization on the one hand, or a

sections of the book I have tried to show that it avoids downward conflation. Van Huyssteen, particularly, picks up the nomenclature "postmodern" to make *not* an antirealist argument, but a postfoundational one. While transversality does not take the suicide pill of downward conflation, neither does it drink the hubris-forming wine of upward conflation.

No discipline or field (not even theology) can stand at the peak of reality, possessing the universal foundations of reality. This has been the heavy-handed and not always fair critique directed toward the Chalcedonian perspective. Transversality agrees that there is no universal locale in which human beings (or their fields and disciplines) can stand to know fully or even possess reality. This is not possible (for the creature is not the creator), which means that interdisciplinarity is always needed. *Interdisciplinarity is needed in practical theology not for academic purposes, but for confessional ones. A Christopraxis practical theology must turn deeply to interdisciplinarity because of its attention to divine action, because it believes divine action is real and human action (our justification perspective says) cannot foundationally possess this reality (we must live with ex nihilo). Therefore, because of a Christopraxis commitment to divine action as a realism, a case for interdisciplinarity can be made from within attention to divine action itself. We turn to interdisciplinarity because of our very experiences of the mystery of reality and our confession of our finitude in knowing reality.*

So van Huyssteen is not so much a postmodernist as he is deeply opposed to upward conflation, asserting that it is not universality that is indispensable, but transversality. Because we cannot stand at the peak of reality, we can never stand on foundations; we must rather, through our experience, be always moved into transversal discourse because we always experience reality as a mystery that is more than any of our thought conceptions. The very shape of ontological realism and our experience of it make transversality a helpful interdisciplinary organizing perspective in practical theology.

This may be even more so because the very shape of practical life itself is more like transversality than foundationalism. In practical life we enter into conversation as a way to enter into each other's lives, sharing perspectives and ideas (and our very selves) as a way to help each other solve problems and understand our own being in the world.[32] These moments of sharing (especially ministerial sharing) are much like transversality; they are the layering

pluralism of culture-spheres, particularized language games, and relativized moral claims on the other hand. A postfoundationalist notion of rationality thus creates a safe space where our different discourses and actions are seen at times to link up with one another, and at times to contrast or conflict with one another. It is precisely in the hard struggle for interpersonal and interdisciplinary communication that the many faces of human rationality are revealed." *Shaping of Rationality*, 139.

over of our very lives, transversing our conception of reality with another's. Something like transversality itself (transversality of ideas, perspectives, and other's experiences) leads us into our *normative* commitments (connecting this to human action, as realism has made possible divine action), and these normative commitments (that come not through foundations but from the transversal experiences of reality) motivate our actions in the world.

We can already begin to see then the possibility of the hypostatic personalism in transversality, which therefore leads into the concrete and lived possibility of ministry itself. However, to explore this further we'll need to turn to the second element of transversality, the *rationality*. In this next section we'll deepen and drive further many of the ideas in this one.

RATIONALITY

In chapter 7 we claimed that the third commitment of critical realism is judgmental rationality. This judgmental rationality is *not* the instrumental rationality of upward conflation, for instrumental rationality takes its stand from foundationalism.[33] The instrumental rational act is born from correlation with and support from foundational truth, the truth the human mind has possessed and knows reality completely. An instrumental rational act (or thought) is one that is engendered from these foundations. Yet, critical realism (as well as transversality) is a postfoundational perspective. Transversality and critical realism are connected, in my opinion, not only through their realist commitments but also through their views of rationality. Both claim that instrumental rational foundations cannot be possessed, for the human beings cannot stand at the peak of reality. They do not possess (and neither do their disciplines and fields) the epistemological equipment to have a God's–eye foundational rational view (denying upward conflation).

---

32. "Thus the notion of transversal rationality opens up the possibility of focusing on patterns of discourse and action as they happen in our communicative practices, rather than focusing on only the structure of the self, ego, or subject. On this view it is clear that transversal rationality is not just a 'passage of consciousness' across a wide spectrum of experiences held together by our memory. It is, rather, a lying across, extending over, and intersecting of various forms of discourse, modes of thought, and action. Transversal rationality thus emerges as a performative praxis where our multiple beliefs and practices, our habits of thought and attitudes, our prejudices and assessments, converge." Van Huyssteen, *Alone in the World?*, 21.

33. "There is a common way of summing up the relationship between realist and conventionalist (or, more accurately, instrumentalist) standpoints on truth, which is that realists say useful knowledge is useful because it is true, and instrumentalists say knowledge that is called true is so merely because it is useful." Sayer, *Realism and Social Science*, 42.

We saw that the rationality of critical realism is a postfoundational rationality embedded in experience itself. Experiences with reality lead to rationality.[34] Something is rational because it helps us to make sense of our experience—because it is something that can be believed! *And we are norming, believing animals* who must make rational sense of our lives; we must have things we believe in. We enter into disciplines or perspectives of thought because they are rational conceptions that help us make sense of our experience of reality.[35] "This . . . brings us face to face with the fact that we relate to our world(s) only through interpreted experience, and that the world as a phenomenon shows itself precisely in the manifold forms of human experience."[36] But, again, this rational sense is not foundational but rather embedded in our very experience of reality itself; we trust (have faith) in these rational conceptions, but they cannot be foundationally proven. Nevertheless, embedding rationality in experience does not mean it is caught in a spirit of uncertainly or absurdity that downward conflation cannot stand against.

I may have an experience that I'm really a cat, but this experience has to be brought into the judgment of others' experiences (and even rational disciplined theory) because reality is more than me. From the perspective of downward conflation, it may be weird to say that I am indeed a cat, but because I am only the embodiment of the discourses of society, it is just as possible that I'm a cat as that I'm a heterosexual husband and father living a middle-class life (both are, in the end, only socialized texts).

As we saw, critical realism would rule this out because as a being in reality I cannot possess reality. I nevertheless have experiences that can be judged in

34. "Crucial to a postfoundationalist theory of rationality, then, is a theory of experience that will enable us to reason adequately about the various facets of our human experience. . . . On this view human experience is always interpreted experience, our observations and perceptions are always theory-laden, and they interact with our world(s) in terms of life views to which we are already committed." Van Huyssteen, *Alone in the World?*, p. 13.

35. "Regardless of the extent to which the specific 'reality' we focus on in theology and the sciences may be 'mind-independent' or not (as in the realism/antirealism debate), our knowledge of this reality represents information only yielded in an interpretation of our experience. What is relevant for us therefore depends on how we go about experiencing our world, and how we interact with what we see as reality. For theology and the sciences the depth of the epistemological overlaps they shore emerges only on this level. Furthermore, on a postfoundationalist view of rationality, epistemological fallibilism and rational accountability become viable options only when we realize that our only access to reality is via the construction of theories, models, or world-pictures, in which our intellectual resources have a crucially conditioning and shaping function, precisely because of their embeddedness in interpreted experience." Van Huyssteen, *Shaping of Rationality*, 186.

36. Ibid., 211.

discourse as more or less true, or as possible or misguided. Because reality is something real that I cannot get my arms fully around, I must place my personal experiences into conversation with others for judgment, for some experiences or theories witness to what is real and others obscure it.[37]

Through personal discourse, through confession of my experience with reality next to another's confession, rational judgments can be (provisionally) made. Disciplines and fields themselves are deeply embedded and complicated thought worlds that seek to give rational shape to the experience of reality. Interdisciplinarity is the entering into the rational experiential conceptions of a community of thought. Interdisciplinarity as transversality is moving into another discipline's rational system for a time to explore and judge its conception of reality, gleaning from it what helps us make rational sense of our own experience before our rational conceptions of our own experience move us out of conversation.

In a transversal interdisciplinarity it is this very kind of postfoundational rationality that makes convergence possible or necessary at all. I'm moved into conversations of transversality, laying one theory over another, placing one perspective in conversation with another, because in discourse they give me rational pictures of reality that concur with my experience. I turn to other disciplines for rational reasons: they help me make sense of reality. But my only touchstone with reality is through experience; is it is through my personal experience and the research traditions into which my experience has moved me (like, say, theology) that I turn to sociology to make sense of my concrete and lived experience. Van Huyssteen asserts, "In both theology and the sciences we therefore indeed relate to our world epistemically through the mediation of interpreted experience, but for the Christian believer this interpreted experience will now often include religious experience, where the experiences of divine love, faith, or permanent commitment may be deeply revelatory of what is believed to be beyond these experiences."[38]

I am pulled into personal discourse with others, hearing their theories, but also recognizing that their theories are embedded in a rationality that connects to their experience. This rationality leads me into personal interdisciplinary discourse, but it also may end it. For I may say, *I simply cannot go there with you,*

---

37. Van Huyssteen points to how these judgments of experience are made, adding texture to this perspective. "A postfoundationalist model of rationality is therefore attained when we find a careful balance between, on the one hand, the way our beliefs are anchored in interpreted experience, and, on the other hand, the broader networks of beliefs in which our rationally compelling experiences are already embedded." Ibid., 232.

38. Ibid., 188.

I cannot go with rational choice theory, for example, for though I can see how gain would direct some of my action, it makes no rational sense of my experience of my love for my children or the care of the stranger given to me in my illness. My personal (hypostatic) experience becomes the rational lens I use to make interdisciplinary decisions, all for the purpose of confessing my *belief* in the shape of reality itself that comes to me as lived and concrete experiences.

The danger of the Chalcedonian method of interdisciplinarity in practical theology is that it becomes a kind of theological foundationalism. We relate disciplines and fields through a grammar, but this grammar is so firm that conversation is hard. It is like the grammar of the king's court; it is so ordered that the grammar has the danger of being prioritized over concrete experiential personhood, pushing us to use the grammar to relate things and not subjects. It can become almost irrational: I may use the grammar so firmly (and foundationally) that I ignore or downplay my experiences with reality.[39]

This is what bounced the Chalcedonian method from Christopraxis: its ruled grammar has the danger of downplaying hypostatic personalism. But, then, how does the view of rationality in transversality that I just described connect to hypostatic personalism? In exploring this question we press our interdisciplinary perspective of transversal rationality into ministerial transversal rationality and therefore link it with Christopraxis, where it becomes Christopraxis's interdisciplinary runway.

Into Ministerial Transversal Rationality

A postfoundational rationality, as I said, is bound in our experience, and this experience is not had in an echo chamber, but in and with others. And with others our experiences of rationality must be put into conversations that judge our conceptions and theories of reality. For instance, theories that are used to oppress people (like a theory that poor people are lazy and choose not to work) can often only be overcome by experiencing the personhood of another (being pulled into a ministerial zone of shared humanity) and recognizing that the epistemological conception of this other perspective does not square with one's experience and therefore cannot be correct, for it is disconnected from reality and therefore irrational.

Rationality as experience with reality reminds us that only *personally* can we experience reality, and therefore the personal and rational are fused. Because we are norming, believing animals, we call the rational that which we believe,

---

39. Again I think both VDH and James Loder avoid this trap, but it is in my opinion nevertheless a danger.

but we only believe at all as experiential persons. As hypostatic persons, we are beings that experience reality and experience it personally (Polanyi); we can only experience reality as persons. Through our personal being in reality, we make decisions that we judge as rational.[40] A rational conception is something we personally can experience (emotively or intellectually).

Where foundational instrumental rationality eliminates my need for others, since all I need are the foundations, a postfoundationalism of transversality claims that I'm in ontological need of others. Without others I can make no sense of my experience nor find a rational way of understanding myself—or, just as importantly, reality itself. As hypostatic beings, as persons, we need others (not just our individual sense experience à la Kant) to perceive reality. Rationality itself is born from being norming, believing animals in a reality that is more than us. But as such norming, believing animals, we are beings in need of others with whom to transverse our own experience. For without these others we can make little sense of the shape of reality, and with no sense of what is real, our humanity is lost in delusion.

Hypostatic personalism claims something like transversality at the ontological level; it claims that we have our being as others lay their lives over our own. We are made persons through the relationships that are us. By others laying their lives over our own, our lives transverse, but they are never equated; as in the case of transversing disciplines, the integrity of the other must be always affirmed. In and through these points of personal hypostatic convergence (of hypostatic personal transversality) we experience something real; grieving the death of another, we experience the truth that we are loved as others lay their lives over our own.[41] They transverse their being with our own, ministering to our person through their own person and therefore confessing a

40. Mark Mitchell explains Polanyi's position: "Thus, personal knowledge is a passionate commitment to universal truth made by limited, fallible knowers who strive to make contact with a hidden, indeterminate reality and embrace their findings with universal intent." *Michael Polanyi* (Wilmington, DE: ISI, 2006), 103.

41. Van Huyssteen explains Schrag's view of rationality, which is very close to Archer's own. I contend that the ministerial rationality is nondiscursive. "Schrag distinguished between discursive (the performance of articulation in language and conversation) and nondiscursive practices. The latter specifically refers to the performance of rationality beyond the realm of language and the spoken word." *Shaping of Rationality*, 248. Van Huyssteen also explains, "In revisioning interdisciplinary dialogue as a form of transversal reasoning, human rationality is not seen anymore as a universal and austere form of reasoning, but as a practical skill that enables us to gather and bind together the patterns of all our daily experiences and make sense of them through communal, interactive dialogue. The notion of transversality also enables us to honor the nonhierarchical asymmetry between various disciplines, and specifically between the sciences and theology, and to see human reason as dynamic and practical as we

truth of reality: though our person is broken, it is held, and though we weep, we belong. In and through these *ministerial* hypostatic moments of personal transversality we witness higher strata of reality—we participate in the divine being, who transverses our own being with God's own being at points of ex nihilo.

So transversality and personalism are connected. Or, better, we could say that transversality is built on a view of rationality that follows the postfoundational thought of Polanyi (and others), who reminds us that all knowledge is personal knowledge, that we are personal beings. Because we are these personal (hypostatic) beings, we make rational judgments about reality itself.

This very perspective leads us further, for while transversal rationality becomes an ingenious way to do interdisciplinarity and a way that passes the gatekeeper of ontological realism and the bouncer of hypostatic personalism, we are still left with an important hanging question that moves us back to the beginning of the chapter: what is the motivation for transversality at all?

Exploring Ministerial Transversal Rationality

As the prior paragraphs point to, the very motivation for transversality, from a Christopraxis perspective, is the act of ministry. Because and for the sake of ministry we enter the event of transversality—at least, I would argue, in practical theology. Transversality happens at an intellectual level because disciplines seek to construct epistemologies of reality. Because reality is stratified, we need to glean from discourse with others. But unless one is in such intellectual locales, why would one seek interdisciplinary conversation at all? At the experiential level, at the level of making sense of reality, we do something like transversal rationality, forming our norms and committing to beliefs through the narratives we hear and tell in transversal ways.[42]

---

use it to converse with one another through critical interpretation, through dialogue and rhetoric." *Alone in the World?*, 23.

42. We are narrating animals, as van Huyssteen points out: "In a postfoundationalist notion of rationality, the narrative quality of one's own experience, therefore, is always going to be rationally compelling. And if this is taken seriously, the postfoundationalist notion of rationality itself could never be some sort of superimposed metanarrative, but will itself develop as an emerging pattern that unifies our experience without in any way totalizing it." *Shaping of Rationality*, 177. Van Huyssteen continues, "Rationality thus emerged as a deeply social practice, always embedded in the narratives of our daily lives and contextualized by the radical interpretative nature of all our experiences. In this rich location of self-awareness and consciousness, rationality is then recognized as not only a socially embedded practice, but

This nascent transversality shows the depth of the perspective and its connection to our concrete and lived experience, but it does not explore why a minister, for instance, would turn to the disciplines or fields of certain research traditions to make sense of reality. Interdisciplinarity may be something only for the academic practical theologian. Yet, my Christopraxis perspective and the centrality of ministry within it will not allow me to settle for this position. That is not to mention that if interdisciplinarity is the soul of practical theology and yet its methods are disconnected from those on the ground, then practical theology lives itself out in a performative contradiction.

A transversal rationality may itself have the possibility of connecting directly to concrete and lived practice of ministry. But this can only happen if the minister has normative commitments to the possibility of divine action, which comes to her in and through concrete ministry with the hypostatic other (Christopraxis). In encounter with this other, in doing ministry with him, the minister is called into interdisciplinarity; through this other the minister witnesses the complicated, stratified nature of reality itself. Now in ministry to this other, however, the minister is led into an event of convergence, but this event of convergence is ignited only because of the hypostatic event of ministerial encounter.

As an event of convergence, the concrete need of the other becomes the motivation for transversality. The minister turns to a form of counseling because it assists her in the act of ministry. She uses this perspective for a time, but once it is no longer helpful in ministry, the event of convergence gives way to divergence—the traversal moment is over because the rationality of ministry no longer seeks it. So ministry itself leads one string or stick to be propelled to lay over other; in acting with and for the hypostatic other we use multiple perspectives to help minister to concrete others. We are compelled to seek transversality because of the practice of ministry itself.

The event of convergence is made such because of the event of ministry. The event of ministry, I've argued, is an encounter with the stratified nature of reality. Ministry itself needs these other disciplines—not just for functional reasons but because, in ministering to this other's hypostasis, the minister and this other are pulled into the experience of a high stratum of reality. The minister turns to a form of psychology, but she turns to it only for the purpose of ministry; she seeks convergence but only for the sake of ministerial action. So it is because of ministry that she is led at all into the event of convergence. And because ministry sends her into this event of convergence (this event of laying

a practice that indeed involves the telling of our stories, laden with interpretation, but also containing all-important resources and strategies for critique." Ibid., 181.

over strings or sticks of theory and insight), she does this theologically. She enters the event of convergence with the experiential rational confession that such action of ministry done for this person draws them into a high reality, into an encounter with the divine being. Transversal rationality that is broadened to become ministerial transversal rationality is bound in the *concursus Dei* itself.

And bound here, we can assert that the minister does *not* necessarily experience the divine being through psychology, philosophy, or sociology (and their subtheories), but she does experience the divine being through ministering to the other person. Ministering to this other person often calls her into events of convergence with other (scientific) epistemologies. But she uses these epistemologies only so long as they assist her ministry.[43] If they ever diminish ministry—by for instance pushing her toward an antirealism or antipersonalist perspective—she will need to say adieu and allow divergence to occur. No matter what, at some point divergence will happen, for ministry that attends to divine action (the *concursus Dei*) cannot in the end become psychology or social work; its commitment to reality itself will not allow for this reduction. The minister's normative commitment to divine action, and her experience of it, will keep the boundaries between the fields, given as the minister passionately and freely engages other epistemologies *for the sake of ministry*.[44]

Which perspectives or disciplines the minister engages and takes into the event of convergence is conditioned by the rationality of the minister's experience—the minister's experience with this hypostatic other but also her experience with reality itself.[45] Having normative commitments to divine action bound in her experience, the minister enters the event of convergence with intuition toward a pattern (as Polanyi calls it). She seeks to know what and why something is happening, but because she asks with a normative commitment to divine action, she asks it as a realist, seeking from her lower

---

43. This is something like Hans Frei's ad hoc perspective in *Types of Christology*, but of course with a much more direct ministerial focus.

44. This signals one reason why spiritual formation is so important to theological education: students must be trained for ministry in and through their articulation of their experience (or lack thereof) with God's act and being.

45. This stands in line with van Huyssteen's perspective, "What emerges from this as a criterion for theory choice is the following: we ultimately choose the theory or research tradition which we find the most compelling, and which we judge to have the highest problem-solving adequacy for a specific problem within a specific context. The choice for the problem-solving ability of a research tradition, as for a specific theory, is therefore always a strategy of interpretation." *Shaping of Rationality*, 281.

stratum of reality to enter the complicated layers of existence itself, seeking what and why things are as they are.

In perceiving a pattern, feeling the other's reality, the minister may say to a grieving mother in her hospital bed whose baby was stillborn at eight months, "You know your baby didn't die because you stopped going to church; that's not why." With these words the young mother cries the tears of released shame. Later the minister says to her colleagues, "I don't why I said that; I have no idea where it came from." It comes from her tacit knowledge through her own experience of what is going on, through the Spirit's working in her own experiential rationality that seeks something real. Using her experiential rationality that is bound in her personal sharing with the grieving mother, the minister intuits a pattern, a theory that the mother feels shame and blames herself.[46] In response, the minister experientially, almost reflexively, enters an event of convergence, laying over psychological trauma, shame theory, and a theology of forgiveness, and they all converge for the sake of the event of ministry.[47] The minister engages in this tacit transversality always as a minister, as the one caring for this concrete other.[48] She presents her intuited pattern—the

46. "Polanyi calls this skill intuition, but he notes that this is not some mystical ability. Rather, it is quite similar to perception. When we attempt to perceive an object, we concentrate and perhaps even squint in order better to bring the object into focus. In the same way, this unspecifiable element called intuition 'is a skill, rooted in our natural sensibility to hidden patterns and developed to effectiveness by a process of learning.' Thus, quite contrary to the standard image of a dispassionate scientist, Polanyi argues that the scientist relies on his personal passions as well as the skill of intuition—both of which are not fully explicable. Without these concepts, it is impossible to provide an account of science that adequately reflects actual scientific practice." Mitchell, *Michael Polanyi*, 40.

47. This ministerial intuition is similar to all scientific intuition, as Polanyi shows. Mitchell explains, "In 1945, one year after he was inducted as a Fellow of the Royal Society, Polanyi delivered the Riddell Lectures at Durham University, published the next year as *Science, Faith, and Society*. In these three lectures, Polanyi attempts to show how the practice of science—in marked contrast to the commonly accepted account—actually depends on both tradition and the authority exercised by a community of practicing scientists. Furthermore, he argues, scientists do not conduct their business in a purely explicit fashion. Instead, they rely on hunches and intuition as they seek to gain a clearer understanding of an externally existing reality, which they believe can be known." Ibid., 15.

48. This tacit knowledge as well as the whole interdisciplinary process I have tried to show is deeply connected to my commitment that human beings are norming, believing animals. And it is this conception of knowledge as tacit that highlights *animal*, the embodied element of this perspective. Mitchell explains Polanyi by saying, "Because the proximal component of tacit knowing is rooted in our bodies and extends out from them, all thought is rooted in the body. That said, we are generally aware of our bodies only subsidiarily, and those things we employ subsidiarily while attending to the focal targets of our attention are in effect extensions of our bodies. Thus, 'our body is the ultimate instrument of all our external knowledge, whether intellectual or practical.' Indwelling, then, indicates the extension of the body in the process of knowing." Ibid., 77.

baby didn't die because you've missed church—not for academic reasons but for the sake of ministry (for the sake of sharing in the other as witness to something real). In ministry, reality in its mysterious stratified nature is revealed, and epistemologies of the social sciences are drawn into partnership with divine action itself.

The mystery of reality, and her engagement with it, sends the minister into reflection, a reflection that is always bound to the concrete other to whom she ministers. The minister searches her own experience and feelings to seek a pattern of interpretation and action that might direct her. Through this imaginative intuition toward a pattern for the shape of reality, she moves into interdisciplinary convergence. Caring for the elderly man, she sees a pattern, a reality that becomes clear to her. She discovers, like a revelation, that he is an alcoholic. Now following this intuition that reveals more deeply the humanity of this hypostatic other, she enters the event of convergence, turning to social science to help understand alcoholism. She takes ministerial actions to set the space for the elderly man to find reconciliation with his estranged family. She takes this step for the purpose of ministry because God's own ministry is one of reconciliation. Now in this action an event of convergence happens, for she knows there can only be reconciliation, which witnesses to divine action, if she understands how it is that an alcoholic's systems work, seeking best practices from group therapy to be used in her own ministry.

Therefore, the training of pastors is aimed not necessarily at engulfing them in social-scientific research traditions but rather at helping them reflect on the intuition of their own persons so that they are able to access their tacit knowledge and therefore follow their questions and intuitions into events of convergence. Of course, having some particular knowledge will be important, but more important is fostering the imaginative creativity of seeking patterns of reality that lead to events of ministerial convergence.

The minister senses a reality and therefore believes that in turning to this or that discipline or perspective she might love the other, that she may enter a higher stratum of reality with and for the other. Ministry forces a reach for rational support from other disciplines, but both the convergence and divergence of these disciplines is conditioned by the act of ministry itself. By the ontological realist confession of divine action as God's being as becoming in ministry, and by the hypostatic personalism that holds together act and being as the locale for human action's participation in the divine being; it then is through a ministerial transversal rationality that we glimpse what might be an interdisciplinary model for a Christopraxis practical theology of the cross. And it is with this in place that this project finds its conclusion.

Bibliography

Anderson, Elijah. *Code of the Street: Decency, Violence, and the Moral Life of the Inner City.* New York: W. W. Norton, 1999.

Anderson, Ray S. "Christopraxis: The Ministry and the Humanity of Christ for the World." In *Christ in Our Place: The Humanity of God in Christ for the Reconciliation of the World; Essays Presented to Professor James Torrance,* edited by Trevor Hart and Daniel Thimell. Exeter, UK: Paternoster Press, 1989. Reprinted in Ray S. Anderson, *Ministry on the Fireline: A Practical Theology for an Empowered Church.* Pasadena, CA: Fuller Seminary Press, 1993.

———. *On Being Human: Essays in Theological Anthropology.* Pasadena, CA: Fuller Seminary Press, 1982.

———. *The Shape of Practical Theology: Empowering Ministry with Theological Praxis.* Downers Grove, IL: InterVarsity, 2001.

———. *The Soul of Ministry: Forming Leaders for God's People.* Louisville, KY: Westminster John Knox, 1997.

———. "A Theology for Ministry," in *Theological Foundations for Ministry: Selected Readings for a Theology of the Church in Ministry,* edited by Ray S. Anderson. Edinburgh: T&T Clark, 1979.

Anatolios, Khaled. *Athanasius: The Coherence of His Thought.* London: Routledge, 1998.

Archer, Margaret. *Being Human: The Problem of Agency.* London: Cambridge University Press, 2000.

———. "Models of Man." In Archer, Collier, and Porpora, *Transcendence.*

———. *Realist Social Theory: The Morphogenetic Approach.* London: Cambridge University Press, 1995.

Archer, Margaret S., Andrew Collier, and Douglas V. Porpora. *Transcendence: Critical Realism and God.* London: Routledge, 2004.

———. "What Do We Mean by God?" In Archer, Collier, and Porpora, *Transcendence.*

Barth, Karl. *Church Dogmatics* I.1. Edinburgh: T&T Clark, 1936.

———. *Church Dogmatics* III.2. Edinburgh: T&T Clark, 1960.

———. *Church Dogmatics* III.3. Edinburgh: T&T Clark, 1960.

Bass, Dorothy C. *Practicing Our Faith: A Way of Life for Searching People.* San Francisco: Jossey-Bass, 2010.

Bass, Dorothy, and Craig Dykstra, eds. *For Life Abundant: Practical Theology, Theological Education, and Christian Ministry.* Grand Rapids, MI: Eerdmans, 2008.

Beaudoin, Tom. *Witness to Dispossession: The Vocation of a Postmodern Theology.* Maryknoll, NY: Orbis, 2008.

Bonhoeffer, Dietrich. *Act and Being.* Minneapolis: Fortress Press, 1961.

———. *Christ the Center.* San Francisco: HarperCollins, 1978.

Bradbury, Roslene. *Cross Theology: The Classical Theologia Crucis and Karl Barth's Modern Theology of the Cross.* Eugene, OR: Pickwick, 2011.

Browning, Don S. *A Fundamental Practical Theology: Descriptive and Strategic Proposals.* Minneapolis: Fortress Press, 1991.

Browning, Don S., Bonnie Miller-McLemore, Pamela Couture, Brynolf Lyon, and Robert Franklin. *From Culture Wars to Common Ground: Religion and the American Family Debate.* Louisville, KY: Westminster John Knox, 1997.

Cahalan, Kathleen. *Introducing the Practice of Ministry.* Collegeville, MN: Liturgical Press, 2010.

Calahan, Kathleen, and James R. Nieman. "Mapping the Field of Practical Theology." In Bass and Dykstra, *For Life Abundant.*

Caputo, John. *How to Read Kierkegaard.* New York: W. W. Norton, 2007.

———. *The Weakness of God: A Theology of the Event.* Bloomington: Indiana University Press, 2006.

Charry, Ellen. *By the Renewing of Your Mind: The Pastoral Function of Christian Doctrine.* New York: Oxford University Press, 1997.

Chaves, Mark. *American Religion: Contemporary Trends.* Princeton, NJ: Princeton University Press, 2011.

———. "SSSR Presidential Address Rain Dances in the Dry Season: Overcoming the Religious Congruence Fallacy." *Journal for the Scientific Study of Religion* 49, no. 1 (2010): 1–14.

Collier, Andrew. *Critical Realism: An Introduction to Roy Bhaskar's Philosophy.* London: Verso, 1994.

———. "Realism, Relativism and Reason." In Archer, Collier, and Porpora, *Transcendence.*

Conner, Benjamin. *Practicing Witness.* Grand Rapids, MI: Eerdmans, 2011.

Dean, Kenda Creasy. *Practicing Passion: Youth and the Quest for a Passionate Church.* Grand Rapids, MI: Eerdmans, 2004.

DeHart, Paul. *Beyond the Necessary: Trinitarian Faith and Philosophy in the Thought of Eberhard Jüngel.* Atlanta: Scholars Press, 1999.

Emerson, Michael, and Christian Smith. *Divided by Faith: Evangelical Religion and the Problem of Race in America*. Oxford: Oxford University Press, 2000.

Erlaer, Rolf Joachim, and Reiner Marquard. *A Karl Barth Reader*. Edinburgh: T&T Clark, 1986.

Forrester, Duncan. "Can Theology Be Practical." In Schweitzer and van der Ven, *Practical Theology: International Perspectives*.

Fowler, James. "The Emerging New Shape of Practical Theology." In Schweitzer and van der Ven, *Practical Theology: International Perspectives*.

Frei, Hans. *Types of Christian Theology*. New Haven: Yale University Press, 1992.

Fulkerson, Mary McClintock. *Places of Redemption: Theology for a Worldly Church*. London: University of Oxford Press, 2007.

Ganzevoort, R. Ruard. "Narrative Approaches." In Miller-McLemore, *The Wiley-Blackwell Companion to Practical Theology*.

Gerkin, Charles. *The Living Human Document: Re-Visioning Pastoral Counseling in a Hermeneutical Mode*. Nashville: Abingdon, 1984.

Graham, Elaine. *Transforming Practice: Pastoral Theology in an Age of Uncertainty*. London: Mowbray, 1996.

Hall, Douglas John. *Confessing the Faith: Christian Theology in a North American Context*. Minneapolis: Fortress Press, 1998.

———. *Lighten Our Darkness: Toward an Indigenous Theology of the Cross*. Lima, OH: Academic Renewal Press, 2001.

———. *Thinking the Faith: Christian Theology in a North American Context*. Minneapolis: Fortress Press, 1991.

Hastings, Thomas John. *Practical Theology and the One Body of Christ: Toward a Missional-Ecumenical Model*. Grand Rapids, MI: Eerdmans, 2007.

Hawkes, Gerald. "The Role of Theology in Practical Theology." *Journal of Theology for Southern Africa* 49 (December 1984): 38–48.

Heller, Karin. "Missio Dei: Envisioning an Apostolic Practical Theology." *Missiolog: An International Review* 37, no. 1 (January 2009): 47–61.

Hunsinger, Deborah van Deusen. *Theology and Pastoral Counseling: A New Interdisciplinary Approach*. Grand Rapids, MI: Eerdmans, 1995.

Huyssteen, Wentzel van. *Alone in the World? Human Uniqueness in Science and Theology*. Grand Rapids, MI: Eerdmans, 2006.

———. *The Shaping of Rationality: Toward Interdisciplinarity in Theology and Science*. Grand Rapids, MI: Eerdmans, 1999.

Jennings, Willie. *The Christian Imagination: Theology and the Origins of Race.* New Haven: Yale University Press, 2010.

Jones, Gregory L., and Stephanie Paulsell. *The Scope of Our Art: The Vocation of the Theological Teacher.* Grand Rapids, MI: Eerdmans, 2001.

Johnson, Keith. "The Being and Act of the Church: Barth and the Future of Evangelical Ecclesiology." In *Karl Barth and American Evangelicalism*, edited by Bruce McCormack and Clifford Anderson. Grand Rapids, MI: Eerdmans, 2011.

Jüngel, Eberhard. *God as the Mystery of the World.* Grand Rapids, MI; Eerdmans, 1983.

———. *God's Being Is in Becoming: The Trinitarian Being of God in the Theology of Karl Barth.* Grand Rapids, MI: Eerdmans, 2001.

———. *Justification: The Heart of the Christian Faith.* Edinburgh: T&T Clark, 2001.

———. *Theological Essays I.* Edinburgh: T&T Clark, 1989.

Karkkainen, Veli-Matti. *One with God: Salvation as Deification and Justification.* Collegeville, MN: Liturgical Press, 2004.

La Montagne, Paul. *Barth and Rationality: Critical Realism in Theology.* Eugene, OR: Cascade Books, 2012.

Latini, Theresa. *The Church and the Crisis of Community: A Practical Theology of Small-Group Ministry.* Grand Rapids, MI: Eerdmans, 2011.

Leithart, Peter. *Athanasius.* Grand Rapids, MI: Baker, 2011.

Loder, James. *The Logic of the Spirit: Human Development in Theological Perspective.* San Francisco: Jossey-Bass, 1998.

———. "Normativity and Context in Practical Theology: 'The Interdisciplinary Issue.'" In Schweitzer and van der Ven, *Practical Theology: International Perspectives.*

———. *The Transforming Moment.* Colorado Springs: Helmers and Howard, 1989.

Luhrmann, T. M. *When God Talks Back: Understanding the American Evangelical Relationship with God.* New York: Vintage, 2012.

Madsen, Anna. *The Theology of the Cross in Historical Perspective.* Eugene, OR: Pickwick, 2007.

McCormick, Bruce. *Karl Barth's Critically Realistic Dialectical Theology.* New York: Oxford University Press, 1997.

Mercer, Joyce. *Welcoming Children: A Practical Theology of Childhood.* St. Louis: Chalice, 2005.

Mikoski, Gordon. "Mainline Protestantism." In Miller-McLemore, *The Wiley-Blackwell Companion to Practical Theology*.

Mikoski, Gordon, and Richard Osmer. *With Piety and Learning: The History of Practical Theology at Princeton Theological Seminary*. Berlin: LIT, 2012.

Miller-McLemore, Bonnie. "Introduction: The Contributions of Practical Theology." In Miller-McLemore, *The Wiley-Blackwell Companion to Practical Theology*.

———. "Misunderstanding about Practical Theology: Presidential Address to the International Academy of Practical Theology." Presented at the 2011 Conference of the International Academy of Practical Theology, Amsterdam, 2011.

———. *Christian Theology in Practice: Discovering a Discipline*. Grand Rapids, MI: Eerdmans, 2012.

———, ed. *The Wiley-Blackwell Companion to Practical Theology*. Oxford: Wiley-Blackwell, 2012.

Mitchell, Mark. *Michael Polanyi*. Wilmington, DE: ISI, 2006.

Moltmann, Jurgen. *The Source of Life: The Holy Spirit and the Theology of Life*. Minneapolis: Fortress Press, 1997.

Murphy, Nancy. *Theology in the Age of Scientific Reasoning*. Ithaca, NY: Cornell University Press, 1990.

Niebuhr, Reinhold. *The Nature and Destiny of Man*. New York: Charles Scribner's Sons, 1942.

Nimmo, Paul. *Being in Action: The Theological Shape of Barth's Ethical Vision*. Edinburgh: T&T Clark, 2007.

———. "Karl Barth and the Concursus Dei—A Chalcedonianism Too Far?" *International Journal of Systematic Theology* 9, no. 1 (January 2007): 58–72.

O'Donovan, Leo. "The Mystery of God as a History of Love: Eberhard Jüngel's Doctrine of God," *Theological Studies* 42, no. 2 (1981): 251–71.

Osmer, Richard. "Cross-Disciplinary Thinking in Practical Theology." Unpublished article.

———. *Practical Theology: An Introduction*. Grand Rapids, MI: Eerdmans, 2008.

———. *The Teaching Ministry of Congregations*. Louisville, KY: Westminster John Knox, 2005.

———. "The United States." In Miller-McLemore, *The Wiley-Blackwell Companion to Practical Theology*.

Pattison, Stephen. *The Challenge of Practical Theology*. London: Jessica Kingsley, 2007.

Paulson, Steven. *Lutheran Theology*. Edinburgh: T&T Clark, 2011.

Pedraja, Luis. "The Infinity of God: A New Possibility in the Thoughts of Whitehead and Jüngel." *Encounter* 58, no. 2 (Spring 1997): 151–70.

Polanyi, Michael. *Personal Knowledge: Toward a Post-Critical Philosophy.* Chicago: University of Chicago Press, 1962.

Porpora, Douglas. "Judgemental Rationality and Jesus." In Archer, Collier, and Porpora, *Transcendence.*

Price, Daniel. *Karl Barth's Anthropology in Light of Modern Thought.* Grand Rapids, MI: Eerdmans, 2002.

Purves, Andrew. *Reconstructing Pastoral Theology: A Christological Foundation.* Louisville, KY: Westminster John Knox, 2004.

Root, Andrew. *Revisiting Relational Youth Ministry.* Downers Grove, IL: InterVarsity, 2007.

Root, Andrew. *The Relational Pastor.* Downers Grove: IL: InterVarsity, 2013.

Rubin, Herbert J., and Irene S. Rubin. *Qualitative Interviewing: The Art of Hearing Data.* Thousand Oaks, CA: Sage, 1995.

Sayer, Andrew. *Realism and Social Science.* Los Angeles: Sage, 2000.

Searle, John. *The Construction of Social Reality.* New York: Free Press, 1995.

Schweitzer, Friedrich, and Johannes A. van der Ven, eds. *Practical Theology: International Perspectives.* Berlin: Peter Lang, 1999.

Smith, Ted. "Theories of Practice." In Miller-McLemore, *The Wiley-Blackwell Companion to Practical Theology.*

Smith, Christian. *Moral Believing Animals: Human Personhood and Culture.* Oxford: Oxford University Press, 2003.

———. *What Is a Person?* Chicago: University of Chicago Press, 2010.

Spjuth, Roland. "Redemption without Actuality: A Critical Interrelation between Eberhard Jüngel's and John Milbank's Ontological Endeavours." *Modern Theology* 14, no. 4 (October 1998): 505–22.

Swinton, John, and Harriet Mowat. *Practical Theology and Qualitative Research.* London: SCM, 2006.

Swinton, John. *Resurrecting the Person: Friendship and the Care of People with Mental Health Problems.* Nashville: Abingdon, 2000.

Tanner, Kathryn. *Christ the Key.* London: Cambridge University Press, 2010.

Taylor, Charles. *A Secular Age.* Cambridge, MA: Belknap Press of Harvard University Press, 2007.

Tillich, Paul. *Systematic Theology: Reason and Revelation. Being and God.* Chicago: University of Chicago Press, 1951.

Volf, Miroslav, and Dorothy C. Bass. *Practicing Theology: Beliefs and Practices in Christian Life.* Grand Rapids, MI: Eerdmans, 2002.

Ward, Pete. *Participation and Mediation: A Practical Theology for the Liquid Church.* London: SCM, 2008.

Watts, Graham. *Revelation and the Spirit: A Comparative Study of the Relationship between the Doctrine of Revelation and Pneumatology in the Theology of Eberhard Jüngel and of Wolfhart Pannenberg.* Milton Keynes, UK: Paternoster, 2005.

Weber, John B. *Eberhard Jüngel: An Introduction to His Theology.* London: Cambridge University Press, 1986.

Wolfteich, Claire E. "Re-Claiming Sabbath as Transforming Practical: Critical Reflections in Light of Jewish-Christian Dialogue." In *Religion, Diversity, and Conflict,* edited by Edward Foley. Berlin: LIT, 2011.

Wright, Terry "Reconsidering Concursus." *International Journal of Systematic Theology* 4, no. 2 (July 2002): 205–15.

Wuthnow, Robert. *After the Baby Boomers: How Twenty- and Thirty-Somethings Are Shaping the Future of American Religion.* Princeton, NJ: Princeton University Press, 2007.

Zizioulas, John. *Being as Communion.* Crestwood, NY: St Vladimir's Seminary Press, 1985.

———. *Communion and Otherness.* Edinburgh: T&T Clark, 2006.

Index of Names and Subjects